# Creative R & D Leadership

# Creative R & D Leadership

## Insights from Japan

### JAMES L. BESS

**QUORUM BOOKS**
Westport, Connecticut • London

**Library of Congress Cataloging-in-Publication Data**

Bess, James L.
    Creative R & D leadership : insights from Japan / James L. Bess.
        p.   cm.
    Includes bibliographical references and index.
    ISBN 0–89930–915–1 (alk. paper)
    1. Research—Economic aspects—Japan. 2. Research, Industrial—
Japan. 3. Science and industry—Japan.   I. Title.   II. Title:
Creative R and D leadership.
    HC465.R4B46   1995
    001.4'0952—dc20          94–46199

British Library Cataloguing in Publication Data is available.

Library of Congress Catalog Card Number: 94–46199
ISBN: 0–89930–915–1

First published in 1995

Quorum Books, 88 Post Road West, Westport, CT 06881
An imprint of Greenwood Publishing Group, Inc.

Printed in the United States of America

∞

The paper used in this book complies with the
Permanent Paper Standard issued by the National
Information Standards Organization (Z39.48–1984).

10 9 8 7 6 5 4 3 2 1

**Copyright Acknowledgments**

The author and publisher are grateful for permission to reprint portions
of the following copyrighted material.

McWilliams, Wilson C., 1973. *The Idea of Fraternity in America.*
Berkeley: University of California Press. Copyright © 1973 The
Regents of the University of California.

Rohlen, Thomas P., 1975. "The Company Work Group," in Ezra F.
Vogel (ed.), *Modern Japanese Organization and Decision-Making.*
Berkeley: University of California Press. Copyright © 1975 The
Regents of the University of California.

To Nancy

**MUNEN MUSOO DE ARU**
"to be free from all worldly cares"

# Contents

# Exhibits

# Preface

In 1986–87, I was scheduled for a sabbatical leave from my university. Having taught and written about the subject of organizational theory for many years, particularly in its applications to colleges and universities, I had heard and read much in the popular and academic literature about Japanese management techniques and their potential for improving American organizations. My first thought for a research project was that I would study Japanese universities to see if and how those techniques had found their way into Japanese higher education. The results would certainly help improve the management of American higher education, itself a fertile and still relatively untilled field for organizational study and analysis. Preliminary research on the topic, however, resulted in a quick rejection of that notion. In point of fact, for reasons I discuss in some detail in the book, Japanese universities are not among the best managed in the world, though they have other strong merits. I then turned to the obvious success of the Japanese in developing high-quality, marketable products and to the R & D processes to which that success can in part be traced. Since R & D also plays an important role in universities, at the very least, I reasoned, I could study university R & D and its management to see if there were lessons to be learned in that setting. Again, as I detail later, to do the study properly, I also decided to compare university R & D management with R & D management in two other sectors—corporations and government institutes.

What was also intriguing about this idea was that I would be able to look into some especially fascinating but perennially controversial and still only partially understood concepts from the field of organizational theory. These included leadership and conflict management and their effects on worker motivation, satisfaction, commitment, innovation, and risk taking. Studying them in a setting where cultural conditions are so different would, I hoped, afford a

fresh insight into what those terms and their relationships really mean in our
own culture.

What I discovered and will detail in the book was the unique manifestation
of leadership practiced in Japan. It reflects the emerging recognition of the limitations of rational, linear thinking that have long been the basis of Western
conceptualizations of leadership and are now being challenged by many post-
modern thinkers. It also embodies the still-developing conceptualizations of self-
managing teams, in this book partially explained by a canonical theory of group
relations. The theory to be laid out in the book refers also to the beginnings of
an expansion of the emerging conception in Western social science literature
that leadership is carried out by more than a central charismatic figurehead, and
that leader behavior is a function of his/her interactions not only with his subordinate leadership team, but of the latter with their subordinate workers and,
in turn, of them with each other.

As will be seen, these leadership conceptualizations incorporate some of
George Graen's ideas about leader-member exchange but are expanded in the
conceptual framework to include some theories from the literature on groups,
in particular the cultural and normative constraints on behavior. As many have
reported in the literature, unpacking the meaning of the extremely tight constraints of culture on worker behavior, as in Japan, is critical to understanding
all organizational behavior. Much of the material in early chapters reports the
main features of this culture that seem most relevant to understanding the conduct of leadership.

It is important to point out that though the focus of the research was Japanese
leadership, and the data were collected in Japan, this book is not intended to
provide new insights about Japan and Japanese culture in general. Many others,
particularly Asian scholars, have written such books and continue to do so.
Rather, Japanese culture and organization is used as an heuristic to inform Western understanding of our own culture and organizational behavior (this despite
published caveats arguing against such efforts). Even if there are occasional
misinterpretations of Japanese life (for which I apologize to my Japanese
friends), I believe that some complexities of Western management and leadership puzzling researchers and practitioners here are usefully unraveled in ways
that would not have been available from exclusively homegrown empirical data
and perspectives.

Part I of the book begins with a discussion of key elements of Japanese
society in general in order to give some sense of the cultural and social environment which so critically bears on leadership practices in Japan. These broad
observations are followed (in Part II) by a summary of educational practices in
Japan, since, again, the learned patterns of behavior reveal much about how the
Japanese relate to their leaders. For example, both lower and higher education
function as formative influences in the career selection and upward mobility
paths that workers in Japanese organizations take.

Following this introductory propaedeutic, I present, (in Part III) a summary of how Japanese organizations are structured, how decisions are made, and how people behave. In addition, since the concern here is with research and development, I next consider some aspects of technology and technological innovation. Further, the government of Japan plays a significant role in the management of technological change. I report on that as well.

Part IV introduces two central variables in the study: leadership style and conflict management. In each chapter the origins of the theoretical bases of the design for the empirical phases of the study of R & D managers are discussed.

Most of the above is by way of introduction. In Part V, the findings from the study are reported. I focus on three concerns at the micro-organizational level—namely, leadership and conflict management and their individual and joint effects on worker motivation, commitment, risk taking, and satisfaction. Added to this are some related structural and attitudinal variables that speak to the dynamics of leadership behavior—source of control/authority, ego gratification sources, information flow, social hierarchies, types of sanctions, and risk propensity. In Part VI, the book concludes with observations on both a practical and theoretical level.

In sum, the book addresses key questions that this country continues to ask of itself. The Japanese answers extracted through my research may not translate to our own problems one-for-one, but they make for intriguing speculation.

# Acknowledgments

Completion of a project of this scope could not have been managed without the help of several highly supportive institutions and a large number of talented and unselfish people. Three organizations deserve special mention. One is the National Institute for Educational Research (NIER); another, the National Institute for Research Advancement (NIRA), both in Japan. NIER is a premier government-supported educational research agency, located in Tokyo. In the spring of 1986, New York University, my home institution, had hosted a Fulbright scholar, Tatsuo Yamada, from NIER. In the fall of that year, NIER reciprocated by allowing me to spend a year as a visiting scholar in Japan. Generous in kind as well as spirit, NIER provided me with a large office, typewriter, computer, supplies, telephone, and mailing privileges. As a member of the NIER "family," I also was allowed, indeed encouraged, to join in the various social and recreational activities of the organization, including tennis on their own court, ping pong, a tennis competition with other research organizations, festivals which mark the Japanese calendar, and occasional after-hours bar-hopping adventures. I will be forever grateful to NIER, to its directors while I was there—Hiroshi Kida and Isao Suzuki—and to Dr. Katsuhiro Arai, a kind and most knowledgeable source of information. But I am especially beholden to my special host, Mr. Tatsuo Yamada, whose extraordinary generosity and care for me and my family was perhaps the best introduction to Japan and its people that one could have.

I was also fortunate to receive a grant from NIRA. NIRA is a think tank in Japan which makes external policy research grants and, to a limited extent, conducts in-house economic and social scientific research. In addition to a stipend, NIRA provided me with an office, secretarial assistance, translation and interpreter services, and research assistance of all kinds. Further, through NIRA

I was able to establish contact with the major figures in the scientific community in the university, government, and corporate sectors. My sincere thanks to Mr. Atsushi Shimokobe, president of NIRA. Ms. Yumiko Iwahara provided able translation of the questionnaires, and Ms. Yoriko Soma coordinated my many visits and otherwise made my life at NIRA most efficient. I save my last and greatest debt of gratitude at NIRA for Ms. Kiyoko Ishikawa. I have never met a more dedicated, hard-working, and committed individual. Her superior intelligence, as well as her capacity to relate to a foreign researcher with a complicated set of expectations about how Western social science should be conducted, was truly amazing.

The third organization that helped me realize the goals of the project was the United States Information Agency's Fulbright Commission. In 1987–88, I received a Fulbright grant to conduct research in Japan. Not only was the grant itself extremely important in providing travel and subsistence allowances, but the staff of the commission helped me to make connections with key persons in the Japanese R & D system. Jennifer Keefe was instrumental in facilitating my application. I am especially grateful to Mrs. Caroline Mitano Yang, executive director of the commission, who was most gracious and helpful throughout my time in Japan. Ms. Atsuko Miyawaki, also of the Fulbright office, not only provided able assistance in Tokyo, but after she moved to New York, continued to help directly in the translation of open-ended comments from respondents to the questionnaires.

Still another source of assistance was the Recruit Company's Testing Research Division, under the able direction of Mr. Hideyuki Nimura (now vice president of the Human Resource Research Institute in Tokyo). Mr. Nimura and his staff were a constant source of information and direct aid in the translation of the Myers-Briggs questionnaire (which had been translated previously by Recruit) and in the refinement of the Thomas-Kilmann conflict management instrument.

Assisting me at NIER and subsequently was an extraordinarily bright and knowledgeable graduate student at that time completing her studies in the physics of superconductivity. Ms. Keiko Aoki gave of her time and energy and intelligence far above what I as an American would have thought commensurate with the meager compensation I was able to pay. Her sensitivity to the nuances of Japanese society and to the difficulties of conducting research in a foreign culture saved me over and over from small and large errors in protocol, not to speak of substantive errors in the research. I owe her a great many thanks for her many kindnesses.

The processing of the data and its analysis was a significant undertaking. Rescuing me frequently and with cheerful alacrity from the entanglements of statistical conundrums was Burt Holland at NYU's Academic Computing Center. Another resource of inestimable value was the office staff at NYU, particularly Charmaine Baptiste, who patiently endured my many memory lapses. I wish to thank also Julia O'Brien, who so elegantly crafted my tables and exhibits.

Lastly, I turn to my family—wife Nancy, and sons, Isaac and Ivan—who took on with great enthusiasm and insouciance the rigors of living and learning in Japan for a full academic year. Through their initial courage and subsequent involvement and excitement, I was able not only to do my own work, but always to be uplifted and energized through the diurnal recapitulation of our adventures in this wonderfully unique land.

I hope all of these fine people will take at least partial credit for whatever value this book may have. They deserve it and my everlasting thanks.

# I

## Introduction

# Introduction and Background

## BACKGROUND OF THE PROBLEM

Currently among the most salient of concerns for government leaders in industrialized nations is the proper policy for the development of technology that will maintain and enhance national economic growth. One source of new technology lies in the sustained creativity of trained scientists who work in industry and of scholars laboring in university and government laboratories. While institutions of higher education in the United States act as major producers of new knowledge to be used both in science and industry and in the continuing advancement of the general culture, in some national systems (as in Japan) the knowledge production function has been substantially decentralized to the industrial sector. Often well-supported directly and indirectly by government funds (in recent years over $62 billion, or 3.5 percent of GNP in Japan), research and development units in business and industry have historically borne the major burden of invention and adaptation of new ideas and products. ''Big science'' (de Solla Price 1963; Graham 1985) in Japan is not typically performed at university centers, though the situation seems to be changing of late, especially as collaboration between universities and industry increases (cf. Ushiogi 1993). Most big science research is corporate-based or carried out at research institutes, though less than 15 percent goes for ''basic'' research (Ushiogi 1993, 313). In part, this is because of a tradition of government support for private industry in the national interest and in part because, for a variety of reasons, a long-term perspective on investment returns is more acceptable in the Japanese corporations than in the United States.

Approximately 40 to 50 percent of the some 400,000 research workers in Japan are employed in universities. About two-thirds of these work in the natural sciences. Thus only roughly 30 percent of the natural science research personnel in the country are in universities, versus 49 percent in private industry. While this distribution of talent may have been functional in earlier times, some questions are now being raised about its effects on the productivity and effectiveness of both education and industry (Anderson 1984; Turney 1984). Indeed, the paucity of funding for academic researchers leaves the prospect of serious productivity very doubtful.

The research design that guided this research looks critically at the question of scientific and technological innovation in developed countries. In contrast to many current studies, however, it focuses not so much on the "idea-to-market" or technology transfer processes (e.g., integrating research, engineering, production, and marketing staffs) as on more general personnel issues that explain how the creativity that antecedes innovation is fostered and made more effective. More specifically, it examines the important aspects of leadership and conflict management styles in scientific research and development units in academic, industrial, and government sectors in order to identify which approaches or styles have had the most positive effects on worker motivation and on a related set of variables surrounding the behavior of individual research workers.

## ORIGINS OF THE PROBLEM

Organizational success can be interpreted in many ways, but there seems little debate that the special and unique modes of industrial organization and management in Japan have enabled it to make enormous gains in productivity since 1945. The lessons for the West are still being gleaned. There has been much written about styles of Japanese industrial management, and much research continues to be conducted on the subject. Similar successes in the management of R & D in Japanese higher education, on the other hand, have not been forthcoming. Research indicates that college and university organization and management in general in Japan is not as efficient or productive as it might be (Cummings 1979; Wheeler 1976; Zeugner 1984; Sato 1991). The reason, some argue, is that the historical cultural constraints of the educational and occupational systems render higher education relatively impotent and, indeed, unimportant (save as a screening/classifying agency) in the overall social and economic organization of the country. On the research side, the peculiar eccentricities of the departmental organization system in the university (the *koza* mechanism—see Chapter 9) have resulted in a degree of research stagnation.

Recently, critics have also begun to express some doubt as to the continued viability of the structure and processes of research on the industrial side as well, despite Japan's exceptionally strong record (Kagano, Nonaka, Sakakibara, & Okumura 1983–84; Ohmae 1985). They question the ability of the system to be technologically creative as well as adaptive in the increasingly competitive world markets. Since Japan is so dependent on those markets, the issue is a serious one.

More specifically, the question is raised as to whether the critical ubiquitous characteristic of Japanese society—namely that its "groupism" (Befu 1980; Ouchi 1981) imposes serious limitations on the capacity of the system to be sufficiently innovative and creative. Further, Japan's associated structural and processual organizational support systems (e.g., bottom-up—*nemawashi*—decision making, free and extensive information flow laterally and vertically, nonspecialized career paths, job rotation, group evaluation, job security for life— cf. Marsland 1980; Pucik & Hatvany 1983) are seen to be not unconditionally beneficial. While they may, indeed, promote harmony and communal spirit, as is noted in later chapters, they also tend to suppress the individual growth and development, creativity, and motivation which may be needed for organizational effectiveness in the new international markets (Christopher 1983; though see Shimada 1985). In still other words, the question revolves around the issue of the proper balance among the demands of "market, bureaucracy, and clan" (Ouchi 1984). The close-knit group may foster so much conformity that it inures the members to outside stimulation (cf. Janis 1982) and inhibits its members from standing up for and pressing for adoption of creative ideas that might make the organization more productive and competitive (cf. Weisz, Rothbaum, & Blackburn 1984). How the Japanese deal with this dilemma will also be of use to Western management.

There are, then, quite obviously some aspects of R & D leadership in Japan (as well as in the United States) that are of value and others that need remediation. The research described in this book was intended to discover leadership orientations and patterns of management that were especially successful in leading to greater motivation, independence, and innovative disposition among workers. That is, the focus was on the characteristics of leadership behavior in organizations that bypass the constraints of tradition and culture on worker dispositions and behavior.

The units identified for special study were key national organizations concerned with industrial and social advancement, such as scientific research and development laboratories and institutes. While the search for anomalous success in general is certainly not a new research method (see, for example, Likert 1967), the prospects here are enhanced by the choice of a unique set of variables examined for the first time in cross-cultural perspective. The study followed in the tradition of Haire, Ghiselli, and Porter (1963) and Bass, Burger, Doctor, and Barrett (1979). The conception of leadership in this book is a complicated one, having evolved over the course of the research rather than having been totally preconceived, maintained, and tested throughout. Many theoretical alternatives were available (see the detail in Chapter 13).

The academic study of leadership has proceeded from investigations of qualities of individuals that may account for extraordinary achievement, to considerations of behaviors of great and poor leaders, to analyses of situations that bring forth individuals who perform well in those situations, to examinations of the "match" between leader and situation, to perspectives on contingencies that must be taken into account in making the match, to "substitutes for leadership" (particularly in the organizational culture, as part of the evolving conceptions of the "indirect" nature of leadership influence) (Hunt 1991, 36), and finally (to date) to the expansion of leader-member exchanges in the social-psychological tradition to group/team leadership.

The impetus for this book began with the search for a theory of leadership that could explain the extraordinary success that Japan seemed to be experiencing in its remarkable rise to a position of economic superiority in the modern world. Surely, there must have been some unique modes of leadership exercised to map out the paths for progress and to assure that the work force in the long and arduous journey stuck to the paths or detoured at appropriate times and places. In an attempt to find the broadest and most comprehensive conceptualizations of leadership, the grounding of the framework was set in a systems perspective. Any true understanding of leadership must comprehend the totality of the needs of the system and the functions of the leader in attending to them, either personally or indirectly.

The initial quest for an appropriate systems perspective led to the master sociologist, Talcott Parsons, whose postulation of "system prerequisites" (Parsons 1951) seemed to lend itself to the parallel notion that the exercise of leadership must attend to each of them (Bess 1984). The dichotomizations by Parsons of system needs into internal and external prerequisites on the one hand, and instrumental and consummatory prerequisites on the other, are especially helpful. They reflect the organization's, and hence the leader's need to attend to the dynamics of internal efficiency, including issues of individual motivation and interpersonal/intergroup collaboration, as well as the necessity for responsiveness to cross-boundary external conditions, both in terms of identifying and setting markets and goals and securing and distributing resources pursuant to the achievement of those goals.

A review of the literature, however, revealed few theories of leadership that were comprehensive enough to capture these requisites. Nor was there any instrumentation extant. There was, however, a related conceptual framework which, coincidentally (and apparently accidentally) overlapped with that of Parsons. Carved out in the research and writings of Ian Mitroff and Ralph Kilmann (Mitroff & Kilmann 1975; Mitroff 1983), the theory sought to move from the individual level of managerial "dispositions" to the "behaviors" associated with those dispositions as the latter may be directed toward different organizational objectives.

Kilmann found that there were four distinctive orientations or preferred foci of managerial behavior—namely, toward: (1) internal efficiency; (2) internal effectiveness (e.g., motivation of employees); (3) external efficiency (e.g., market share, niche); and (4) external effectiveness (e.g., social welfare). Each of these orientations could be traced to basic personality dispositions. Kilmann's inspired source of the theory was the macropsychology of Carl Jung's "archetypes'' (Mitroff 1983). Gathering empirical data by means of the Myers-Briggs Type Indicator (MBTI) (Myers & Briggs 1962), these authors ascertained that most managers fell into one of the four groupings. At the individual level, the manager's psychological disposition to be primarily oriented toward any one of the above four was based on the Jungian and Myers-Briggs contention that individuals access information in one of two ways—by sensation or intuition—and process that information once received, again in one of two ways—by thinking or feeling. For example, managers who take in information in discrete sensory units and use cognition to process it are ''sensation-thinking'' types.

For this study, the Kilmann typology appeared to be especially promising in an exploration of Japanese leadership, particularly as compared with leadership style preferences in the United States. Since the Japanese have been successful on both the external (e.g., market share) and the internal (e.g., motivation) dimensions, the mix of personality dispositions and concomitant behaviors that make that success possible would be particularly intriguing. Operationalization of the theory required a translation of the Myers-Briggs Type Indicator into Japanese. This required some elaborate negotiations with early Japanese users to gain permission to use the instrument and some changes in the instrument to accommodate it to the Japanese R & D setting. This activity is described more fully in Chapter 14.

After the data were collected and partially analyzed, however, it became evident that the theory itself was not entirely adequate to describe leadership in Japan. As Chie Nakane (1988), the extraordinary Japanese sociologist, points out:

The Japanese language has no term for the word leadership. . . . Responsibility is diffused through the group as a whole and the entire collectivity becomes one functional body in which all individuals, including the manager, are amalgamated into a single entity. . . . The strength of this structure lies in its ability to efficiently and swiftly mobilize the collective posture of its members. The importance of its contribution to the process of Japanese modernization is immeasurable.

Indeed, studying the Japanese organization in cross-cultural perspective permitted and initiated the need for a more comprehensive theory that would be applicable not only to Japan but universally. Once again, help was available in the literature. Mitroff himself (1983) found that to understand the dynamics of hierarchical leadership it was necessary to consider more than the trait approach that the MBTI typology offered. As he notes:

One of the most offensive things about any typology is that it ''types'' people, a consideration that Jung was painfully aware of and went to great lengths to avoid. Throughout his various descriptions of the types, he repeatedly cautions against putting people into ''neat little boxes.'' (Mitroff 1983, 65–66)

Mitroff believes that despite predominant personality dispositions, individuals may vary their behavior depending on the situation in which they find themselves (others, e.g., Fiedler, would differ). Although there is some considerable debate on the subject of the variance or invariance of personality in alternative contexts (see, for example, Bem & Allen 1974), it seemed appropriate to accept, at least hypothetically, the notion that people, including leaders, do act differently depending on the person or group with whom they are interacting. The decision to add this contingency seemed especially wise in view of the consistent image of the Japanese psyche that prevailed in the literature. As explained in Chapter 7, the Japanese sensitivity to others and the need not to offend have implications both for leadership and followership. The refraining by leaders from openly initiating behaviors (e.g., planning, structuring, or restructuring the organizational design) and from offering direct critical feedback of peers or subordinates results in an exchange, or at least a sharing, of the usual responsibilities for leadership among leaders and followers.

This other-directedness must be placed in the context of a long cultural tradition in Japanese society in which familial relationships and most social interactions are rigidly hierarchical. Hence, to some degree, the other-directedness in leadership dynamics must also be conceptualized in terms that lean heavily on the role and authority framework of the nuclear family (see Chapter 5). The transactional analysis theories of Eric Berne (1961; cf. Bennett 1976; Villere 1981) help extend the Mitroff thesis. Again, the utility of tracing the sources of Japanese leadership style back to cultural, educational, and family conditions will be seen to offer insights into why Western leadership patterns are similarly constrained by antecedent factors and, in turn, what difficulties will be encountered in attempting to make changes that are acceptable both to leaders and followers in Western societies.

## LEADERSHIP IN GROUPS AND ORGANIZATIONS

The setting for the empirical phase of the study of leadership in this research was Japanese R & D laboratories of 15 to 40 workers, which are small enough to examine leadership in face-to-face settings yet are subject to external organizational demands. While it is generally agreed that R & D is a unique enterprise, there is considerable disagreement about the kinds of management that are likely to result in effective operation. Indeed, popular opinion (perhaps inspired by petulant researchers) is that researchers do their best work when simply left free of external constraints such as leadership. Some research (e.g., Pelz & Andrews 1976; Kanter 1983, 248 ff.) suggests the contrary—namely, that some constraints on researcher freedom actually enhance both creativity and effectiveness. In point of fact, creative ideas originating in the organization's environment are often communicated by an alert, externally oriented administration, while those from the laboratory are generated largely by the research staff. They are merged in subtle ways and supported by formal and informal organizational design and authority. Despite the hierarchical nature of society and organizations in Japan, the popular image of Japan as rigidly authoritarian is misapplied. Top-down directives or interventionist leadership is not considered appropriate and is usually avoided. To the contrary, though authority in Japan is formally vested in the bureaucratic hierarchy, the responsibility for decision making lies in the many formal and informal processes of interaction which take place in the work setting (see Chapter 8).

Yet the notion persists (both in Western and Eastern societies) that formal leaders do, after all, have ultimate responsibility for their organizations and that their activities are therefore critical to the continuing productivity of the organization. How it is exercised is, of course, the subject of both debate and research in academic circles. Alternative explanations seem to turn in part on the conceptualizations of the meaning of leadership and in part on the behaviors that are said to comprise it. Most social scientists conceive of leadership as an influence process. Leaders, both formal and informal, are able to move their organizations and their workers in directions thought to be desirable, both for the organizations and for the workers. The modes of influence are quite varied. Some leaders do actively direct workers and impose their wills on them. In a military or emergency situation, for example, such leadership may, at times, be appropriate. Others are able to ''transform'' their workers by helping them identify with and work toward organizational ends that transcend their personal spheres.

Following the Parsonian model noted above, it can be seen that other kinds of influence in an organization can also be labeled good leadership. For example, some leaders are particularly adept at cross-boundary relations. Their special skills lie in establishing and extending the relationship that their organization has with other sectors with which the organization has contact. One type of good leader here might be able to show how ideas generated in an R & D laboratory have or could have an important bearing on the larger organization's existing or potential clienteles. This leader can show how the work of his R & D unit is useful. Further, by convincing others, he can sustain or produce necessary funding. Along these same lines, another kind of cross-boundary leader might be effective in identifying needs of the clienteles of the organization (the outside society, the government, the customers, etc.) and in translating those needs into researchable projects.

Still other kinds of leaders are good at creating a positive work ''climate'' within the work section—a climate that encourages strong individual motivation and commitment, as well, perhaps, as risk taking. In the latter case, the leader must create conditions in the organization that identify and encourage radical, novel ideas, with rewards for toleration of viewpoints that may appear ''deviant'' to the majority. Recognition by the leader of the *kind* of climate that may be appropriate for the organization is also a leadership skill. A conservative climate may be needed at one point in an organization's history, but a more adventurous climate may be required at other times. For example, a corporation that has had a large share of the market for many years may find that it is useful to find ways to make incremental improvements in the product so as to preserve that share. Later, when the market domination has eroded, the same corporation may prefer to have its R & D organization take more risks in the development of new products. Whether the same leader can be effective either in generating the climate or behaving in it is a question to be answered.

These latter components of climate have to do with values and norms of work as they affect individual worker attitudes toward the work itself. Other norms and values are concerned with the interpersonal processes that take place in the work setting. Hence, another kind of good leader may be adept at promotion of a climate of cooperation and collaboration. Clearly, the ways that workers choose to interact with one another are subject to influence from many sources, one of which may be the formal leader. And even when disagreements occur, the skilled leader may be the one who can adjudicate conflicts without causing either party to lose face. Research has shown that at the applied and developmental end of the R & D research agenda, the establishment of highly collaborative efforts is critical, since many different backgrounds and skills must be brought together (cf. Thompson & Tuden 1959). The good leader, then, might be especially good at the subtle suppression of both ideas and persons who will upset the flow of the work. On the other hand, fostering good *basic* research—research that challenges existing ideas—may require a leader who is able to get new ideas into the open, forcing an obvious clash of new and old, without destroying the minimum organizational stability and comity needed for work to be carried out.

As a final example, there are some kinds of leaders who are good at managing the flow of information inside their organizations or at designing the work tasks so that they can be performed efficiently. This type of leader is oriented toward internal efficiency matters, such as just-in-time inventory practices, or toward internal effectiveness, such as personal counseling to facilitate individual productivity.

## MAIN TOPICS FOR RESEARCH

The use of the singular and presumably formal designation of "leader" should not be interpreted to mean that the research for this book concentrates only on this role, though indeed, at the outset, that was the focus. As noted earlier, in the course of the research, it became evident that leadership was exercised throughout the R & D laboratory. Its multiple and complex manifestations are represented by canonical correlations of attitudinal variables among all the workers—formal leaders, informal leaders, and working staff.

Three variables form the heart of the research: (1) psychological makeup or leadership orientation; (2) conflict management style, and (3) subordinate motivation and behavior. The conceptualizations of these factors derived initially from prior published research and the measurement of them from established questionnaire instruments. These processes are discussed at length in Chapter

14. Leadership orientation is conceived here largely through the idea of "psychological type" and was measured in the empirical research with the Myers-Briggs Type Indicator (Myers 1962; McCaulley 1981). It was further operationalized for statistical analysis by utilizing the Mitroff and Kilmann conceptualization noted above, as well as in a post hoc construction generated from the data. Conflict management style was measured by the Kilmann-Thomas "MODE" instrument. The dependent variable of worker motivation was conceptualized via the theory of Hackman and Oldham (1976; 1980) and tested through the administration of their "Job Diagnostic Survey." The latter provides, in addition, measures of perceived "job characteristics" conducive or deleterious to motivation and of "growth need strength" of workers. All of the instruments were carefully translated into Japanese.

Leadership theory (see Chapter 15 for a fuller discussion) has long virtually ignored the utility of "trait" approaches on the strength of (some say misinterpretation of) Stogdill's finding that no set of traits consistently predicted high group performance across all situations. But as Bass (1985) notes, Stogdill did not mean to cut off all research on traits; only to suggest that to the date of his summary, valid relationships had not been found (cf. Kenrick & Stringfield 1980).

The work of Kilmann and Herden (1976), Hoy and Hellriegel (1982), and Thamhain (1987; Thamhain & Gemmill 1974; Thamhain & Wilemon 1977; cf. Conger et al. 1988; Cummings & Staw 1990) has reinvigorated the search for leader traits that seem to work under different contingencies. Hellriegel and Kilmann, for example, found behavioral correlates for some traits that could be related to organizational conditions in different phases of the organizational life cycle (cf. Cameron & Whetten 1984; Parsons 1951; and Bess 1988).

## RESEARCH QUESTIONS

Thus, there is a wide variety of different kinds of leadership that can have varied effects on workers. As noted above, prior research has demonstrated that most research workers are more productive under conditions in which some constraint is put on their freedom. But the literature is not clear as to what kinds of constraints are best—for example, what kind of influence (leadership) is needed under what conditions.

There is also some confusion and/or controversy in the literature about the distribution of leadership in an organization. Although there may be only one "formal" leader, there are many leadership functions required to be performed in any organization. How many of those functions and which ones can be carried out by the formal leader? Is it possible, for example, for the leader to be both an "inside" and an "outside" person, a considerate, gentle caretaker of subordinates and at the same time, a hard, driving competitor? Or, are different people required for these different roles? Further, can these roles be played by people who occupy "informal" rather than formal positions in their work settings? A personality measure of leadership dispositions, in this case the Myers-Briggs Type Indicator, appears to offer an unusually clear perspective on the priorities of formal leaders, particularly their emphases on efficiency versus effectiveness in both internal and external environments of the R & D unit. The Kilmann-Thomas conflict measure permits an accurate assessment of the balance between leader assertiveness and cooperativeness–competitiveness in conflict management—especially important variables potentially discriminating between successful and unsuccessful laboratories, where group pressures may inhibit creativity. This measure has particularly intriguing possibilities for uncovering the modes in some Japanese laboratories that leaders may use in balancing strong, organizationally normed, cooperative impulses with individual needs for personal success. Finally, the Hackman-Oldham questionnaire assessing worker motivation yields critical data about worker attitudes toward the design of work, their leaders, and other conditions of the work setting.

We turn now to a more specific discussion of the research questions. Two major kinds of questions guided the design of the study and the manipulation of the variables. The first set was intended to provide descriptive data about the field of interest. The second set was addressed to the more theoretical concerns of the research. Both are noted in some detail below.

**Descriptive Questions**

1. What are the psychological characteristics of effective academic and industrial research leaders? Are certain traits more successful? For example, are leaders with concerns for *internal* efficiency or effectiveness (measured by a combination of MBTI traits) more or less effective under certain conditions (e.g., laboratories with different funding sources—university, government, corporate—or in different phases of a growth/decline cycle)? Should such leaders give way to others when market share or social responsibility pressures mount?

2. What styles of conflict management predominate in effective and ineffective leaders? Research using the Thomas-Kilmann MODE instrument reveals distinctive approaches to conflict resolution (e.g., accommodative, competitive, compromising, avoiding, or collaborating). Do these, in turn, reveal culture-bound and/or specialized academic/industrial dispositions?

3. What is the impact of leader characteristics *in combination with* conflict management styles on organizational effectiveness and subordinate motivation and creativity? Are there specific combinations of psychological characteristics of leaders and group conflict management styles that produce R & D units which are more successful than others and which also promote subordinate satisfactions? Under what conditions is individual motivation enhanced or inhibited?

**Theoretical Questions**

1. The first and most basic question deals in part with the issue of the invariance of personality across situations (Mischel 1983; Bem & Allen 1974; Epstein 1979; Kenrick & Stringfield, 1980). It also deals more specifically with the controversies in the study of leadership over whether leaders can change their styles in varying circum-

stances (e.g., Fiedler vs. Ohio State et al.). If the Jungian types of personality in the Mitroff and Kilmann scheme do not vary under different conditions of organizational stress, then is it likely that modes of managing that stress (or conflict management in this case) will vary? If not, will the research produce a finding demonstrating strong relationships between each of the four personality types and the five conflict management modes (in the Kilmann-Thomas inventory)?

2. The second, more theoretical concern of the research is with the relative importance of intrinsic versus extrinsic sources of reward (Deci 1975; Deci & Ryan 1985; Zuckerman et al. 1978; Staw 1976). The issue lies in the conceptualization of the notion of both "intrinsic" and "extrinsic." Since in Japan, intrinsic, egocentric sources of motivation are habitually subordinated to extrinsic ones, it is necessary to discover in successful research settings how leadership deals with the organizational need to evince individual behaviors which may have positive efficiency and effectiveness consequences for the organization, but potentially negative social/peer consequences for the individual. If, for example, the demands of the environment call for a leader disposition which maximizes the organization's bargaining position in relation to its environment, a mode of conflict management may be required which may not attend to the organization's needs for pattern maintenance and tension reduction, to use the Talcott Parsons's terminology (Parsons 1951). The crumbling of the organization's unified, singular identity, which employees use as an alter ego, may have consequences for the organization quite different from those desired by the leader.

In addition to the key variables of leadership, conflict management, and motivation, several additional moderating or controlling variables were investigated (though not all are reported in this book):

1. Industrial or scientific field (chemicals, transportation, communications, and iron and steel)
2. Resource availability (expanding, steady state, or contracting fields)
3. Social sector (corporate, government, or university)
4. Research orientation (basic, applied, developmental)
5. Institutional effectiveness (here defined as patents applied for, reputational status, or financial rank in field)
6. Institutional characteristics (size, age, diversity)
7. Cultural and/institutional values (sources of organizational authority, rewards, information flow, employee social status, sanctions, risk taking)
8. Unit characteristics (size, discipline)
9. Aggregate individual characteristics (homogeneity and/or diversity in age, education, socioeconomic status, and training and education patterns)

The focus of the research, then, was the management of the scientific research and development laboratory in three distinctive settings—corporations, universities, and governmental institutes. There has been much written about styles of Japanese industrial management, and much research continues to be conducted on the subject. It is probable that these same modes and management styles, which inhere in the wider industrial sector, obtain as well in research and de-velopment, accounting perhaps for some of the overall Japanese success. There are, however, hypothetically important differences across the organizational types in which R & D takes place. Goal foci, role definitions, organizational complexity, and other conditions suggest that university R & D may be quite different in many ways from that in government and corporate settings.

Some considerable controversy also exists in the literature on the cross-cultural validity of social science. The research described in this book helps sort out some of the confusion. Contrasts among the Japanese and the United States are useful for exploring these questions, since there are so many cultural and social differences which, in turn, have a profound effect on how R & D can be managed. While leadership and conflict management styles in either country may be effective, it is naive to believe that the methods employed can be ex-ported wholesale, without change, to another culture. Some of these differences are reflected in the research design for this study. Again, these will be considered later.

Another issue of interest in the research is concerned with the interplay of group and individual identity (cf. Befu 1986). Since sustained motivation de-pends in some way on achievement as an internal reward, there is some question as to the appropriate levels of salience of alternative signs and symbols of achievement to individuals and groups. Clearly, practices differ in countries with individualistic versus collectivist cultures, Japan bending more toward shared rewards and the United States toward separated individual merit assessments with some group participation.

An interesting problem thus created for this research, then, was the degree to which individuals in each culture can and do differentiate themselves from the group and hence find meaning and motivational sustenance from rewards avail-able to each. To ask a Japanese worker to give his *honne* (his innermost feeling) presumes both that some difference exists between *honne* and *tatemae* (his ex-pectation of what his peers expect) and, further, that he can make the distinction in his mind between his own and his group's identity. To be sure, each person regardless of culture or society is a unique individual. Hence, there is always some distance between self and others. In Japan, a culturally homogeneous so-ciety, the variance in the social and background characteristics of the population is smaller than in this country, and cultural/national norms stronger and more easily apprehended. Hence, the Japanese person can more easily know how he should behave. But he may be less able to differentiate his own feelings from the group or culture with which he identifies. For the group leader seeking to encourage creative deviant ideas, this merging of self and local or larger social system creates problems well beyond simply recognizing and rewarding the new and different. For the researcher, furthermore, problems of validity arise in in-terpretation of leadership attitude and behavior data.

America, with its cultural diversity and increasing heterogeneity, faces the same problem at the other extreme. Too many individual differences and cultural pressures to preserve them make collective action more difficult to achieve. The movement toward the center and away from dysfunctional collectivism that has evolved in the Japanese experience may also provide clues that will help facilitate the movement in the opposite direction in America. Issues of validity, however, must be accounted for in this setting as well.

Still another methodological question for the research revolves around the balance of individuality and collectivism in societies. In more Westernized societies, individuals can be asked how they will behave under certain conditions. Westerners are able to answer these questions, since they believe (though it may not be true) that their personalities are relatively invariant over different situations. That is, they believe themselves to be consistent in their behavior, since they think of themselves as individuals—indeed pride themselves on their individuality. In other societies, such pride may not be as highly prized. Other values, such as adaptability over different settings, may be more paramount. So, for example, in Japan, it may not be possible to ask formal leaders hypothetical questions calling for their prediction of their probable behavior under broad and general organizational conditions. The Japanese respondent will want to know the concrete social environment and other specific conditions of the setting, including, most importantly, the nature of the person or persons in the interaction.

## SUMMARY OF THE RESEARCH

This book is a report of the results of an empirical inquiry into the characteristics of scientific research and development laboratory leadership in Japan. The study arose out of the recognition that research and development in any developed country are critical to the continued well-being of the country's economy and to the long-term welfare of its people (Johnson 1983). The data were gathered in Japan from 1986 to 1988, during the author's sabbatical and subsequent year under a Fulbright grant. Data analysis began in the fall of 1987 and has continued as new data are collected.

The research involved an investigation of the nature and forms of leadership and conflict management as they may bear on the characteristics of a variety of conditions in the workplace and on worker attitudes that are commonly the concern of leaders seeking greater productivity (e.g., job clarity, collaboration, worker motivation, organizational commitment, and risk-taking propensity). The research is the first phase of a planned three-country comparative effort—the other countries being the United States and Great Britain.

2

# Conceptual Framework

## INTRODUCTION

As noted earlier, the intellectual/conceptual base for this study relied on theories and reports in the literature of empirical research on leadership, conflict management, and motivation. Variables from that research were operationalized in the form of translations of three published, well-tested, and well-regarded questionnaire instruments developed and tested in this country. In addition, other features of the R & D context were explored. The three main organizational constituents identified above had never been conceptually linked in cross-cultural conditions, though some combinations of parts had.

The leadership issues examined here utilized the Jungian psychology originated by Kilmann and Herden (1976); the conceptualization of alternative modes of conflict resolution was derived from the work of Kilmann and Thomas (1975); and the motivational variables came from the "job characteristics" theory developed by Hackman and Oldham (1976). Operationally, the three sets of independent variables were measured as follows:

1. *Leadership style*—the Myers-Briggs Type Indicator (MBTI) (Myers 1962; McCaulley 1981; Kilmann & Herden 1976)

2. *Conflict management style*—the Thomas-Kilmann "MODE" instrument

3. *Managerial attitudes*—original scales developed for this research

The dependent variable of primary interest, worker motivation, was tested through the administration of the Hackman and Oldham Job Diagnostic Survey (which provides, in addition, measures of perceived job characteristics conducive or deleterious to motivation). Other dependent variables included satisfaction, commitment, and risk-taking propensity.

Two of the published instruments had been used previously in Japan, and psychometric data on the properties of the scales were available. All of the English language questionnaires were translated into Japanese, then backtranslated to assure at least minimal validity, subject to empirical testing and other validation techniques. A third instrument was translated during the period of research, and its psychometric qualities are still being examined. The questionnaire used in the research also incorporated a number of other variables which were thought to be of interest and relevance and/or which can be used as controls.

The unit of analysis for the study was the R & D laboratory "section," defined as a subunit of 15 to 40 workers. This choice was dictated by the need to circumscribe the research to cover "face-to-face" leadership (*ore no kao ni menjite*[1]), rather than the more distant leadership that might be tapped by examining laboratory leadership at the top. Clearly, there are important questions about leadership in Japan in these macrosocial areas, some of which are connected to group leadership, but for a variety of reasons the research conducted for this book was limited to the more intimate, direct relationships that Japan's work group leaders have with the members of their groups. In this case, scientific research and development laboratories in selected industrial, governmental, and university organizations in Japan were chosen for investigation. The specifics of the sample are given later. Below, the questions outlined in the previous chapter are posed more concretely and in some greater detail, with the variables of concern clearly labeled.

## INDEPENDENT VARIABLES

### Leadership Style

What kinds of leadership types exist in different laboratory organizations (university, corporation, government institutes) and in different fields (e.g., electronics, iron and steel, chemicals, and transportation)? (See below for detail.)

### Conflict Management Modes

What are the various modes through which interpersonal conflict (in many forms) is productively resolved—and how do these differ over types of laboratory organizations and fields?

### Managerial Attitudes

*Control of Work.* In different kinds of laboratories, what is the leader's attitude toward worker versus management control over choice of projects and project methods?

*Focus of Rewards.* To what extent are individual versus group achievements valued and rewarded. How is this focus manifested in leadership behaviors?

*Norms of Information Flow.* Is information used more to advance individual or group objectives? Are workers encouraged by management to share discoveries freely or to keep them secret?

*Social Status.* Do manifest and latent values concerning worker status facilitate or inhibit achievement and especially worker creativity? Does management practice a hierarchy of status relationships, or is the pattern more egalitarian?

*Nature of Sanctions.* Are positive or negative sanctions typically applied by managers?

The answers to some of these questions are still under investigation and are not reported here.

## DEPENDENT VARIABLES

### Motivation, Satisfaction, Commitment, Risk Taking

What levels and types of worker motivation and satisfaction exist, how much commitment to the organization and its goals is there, and to what extent are workers willing to take risks in their research endeavors?

## CONTROLLING OR ANCILLARY VARIABLES

### Sector of Control

Are there different patterns of control and leadership in corporate, university, and government laboratories?

### Research Orientation

When an R & D organization emphasizes "basic," "applied," or "developmental" research, what kinds of leaders and conflict management are the most effective?

### Field and Economic Conditions of the Market

To what extent and in what way do industries in declining, steady state, or expanding markets differ in R & D leadership? What differences exist among organizations in the fields of electronics, iron and steel, chemicals, and transportation, the fields chosen for analysis in the Japanese phase?

### Laboratory Age/Research Project Stage

What is the relationship between R & D management style and the age of the laboratory and stage of development of a project?

**Demographic Characteristics of Leaders**

How are age, education, and employment history related to R & D management style?

What follows is a brief discussion of the three central conceptual domains in the research as they were utilized in the generation of these questions. Each of these domains is addressed in detail in separate chapters that follow.

## LEADERSHIP

Conceptualizations of the nature of leadership have shifted only incrementally since World War II (see Chapter 14). As has been well documented (cf. Bass 1990; Cummings & Staw 1990; Kellerman 1984; Vroom 1984; Misumi & Peterson 1985; Hunt, Hosking, Shriesheim & Stewart 1984; Hunt, Baliga, Dachler & Schriesheim 1988; Hunt 1984), researchers have moved from an examination of leader traits or dispositions (and recently back again) to leader behaviors, to more contemporary theories of normative behavior contingent on situations and/ or larger contexts. Successful leadership is alleged to involve the management by creative and appropriately disposed individuals of the demands of the competing and sequentially staged demands of two forces: on the one hand, the environment external to the organization which requires adaptive organizational behavior that will ensure survival and growth, and, on the other, the intraorganizational needs of its members who require sufficient psychological support to sustain their motivation, creativity, and commitment to each other and the organization's goals. The successful leader, often with help from a properly disposed lieutenant, makes a payoff to the demands of each constituency and balances the two over time. Indeed, where with the creative assistance of leaders, the cross-boundary, system-sustaining demands are transformed for and by employees into challenges rather than threats to self-fulfillment, the objectives of organization and individual are merged (Argyris 1987). It should be noted that the "organization" referred to here can be any bounded social system, formal or informal, including R & D units within a larger organization.

Whether it is possible for any *one* person to carry out successfully all of the requisite leadership tasks (cf. Hunt 1991, 71) has been questioned. Fiedler, Chemers, and Mahar (1976; cf. Fiedler & Garcia 1987), for example, suggest that since personality or psychological traits are relatively intractable, the successful leader will be that person who is able to change the *situation* to meet his/her leadership predispositions or who sees the need to and does leave the organization to find a more compatible situation. Some recent theorists have suggested that leaders must be matched to organizational phases of growth and decline (Bess 1982; Cameron & Whetten 1984). Other currently salient theories indicate that there are "substitutes for leadership" and that the proper "management of culture" successfully utilizes those substitutes. Still others deal with different theoretical resources: self-efficacy theory (Bandura 1982), charisma (Conger, Kanugo, & Associates 1988), and symbolic leadership (Hunt 1984).

A central thesis of this book is that in Japan the culture itself creates conditions that may invalidate traditional Western notions of leadership. That is, the conceptual frameworks that fall broadly into such older frameworks as the Ohio State behavioral model (initiating structure versus consideration), Hersey and Blanchard's addition to it of the subordinate maturity contingency, or Fiedler's combination of trait/situation contingencies, as well as the "vertical dyad linkage" or, more recently, "leader-member exchange theory" tradition of George Graen and his associates (cf. Graen & Cashman 1975; cf. Dienesch & Liden 1986; Schriesheim, Scandura, & Neider 1991) are less valid in most foreign settings. In Japan, it would be difficult to find leaders with sets of the requisite Western traits, dispositions, or behaviors identified in past research reports as leading to effectiveness. The absence of empirical replication of Western-style leadership in Japan calls for new paradigmatic reconceptualizations of leadership which will not only describe leadership in other cultures but will inform the thinking of Western leadership scholars and practitioners.

As noted above, obviously manifested individuality and assertiveness in Japan are subject to severe social sanctions. What has evolved in their place is a much more subtle nexus of "influence" roles played out by different parties (e.g., formal and informal leaders and workers) at different times, depending on the external and internal demands extant inside and outside of the organization. Such evolving role enactment goes well beyond the Balesian role-distribution model proposed some years ago (Bales 1950). Moreover, the very subtlety of the role playing makes the analysis of the character of the persons who play them difficult to discern. Hence, it is necessary to assess the nuances of personality and those that predispose individuals to be more or less attentive to the demands of the situation and of the subtleties of their behavior as they act out leadership roles. As will be seen, it is also critical to understand how individuals become team leaders with personalities and behavior repertories complemented by subordinate worker role players. Discussion in later chapters explores the modes by which organizations in Japan institutionalize these roles.

Another problem with most current leadership studies is that they tend to ignore the social construction or definition of the situation by the manager. All managers make assessments of both the external and internal demands on their organizations. The personality of the manager, however, ineluctably predisposes him to define the needs of the situation narrowly—according to his personality. For example, those whose talents and interests lie in cross-boundary problems tend to lay emphasis in that domain rather than in internal matters. A leader, then, is at least partially successful by virtue of his organization's sagacious recognition of the match of his leadership predilections and the currently salient exigencies—external versus internal—of the organization. Such leader selection decisions limit most organizations to solving present-day problems and leave them less ready to anticipate the future. The multiple leader configuration in the Japanese organization, on the other hand, keeps the organization sensitive to both present and future needs as the phases of internal and external emphases shift.

The research described in this book examined the manager's "psychological frames of reference" (Shrivastava & Mitroff 1983). The measurement tool chosen to examine leadership predispositions, the Myers-Briggs Type Indicator, was modified by some leadership researchers to permit differentiation among persons who are internally versus externally oriented and who are either primarily "people" versus "thing" oriented in their approaches to problem solving. The construction was developed out of the Jungian typology of information acquisition and information processing by Kilmann and Herden (1976), Mitroff (1983), Nutt (1989), and others and provided useful diagnostic categories for understanding managerial dispositions (and, more recently, organizational dispositions and leadership—cf. Bridges 1992; Hirsch & Kummerow 1989). Basically, managers whose preferred style is to take in data by sensing and to act on it by thinking (STs) tend to be oriented toward goals of internal efficiency, while others (SFs) look to the more individual personal concerns of subordinates as measures of success. Still others (NTs and NFs) tend to look beyond the borders of the institution to seek respectively either organizational achievements of a diverse and somewhat impersonal kind or of a more global, humanistic nature. (These concepts are discussed more fully below.)

The relationship of alternative leadership styles to organizational effectiveness in Japan was the special focus of concern here. While there are numerous other possible psychological approaches to the study of leadership or/and decision making (cf. Miller 1986; Kets de Vries 1984; Driver 1984), the Kilmann and Herden mode lent itself to the search for answers to the questions of the advantages and limitations of Japanese and American management. For example, it may well be that, given the domestic and world market conditions for a given country from 1945 to, say, 1980, the special mix of Jungian types which emerged in the country may have fit certain of the external contingencies. Thus, Japan's particular concern with internal effectiveness and efficiency during this period may have demanded STs and SFs, which apparently were in abundant supply. On the other hand, those same managers in today's more competitive international environment may be inappropriate (Cameron & Whetten 1984; Bess 1983). Similarly, it may be that while these managers may have been internally responsive, evidence from the United States suggests that managers' emphasis here on short-term external adaptiveness may have resulted in the neglect of internal exigencies.

At any rate, as will be seen, the instrument chosen was effective in testing these notions. As Hoy and Hellriegel (1982) note, the MBTI "represents a safe but powerful means for assisting a group of small business managers to gain self-insight into their natural inclinations and the manner in which this insight might influence the problems and goals they emphasize. . . . " (For a dissenting view, see Pittenger 1993.)

The first conceptual framework, then, comes from the work of Ian Mitroff and is based on the psychological principles of Carl Jung's "archetypes" (Jung 1923; cf. Benfari 1991). Jung believed that it is possible to categorize all people into a reasonably small number of types, namely:

The archetype is a symbolical formula, which always begins to function whenever there are no conscious ideas present, or when such as are present are impossible upon intrinsic or extrinsic grounds. The contents of the collective unconscious are represented in consciousness in the form of pronounced tendencies, or definite ways of looking at things. They are generally regarded by the individual as being determined by the object—incorrectly, at bottom—since they have their source in the unconscious structure of the psyche, and are only released by the operation of the object. (p. 476)

Understanding these types permits the prediction of behavior, Jung claimed, with a satisfactory degree of reliability. Mitroff (and, subsequently, others) adopted the Jungian typology and tested it with various samples of leaders, with the finding that the Jungian personality types could be used to describe different kinds of leaders.

In particular, they postulate that there are four predominant leader types as noted in Exhibit 2.1. The questionnaire instrument to measure these four types consists of paired self-description adjective comparisons. The instrument is an abbreviated version of the Myers-Briggs Type Indicator and was translated for use in Japan. (See Chapter 13.)

## CONFLICT MANAGEMENT

The second concept adopted for the research was conflict management style. The issue of the health or divisiveness of conflict has largely been settled in the literature, but only for Western-style management structure and process. The consensus seems to be that "managed conflict" is necessary— that is, the encouragement in an organization of conflict which is organizationally, rather than personally, focused and which is manifest, rather than latent (Pondy 1967; Deutsch 1973; Thomas 1976; Greenhaigh 1986). The literature is controversial, however, when cross-cultural applications are considered. Some of the difficulty stems from semantic problems. A group of observers, especially in Japan, would insist that no conflict of any importance exists, since the structure and processual dynamics of most Japanese organizations prevent it from occurring. In point of fact, however, the early stages of the Japanese extensive lower-level discussion processes (see *nemawashi* discussed later) are essentially equivalent to one form of functional conflict— disagreements which are permitted to surface and be resolved. Whether there are latent conflicts which undermine the effective functioning of organizations in both countries is a largely unexamined question.

The Thomas model, as operationalized in the Thomas-Kilmann Conflict Mode Instrument, was derived in part from the conceptualizations of Blake and Mouton (1964). The model allows the identification of five conflict management

**Exhibit 2.1**
**Variables in the Leadership Framework**

1. **Orientation Toward Maximizing Internal Efficiency**
   Here the leader is concerned with costs, productivity per worker, wastage, office management

2. **Orientation Toward Maximizing Internal Effectiveness**
   The disposition of this leader is toward keeping workers motivated, creating a supportive climate, engendering positive worker attitudes toward the organization, facilitating good interpersonal relationships

3. **Orientation Toward Maximizing External Efficiency**
   This leader is concerned with improving the organization's bargaining position with agencies outside, with assuring that products are used by the maximum number of people, with new product development, and with the identification of new users

4. **Orientation Toward Maximizing External Effectiveness**
   This leader's primary orientation is toward societal satisfactions, solving current and emerging social problems, improving the quality of life, and with the impact of his organization on the environment as a whole

approaches which are generated out of an analysis of the dispositions of respondents to two basic orientations: the desire to maximize one's own satisfactions in a conflict dispute and the desire to cooperate with others in a dispute. These are conceived as independent dimensions such that different persons may score high or low on each. Each of the modes of conflict resolution is appropriate for different contextual conditions (Thomas 1976) as follows: competing (when quick, decisive action is important); collaborating (when the interests of the parties in dispute are seen as too important to be compromised); compromising (when goals are deemed important, but preservation of interpersonal harmony is believed to be critical); avoiding (when the conflict is over apparently trivial matters); and accommodating (when one party's stake in the conflict outcome appears minor and the desire to cooperate with others predominates). For the samples in this research, it was intriguing to speculate at the outset which were the predominant modes among managers in R & D organizations. For example, as the notes which accompany the Thomas-Kilmann instrument indicate:

As behaviors, collaborating and compromising are quite different. Collaborating means working with the other to seek solutions which completely satisfy both parties. This involves accepting both parties' concerns as valid and digging into an issue in an attempt to find innovative possibilities. It also means being open and exploratory. In contrast, compromising means seeking an expedient settlement which only partially satisfies both people. It doesn't dig into the underlying problem, but rather seeks a more superficial arrangement—e.g., splitting the difference. It is based upon partial concessions—something to get something—and may be played close to the vest.

It was hypothesized that Japanese conflict management styles were quite different from those in the West, marking different emphases on what Thomas calls the "integrative" (increasing the size of the pie) versus "distributive" (cutting up the pie) dimensions of conflict resolution. Hypothetically, so also are there differences across institutions with different types of control (corporate, government, and university). Further, what was of interest was the interaction of the psychological type noted above with conflict management style (cf. Kilmann & Thomas 1976; Mills 1985; Chanin 1984; Wommack 1988) as well as the effect of both on the success of the organization (e.g., external success rankings of the unit and/or the collective internal motivation of the workers).

The Thomas-Kilmann conflict instrument has been extensively tested and found to be valid and reliable (see, for example, Kilmann & Thomas 1977). The instrument comprises only 30 items and has been successfully translated into French and Spanish. In the first phase of the research conducted for this study, it was translated into Japanese.

The five conflict management modes are generated out of an analysis of the dispositions of managers to two basic personality orientations: the desire to maximize one's own satisfactions in a conflict dispute through assertive behavior and the desire to cooperate with others in a dispute. These are conceived as independent dimensions such that different persons may score high or low in each. This research provided a first opportunity to examine these conflict management modes in cross-cultural comparison with the Japanese, whose conflict management modes, as noted above, are quite distinctive. Crossing these two axes of disposition in a two-by-two table results in a questionnaire instrument (the Thomas-Kilmann MODE) that permits the researcher to assess situationally the presence of five alternative types of conflict management behavior or, more precisely, approaches to conflict management. These are noted in Exhibit 2.2.

## MOTIVATION

The third and last conceptual framework employed in the research was derived from the work of Hackman and Oldham (1980). The theoretical underpinnings of their research are drawn from the literature on intrinsic/extrinsic motivation (and further on need and expectancy theory and developmental psychology). The subject of employee motivation has received considerable attention among industrial and organizational researchers (see, for example, the reviews in Lawler 1973; Steers & Porter 1975; Staw 1983; Pinder 1984; Algera 1990; Idaszak & Drasgow 1987; Katzell & Thompson 1990; Kanfer 1990; Idaszak, Bottom, & Drasgow, n.d.). Less work has been done on faculty and/or professional researcher motivation (but see Hagstrom 1965; Gaston 1978; Pelz & Andrews 1976; Andrews 1979; Bess 1977, 1982; Lewis & Becker 1979; Fulton & Trow 1975; Staw 1984). Theories of work motivation are frequently classified as "content" theories (usually, need/drive approaches; e.g., McClelland, Maslow, Alderfer, Herzberg) and "process" theories (commonly oriented

**Exhibit 2.2**
**Variables in the Conflict Management Framework**

1. **Competing**
   The leader's behavior in this mode is toward pursuing his own concerns at the expense of others. This is a power-oriented mode.

2. **Accommodating**
   Under this mode, the leader neglects his own concerns to satisfy the concerns of others. He usually obeys another person's orders when he prefers not to. He yields in most cases.

3. **Avoiding**
   The behavior of this kind of leader does not address conflict. The leader does not immediately pursue either his own concerns or those of the other person.

4. **Collaborating**
   Here the leader is both assertive and cooperative. The leader attempts to work with the other person to find some solution which fully satisfies the concerns of both parties.

5. **Compromising**
   This is a mid-point mode, between collaborating and accommodating. It represents behavior in which the leader tries to find some expedient, mutually acceptable solution which partially (but not fully) satisfies both parties.

toward explaining the elements which initiate and sustain or change behavior; e.g., Porter & Lawler, Vroom, Adams).

In this study, the job characteristics model (Hackman & Oldham 1980), which incorporates parts of both approaches, was utilized. It is built in part on Maslow's (1943) need hierarchy and in part on the more cognitive expectancy theories, thus reflecting the intimate, subtle, yet critical linkages between intrinsic and extrinsic sources of motivation. Though not without methodological faults (cf. Roberts & Glick 1981; Aldag, Barr, & Brief 1981; Pierce, McTavish, & Knudsen 1986; Fried & Ferris 1987) and in recent years having been subjected to suggested revisions, the original model and instrumentation were determined to be suitably chosen for this kind of cross-cultural research.

Hackman and Oldham found through empirical research that the design of work in organizations profoundly affects the psychological state of mind of workers. In turn, these states of mind determine the motivation and commitment of workers to the organization and task and to the quality of the work output. Not all workers, however, are equally affected by the conditions at work. Some have a higher growth potential, or growth need strength, which further accentuates the effects of working conditions.

The Hackman and Oldham model recognizes the influence of the management decisions about the design of work conditions, especially decisions having to do with styles of organizational control and task or worker autonomy and/or interdependence. As noted earlier, these are key variables that may differenti- ate R & D, particularly in view of different knowledge and technology trans- fer modes in different countries. Using the data from the Hackman and Oldham Job Diagnostic Survey (JDS), R & D job characteristics and research worker psychological states can be correlated with leader types and conflict modes. Another value of the JDS instrument is that it yields a "motivating potential score" which is "a means for summarizing the overall degree to which a job is objectively designed in a way that maximizes the possibility for internal motivation on the part of the people who perform it." (Hackman & Oldham 1974, 25).

More specifically, the Job Diagnostic Survey measures workers' perceptions of five core task attributes: skill variety, task variety, and task identity (summed) which are multiplicatively related to autonomy and feedback to yield the mo- tivating potential of a job. The authors suggest that three psychological states intervene to moderate or explain the effects of job characteristics on motivation. These states are "experienced meaningfulness of the work," "experienced re- sponsibility for outcomes," and "knowledge of results." Finally, the dependent variables are the strength of internal worker motivation, the commitment to high quality and high quantity work output, and the extent of absenteeism, accidents, and turnover. The model used to describe this motivational framework is given in Exhibit 2.3. While all of the questions tapping the independent variables in the Hackman and Oldham model—job characteristics, psychological states, and worker motivation—were included in the survey instrument used in the research, since the objective was to determine the impact of leadership and conflict man- agement on motivation, neither the job characteristics data nor the psychological states are reported in the findings in later pages. (This is *not* to suggest, of course, that job design is not one of the means that leaders use to carry out their influence. Indeed, in Japan, this is certainly the case.)

It is necessary here to anticipate a possible objection to this design. As will be noted, the dependent variables (e.g., various types of motivation) described above are "internal" to the organization. That is, the inference will be made that, hypo- thetically, certain types of leadership and conflict management will result in higher levels of motivation. The latter, however, may or may not be related to the external effectiveness of the laboratory or institution measured in the system sur- rounding the organization (regardless of the definition of "effectiveness"). There is no guarantee, in other words, that simply working hard within an organization will result in organizational success in its competitive environment.

While there is some support in the literature that there is a moderate corre- lation between high motivation, commitment, and satisfaction in workers and institutional effectiveness as a whole, an additional measure of external success of the R & D laboratory should be added to the design for the research (cf. Azumi, Hull, & Sakakibara 1986). Although the specific criteria differ in dif- ferent countries, in Japan there are effectiveness rankings of firms and univer-

**Exhibit 2.3**
**Variables in the Motivational Framework**

| Core Job Dimensions | Critical Psychological States | Personal and Work Outcomes |
|---|---|---|
| Skill Variety | | |
| Task Identity | Experienced Meaningfulness of the Work | High Internal Work Motivation |
| Task Significance | | |
| Autonomy | Experienced Responsibility for Outcomes of the Work | High Satisfaction With the Work |
| Feedback | Knowledge of the Actual Results of the Work Activities | Low Absenteeism and Turnover |

Employee Growth Needs Strength

*Source:* Hackman & Oldham (1976, 250–279).

sities (though not of independent laboratories) (see, for example, Arimoto 1978; Jones, Lindzey, & Coggeshall 1982; Toyo Keizai 1985; *Japan Times* 1985; Fortune 500 1987). Post-hoc assignment of industry or university rank to the randomly sampled institutions might permit an analysis of the relationship of the key variables to external measures of effectiveness. Such an analysis was not done, however, and the results reported below must be understood as internal measures of effectiveness only.

## RELATIONSHIPS AMONG THE CONCEPTUAL FRAMEWORKS

It is now necessary to consider how the three theoretical foundations of the research are related hypothetically. While there are actually a great many individual item variables in the questionnaire which are used for control or enrichment purposes, the essential components of the model for the research can be portrayed by displaying the frameworks adjacent to one another and considering the alternative possible findings. The omnibus model is noted in Exhibit 2.4.

As the model shows, the leader personality types can be combined with the conflict management styles in as many as twenty combinations (four leader types [A–D] multiplied by the five conflict management modes [1–5]). These in turn can be associated with each of the four dependent variables: high motivation, high quality work, high commitment, and low absenteeism (W, S, Q, and AT.)[2] In point of fact, as the data were analyzed, these theoretical relationships were modified and expanded.

**Exhibit 2.4**
**Composite Model for the Research**

| Characteristics of R & D Leaders | | R & D Research Workers |
| --- | --- | --- |
| Leadership Styles | Conflict Mgt. Modes | Outcomes |
| | Competing (1) | |
| Internal Efficiency (A) | | Internal Work Motivation (W) |
| | Accomodating (2) | |
| Internal Effectiveness (B) | | Quality of Work Performance (Q) |
| | Avoiding (3) | |
| External Efficiency (C) | | Satisfaction With Work (S) |
| | Collaborating (4) | |
| External Effectiveness (D) | | Absenteeism and Turnover (AT) |
| | Compromising (5) | |

The directions in which hypotheses regarding these variables should be framed is not at all clear. It may be, for example, that in an industry experiencing a condition of basic decline (e.g., iron and steel in Japan), the type of leadership and conflict management which is effective in producing the desired W, S, Q, and AT is quite different from what is required in a rapidly expanding field, like computers. Moreover, it may be that the R & D manager in a department oriented toward applied or developmental research may be different from one in a basic research laboratory. There is no prior published research which can provide assistance in predicting the nature of the relationships among the variables. Hence, no directional hypotheses were formulated.

Clearly omitted in this research are several key organizational variables which surely have some influence on effectiveness and subordinate motivation. As Pelz and Andrews (1976; cf. Pelz 1978; Andrews 1979; Lambright & Teich 1981) so well revealed, scientists in organizations (at least Western organizations) do not function optimally with complete autonomy. For maximum creativity as well as productivity, they need a mix of hierarchical control and freedom. Though measures of bureaucratic control structures and processes (Ouchi 1978) in the units under investigation were not explicitly addressed in the study, they were indirectly recorded through the Hackman and Oldham measures (though see the current concern about the confusion of worker independence/interdependence with worker autonomy or discretionary authority in Breaugh 1985, 1989, and Dossett & Lee 1991).

Also of consequence but not considered here is the subject of "organizational," as contrasted with "national" culture (Selznick 1957; Schein 1985; Deal & Kennedy 1982). While variance in the dependent variable among different units as a result of organizational climate and value differences must surely exist, in this research other sources of explanation were sought. More particularly, the key assumption here is that national cultures and values will have a profound effect on the nature of managers, the nature of conflict management, and the resultant strength of motivation of subordinates (Haire, Ghiselli, & Porter 1963; Hofstede 1976, 1980b, 1984; Kraut 1975; Barrett & Bass 1976, though see Whitely & England 1977 and England & Negandhi 1979). While the measure of success or effectiveness in this study is internal to the national culture (i.e., the quality rankings within each country and may even vary *in definition* across institutions within them), the question is begged of the long-range "fit" of organizational internal success to national survival and continued health. If, however, it can be shown that employees in organizations at the tops of their fields are found to have high motivation and productivity, it is reasonable to assume that national welfare will be enhanced if similar policies are adopted in organizations lower in the effectiveness ratings.

Criticisms of the job characteristics approach and of the Hackman and Oldham instruments (Dunham, Aldag, & Brief 1976; Roberts & Glick 1981; Aldag, Barr, & Brief 1981; Breaugh 1985), as well as the potential bias from subjective reports of job characteristics (Van de Ven & Ferry 1980, 59–62) have been partially addressed (Oldham & Hackman 1981; Glick, Jenkins, & Gupta 1986; Fried & Ferris 1987). Moreover, the concern in this study was primarily with the dependent measures in the model, that is, internal work motivation and various kinds of satisfactions (growth, social supervisory, security, pay, and general), which would seem to have been sufficiently validated in the development of the instruments.

It should also be pointed out that the study is primarily concerned with horizontal conflict among peers, not with conflict between levels in an organizational hierarchy. However, it is addressed to the leadership dynamics of the resolution of that conflict, which are at least formally hierarchical. That is, the primary objective is to identify the dimensions of leadership personality and conflict management preference modes in general. There is only minimal and anecdotal description of the concrete behavioral components of the processes, though such research is certainly needed.

Finally, it should be noted that this study is descriptive at the organizational level, not normative at the cultural level. It is not the intent to make judgments about the values of the national culture or of the organizational dynamics which may follow from it. Sullivan's (1983) discussion of industrial clans and humanism, for example, is only tangentially related to the central concerns of this study.

The conceptual framework for the research thus having been presented, it is necessary next to turn more substantively to a fuller description of the societal and organizational contexts for the exercise of leadership in Japan—more specifically, to education and family life as the backdrop for understanding the social relations in organizations and to the evolution of business and educational organizations in Japan to their present structures and functions.

## NOTES

1. Translations of key English terms into Japanese are given from time to time to provide Japanese readers a better basis for understanding their meaning and use in this context.

2. Not shown above, but also considered in the research, are controlling variables such as industry or field of study and differences among R & D units which are oriented toward basic, applied, or developmental research.

## II

# The Japanese Sociocultural Environment

# 3

# Japanese Society and Culture

It is incontrovertible that in all societies culture is a powerful determinant of individual behavior. In more homogeneous societies, the national culture exerts a greater influence than in societies with more diverse subpopulations, each with its own set of values, mores, and folkways. Since Japan is extremely homogeneous, it follows that the press of its culture is profound, coherent, and consistent. In the United States, in contrast, the national culture is amorphous and multifaceted, with its impact less critical to individual decision making. In each case, the culture accentuates respectively either the pull toward individuality or toward collectivism. The strong culture in Japan reinforces the nomothetic, while the diverse U.S. culture sustains the values of individuality. Leadership and followership, as might be expected, are bound up in cultural conditioning, especially in a society so weighted with a singular and strong culture.

It is important at the outset, therefore, to describe some key cultural features of this complex nation to set the context for understanding the findings from the research on leadership. Many observers and authors, especially native Japanese, have provided extensive emic and etic analyses of the culture. (See, for example, Befu 1971; Lebra 1976; Mouer & Sugimoto 1986; Najita & Koschmann 1982; Hamabata 1990; De Vos 1985; van Wolferen 1989; Dore 1967; Krauss, Rohlen, & Steinhoff 1984; Hayashi 1988; and the Graubard 1990 publication, ''Showa: The Japan of Hirohito.'') Hence, what is offered here are those more salient elements of Japanese culture that especially illuminate the unique patterns of R & D leadership. As with all generalizations, these are not to be taken as universally applicable nor by any means to account for the intricate nuances that exist.

Harumi Befu (1971) identifies four main features of Japanese cultural style that express the significant characteristics of Japan: subtlety, simplicity, indirection, and suppression of verbalism. Each of these affects importantly how leadership is exercised. In various forms, we take them up below.

Japan is a country geographically not quite as large as California with twice its population and with an historic tradition at least five times as old as that of the United States, where almost all of the population has deep roots in a common ancestry comprising a unique aggregation of long-standing indigenous institutions, many derived from the rich oral and written traditions of Chinese culture. It is a country where there are virtually no minorities; where the central government dictates most of the curriculum in the schools; where nonconformity to expected behavior carries exceptionally strong negative sanctions from peers; where fathers are feared and respected, yet absent from the home most evenings and many weekends; where homes are so small that privacy rarely can be found; and where public places are so crowded that people are forced both to ignore one another as well as to be extremely conscious of the necessity to be civil, cordial, polite, and deferent.

Japan is also a country of incredible natural beauty, with mountains and seascapes of extraordinary splendor. Its people possess tremendous energy, intelligence, and esthetic sensitivity which is applied with diligence and dedication to education, work, art, and play. The Japanese are a trusting, caring, devoted people, full of generosity and kindness, reverent of their elders, highly patriotic, proud of their heritage, and loyal to their leaders. The uniformity of the culture, however, does not necessarily render it easy to understand. Because Japan's history is long and its customs and traditions deeply ingrained in its social conditions, and because it has long resisted scrutiny by outsiders, it remains at least partially inaccessible, especially to Westerners. For example, it embodies a pattern of seemingly incompatible philosophic or value contrasts as well as social and cultural artifacts that coexist without outwardly apparent conflict. Japan is simultaneously subtle and understated, while brash and busy; bland and undistinguished while beautiful and unique; democratic and egalitarian while hierarchical and status-oriented; competitive at the same time it is collegial; and rooted firmly in tradition and ritual while fresh with the innovative and pioneering spirit of the present.

This is not to say that Japan manages these contrasts without strain. Indeed, many of the trade-offs that Japan as a society and the Japanese as a people must make for the positive gains it has achieved would make a Westerner extremely uncomfortable. Perhaps most basic to the differences between the two cultures is the apparent submersion of individualism in Japan, about which more will be said later (see Chapter 6). To the outsider, Japanese individuality is inhibited, Japanese autonomy is restricted, Japanese personal initiative is frowned upon, Japanese aggressiveness is seen as offensive, Japanese personal competitiveness for self-aggrandizement is cause for opprobrium. The Japanese have an expression that captures some of this notion: "*Deru kugi wa sugu utareru*"—"the nail that protrudes is soon pounded back down." While this metaphor, now a cliché among Japanese observers, overstates the forcefulness and ignores the subtlety of the collective response, it does convey the negative psychological environment for sustained deviance. Van Wolferen (1989, 23) suggests that the Japanese are controlled by teachers and bosses "in the way a landscape gardener treats a hedge; protruding bits of the personality are regularly snipped off." Along these same lines, Robert Christopher (1983, 74) points out:

self-assertion comes close to being the ultimate no-no in Japan. To proclaim openly your right to special rewards for a job extraordinarily well done or to individual credit for what was nominally a group effort frees your colleagues of any sense of guilt toward you and hence is destructive to your prestige and influence.

Christopher (1983, 73) also notes that guilt is probably the most critical motivational lever, controlling most interpersonal relationships in Japan. The avoidance of guilt, then, becomes an all-consuming passion of the Japanese and one to which Japanese leadership is highly attentive. To be sure, in more moderate forms, guilt is also a powerful force in Western society. According to one psychoanalytic interpretation (McWilliams 1973, 17):

Fraternal solidarity in patrilineal societies, Freud argued, must be based in part on guilt; having idealized the father, sons feel remorse for his murder and need their brothers as sharers of the burden and sources of encouragement and affection.
    A society may seek to protect the father and his authority by surrounding him with taboos which make competition for his favor and status impossible, although they also make his authority irrelevant for much of day-to-day life.

So also in Japan, there are taboos that not only inhibit competition but that result in a kind of leadership which replaces parental-type "authority" with a uniquely Japanese style of shared decision making. Furthermore, the inhibition of competition has important implications for the management of creativity and innovation, which are, themselves, stifled. As in all human cultures, the Japanese is composed of certain ubiquitous values, some of which are common to other cultures (cf. Linowes 1993). The ones noted below exceed in strength what is found in most other countries. These include dependence (*amae*), duty (*on*), social obligation (*giri*), and human feeling (*ninjo*) (Sethi, Namiki, & Swanson 1984, 7). As will be seen, each bears importantly on the leadership question.

Takeo Doi, perhaps the most well known of Japanese authors, illuminated the concept of *amae* or dependence most prominently (especially in his *The Anatomy of Dependence*, 1973). Dependence for the Japanese, he says, begins with the child's relationship to its mother. Japanese mothers attempt to engender in their children a sense of complete dependence on them. At the same time, they indulge their children in the child's whims and tantrums. The child soon comes to see, feel, and understand that the mother is the source of all good things and to want to please that source. Doi suggests further that when a condition of *amae* exists, the child is attempting to deny the actuality of separation from its mother (p. 75). The one and the other are inseparable (cf. Buber 1970). It is this curious combination of dependence on others and at least partial denial of separation from mother and surrogate mothers in adulthood that carries over to the world of work in Japan, where the organization takes over many of the roles played out in the Japanese family. Indeed, the government itself further mirrors some of those family-like responsibilities.

Hence, in the context of the organization, the Japanese worker feels both dependent on the good will of the organization and confident in its benevolence. At the same time, he is usually unaware of or at least inattentive to differences between his own attitudes and values and those of the organization to which he belongs. This individual-organization isomorphism of values serves both, to reduce conflicts that might not be in the best interest of one or the other. On occasions when contradictory obligations do emerge and appear to the worker to conflict with organizational or societal norms, he feels disloyal and threatened. He questions both himself and his fealty to his support system. If questioned about his ambivalence, almost invariably he will give a response (his *"tatemae"*) that is ideologically identical with organizational "line." In other words, the Japanese worker, "unconsciously," melts into his organization. Indeed, since he is often unaware of the difference between *"honne"* (his innermost feelings) and his *tatemae*, the answers to questions that he gives are sometimes confusing or contradictory, especially to foreigners. That is because his desire is not to offend, and he molds his response accordingly. His self-concept and sense of his acceptability as a human being "depends" on his success at fitting in. Further, as discussed later, the Japanese are less aware of and more dispositionally tolerant of intellectual and emotional intrapsychic contradictions. Ignoring the latter in the interests of harmonizing self and social system—society or organization—is thus more easily effected and with less trauma.

In terms of the research conducted in Japan, this sense of *amae* was critical to the understanding of the kinds of leadership that might be most effective there. If the worker gives credit for his achievements to his colleagues—or, more likely in Japan, to his superiors—he frees himself from guilt and generates an obligation from them. This practice is functional for the Japanese worker and is strongly reinforced through the norms of the workplace. Hence, even if a Japanese worker were willing to accept some guilt, it would be extremely awkward for him socially if he were to claim credit for some innovative idea. Again, the problem this creates for leaders of research and development units desirous of motivating employees is formidable, as is discussed in later chapters.

The concept of *on* or "duty" is also critical to understanding the meaning of leadership in Japan. For Japanese workers, the generalized norm of obligation to others is a fact of life and a not inconsiderable ongoing burden. There is a universal agreement that one owes others for their kindnesses. To prevent this feeling from becoming overwhelming, Japanese people are constantly giving, constantly fulfilling their obligations to their fellow workers, to their families and friends, to their organizations, and to their community. (The very old philosophic conundrum that all behavior is essentially egocentric should not be invoked here to infer that the Japanese are not genuinely altruistic. They are.)

For workers in organizations, the repayment of perceived debt of *on* is accomplished through *giri*—by becoming an obedient and loyal subordinate, providing unquestioned service (Befu 1980; De Mente 1981, 46). *Giri*, then, represents the ongoing interdependence of people with one another—the sense of a mature, continuing relationship that will permit the expiation of any excess of accrued obligation. Clearly, this characteristic of the Japanese is critical to understanding how and why groups in Japanese organizations operate and hence, how leadership roles will be carried out in part by taking advantage of both *on* and *giri*. While the culture strongly incorporates these values, their reinforcement through organizational norms is one of the prime functions of leadership. In contrast to some Western notions of organizational health which argue for the possibility of mutual individual and organizational personal development and growth, and for a leadership stance that integrates each (e.g., Argyris 1957), the Japanese leader must understand and rely on guilt as a driving force in maintaining the solidarity of the organization. As De Mente (1981, 46) notes,

Both *on* and *giri* are reciprocal in nature, and derive from a relationship in which the subordinate is expected to extend service and loyalty to the superior, and the superior is obligated to demonstrate responsibility and gratitude to the subordinate. Without *giri*, the *on* system would disintegrate.

The fact that Westerners see guilt (or at least excessive guilt) as a condition of psychological stress in a group setting, while in the East this same feeling may be perceived as psychological health, speaks to the enormous cultural differences between Japan and the United States. Understanding what effective leadership means, consequently, must consider these culturally biased interpretations.

The last concept that is important to understand is *ninjoo* or the conscious operationalization for each Japanese worker of the collective obligations one has. *Ninjoo* represents for the Japanese person a compelling feeling of being obligated not to one person, but to a collectivity, the totality of which constitutes a virtually unappeasable force. That is, it is the sum of the *on* or duty that can never be completely assuaged through *giri* or service. Just as the *amae* that was engendered through early childhood dependence can never be completely eradicated in the Japanese worker, so also, *giri* remains a critical condition of Japanese organizational life. There is simply no way that the Japanese worker can assuage his guilt at receiving what is perceived to be more than his due share from his surrogate mother, the organization. The positive psychological benefit, of course, is that the organization is perceived as forever supportive and protective.

The confidence of the worker in the probability of the continuity of "hygienic" conditions in the organization—provision for basic, lower need satisfactions such as employment security and good working conditions (cf. Herzberg 1966; House & Wigdor 1967) has quite different effects on the Japanese worker than on the Westerner. In the West, given such security, workers shift from external sources of motivation to internal ones. They are freed to focus on higher-order need satisfaction, particularly at the ego level. In Japan, the worker is not so "released." The constraint to produce still derives from organizational pressures, though of a different kind. There is no differentiation between hygienes and motivators. Motivation in Japanese society stems largely from the *amae*, *on*, *giri*, and *ninjoo* which depend on the merging of the identities of individual and social system and the impetus to action when the two threaten to diverge. As will be seen in later chapters, the meaning of "leadership" in this context becomes significantly different from that in the West.

Finally, a word on the culture of creativity and innovation in Japan. It must be stressed that the "new" in Japan is seen as continuous with the past—a powerful implicit denial of postmodernism at its heart. David Mura (1988) points out that "for Japanese aesthetics does not place the value we do on the original, the primary source, and the proclamation of the copy is at once the open announcement of Japanese aesthetics and its hidden secret." Thus, the urge of an individual to become known as the discoverer of the new is dampened not only by social contexts and norms inhibiting deviance, but by the very deepseated values of a culture that sees change as gradual and incremental.

# 4

# Education in Japan

As in any society, the social institution of education in Japan assumes a critical role. In most Western societies, schools play both manifest educational roles and latent socializing roles. They transmit knowledge, develop skills, and communicate the generalized expectations of society as to proper behavior in a variety of settings. In Japan, the school is far more profoundly and explicitly a socializing agency. As Benjamin Duke (1986) points out, from the child's first day, the school begins "the formal process of group training, Japanese style, that is, developing ties that bind the individual to his group in order to achieve the ultimate goal, group harmony." Most relevant to this study is Duke's further judgment that:

It is in every sense, the initial stage in school in the long task of preparing the future Japanese worker for the harmonious adjustment of employer-employee relationships characteristic of labor relations within Japanese industry. (p. 25)

This is not to deny that in the United States, for example, schools do not engender values and beliefs and do not institutionalize behavior in socially acceptable ways. But because of the heterogeneity of the backgrounds of Americans, there is a constant strain between the need to emphasize what is common to all and what is permissibly, indeed, desirably different. In Japan, where backgrounds are common and the society as a whole is more dependent on conformity to expectation, the place of the school in inculcating proper attitudes and modes of behavior becomes more critical. This belief is reflected in a history of extremely powerful, centralized governmental policy making and control (Kitsuse & Murase 1987; Horio 1988; Passin 1965; Fiske 1987a, 1987b). Further, insofar as school-inspired attitudes and behaviors are carried forward into the work setting, it is critical to understand them and to anticipate their relevance to the question of leadership in organizations.

This chapter will look at a number of features of the Japanese educational system including such issues as organization and hierarchy, authority and discipline, learning, information exchange, group consciousness (*shuudan ishiki*), collaboration and competition, achievement, talent distribution and recognition, and effort (*gambaru*; *doryoku*).

## ACHIEVERS AND NONACHIEVERS

The modern era of education in Japan is said to have begun with the end of the Tokugawa era and the beginning of the Meiji restoration. Reischauer (1988, 187 ff.) points out that with the restoration came a completely new orientation to education, unencumbered by the parochial or religious educational structures of the previous era and committed primarily to the less prestigious but critical foundation of elementary rather than higher education. Subsequent developments of the early part of the twentieth century, however, provide the direct antecedents of contemporary education that are especially meaningful for the understanding of leadership in Japan (cf. Shimahara 1979, 44–77). The system became legally more egalitarian and closely connected to national needs. After the war, the system was again reformatted to be somewhat less preferentially hierarchical in its admissions policy.

Nevertheless, education in Japan, reflecting the practical requirements for successful economic growth and political stability, is meritocratic. One important feature is the institution of "streaming." Since high-quality, upper-level schooling was limited, it became necessary to identify talent at an early age and to assure that those individuals so identified could proceed to advanced educational opportunities. Not only did the streaming include discrimination by gender (boys and girls went to different schools), but access to progressively higher levels of education required termination at the middle school level and/or separation of students into vocational, technical, and normal schools (Passin 1965, 104). Passin also reports that further upward, educational mobility was even more restricted:

Because facilities for higher education were far below demand, competition was ferocious and ruthless. Only one out of 13 middle school graduates could expect to enter higher school, and only one out of 25 was admitted to the prestige higher schools that opened the way into the Imperial universities. Normally, there were about seven times more applicants than openings. The gateway to higher education was therefore a very narrow one. (p. 104)

This narrow triangle representing the schooling system continues today, although in less severe form. More importantly for this book, streaming is a mechanism of meritocracy that occupies a legitimized and important place in the industrial sector. As will be seen, the gateway to prestigious organizations and upward mobility in them requires the recognition of talent early in the careers of competing workers, no matter how subtlely that competition is exercised.

## EFFORT AND MOBILITY

Manifestly, not everyone can reach the top in a hierarchically structured society or organization. Yet it is necessary to encourage effort toward the more desirable positions at the top and to offer socially acceptable reasons for differential degrees of success. One important by-product of the limited access system in a meritocracy is the value attached to hard work as the sine qua non for achievement. *Gambaru*, or persistence or sincere and intense effort, is stressed in the schools. The Japanese believe that the internal characteristics of personhood are shaped by powerful forces (variously called *ki, konjoo, kokoro, tamashii,* and *seishin* (Befu 1986, 24). To utilize the forces, the individual must experience hardship and overcome it through hard work. Indeed, in elementary classrooms, individual goals for self improvement (*gambari-hyo*) are posted. These, by the way, include goals that have social consequences (e.g., cooperating more with others).

In order not to cast aspersions on those who may not have been born with the necessary intellectual or other abilities to succeed, the Japanese ascribe virtually all success and failure to the degree of willingness of persons to strive to the utmost. Failure, in other words, is the result of, or at least attributed to, a lack of persistence.

Thus, on the one hand, the social system provides the carrot of opportunity inducing hard work among all. On the other hand, there is the recognition of limited access to the top of the organizational pyramid. It is important to see these rather anomalous, if not contradictory, views as characteristic of the Japanese person's capacity for tolerating divergent perspectives to preserve cherished values in each. It is clear to the Japanese (if at a somewhat less than explicit level) that there is an unequal distribution of talent in the society (Tobin, Wu, & Davidson 1989, 25) and that it is necessary to screen out, through the streaming process, those who are most likely to benefit from higher levels of education. On the other hand, it is equally manifest that the society requires egalitarian treatment to encourage the diligence among all citizens that makes it more successful. As Merry White (1987) notes:

When engaged effort is valued over ability, the environment of study or work is more truly egalitarian than it would be if the ceiling on a person's efficacy were set by ability alone. If you commit more hours and more sweat to a task, your identity as a good worker will be enhanced without invidious comparison. (p. 52)

What the streaming process does is to ensure that the most dedicated workers, not necessarily the most talented, rise to the top of the occupational hierarchies.

The economic and social function of this policy is that it encourages assiduous dedication to the tasks at hand, regardless of talent. The potential dysfunction is that the most creative and talented may not reach the top leadership positions. However, the system adjusts readily for the disjuncture between talent and formal position through its structure and forms of decision making (of which more will be said later). The processes of leadership in Japan, in other words, necessitate the recognition of the Type I and II errors that occur in the selections for responsible positions—errors that erroneously identify workers as potential leaders and that do not recognize leaders who are capable. The system of leadership in Japan, however, in its canonical form, utilizes all or most of the talent that is available, regardless of formal title.

It should be pointed out that though the school system structurally permits tracking, within the schools the practice is to avoid it. Indeed, the deemphasis on individual achievement demands that groups qua groups, not individuals qua individuals within groups, reach for high levels of performance. As will be seen below, many practices in the schools are directed at improved group performance, with students themselves responsible for the group, rather than their individual achievement. It becomes in the interest of the more skilled in the group, therefore, to assist those less skilled in order to enhance group performance. One useful by-product of this educational practice is that in their early academic experience, future leaders develop interpersonal skills in assisting others. While the low variance across individuals in levels of achievement allows the development of single curriculums that are addressed to all members of the class, the deemphasis on individual achievement in some ways removes the incentive to achieve in excess of group norms. Since dependence is so critical a disposition in Japanese society, the mother, in the preschool years, works very hard to build in the child a feeling that she is needed. As noted earlier, Japanese children's emotional outbursts and excesses are frequently indulged to accomplish this aim. (This same indulgence pattern can be seen later in organizational settings, as longer-tenured employees [*koohai*] tolerate initially the emotional excesses of the newer employees [*sempai*]).

The transition from toddler environment to the more organized social setting of the school or preschool is often a major problem (Peak 1991). From a ratio of one child to one parent, three- or four-year-olds move to a classroom setting in which as many as 40 or 50 children (a *kumi*) come under the jurisdiction of one teacher. This ratio is not necessarily forced by budgetary constraints, but is, instead, a considered pedagogical policy choice based on the recognition of the need to engender more group identity. From an attitude of "me-first" to one of "group-first," Japanese children must undergo a major transformation of the individual psyche—from reliance on the one (the mother) to reliance on the many (the group or co-workers). Part of this movement is accomplished through the structure of the pedagogy and reward system. Rather than making the teacher the center of the learning experience, Japanese education focuses on the group as the source of information, social support, control, and reward.

Again, as will be seen, this practice is mirrored in formal organizational settings later in life.

In Japanese classrooms, children are encouraged to take responsibility not only for themselves, but for others in the class. Matters of discipline as well as learning that are directed toward the teacher are deflected in subtle ways back to the group. As Holloway (1988) notes:

In the classroom, overt control by teachers is more likely to result in feelings of powerlessness by students and less emphasis on controllable factors as determining outcomes. Controlling events—including rewards, deadlines, and surveillance—may undermine intrinsic motivation by focusing attention on external sources as the reason for engaging in the activity.

Interestingly, the objective is to develop an internal locus of control (cf. De Vos, 1986), and the outcome is a society in which individuals feel very much in control of their destinies through their own hard work (though more than in other countries, they ascribe some of their good fortune to luck) (see Lewis 1986). Yet they remain dependent on others for approval of their performance.

Recalcitrant or noncontributing children are brought into the fold not by the teacher but by members of the group. "Mothering" behavior by the teacher, permissible in early years, is rare and frowned upon after the third or fourth grade. Indeed, "emotional confrontations of any kind between teacher and student are usually avoided, both to allow the teacher to remain a benevolent and accessible (though perhaps somewhat affectively neutral) figure . . . '' (Tobin, Wu, & Davidson 1989, 43-44). This pattern of the teacher's relationship to the group as a whole, rather than to individual children, the deflection of responsibility for discipline and control back to the group, and the absence of succorance by the teacher are also found in Japanese organizations. As will be discussed in Chapter 12, organizational leaders treat workers in the same dispassionate style (though not without compassion), assigning responsibility for initiating work and for direct consideration or stroking behaviors to others.

Toward the end of equalizing opportunity and deemphasizing differences among students, Tobin, Wu, and Davidson (1989, 25–26) report that teachers "speed up and encourage slower learners and at times . . . *slow down more talented members of the class*" (emphasis added). They teach to the "average" student, spending the least time with the best students (cf. Willis & Horvath 1988). Carried over into the industrial world, such dampening of potentially creative deviance has clear negative effects on the effectiveness of R & D, especially in the basic sciences. As Duke (1986, 33) notes, "as the child progresses through the school, spontaneity, original ideas, and innovative thinking fade away." Creative thoughts generated by individuals are "de-anchored," and new ideas are given to the group for further development and "ownership." Creativity is lauded for its contribution to group productivity, not for the imagination, skill, or daring that it took.

## ACTIVITY, ORDER, AND CONTROL

Japanese classrooms are full of activity, especially activity requiring participation of all children in group behavior. Teachers encourage students very early
in their education to make individual verbal presentations of ideas to the rest of
the class. They also call on students to give their answers to questions, making
certain to spread their requests of students equally. These practices tend to give
students confidence in their public performance, but since they are usually presenting ideas other than their own, learned by rote, the pedagogy works disad-
vantageously, inhibiting contributions based on spontaneous, creative thought.

Equally important, perhaps, in the Japanese educational philosophy is the
practice of breaking the class into small groups (*han*) to solve teacher-assigned
problems. Through these exercises, Japanese students learn how to communicate, collaborate, give assistance, compromise, and play different roles. Each of
these is a practice highly valued in Japanese organizations. In a sense, then, the
practices in the corporation mirror those in the classroom, just as in America
the more teacher-centered, individualized classroom is captured in the corporate
sector in this country.

Indeed, early practice in leadership begins in the school. Each class (*kumi*)
and each small group elects is own leader (*han-cho*). Once elected, the student
comes to understand (with the help of the teacher) that he can not present himself
as different or better. His prime responsibility is to facilitate the harmonization
of the group, at least in part by ensuring that in all decisions, full participation
takes place. He learns how to sense the subtle cues that reflect latent disagreement, to delay the final decision until consensus is achieved through his individual, behind-the-scenes activity (Duke 1986, 25 ff.).

Order is important for the Japanese classroom, in part because it is consistent
with the educational philosophy, and in part because the socialization effects are
important to the smooth functioning of the society. Japanese teachers spend far
less time controlling behavior than do American teachers. Cummings (1980,
111) suggests that if one uses an estimate of 20 percent of the teacher's day to
represent Japanese teacher time spent on order activities, one could assign a 60
percent figure to American teachers (cf. Stevenson & Stigler 1992). In point of
fact, of course, the delegation of authority for control to the students may be
somewhat misleading, since the teacher has not relinquished authority. Perceived
responsibility, however, has shifted downward, just as it does in the formal
organization in Japan.

Many structural mechanisms exist for enabling students to recognize the self-
interest or/and group interest in maintaining order. One, for example is:

to establish a hectic pace of activity in the classroom composed largely of things that
the students want to do—opening texts, reciting, performing exercises, singing songs.
Thus the students are left with little time to become disorderly. (Cummings 1980, 110)

Translated to the work setting once again, it can be seen that the "busyness" of the Japanese organization is a reflection of the classroom. Work is often assigned to more than the one person who is able to do it, at least in part to avoid free time that might be utilized toward nonorganizational ends—either frivolously in play or in activities that may not have yet received complete approval. Neither Japan nor the United States seem to have solved the problem of how to control use of organizational slack among personnel.

This is not to suggest that a completely ordered and disciplined classroom is a desideratum. In point of fact, a considerable amount of chaos (*yochien* or *hoikuen*) is considered useful. Out of the chaos, order emerges, partly by teacher design.

A number of Japanese educators worry somewhat about the tendencies toward conformity in Japanese education, preferring instead at least some encouragement of individuality. Tobin, Wu, and Davidson (1989) quote a preschool teacher they interviewed: "It's easier to teach a mischievous child to behave than to teach a too-good child to be naughty" (p. 32), or, as will be seen, to teach a too-conformist researcher in R & D to stretch into unknown areas.

Children in schools who are initially nonconforming, on the other hand, are not singled out as deviant. Rather, their misbehavior is ascribed to memory lapses or misunderstandings of expectations, to external circumstances or even to an as yet inadequately developed ability to be sensitive to others. Such ascriptions encountered as an adult are serious blows to the fragile Japanese psyche.

The importance of the mother in Japanese society was noted in the previous chapter. Here it is necessary to discuss (again far too briefly) the assumptions about human nature that inhere in the Japanese educational system, since these assumptions also carry over to the organizational setting. Merry White (1987; cf. Shigaki 1983; White & LeVine 1986) captures the essence of these as follows. A good child, she notes, is

*otonashii* (mild or gentle), *sunao* (compliant, obedient, and cooperative), *akarui* (bright, alert), and *genki* (energetic and spirited). *Sunao* has frequently been translated as "obedient," but it would be more appropriate to use "open minded," "non-resistant," or "authentic in intent and cooperative in spirit." The English word "obedience" implies subordination and lack of self-determination, but *sunao* assumes that what we call compliance . . . is really cooperation, an act of affirmation of the self.

## LEARNING RULES AND BUREAUCRACY

Japanese teachers spend much of the beginning weeks of the semester in elementary schools in teaching "procedural skills" such as how to wash hands, arrange the contents of desks, sit, stand, and walk (Holloway 1988). These procedures that emphasize repetitive tasks and reliance on "proper" channels and methods set up the young Japanese to accept and reinforce the similar requirements in the strict bureaucratic structures in Japanese organizations. Sometimes called petty educational rules (*kari kyoiku*), these rituals enhance conformity to authority (Shishin 1988).

Despite some recent new developments in the teaching of science, much of Japanese education takes place in classrooms where rote memorization is the predominant form of instruction, even at the high school level, where students struggle for entrance into prestigious universities. Japanese children are encouraged more to absorb a body of material than to understand or to question it. While some contemporary efforts in Japan are aimed at freeing up the heavy-handed structure of the federal and state systems of education that are manifested in didactic classroom pedagogies, there is a long tradition to be overcome. The individual learning skills that "count" to Japanese teachers (and parents), according to White, are (1) "learning to gather and use large amounts of information," (2) "learning to work diligently and in an organized manner," (3) "learning to do things with sincerity (*seijitsu*), also translated as 'wholeheartedness' or 'mindedness,' " (4) "learning to be a 'quick study'," and (5) "learning to develop *kan* or a 'grasp' " (White 1987, 43–44). As will be seen in the chapter on leadership (Chapter 12), these are requisites of leadership to be exercised propitiously as required by the situation. The first of these, the application of thought to inanimate objects, corresponds to a distinctive leadership style that is appropriate for certain types of organizational problems, not necessarily those associated with research (though more so with applied than basic research). The last two, similarly, relate to more affective, or intuitive, rather than intellectual or rational, apprehensions of either things or people. Once again, these skills are required in certain problem-solving circumstances in organizations. What is interesting about these desirable skills is that in the Japanese educational philosophy, the belief is that all students can and should acquire them. In the United States, too, uniform sets of desirable skills are taught. But here the strong belief in individuality and personality differences suggests that not all individuals will be equally adept at acquiring or using them. The implications for leadership are that the differing skills of leadership in Japan can be engendered in each child, while in this country, we expect that different children will acquire and use them at differential rates. When organizational leadership in the two countries is called for, then, these different cultural or educational assumptions will be seen to be manifested. Here, we expect the superleader, endowed with all the requisite skills; in Japan, deficiencies in leadership may be made up through talents readily found in the group. Importantly, in contrast to this country, such reliance on subordinates is expected and positively sanctioned, rather than seen as a failure of the leader.

Group discussion and group dynamics are thus most important in Japanese schools. The values of the society are inculcated through techniques calculated to engender extremely strong group pressures for conformity. For example, in each classroom, students are aggregated in small groups (in Japanese, *han*) intended to help build group identity. Pedagogy as well as activities outside of the curriculum are designed to imprint the service ethic to group and society. For example, Japanese schools have few or no maintenance staffs; the children take on these responsibilities as groups.

Though egalitarianism predominates throughout the school years as a pedagogical philosophy, it breaks down in practice at the social level where, as noted above, limited opportunities for higher education and the upward mobility advantages it offers makes competition a more powerful force. Especially as promoted by families who have high aspirations for their children, many Japanese children (almost half of junior high school students) (Simons 1987) attend *juku* or extra classes after school to give them an added advantage in school. Later, with examinations to gain admittance to colleges (the "examination hell"), competition is rife. As Holloway (1988) reports, the student's score on the entrance examination is seen as a reflection of the worthiness of the family, low scores signifying parents who presumably have failed to instill a sufficient spirit and drive for achievement. Families, then, are in competition, as are separate schools (Vogel 1979, 165). Vogel goes on:

By the time the Japanese student enters a good high school or good university, he has internalized attitudes about hard work. He may not have enjoyed the pressure of examination hell, but he has learned discipline as well as mastered a body of knowledge. For all the excesses of the entrance examination system, the desire to succeed on them maintains group solidarity and the motivation to study. (p. 166)

High school preparation for college or postgraduate life has many of the same characteristics of the lower schools. As Rohlen (1983) notes, "How schooling shapes the regular habits and life patterns of millions of people is of greater significance than what teachers say about political truth or even how much equal opportunity the system offers" (p. 271). In contrast to the United States, he asserts, where young people are "discovering" who they are or might be, "maturation" in Japan consists of intensification of study routines preparatory to the examinations for college and learning how to become integrated into the larger society. Hence, it is important to see how the socialization processes carried out in high schools prepare individuals for corporate life and for the leadership roles that they accept or perform.

The first observation is that high schools are spare and simple. Little embellishment of bare walls and vacant halls is permitted. The pedagogy is similarly simplistic. One teacher lectures for an hour to 40 or 45 students, with teachers of different subjects rotating through the same classroom. All of the homerooms of students in the same grade are on the same floor so as to cement relationships among these peers. As Rohlen puts it, "Schools everywhere are like egg cartons, with each compartment a classroom" (p. 150). These spatial arrangements are designed to ensure that the essential identification with a group is accomplished.

The pace of the school day teaches students what it will be like after graduation. The rigid routine of hour-long, didactic lectures is rarely violated. The curriculum is circumscribed by the boundaries of conventional subject matter. Since teachers rotate across classes, they do not come to know the students as individuals.

The routine from day to day does not vary. Rohlen notes, "as socialization in orderliness, nothing could be more effective" than the patterns of routine activities (p. 158). It begins from the day of entrance. Describing one Nagoya high school's annual procedure, Shimahara (1979) reports:

Group training begins from the first day of attendance for the tenth grade students. On the first sunny, spring day in April, 350 tenth graders, all wearing identical white caps, line up on the athletic ground of the school. They are divided into groups of about 40, the leaders of which were selected to coordinate group activities. These new *Saigoo* students are unfamiliar with the training but appear quite anxious, since many of them have heard rumors about what some of them identified as "Spartan education." (p. 98)

There is also an initiating ritual involving the first of many off-campus excursions by the smaller groups. The students and teachers engage in group-building exercises such as mountain climbing, visiting shrines and temples, living together away from their home cities. These patterns of extracurricular activities and the reinforcement of group identity are replicated later in organizational life as workers go off together after formal work hours.

Interestingly, education in college is almost a mirror image of earlier Japanese schooling and later life in the corporate world. Despite significant expansion of educational opportunity and conscientious attention to the need for structural and pedagogical reform (see, for example, MOMBUSHO 1965; B. Clark 1979), Japanese college freshmen still identify college campuses as "leisure land." Japanese colleges, with some notable exceptions and less so in engineering and the hard sciences, are easygoing, undemanding, virtual vacations. They present opportunities for Japan's most talented to relax from the rigors of examination preparation in high school and to cement relationships with peers with whom they will have continuing contact for the rest of their lives.

Education and training continue beyond school and college. A major portion of continuing education takes place in the corporate sector: "Graduate education in Japan is an anomaly, a marginal segment in an otherwise highly developed system of education" (Ushiogi 1993). Relatively few Japanese (about 4 percent of college attendees versus about 11 percent in the United States) are in graduate schools (*U.S. News and World Report*, 1987). A new type of graduate school, begun in 1989, centers education directly within six research institutes administered by the Ministry of Education. It is too soon to evaluate the results of this innovation.

The implications for leadership in organizations here are important to remark. As Singleton (1989) notes,

The real content of any educational process is *seishin* (individual spirit and character development) and *shuudan ishiki* (group consciousness, belongingness) or *dantai ishiki* (organizational consciousness). It underlies the wide public and government support for school-based moral education and guides the corporate training programs for new employees. (p. 11)

Thus, as with the family, the Japanese educational system builds into the Japanese worker an expectation about leadership and followership. Workers tend to be more accepting, less questioning, more compliant, less willing and able to tolerate conflict (Sato 1985), but at the same time, more peer-related, cooperative, collaborative, and committed to group ends. As will be noted in the next chapter, organizational life and leadership also reflects the character of family life in Japan.

# 5

# Family Roles and Interactions

Some considerable proportion of the explanation of adult psychological dispositions and behavior among workers in organizations in all countries can be understood as a product of the typical structure, relationships, and interactions among family members (Hochschild 1983, 156 ff.). In Japan, these family characteristics evolved slowly throughout a long history (Murayama 1982) and are manifested in some obvious and some quite subtle ways in contemporary society. Since World War II, the Japanese family has undergone significant changes, particularly as a result of the disruption in the first postwar generation which suffered not only from the war but from the impact of the Allied occupation. For example, the quondam traditional and extraordinary emphasis on education was somewhat vitiated, with the result being a second and third generation who today operate in a context of significantly different values, if not a vacuum or anomie of values. Nevertheless, the impact of the Japanese family member interactions and child-rearing patterns on later life and work relationships is still profound and deserves special note.

While there have been some cautions about the dangers of overusing the family as a metaphor for understanding the dynamics of interpersonal relationships in Japanese organizations (cf. Befu 1980), there are some quite compelling reasons to do so (Hamabata, 1990). As Nakane (1986) notes, the work organization "provides the whole social existence of a person and has authority over all aspects of his life; he is deeply emotionally involved in the association."

There can be no argument that the traditions of family life are strongly rooted in the traditions of Japanese culture as a whole—and the reverse (Hsu 1975). As in other cultures, the young Japanese is imprinted early with patterns of interaction in the family (Roman & Raley 1980; Bernstein 1985). In contrast to some other cultures where children and adults have some degree of flexibility and are expected to carve out unique roles and relationships, in the Japanese setting these are less subject to idiosyncratic or even to individual family interpretation. The rules are fixed and immutable by historical custom, and so is expected behavior. The young Japanese person comes not only to obey the rules, but to see them as a source of predictability and stability in his life both within and outside the family. Bowring and Kornicki (1993, 238) report that the Japanese word for child-rearing is *shitsuke*, which also translates into "tacking a kimono into shape and teasing rice seedlings into upright position."

The psychological development of young people also differs. In some other cultures, as young persons move through adolescence and early adulthood, there is a pattern of rebellion both against the rules and against the persons or symbolic persons (surrogates) exercising them. Indeed, it is claimed in the West, for example, that the rebellion is functional for the freeing of the ego or individuality that allegedly lies latent in each person.

In Japan, on the contrary, because of the characteristic need for "dependence" described in earlier chapters (cf. Doi 1973), it is important for the Japanese person to be able to continue to believe in the validity of the relationships established so firmly in childhood. Hence, it is critical that his organization create surrogate, family-like roles (*kazokushugi*). Organizations understand and accept this responsibility. One president of a Japanese company (Idemitsu Petroleum) is alleged to have asserted,

The Philosophy of Idemitsu is, to put it briefly, application of Japanese home life to enterprise. Since the first day of our business we have endeavored to bring our employees up men of good character, because they were left to us by their parents. (Ballon 1969, 61)

In particular, two important features of the family that are reflected in the Japanese work organization will be considered here. The first is the pattern of role relationships. The second is the impact of the dominance of the female role on individuality, deviance, and creativity.

Intergenerational relationships are especially strong and age-dominated in Japanese families. *Oya* (parent) and *ko* (child) represent the older and younger generations respectively. As Nakane (1988) notes:

Most Japanese, whatever their status or occupation, are involved in *oyabun-kobun* (boss-subordinate) relationships. The *oyabun-kobun* relationship comes into being through one's occupational training and activities and carries social and personal implications, appearing symbolically at the critical moments in a man's life. The *oyabun* often plays the role of the father, and it is by no means exceptional for him to play an even more important role.

Historically, interpersonal and group behavior of the typical household or *ie* arrangement were linked with the family as an economic work unit (Kondo

1990, 121 ff.). As such, the household unit was constituted of at least two quite separate parts: the *oku* and the *omote* (Morioka 1986). The former was the intimate core of family life and relationships closed to public scrutiny, while the latter represented the family in its public mode. The physical arrangement of the house itself accentuated these differences, with the *oku* activities taking place in back and bedroom locations, while the *omote* centered around the entrance.

The physical arrangement was matched by the emotional. As Kondo (1990) notes,

The term *uchi* describes a located perspective: the in-group, the "us" facing outward to the world. It is the *ie* or other group to which one belongs. While the notion of *ie* highlights continuity, generation after succeeding generation, *uchi* focuses on the household in close-up, as a center of belonging and attachment. *Uchi* defines who you are, through shaping language, the use of space, and social interaction. (p. 141; cf. Hamabata 1990, 46–47, on the distinction between *ie*, *uchi*, and *otaku*)

Hamabata (1990, 34) remarks that the *ie* "looks less like a family and more like a corporate group with a variety of options available to fill positions and thereby guarantee organizational survival." (The traditional conceptual foundations for analyzing the Japanese household continue to undergo some serious questioning. See, for example, Kitaoji 1971; Bachnik 1983; Bachnik & Quinn 1994).

The intimacy of the *ie* system extends not only throughout generations but across families. As might be expected, such patterns have historical explanations. Whereas prior to the Meiji Restoration, the vast majority of organizations were family owned and staffed with family members, with the industrial revolution and modernization period, larger and more bureaucratic organizations evolved. Prerestoration Japan was thus dominated by the *ie* or household pattern of relationships (Morioka 1986). Even by the early twentieth century, the extended family of households remained connected with one another. However, as modern commercialism found its way into the country, these linkages became weaker. Indeed, there came to be a view that in the family system, *ie* was "an evil, feudalistic growth obstructing modernization" (Nakane 1986). In its place came boss-subordinate relationships which mirrored the older *oya* and *ko* (parent-child) patterns of the *ie*.

After the Meiji Restoration, the more feudal character of the hierarchical relationships became significantly attenuated, but the basic family unit remained. Emerging to replace the interfamily connections were the modern, economically more efficient units of business and industry. The *oya* and *ko* pattern of interpersonal relations were retained to ease the transition.

By the early twentieth century, as Morioka (1986) notes, a "managerial paternalism" had developed that incorporated the idea of the entire country as a large family, headed by the emperor. The authority of father-son relationships, borrowed from the earlier *omote*, was found to be particularly useful in the organization and management of business enterprises.

Traditionally, the *ie* was "patriarchal, patrilineal, primogenitural, and patrilocal" (Hamabata 1990, 33). However, it should not be inferred from this historical evidence that contemporary society is predominantly patriarchal, though most assuredly it is ostensibly so. As noted earlier, the father in the Japanese family is feared and revered, but the strength of women in the society is nonetheless formidable, even if it is expressed much more subtlely (Kawai 1960). Japanese society, according to Lebra and Lebra (1986; cf. Lebra 1976, 1984) has in fact always been "maternal," in contrast to the paternalism in Europe and the United States, the distinction being the degree of nonjudgmental love that obtains. In postwar Japanese society there has been an increase in maternal control (Kawai 1960).

In point of fact, since the father is so seldom present in the typical family, the mother constitutes for the children both an authority figure and a nurturing source. The role of women in Japanese society does not (yet) permit most to see themselves in organizational careers. And despite the increasing use of labor-saving devices in the home, they still conceive of their primary role as mother and, importantly, educator of "good children" (sometimes, according to one author [Kawai 1960], so dominating the children as to create psychic disorders; cf. Kumagai 1981). Indeed, the prime satisfactions of most Japanese women come from their ability to engender in their children the correct spirit of industry and dependence that will advance them through the educational system and ultimately through life. These objectives, however, may be done a disservice when the psychological needs of the mother overwhelm the very objectives they seek to achieve in their children (cf. Lebra 1976, 57-60).

The role of the woman as mother, then, is clearly prejudicial in both a good and bad sense in the patterning of expected relationships and behavior later in life. With the advent of labor-saving devices and the reduction in the number of children per family, Japanese wives now must spend far less time attending to matters of general household concern and can devote themselves even more to their children. The result of the dominance of women in the home is that Japanese boys come to be more compliant toward women, although the society as a whole places great emphasis on the apparent dominance of men. This anomaly is perhaps best captured by the practice in the homes of most salaried employees ("salarymen") of having the paycheck from work given in toto to the wife who then returns a weekly allowance to the husband. (This practice may well change with the advent of plastic credit cards in Japan, which are quickly finding their way into the economy.)

## FAMILY ROLES AS MANAGEMENT STRUCTURES

Family roles provide important clues as to the nature of leadership in the R & D laboratory. The imprinting of family roles is so uniform and so heavily constrained by tradition that it is inevitable that they have critical impacts on behavior in adult life. As will be seen, the roles played by various persons in the laboratory tend to take on those found in the family. For example, there is usually in every Japanese organization a *nyooboo yaku* or wife figure, whose responsibility for leadership turns out to be critical. Further, the occasional mild excrescences of irrationality in male office managers can be traced to the petty tyrant (*teishu kampaku*) proclivities of Japanese husbands who make unreasonable and peremptory demands for domestic services from subservient wives.

There are many aspects of the Japanese firm that mirror family life. Indeed, it serves *in loco parentis* (Kondo 1990, 178 ff.). For example, there are "company housing, hospital benefits, family-recreation groups for employees, monetary gifts from the company on the occasion of marriage, birth, or death, and even advice from the company's consultant on family planning." There is also the parallel of the patterns of compensation in the firm which resemble the family allowance (Nakane 1986). The widespread practice of lifetime employment, incidentally, arose as a result of government restrictions on labor mobility during World War II. At that time, the factory was to become a surrogate family for the worker, providing for material and socioemotional needs.

As Hsu (1975) points out, "what the Japanese does is to carry his kinship structure, and especially its content, into his secondary grouping," the organization. Further,

The principle of solidarity on which *iemoto* is built is what may be called kin-tract. By this term, I refer to a fixed and unalterable hierarchical arrangement voluntarily entered into among a group of human beings who follow a common code of behavior under a common ideology for a set of common objectives. It contains elements of what Nakane . . . terms *ba*. It is partly based on the kinship model so that, once fixed, the hierarchical relationships tend to be permanent, and partly based on the contract model, since the decision for entering, and occasionally for quitting a particular grouping rests with the individual. (p. 62)

Thus, in the Japanese organization today will be found the equivalents of fathers, mothers, uncles and aunts, grandparents, and elder and younger siblings. There are unwritten rules guiding the worker's relationship to each of these roles. Hsu (1975, 125) describes this as a "controlled diffuseness rather than unfettered diffuseness."

[A]lthough the scope of Japanese life patterns (including language) is wide and full of incongruities, the actual tasks for various individuals are extremely specific, and very clearly designed and executed. There is no evidence of diffuseness in them. (Hsu 1975)

Paradoxically, then, the role relationships among members of the family are simultaneously rigid and loose, depending on the function of the interaction. For manifest purposes of giving and receiving respect and thus reinforcing the security of the status quo, hierarchical, given roles are rigidly determined. On the other hand, for purposes of solving problems in the workplace, role definitions within hierarchical rank are loose enough to permit virtually any knowledgeable or skilled worker, regardless of formal role, to contribute to the task at hand. In short, within the family, an uncle knows exactly what the bounds of his role can be vis-à-vis different members of the family (e.g., aunts and grandfathers), but he also knows that he need not play his uncle role exactly as other uncles play theirs. In the organization, this lateral looseness in role definition, combined with commitment to the organization as family, permits much individual adaptive behavior in service of organizational ends. It also partially removes the threat to superiors of underling success (though, as noted earlier, not infrequently Japanese workers find ways to fulfill an inadequately played role of their superiors without revealing his incompetencies).

In sum, at the formal level of hierarchical interactions in the Japanese firm, the role relationships are powerfully communicated, though with utmost subtlety. Violations of the order of interaction are sanctioned negatively. Since the early imprinting in the family is so strong, however, the Japanese are often able to walk through the role playing without consciousness of the need to fulfill expectations. They do not "play" the role; they act it existentially. Their behavior and the behavior predispositions based on role preparation in the family are isomorphic. On the other hand, as noted earlier, functional lateral work relationships are diffusely defined.

To understand the dynamics of the leadership process, then, it is important to see how the management of creativity is carried out within the context of family-like role relationships. As will be stressed throughout this book, the leadership role is distributed widely across many persons in the Japanese organization. The relationships of various leaders to followers take two forms—one dyadic (between formal and informal leaders [plural emphasized]), the other, person to group. In the first instance, individuals establish over time the roles they occupy vis-à-vis one another and act out those roles as they carry out their organizational duties. In the second instance, the leader relates not to any one individual, but to the group as a whole. As noted in the previous chapter, this resembles closely the Japanese teacher in elementary and secondary schools who more frequently than not establishes a relationship between herself and the pupils as a whole, rather than between herself and each individual. The dyadic role relationship varies combinatorially with the number of role relationships possible—primarily, husband/wife, father/son, mother/son, brother/brother (Hsu, 1975) and secondarily, grandfather/son, grandmother/son, and so on. As McWilliams (1973) notes, the fragility and yet utmost significance of family relationships shape human relationships profoundly:

A brother is, however, not simply one who shares a father: in the most absolute sense, he is one who shares a mother as well (*bruder* once implied one of the brood, a product of the same litter or womb). To be fully one's brother, he must share ties to feminine things—to affection, to gratification, to welfare, and to community. A brother is in this sense the only person who shares both the authorities to which men are subject, flesh and spirit, birth and death, community and the outer world. (p.18)

Of all human relationships, fraternity is the most premised on imperfection, the most fraught with ambiguity, the least subject to guidance by fixed rules, the most dependent on choice. (p. 18)

The process of individual development begins with the emotions and with the primary social groups which serve them. Society may satisfy basic material and erotic needs sufficiently to enable the individual to doubt society's purposes, to allow ego to put eros to the question. It is then that the influence of society becomes perilous, for morally and psychologically the individual must face the dilemmas that Socrates poses in the *Crito*. The individual is in a position to challenge society because society has made him so, and (his moral debt to society aside) he will hesitate to move into a new world at the cost of the goods of the old. Indeed, he cannot do so: eros threatened tends to become eros sovereign, and to go beyond society requires the individual to find new support and security. (p. 58)

It is in this situation that man finds a need for brothers, for the "true friends and genuine contemporaries" who share his values and with whom he experiences the encouragement of affection and rivalry. The individual does not find "identity" through his brothers, for identity is not vouchsafed to men in this life. To know the self is to know the whole of which the self is a part; to know identity, one must not only know the self at a given time, but the self over time, something which man cannot "know" until the end. (p. 58)

In other words, the Japanese ego is subordinated to eros, played by the mother, while his ego finds avenues for enhancement through his engagement with his co-workers, his brothers.

The role of the female in Japanese society and organization is intimately tied to the role of the mother and wife in the family. Lebra (1976) says it best.

The mother remains a lifelong object of attachment, not only because she is the source of all kinds of gratification, but also because she symbolizes the weakness and inferiority of the female sex in a male-dominant society.

This is another reason why the Japanese adolescent does not feel his male ego threatened by his attachment to his mother. This curious mixture of dependability and inferiority seems to make the mother the most idealized cultural heroine—one who is, simultaneously, the object of yearning, sympathy and guilt. (p. 59)

The wife role in the family is acted out differently, depending on where the interaction between spouses takes place. While in the external community the wife manifests the subordinate, dependent role, while in the household itself she becomes dominant. Although nominally the "unchallenged boss" (Christopher 1983, 65), the husband depends on the wife for economic and personal care and for emotional succorance. Indeed, the wife will tolerate spousal irresponsibility, much as she indulges willingly the excesses of her children (Lebra 1976, 62).

Japanese children, needless to say, are socialized into these traditional role relationships and carry their expectations into the workplace. As Christopher notes, ''Japanese men are always unconsciously trying to find someone who will love and cherish them as uncritically as Mama professes to—which, in most cases, is obviously a foredoomed effort'' (1983, 68).

This issue of family role playing in the organizational context is taken up in greater detail in Chapter 11. In the chapter just following, however, we turn to one of the most profoundly influential foundations of Japanese organizational life—the orientation toward collectivism.

# 6

# Individualism and Collectivism in Japan

One of the most important qualities of any culture that must be examined in order to more fully understand the nuances of interpersonal and group behavior is the mode by which individuals adjudicate the often competing claims on their behavior—claims from their inner selves and from other persons. Although the strength of each claim varies by individual and culture, there is a wave-like, cyclical though sometimes simultaneous, psychic tension experienced by every individual as a unique person and as a member of a social system with both positions making claims on behavior (Getzels & Guba 1957; Parsons 1951). The emphasis on one or the other and the necessary balance between them (to prevent psychic disorders) is affected partly by the education and socialization processes of the culture, which in turn generate in varying degrees the development of a separate identity. In some cultures, individuality is stressed (cf. Gans 1988); in others, the collectivity (cf. Erez & Earley 1993, 77 ff.).

Identity is manifested in and reinforced by behaviors reflecting acquired habits of satisfying activity and by cognitive appreciations of the potential sources of continuing satisfaction. People tend to perpetuate hedonistically the anticipated pleasurable activity. As will be noted below, Japanese culture, in contrast to some other cultures, lies on the collectivist or more socially constrained side of this equation (Barnlund 1975). In contrast to some other cultures, personhood in Japan is not as important in human development practices and is more constrained in everyday life. Indeed, Sampson (1988) refers to this as an "embedded" or "ensembled" form of individualism in which the boundary between self and other is ambiguous and blurred, both in terms of norms of the culture and the awareness of the individual (Heelas & Lock 1981). Sampson remarks further:

As has often been noted, the Japanese consider the idea of an individual who is defined completely apart from the environment to be a very foreign notion (e.g., Kojima 1984). Confucian thought (e.g., Ho 1985; Tuan 1982) further illustrates the fluidity of the self-other boundary and the embedding of the person in a larger field of forces: Individuals do not define themselves as detached from their family and society; persons' obligations are to sustain harmony within the social order.

It is important to understand how this conception of "obligation" to others in Japan differs from the Western sense of the concept. Here, obligation stems from norms of reciprocity which, in turn, are based on the assumption of separate identities, whereas in Japan, the obligation results from a social bonding that takes the "other" as an unconditional part of self.

Within Western organizations, the balancing of the apparently competing claims on behavior from the social system and personality is critical to the effectiveness of both individual and organization (Barnard 1986; Parsons 1951, 134 ff.). While the organization requires stability and predictability among employees, it also needs the prods of divergent thinking and action to help it change direction in organizationally relevant ways (Knoke & Wright-Isak 1982). The individual needs the stability of his ties to the organization, but also the freedom to dedicate himself to tasks that enhance his sense of himself as a unique and productive person. Too strong an identification with and commitment to the group may result in the submersion of the person to the group—its values, goals, norms, and formal decision-making patterns. The resulting deindividuation may result in a reduction in effort and/or creativity (Greenwald 1982). On the other hand, too much attention to the self may result in behavior that does not contribute to group comity or to group effectiveness and efficiency. Creativity in research and development may be thus labeled as "deviant" behavior in the traditional functionalist perspective or, using the other side of the functionalist argument, as "adaptive" (cf. Alexander & Colomy 1985).

In Japan, where self and other lines of demarcation are less distinct, leaders must find a way to defuse the strong negative connotations of the deviant labeling, or the worker will not be inclined to take the risks necessary for creative breakthroughs. The challenge to the leader is to find ways both to permit the individual to detach himself as an individual identity and then to "encourage" (give courage to) the deviant individual by reinforcing group rewards to individual ego satisfaction, thus defusing the threat of ostracism by the group. Leadership, in other words, involves both leader-worker and leader-group activities. More on this in later chapters.

It has been argued (Knoke 1990) that there are three prime sources that motivate individual behavior: rational cost-benefit calculations; emotional concern for others; and conformity to group norms. The means of manipulation of these incentives varies in collectivist versus individualist societies, as do, by consequence, the tasks of leadership. The purpose of this chapter, then, is to elucidate the nature of individualism and collectivism in Japan and to show how the management of deviance bears on the leadership question, especially as it affects creativity in research and development. (The approach takes a more sociological than psychological slant: the "self" as a psychological construct will not be explored in depth. For this latter perspective, see De Vos 1985; 1976.) Further, analyses of the role of individuality in Japan benefit from an emic rather than etic mode of social science analysis.

The differences between allegedly individualist versus collectivist cultures have been a topic of research and discussion for some time (de Toqueville 1966; Dewey 1929; Riesman 1961; Hofstede 1980a; Wagner & Moch, 1986; Goleman 1990; Triandis, McCusker, & Hui 1990; Triandis, 1990; Watt 1989; Bellah 1985; Bellah et al. 1987; Gans 1988). In more individualist cultures, for instance, normal compliant and cooperative social behavior stems from the egocentric recognition that others are needed to enhance one's own well-being. In more collectivist societies, such behavior is more motivated by the satisfaction received from seeing others (or other entities) with whom (or which) one has identified achieve their goals (see Befu 1980, 180ff). Here, the self is enlarged (some would say submerged) to include the other(s) (cf. Aron et al. 1991). The importance of this measure in explaining organizational behavior can not be underestimated. It explains the design of the organization, its motivational system, and its forms of leadership. Each of these organizational elements both implicitly and explicitly recognizes the cultural bias that inheres in the organizational system. For example, with the advent of technologies that require task interdependencies among workers, sociotechnical systems design of organizational structures must incorporate the prevailing individualistic or collectivist belief system (Trist et al. 1963; Morishima & Minami 1983). Collectivist organizational structures will recognize formally and informally the necessity for participative decision making, group and organizational pride in achievement, rewards that do not single out individual accomplishments, and leaders whose behaviors are explicitly understated and modest. Individually oriented organizations will be the opposite, emphasizing individual decision making and rewards and promoting leaders who are obviously dynamic and explicitly powerful. As has been noted, Japan is clearly in the former category.

Collectivist cultures like Japan also constrain the expression of individuality by the very design of the work. As Morishima and Minami (1983) note, in Western work settings, individuals are assigned work and are expected to complete the jobs autonomously, on the bureaucratic, scientific management assumption that, through specialization of labor, there will be no need for outside consultation or collaboration. In Japan, the opposite is true. Work is designed with the expectation that individuals will consult with others and will call upon others for assistance in the completion of the task. As noted in Chapter 5, Japanese workers come to feel that they are "dependent" on others—indeed, that they are not responsibly attending to the work if they do not demonstrate their dependency. Hence, a claim for individual creativity would be viewed by the group as a violation of the norm of needing, asking for and admitting to assistance from others. In addition, after some time, the competitive strain serves to weaken overall motivation (Parsons 1951), especially among those who do not expect to rise in rank.

Despite its relatively large size, Japan has the characteristics of a *Gemeinschaft* social system (Tonnies 1957)—a set of ongoing, close, interpersonal relationships contained in a small social setting. Japan, according to Sakuta (1978), has also become a hierarchical community (*kyoodootai*) that has added to *Gemeinschaft* the elements of *giri* and *ninjoo* moral obligations and human feelings. Kawashima Takeyoshi says *kyoodootai* is a:

fixed, inclusive, functionally diffuse type of relationship that so dominates all facets of each member's life that private life is not permitted, or at least is severely curtailed. Personal bonds are particularistic and emotional and encompass the total personality of each member rather than serving only a limited, specific purpose. "Face" is of utmost importance, not only in terms of personal influence or prestige, but also in the literal sense of "face-to-face" contact. (Sakuta 1978)

The concern of the Japanese to fit in is in some ways matched by the need not to be physically alone. The Japanese person desires at once to be seen and known and, indeed, is uncomfortable without constant observation of his commitment and service. He wants to be completely surrounded or enveloped— *marugakae* (Singer 1973). As Frost (1987) notes,

One feature of Japan's group behavior that often unsettles Americans is a high degree of mutual watching, which has been attributed to an intense concern with one's standing in the group, combined with a habit of waiting to see what others will do.

One purpose of mutual watching is tactical or competitive. From the game of *go* comes the expression *okame hachi moku*, freely translated as "he who is watching can see eight moves ahead," or "the bystander has the advantage." (p. 69)

The need not to give offense to others has its corollary in the need to conceal one's innermost thoughts, beliefs, and very personality from others. A Japanese woman, for example, will often wear under her kimono an extremely brightly colored, almost flamboyant garment which cannot be seen by anyone. This "secret" self is suppressed, yet a source of pleasure to the wearer.

It almost goes without saying, of course, that such containment of self is not unique to Japanese society. Philosophers and social scientists report this restraint as a fundamental prerequisite of organized social systems. However, Hsu (1975; cf. Epstein 1979) asserts that the notion of a unique personality that exists independent of both the society and other individuals is decidedly Western. As Befu (1986) notes with respect to American concepts of self, individualism in this country connotes images of pioneers, competition, and independence—in short, "rugged individualism" (p. 22). The concept is even more powerful in Sweden, where life is portrayed in terms of "forced" individualism, such that "individuals simmer in a greasy broth of institutionalized helplessness" and are afflicted with a "curse of isolation" (Guillet de Monthoux 1989; cf. Hofstede 1980a). In Japan, however, the system bends the individual in the collectivist direction. As De Mente (1981) reports, "The Japanese, especially those born before 1945, tend to have shallow and fragile concepts of themselves as individual entities," a sort of self-denial ( *jibun ga nai*) or even self-abnegation.

The threat of ostracism or of being alone or on one's own is probably the most significant motivator of all behavior in Japan. The concept of self as distinct from a group, when it is forced into consciousness, is highly threatening to the Japanese. The possible legitimacy of such a circumstance is itself repressed, with social norms reinforcing the repression, and behavior following accordingly. The language, too, reflects this. The Japanese in formal and informal conversation for the most part avoid the use of the personal pronouns "I" and "you" (*watakushi* and *anata*), and they prefer to use the passive rather than the active voice (cf. Suzuki 1978; Kondo 1990, 25–33).

For these reasons, it might be concluded by some that the Japanese individual lacks ego strength. In point of fact, this is not true. As Allport (1979, 459) defines it, ego or ego-involvement means being "personally, perhaps excitedly, seriously committed to a *task*." The Japanese have just as intense drives, needs for achievement, pleasures in accomplishment, disappointments in failure, and concerns for advancement. The difference between American and Japanese egos is that the latter are engaged with the larger organization. For the Japanese worker, the personal ego and that of the organization personified are almost indistinguishable. The worker identifies intimately with the organization and with its workers, and a sense of singular oneness suffuses the organization. Workers, consequently, have difficulty differentiating their own needs and satisfactions from the organization as a whole and from other workers with respect to the achievement of organizational goals and the means leading to them. Hamilton and Sanders (1992, 53) refer to this phenomenon as a variety of "contextualism."

However, in Japan, each person is simultaneously (or alternately) both extremely private and completely public (cf. Barnlund 1989). As Kondo (1990) notes,

a human being is always and inevitably involved in a multiplicity of social relationships. Boundaries between self and other are fluid and constantly changing, depending on context and on the social positioning people adopt in particular situations. These multiple, infinitely graded layers of selfhood are often described in Japanese in terms of two *end points* of a continuum: the *tatemae*, social surface, that which is done to smooth social relations, and *honne*, "real" feeling. (p. 31; cf. Doi 1986)

Thus, the Japanese person must continually define and redefine himself in terms of the social context in which he finds himself. Hamilton and Sanders (1992), drawing from the terminology of legal anthropology, refer to such relationships as "multiplex" in contrast to "simplex." These authors note that there are as many as fourteen words for "I" in Japanese (p. 57).

Befu (1980) distinguishes between "personhood" and individualism. The latter more properly conveys the social-psychological approach of contemporary interactionists (e.g., Blumer 1969). Here, "self" must be defined in terms of the relationship that one has with others (roughly, *jinkaku shugi*). Befu suggests that "it is the interconnectedness of persons and the quality of this interconnectedness that determines who one is" (p. 23). The Japanese must be understood not only as a person in some intimate connection with his environment, but as one whose consciousness of that relationship lies so deep that it rarely rises to levels of cognitive awareness. David Riesman (1954) spoke of this condition in Western man as "tradition-directed." He notes:

The tradition-directed person . . . hardly thinks of himself as an individual. Still less does it occur to him that he might shape his own destiny in terms of personal, lifelong goals or that the destiny of his children might be separate from that of the family group. He is not sufficiently separated psychologically from himself (or, therefore, sufficiently close to himself), his family, or group to think in these terms.

The elimination of the subliminal projection of a boundary between self and society is a daily mental health maintenance activity. On the other hand, for some very few Japanese, individual identity or autonomous action (sometimes defined as *shutaisei*) connotes a conscious belief that it is possible to assert oneself, even if there is considerable social cost or consequence. There are, consequently, some individuals who manage to remain fiercely independent, despite pressures toward conformity (or, as will be shown later, because of a leadership style and pattern of group norms that can tolerate, if not support such deviance). The typical reaction of group members to such individuals, however, is to isolate them in jobs that do not require task interdependencies. Indeed, they may be given a "window" location that physically removes them from the main stream of activity and interaction. The name for such physical and psychological dislocation is *mado giwa zoku*.

In any country, but especially in Japan, it is difficult for individuals who are truly creative to convince others that their ideas are worthy of consideration. By definition, truly innovative/creative notions are initially either misunderstood or rejected or both. Without the approval of the group, the originator of the idea may be seriously hampered in attempting to develop it further. "It may not be too extreme to say that cutting an overconspicuous figure in a Japanese organization is regarded as a sin" (Sasaki 1981, 5). As a result, only incrementally different rather than paradigmatically different ideas are usually taken up in Japanese groups. This situation is exacerbated by the practice of refraining from criticism of ideas put forth by formal leaders. Here, bad ideas receive currency and hence waste the group's energy and time (cf. Diehl 1984).

The notion of self in Japan must be conceived not only psychologically, but culturally. Anthropologists have begun to recognize the need to conceptualize the idea of self in terms of a particular culture's philosophical and sociological framework (Price-Williams 1985). As explained by Kimura (1973),

The Western concept of "self" refers essentially to the uniqueness of the individual, or the substance of the person, which has maintained its sameness and continuity over time and across situations, although it is recognized as a product of interaction with other humans. Whereas, the Japanese concept of *jibun* refers to one's sharing which is something located beyond a boundary of "self" in the Western sense. The amount of one's sharing varies depending upon the dynamics of a situation. *Jibun* does not have a definite consistent boundary. (Price-Williams 1985, 1007)

It is important to note that the Japanese psyche is not only immersed intimately in the cultural mores and norms of Japan but is also a member of at least one and probably many groups with which it also identifies. As noted above, the sense of self for the Japanese person is virtually inseparable from his identification with the groups to which he belongs. Psychological interpretations of individualism must thus be cast in terms of culture, organization, and work group (cf. Weisz et al. 1984). As Ballon (1969) notes:

True to Japanese mores, human collective considerations take precedence over mere economic individual considerations, as so aptly expressed by the *nenkoo* system. And since man is primarily motivated by the realization of where his main stake is, the Japanese employee is highly motivated by the realization that his main stake is in the enterprise of which he is a member and thereby, also, in the national economy of which his enterprise is but a partial component.

In the eyes of the Japanese, it is not the occupation (*shokugyoo*) that counts, but the place of work (*shokuba*). In other words, it is not *what* a man does that is the important industrial dimension, but *where* he does it.

Finally, the collective orientation of the Japanese is revealed in the language (Hamilton & Sanders 1992, 56–59). For example, the mode of polite, interpersonal introduction of strangers to one another reveals the nestedness of social relationships. It is typical to say something like, "I am Mr. Tanaka of the Hitachi Corporation." The meaning of the self-identification is better revealed in the Japanese language which gives Hitachi possession of Tanaka, namely, *Hitachi no Tanaka desu*—"I am Hitachi's Mr. Tanaka." The first source of identity is thus the organization.

## COLLECTIVISM IN JAPAN

It is important to note that this depiction of the Japanese orientation toward others is somewhat different from other characterizations of Japanese society as extremely "collectivist" (cf. Hofstede 1980a). The collectivist versus individual orientation in different nationalities has been commented on and researched by many (Triandis 1972; Hui & Triandis 1986). As Earley (1989) notes,

Individualism-collectivism determines, in part, an individual's perceived dispensability and expectations of others' actions. Collectivists emphasize the attainment of group outcomes and subordination of personal interests to ensure that group outcomes are attained. Each member of a group is cognizant of individual responsibility for group success and feels he or she has an indispensable part in a group's survival. Additionally, collectivists will contribute freely to group activities and not worry that other group members will fail to shoulder their burdens and will take advantage of them. (p. 568)

Research on "free riding" or "social loafing" (not pulling one's own weight in a group task) (cf. Gabrenya, Latane, & Wang 1983; Latane, Williams, & Harkins 1979; Jones 1984; George 1991) offers additional insights into the effects of individual versus group identification. For example, Earley (1989) found that in the People's Republic of China, a society with a confirmed collectivist culture (similar in a number of, but certainly not all ways to Japan) (see Hofstede 1980a), workers exhibited little or no evidence of social loafing, at least under the work conditions he studied. Workers were not inclined to slack off in their work under the assumption either that they would not be observed or that the work of the group would get done without them. As Bairy (1969) notes:

In point of fact, though Japanese work long and well, their work done *isshookenmei* (with all strength) . . . is commonly equivalent to merely an average performance in the West. More remarkable than any flamboyance of temporary performance is their constancy; faithfully, day after day, hour after hour, they accomplish their assigned tasks with patience and perseverance.

Thus have the imprinting and socialization processes so ingrained themselves in workers that opportunities to work less hard are seen as a shirking of responsibilities with heavy negative social consequences. While there is some strong speculation that Western modernization in Japan has been accompanied by a rise in individualism, there is no direct evidence as yet that significant changes have resulted. As Moeran (1984a) notes, there is sufficient ambiguity in the culture to prevent "Japanese society from jumping—lemming-like—into the abyss of Western individualism, and allows it to retain strong community values."

Thus far, issues related to the individual in society have been discussed in terms of the larger society. This study was concerned with the more intimate social setting of a small work group. It is necessary, therefore, to understand yet another layer of social constraints on behavior—those that are engendered by the norms of the small group. Norms are shared beliefs of members of a group about what actions are expected or acceptable, the degree of conformity to those norms yielding the actor some level of social status in the group. (For other definitions, see Gibbs 1981, 7–21; Ullman-Margalit 1977.)

Interestingly, the Japanese work settings provide some validity to alternative conceptualizations in the controversies over the explanation of social control in groups. Mainstream sociologists tend to conceive of norms as functioning in groups to control their members through sanctions attached to nonconformity.

Critical theorists, Marxists, and conflict sociologists, on the other hand, would ascribe social order to the repressive, if sometimes subtle and hidden, structural and authoritarian characteristics of organizational settings. In Japan, both approaches are helpful in understanding both deviance and creativity in the R & D laboratory. The Japanese worker is compelled to conform because of the extreme normative pressures to which he is subject, but those pressures are reinforced by a management and organizational structure that intelligently molds them more toward service to the organization than with the aim of maximizing personal growth and development or even balancing the two. Jones (1984), for example, notes that "problems of free riding and shirking are most evident when the individual's marginal productivity cannot be measured or monitored." The structure of decision making and the physical layout of the work setting (see Chapter 7) both mirror the philosophic and psychological underpinnings of a collectivist system and render these problems as minimal. Indeed, even in settings where intrinsic motivation is lacking, high visibility—recall that this is not resented, but desired—results in lower social loafing (George 1991).

The dilemma of encouraging constructive deviance in a Japanese organization like an R & D group is further confounded by the repression of open competition. Since group/corporate goals are deemed to be legitimately superordinate to individual ones, no suboptimization will be looked upon favorably. Yet, the system is intensely competitive. Each person, especially in early years, strives to make his mark so as to be promoted to higher status positions—the sine qua non of achievement in Japan. There are two contrasting effects of this latent competition. First, competitors are bound to give evidence of accomplishments only when those latter have been legitimated as institutionally valued. Further, promotion from within (virtually always the case in Japanese organizations) must have peer approval. It is "earned" through long years of service in rank without formal rewards such as large increases (there are very occasional group bonuses that may result in small salary increments) (MacDuffie 1988). Thus, the Japanese worker must strive to show his own colleagues that he is superior, but he cannot do so by showing them up through performance that goes beyond the norms of the group, since that will alienate them and constrain his chance of advancement.

As Takeuchi Yoo (1984) interprets the situation, group effectiveness is facilitated by the management of "homogeneity," not the management of "harmony." Taking his cue from history, Yoo recounts the difference as reflected in the words of Japanese philosopher Ogyuu Sorai (1666–1728), who suggested that harmony meant blending differences without loss of individual distinctiveness, while homogeneity meant merging differences into a uniquely new composite that does not conserve or emphasize any of the component parts. It is becoming evident, even to the Japanese, that frequently the management of homogeneity in R & D organizations stifles the individuality that is needed for creative breakthroughs. Some Japanese firms have instituted elaborate suggestion systems that clearly benefit the organization's operating efficiency. Generally, these systems reward the small groups that were generated out of the enormous influence of William Demming's introduction of quality control through quality circles (e.g., *jishu kanri* at Nippon Steel) (Yamada 1985), but for the most part, the rewards to *individuals* are largely symbolic payoffs for contributions to the organization. While these do induce suggestions, they do not encourage deviance from established formal and informal expectations. Contrast this pattern with the rewards for R & D achievements now making their way into United States corporations (Derra 1989).

### Deviance

As noted earlier, there are important implications of the above discussion of individualism/collectivism for understanding how leadership is played out in Japanese R & D. The action consequences are manifested in "deviant" behavior.

In the case of Japan, however, deviance must be understood not only from the perspective of the system, but as well as the Japanese person perceives it (if he does). As labeling theory in the symbolic interactionism of social psychology suggests, individuals discover over time that they are or are not deviant as a result of the labels they acquire through interactions with others. The frequent and extremely fluid patterns of interactions among workers in Japanese firms permit a constant checking by each individual of the degree to which deviance is dangerously close.

There are many approaches to the study of deviance, including functionalist, interactionist, anomic theory, social and cultural support theory, and social and cultural conflict theories (cf. Farrell & Swigert 1975). As will be seen, none of these by itself quite accurately captures the nature of deviance in Japan, particularly as the Japanese react to it. Moreover, the concern here is both with the negative effects of deviance dampening as well as functional aspects of deviance enhancement (Wilkins 1965). Deviance in an individualist society is conceived as antisocial behavior that endangers the rights of other individuals to pursue their self-interest, while deviance in a collectivist social system is seen as violation of the norms of service to the community good. In other words, in a society like the United States, behavior that appears to be beyond the limits of acceptable standards is considered to be damaging to the ability of others to obtain personally valued goods and services. Resentment arises because of the perception of interference with individual freedoms, rights, and opportunities. In a society like Japan, on the other hand, deviance is conceived as action contrary to the good of the social entity itself. The Japanese member of the system views deviance as an assault on the system and as a personal assault by proxy. His belief in the beneficence of the system and its caretaking role causes him to worry that there will be some obstruction in the harmony and smooth functioning that ultimately will adversely affect him. But the immediate feeling is concern for the system, while in America, the proximate feeling is a personal affront.

The discussion above considers deviance from the perspective of society. From the viewpoint of the individual himself, especially one who sees the need to make some change in the structure, functioning, or value bases of the system in which he works, the social restraint on nonconforming behavior is greater in a collectivist society. The tradition of individualism has not been passed on through the usual socializing institutions, and the society's strictures against deviant behavior are much stronger. The sanctions are much to be feared by a person who has not been raised to be independent and for whom the opprobrium of ostracism bears penalties of loneliness—a serious pain for most Japanese. Indeed, deviant activity if it exists at all takes a much more subtle form in Japan. As Rohlen (1975) notes,

Actions at variance with the expected and required behavior within the group seldom if ever take the form of open confrontation with authority or a refusal to perform required work. Numerous factors, including the ethic of cooperation and the general restraint of expression in Japan, inhibit direct confrontations in the office. Deviance and opposition take more private and qualified yet discernible forms, and the response of the rest of the group to even mild nonconformity is worth considering.

Deviation is most often expressed by withdrawal from participation in the group and with its leader. The individual who is unhappy or in strong disagreement, but who cannot express these feelings, is likely to set himself at odds with group norms in areas of behavior where matters of personal preference and the standards of the group intersect. Some typical examples would be avoiding office social activities, excessive make-up, drinking too much, joining a leftist youth group, and remaining silent during group discussions. These kinds of actions disturb the sense of unity, but cannot be labeled insubordination and summarily dealt with. They are conventional symbols of dissatisfaction and isolation from the group. (p. 193)

But it is highly unlikely that the Japanese can maintain deviant behavior for very long. As Bairy (in Ballon 1969) notes:

Although a supreme Japanese individualist endowed with an adamantine character and an insatiable thirst for independence can be imagined, it is unimaginable that he would be able to maintain his eccentric posture very long in the concrete context of his isolation; he would have to bow sooner or later to the general law.

Interestingly, the modes by which deviance is "managed" reflects the family-like structure and norms of the Japanese organization. Again, as Rohlen points out,

Often acts of "resistance" (*teikoo*) to the group or its leader are understood as analagous to the rebellious behavior of children toward their families, particularly when hurt feelings rather than principles are at the heart of the matter. The individual's natural state of existence is within some group, it is assumed, and resistance is easily interpreted as a sign of unhappiness and an indirect expression of personal need, which should be answered with sympathy and special attention that create a sense of belonging. (p. 194)

How the deviant is brought back into the fold is also relevant to the understanding of R & D creativity. As noted above, cues to the nontraditional deviant scientist to return him to the paradigmatic mold do not take the form of open social ostracism. Rohlen (1975) continues:

The group's members, especially its leaders, experience considerable irritation to be sure, but these reactions should be and usually are repressed. Understanding and tact are required, reminiscent of the general expectation that parents will be flexible and tolerant in the face of their children's recalcitrance. That order and participation begin with individual feelings and cannot be forced through rules and punishments is the crucial assumption. (p. 194)

It is worth wondering whether the unhappiness of the more productive members of the group with an unproductive member differs in any significant way from Western workers' dissatisfaction with a social loafing. It is important to point out, however, that the modes of dealing with the deviant are behaviorally distinctly different. The Japanese recognize that labeling acts as expressly deviant will call attention to an antisocial activity that is morally repugnant to the group. To brand an individual as deviant will not only cause harm to the individual, but will openly reveal a violation of the norms and values of the group, especially those that advocate social comity, reciprocity, and social service. Since the inner "self" of the deviant is very much merged with the group "self," for the group to punish the deviant is to punish itself. As Bairy (Ballon 1969, 51) notes, "In other words, in Japan the promotion of one individual is really the affirmation of the strength and achievement of the group, whose world of concern is small, restricted, and usually undiversified." Further, to blatantly punish the deviant is to legitimize that method of dealing with deviance and to risk having the same treatment befall the critic at a later time.

How, then, can the deviant be dealt with? One answer is that persons who depart from acceptable ways are not labeled as deviant. The Japanese do not see people as immutably set in their ways. They believe firmly that individuals can, with proper coaching, be redirected in their orientations and behavior. As Rohlen again trenchantly reports:

Rarely is a troublesome person treated with anything but sympathy and constraint, and this in turn undoubtedly generates constraint and cooperation from most potentially difficult people. The calm surface of mutuality, however, can be accompanied by much hidden disenchantment and resentment.

Another mode of dealing with the deviant is to remove formal responsibility for failure from any one individual. Just as social loafing, which involves only minimally acceptable productivity, can take place in the anonymity of group behavior, so also less than minimal—that is, unacceptable—behavior can be removed from public scrutiny and obloquy by placing blame at the top. The problem of suppressed individuality in Japan is not only a function of failure to give credit for individual achievement, but partly a result of the protection of the individual against public blame. For an individual to stand up to claim credit for an accomplishment would at a meta level publicly legitimize the practice of singling out and rewarding individuals. In turn this would put pressure on the system to recognize also that "credit" for poor performance would call for negative sanctions. Such a system, however, violates the essence of the Japanese "saving face" (*kau tateru*). Hence, the system's constructive bias, which protects the individuals from being singled out for blame, has a negative counterpart in its constraint on the crediting of personal achievement. The system has adjusted in part by formally shifting both credit (and blame in more subtle form) to the formal leader, thereby preempting the issue of individuality. While it is well-known among Japanese that credit for group performance deeded to the formal leader is pro forma only, the practice also serves the latent function of subordinating individuals to the group and ultimately protecting individuals from explicit blame. How, then, does a leader who wishes to encourage individuality and creativity in research and development do so in a context where both positive and negative performances are socially sacrosanct and immune from reward and punishment? As will be seen later in Part V, there are some unique combinations of traits and behaviors of formal leaders that permit unusual approaches to this problem, particularly through the imaginative delegation of tasks of control to members of the group.

## SUMMARY

Given the intimate connectedness between self and society, organization and group, the alleged subservience to the group in Japan does not really constitute a sacrifice of self to others, since the immersion of self in the group makes the group essentially the *same* as self. This is not to say it is isomorphic; rather, it is to suggest that the Japanese person achieves an "I-Thou" (Buber 1970) relationship with his group that is not cognitive. Hence, when he performs in service of the group, he is also performing in his own self-interest. Clearly, just as the self in Western society can be said to be in conflict, there may also be occasions when the Japanese worker experiences a conflict between his personal ambitions and those of others. We will consider these conflicts in depth in Chapter 11. Before doing so, however, it is necessary first to describe in some detail the nature of Japanese organizations and the place of research and development in them.

# III

## Japanese Organizations

# 7

# Organizational Design

Thus far, some features of Japanese culture and society, family, and education have been presented. With this background, it is now possible to turn to an exploration of their impact on the organization and management of the Japanese organization. As can be seen, the path of the discussion is moving closer to the subject of the empirical research—leadership in research and development organizations.

There has been a great deal written about Japanese organizations, especially in the light of the extraordinary international economic success that the Japanese have enjoyed in recent years (Harvard College 1980). Most of the central features are familiar to both professionals and the reasonably informed lay public. What follows is a recapitulation of some of these characteristics, understanding, of course, that Japanese organizations continue to undergo important changes as Japanese leadership adapts to competitive pressures. The primary internal organizational characteristics have perhaps best been portrayed as "the organizational paradigm" by Pucik and Hatvany (1983). Described in depth by Ouchi (1981; 1984), Pascale and Athos (1981), Sethi, Namiki, and Swanson (1984), Keys and Miller (1984), Vogel (1975; 1979), and Wakabayashi (1987), the allegedly integrated, synchronous nature of the set has, however, been called into question by Sullivan (1983).

According to most of these authors, Japanese firms are generally characterized by at least the following features. First, their primary goal is not profitability but stability and large size, an objective facilitated by an economic infrastructure that supports close articulation between the firm and its input and output networks. Further, consonant with the subordination of obvious personal self-enhancement, individual workers, as noted in the previous chapter, derive much of their status in society from the status of their workplace, in contrast to their personal achievements either within their organization or the society at large. It is most desirable, consequently, to be associated with a large and growing, longstanding and successful organization (Kono 1984, 53 ff.).

Second, since for a substantial percentage of Japanese salaried workers,[1] there is permanent employment (*nenko*) for most of the career, up to about age 55 (somewhat later for top administrators), there is little interinstitutional mobility (Nakatani 1988, 25–35; though see Yoshino 1968, 230–231; Kanabayashi 1988; Tachibanaki 1984; Beck & Beck 1993). Each employee, therefore, sees his career solely in the context of the company that hired him after graduation from school. Knowing that almost all of his colleagues are similarly committed to staying with the organization and that he must work with them for many years, each employee must find ways minimally to accommodate his needs to those of others and optimally to find fulfillment through collaboration with them in the service of organizational goals (Abegglen 1958). It is commonly believed, further, that the pattern of lifetime employment engenders a strong commitment to the organization's goals (though some research evidence would question this) (see, for example, Luthans, McCaul, & Dodd 1985). Of course, there are many downside risks of the permanent employment model. Among them are the loss of stimuli from job changers, who enter organizations with new ideas, and the dissatisfaction of employees "doomed" to remain in one place. Indeed, in 1986, according to a Ministry of Labor survey, fully 45 percent of Japanese workers would change jobs if a better one in another company presented itself (Nakatani 1988, 55).

Third, Japanese firms have a highly developed system of job rotation. Whereas in the United States, organizations prefer to develop highly skilled specialists and, for reasons of efficiency, to lock them into positions that allow performance of those specializations once employees are fully trained, in Japan, the policy is to shift workers at fairly frequent intervals to different parts of the organization. The Japanese conclude that there is no reason to believe that a person is able to specialize in one area only (see Hasegawa 1986, 114–116). Quite the opposite, this flexibility (*shugyo*) is a leadership strength sought for in the recruitment of prospective top managers. As will be discussed later, this focus on system integration, instead of immediate individual productivity, has many latent functions, including the empowerment of workers and the consequent freeing of leaders to work out cross-boundary problems.

The result of this system, furthermore, is not only a work force that has a diversity of skills, but one in which each person has a high degree of direct personal acquaintance with many others throughout the organization. One benefit of this policy is that the suboptimization of goals at the departmental level at the expense of total organizational goals is much rarer. Since workers in Japan are often connected by virtue of prior experience and education with many others throughout the organization, they hesitate to maximize their own gains if that action has negative consequences for others. They share the others' as well as the local unit's goals, values, and perspectives. Indeed, as noted in earlier chapters, the individual's goals are conjoined psychologically with those of the organization as a whole. As Akio Yamanouchi, who headed Canon Corporation's R & D, notes, this feeling of a need for "concord" (*wa*) stems historically from the centralization of Japan's tribal conflicts in ancient times (1986, 145; cf. Nakamura 1987, 146). Indeed, Japanese myths of primitive deities meeting in a divine assembly in a river bed suggests a comity of spirit in conflict resolution (Yamanouchi 1986, 146).

A second benefit of frequent job rotation is that by virtue of the knowledge of others, special skills and knowledge that exist elsewhere can be called upon as needed. There are far fewer barriers to cross-departmental communication and interaction than in this country. Furthermore, the rigidity of the role structure and job specification found here is replaced in Japanese organizations with a fluidity and looseness within hierarchical levels that allow skills and talent to flow more readily to problem areas as they arise. Years ago, Mary Parker Follett (1942) called this practice the "authority of the situation."

The above should not be taken to imply that there is no structure in the Japanese firm. Not only are bureaucratic structural proprieties adhered to, but the processes of decision making are extremely elaborate, both on a formal and informal level. Let us look first at the formal structure through which requirements for decisions and decisions themselves flow.

In Japanese organizations, an explicit hierarchy is critical to the authority structure and to worker motivation. Japanese organizations tend to have taller hierarchies to accommodate the need for more status distinctions among workers (Hamilton & Sanders 1992, 31). The typical Japanese firm is titularly headed by a board of directors, though in actuality this agency exercises little influence over the policies or tactics of the firm. Below the board, the firm is organized in fairly routine, bureaucratic form. There are functional divisions and departments (*bu* groups), sections (*ka* groups) and shops (*katari* groups), augmented by staff groups (cf. Morayama 1982b). Within each formal work entity, workers are assigned to roles by rank (Clark 1979, 104), with the ranks across most firms in Japan closely approximating one another. Listed in Exhibit 7.1 are the typical job titles usually found in a Japanese firm.

As Clark points out, it is important to note that the work responsibilities and authority of all persons with the same job title are not necessarily the same. Some section heads, for example, may have no workers in their section. The rank, then, connotes not so much function performed as status in the company. The utility of this system is twofold: first, it provides each worker with information about the importance of the person with whom he is dealing; second, in classic fashion, it makes the career ladder manifest. In point of fact, there typically is a dual track ladder, with one track terminating at the foreman level, the other permitting further advancement up to the highest level.

As in any organization, the formal decision-making structure is complemented in Japan by the informal system that emerges to connect and regulate personal behavior. On the one hand, this includes the senior-junior (*sempai-koohai*) re-

**Exhibit 7.1**
**Typical Job Titles in the Japanese Organizational Hierarchy**

| | |
|---|---|
| Member of Board of Directors (yakuin) | Member |
| President (sachoo or sohihinin) | Company Head |
| Vice President (fukusachoo or sohihinin-daikoo) | Deputy Company Head |
| Senior Managing Director (senmu torishimariyaku) | Special Duty Executive Director |
| Managing Director (joomu torishimariyaku) | Ordinary Duty Executive Director |
| Director (torishimariyaku) | Executive Director |
| Department Head (buchoo) | Department Head, Division Head |
| Deputy Department Head (jichoo or buchoo daikoo) | Deputy Head |
| Branch Office Manager (shitenchoo) | Branch Office Manager |
| Section Head (kachoo) | Section Head |
| Sub-section Head (kararichoo) | Sub-section Head |
| Foreman (hanchoo) | Team Head |
| Worker (hira-shain) | Ordinary Company Member |

*Source:* Adapted from Clark (1979, 105) and from Sethi, Namiki, & Swanson (1984, 81).

lationship. This hierarchical relationship originates in the varying employment tenure of the cohort groups of employees entering the organization—those entering earlier becoming *sempai* to their later-entering counterparts, the *koohai*. For each *koohai*, all of the *sempai* are treated as superordinate and deserving of respect, though few develop more egalitarian dyadic relationships. The relationship is one of older sibling to younger, mirroring the fraternal relationships in the Japanese home (see Chapter 5). The older person "adopts" the junior (who accepts and welcomes the subordinate, dependent relationship) and provides friendship and assistance. Perhaps more important, the *sempai* acts as a "strict judge of performance and a stern task master" (Rohlen 1975, 197). This important leadership function of controlling subordinate behavior is thus at least partially removed from the jurisdiction of the formal leader, liberating him from responsibility and freeing him to take on other leadership roles that may have conflicted with the succoring role, either for time or behavior. Controlling and consoling, for example, are difficult to effectuate simultaneously by one individual toward another. Rohlen goes onto suggest that

The paternal and familistic philosophies (*onjoo shugi* and *kazokuteki keiei*) espoused by most companies also suggest that leadership should be as sympathetic, protective, and unselfish as good *sempai*. While clearly the ideal may go unrealized, it does establish a set of expectations about proper leader and follower conduct. (p. 198; emphasis in original)

The informal part of the organization also includes another hierarchical relationship—the *oyabun-kobun* pattern of superior-subordinate relationships, though these terms usually refer to more temporary organizational settings in commercial trades, where the members of the organization are not committed to the organization except insofar as it promotes their individual well-being. Hence, the horizontal relationships that are critical and important in large organizations are underestimated in this analysis. The informal solidarity of the firm is ramified into a finely tuned, functional system of authority-subordinate (and lateral) relationships. With a long history manifested in *Samurai*, labor relations, and street gangs, the *oyabun-kobun* mechanism is pervasive in Japanese organizations, though without the negative connotations of exploitive power and authority. This informal relationship, as noted in earlier chapters, is to a considerable extent, parent to child (really father, not mother, to child). It is predicated on a reciprocal relationship in which the parent protects and looks out for the children, while the children are obligated to serve the parent with obedience and loyalty (Bennett & Ishino 1963, 44 ff.).

A key activity that cements the interpersonal relationships in the informal system is the well-remarked practice of after-hours social activity (*tsukiai*) where a significant portion of the conflict suppressed during the day in the formal office setting can be resolved. As Chang (1982) recounts,

After a day's work is over, Japanese managers usually do not go home directly. Instead, they go to bars by groups to eat and drink with each other. Under this relaxed atmosphere, they chat and laugh. But the main topics are related to company matters, and they discuss them informally. Usually the subordinates of these socializing groups speak out or express their complaints to their superiors. These subordinates are very reluctant to raise their complaints to superiors during office hours. In their rigid and structured workday environment, they remain men of conformity. However, socialization at bars and other places after work changes this rigid attitude to a significant degree.

During these informal gatherings, managers and subordinates try to restore respective self-interests and individual aspirations that may have become overlooked during regular work hours. (p. 87)

Interestingly, the role of "parent" is often transposed into *sempai* in these gatherings, thus permitting communications otherwise considered improper in the *oyabun-kobun* relationship.

The Japanese are becoming increasingly aware of a need to vest informal groups with legitimate authority, rather than having them function primarily as a source of suggestions to be decided on by other authorities. Rewards and recognition for autonomous groups follow from high performance. Moreover, there has been a gradual, if slow, movement away from quality circles (sometimes referred to as the "ZD campaign," or "green-cross group") to small, autonomous groups (Odaka 1982).

There are several important consequences of these attributes of Japanese organizations that have bearings on both creativity and performance and on leadership. First, there is now emerging a body of literature that suggests that there are significant downside risks to overly harmonious working groups. Not only do such groups become less open to external ideas, as Janis (1972) suggests, but the social basis of their solidarity makes them less willing to challenge one another's ideas, thus permitting low-quality work to proceed. Second, as will be seen in the chapter on leadership which follows, the anomaly of a formal leader who is dependent on his subordinates for ideas, effort, and commitment, yet is responsible for their well-being, demands a set of leadership traits or characteristics very different from those in the United States. Indeed, the impossibility of any one person, even in Japan, possessing all of the necessary characteristics to fulfill both formal and informal requisites calls for the kinds of dispersed leadership behavior that are found in Japan. This subject is explored in much greater detail in later chapters.

## LEADER IDENTIFICATION

Many Japanese companies have formal educational programs through which all workers proceed at periodic intervals; for example, a newcomer's course, advanced course, middle course, and project leader trainee course (Botkin, Dimancescu, & Stata 1984, 181). Differentiation of individuals, both formally and informally, on the basis of their revealed talent is thus a continuous process, beginning more formally at the fifteen-to-twenty-year status. Promotions are firmly grounded in seniority, rendering them extremely slow and predictable, especially since potential leadership talent is carefully assessed at the point of organizational entry and in the first three years (Wakabayashi, Graen, Graen, & Graen 1988). It takes at least eight to ten years before a worker can achieve the rank of subsection chief, fifteen to twenty years before promotion to department head (Yoshino 1968, 236).

Although norms are eroding somewhat in recent years (Pollack 1993a), little rank jumping on the basis of apparent special skills or achievements is permitted. Potential leaders are observed to identify both task-specific competencies and social interaction skills, most notably as both are put to use in facilitating the achievement of *others* rather than self. (cf. Blau 1964, 126–127. For a discussion of upward mobility in U.S. R & D firms, see Shenhav 1991.) Despite its deference to seniority, however, Dore (1982) reports that the typical Japanese organization is "a more thoroughgoing meritocracy than any except the Eastern European industrial countries."

There should be no misunderstanding, then, about the upwardly mobile ambitions of individual Japanese men in the context of the dominant collectivism of the organization (though see Noguchi 1992). As Chang (1982) notes:

Individualism does play a role in the management system of Japan. . . . There is a word in Japan, *risshin-shuse*, which can be translated as establishing oneself in a successful career. For many ambitious Japanese, this word has become the motto for their self-actualization. The individual Japanese in an organization is concerned with his own promotion and success and is constantly striving to achieve them. (pp. 84–85)

Recent years have seen a significant increase in assisting workers with leadership promise to learn the skills of management. Immediately following World War II, a variety of programs were developed for training supervisory personnel (Yoshino 1968, 243). The current approach is to develop executive training programs within firms as well as to hire outside training groups (e.g., Japan Productivity Center). By far, however, much of the development of talented men for upper management positions is through on-the-job training. Competition for these positions is often fierce, but because of the pressure toward corporate equanimity, such strivings are carried out with extreme care and subtlety and are explicitly overlaid with the expected loyalty and manifest behavioral commitment to the group and organization.

Would-be leaders of Japanese organizations are identified, carefully monitored in their work and the coursework noted above, and groomed early in their careers. By the time there is an opening, virtually all of the workers are reasonably certain who will be promoted (cf. Yammarino & Bass 1990 for a U.S. counterpart), and it is only with their consent (ascertained through informal means by the astute executive staff) that that person will move up the hierarchy. Future "CEO's acquire power as they rise to the top of the organisation through a system that both provides opportunities for the acquisition of power and simultaneously legitimises that power in the eyes of internal and external constituencies" (Bird 1992).

Despite the apparent formal rigidity of the career track, promotions beyond the twenty-year tenure point are, therefore, the result of informal agreement among all peers as well as superordinates as to the merit of the individual to be promoted. Such consensus formation fits perfectly into a Weberian bureaucratic perspective which requires that subordinates' respect for authority stem from their belief in the superordinate's greater knowledge and skills. Vertical conflict is thus largely avoided or vitiated (at least theoretically).

Evaluation procedures for leader identification and advancement have been changing from past practices. Current personnel practices, however, now utilize a formalized evaluation process that includes semiannual appraisals. Increasingly, evaluations seem to be moving away from seniority as the sole criterion and are being weighted toward individual performance with merit ratings (*jinji kooka*) allocated on the basis of accomplishments and a variety of attitudinal factors, including education, ability, and adoption of company values. In recent

years, evaluations are taking more account of output or performance (*gyoo seki*)—
actually a combination of achievement and effort—but the extent of the shift to
date has not been carefully documented empirically (cf. Mroczkowski & Hanaoka
1989). As workers move up the organizational hierarchy, their attitudes also are
evaluated, especially in the area of interpersonal relationships. Special credit is
given for skills in sensitivity, diplomacy, tact, ability to give feedback, and support. As will be discussed in later chapters, there are some who believe that these
interpersonal leadership attributes are accorded so much importance that they prevent the rise of individuals whose creative skills and farsighted thinking might allow for insights into other organizational needs, either within or across R & D unit
boundaries. In research and development, different kinds of leaders may be required, depending on the type of research being conducted. As Rohlen (1975)
notes, "it is ironic . . . that companies . . . regularly place many men in group
leadership positions who lack the capacity to motivate their followers in the highly
personal manner required" (p. 199).

In recent years, evaluations are taking more account of output or performance
(*gyoo seki*)—actually a combination of achievement and effort—but the extent
of the shift to date has not been carefully documented empirically (cf. Mroczkowski & Hanaoka 1989).

It is worth commenting briefly at this point on the role of labor, in the formal
sense of labor-management relations, as it may affect both features of Japanese
organization and the nature of leadership. Some features of labor unions in Japan
are unique:

1. They are originated by employers, not trade unions.
2. Many are local unions, not affiliated with national unions.
3. Consultation for effectiveness and efficiency is carried out through the same mechanism as for negotiation for benefits.
4. 94 percent of companies with more than 1,000 employees have joint consultation
   committees.
5. Many quality circles are formally part of the union structure.
6. 70 percent of companies listed on Tokyo Stock Exchange have an employee share-
   holding system. (Maruo 1982)

## DECISION MAKING

A superficial look at the hierarchical structure for making decisions and the
strict promotion system in Japan might lead to a conclusion that all important
decisions are made by the chief executive officer. The decision-making process
is far more complicated, however, and only approximately 10 percent of decisions are by edict of top management (Tung 1984, 49). While the unit or organizational leader must, indeed, sign off on all major decisions with a formal
affixing of his official seal, such action is preceded by a painstakingly complex

procedure for reaching consensus among members of all ranks. Workers in Japanese organizations typically engage in an elaborate, widespread discussion process prior to every important decision (called *nemawashi*) followed by a formal procedure ensuring acquiescence at all levels (called *ringisei*—literally, "a system of reverential enquiry about a superior's intentions") (Sethi 1975, 511). Under the *ringi* system, draft proposals (*ringishoo*) for alternative decisions available to the firm are prepared by younger members of middle or lower management. Preparation of the proposal involves extensive discussion, along with careful, subtle negotiating and cajoling among colleagues (and occasionally beyond the corporate boundaries) so as accurately to reflect the anticipated consensus of as many as possible, including the chief executive officer. Once it appears that there is widespread, if not universal agreement throughout the organization (or, at least, any serious objections are no longer expressed), the revised proposal is distributed to all units that will be affected by the proposal. At each level in the organization and for each subunit, the managers sign by stamping their names using their personal seals (*hanko*) on the document (De Mente 1981, 83).

The extensive discussion above reflects the two major criteria claimed in the literature as necessitating participation of employees to improve efficiency and effectiveness of decision making: stake in the outcome and expertise (Vroom & Yetton 1973; Hoy & Miskel 1991). In the first place, it permits all persons with a stake in the decision and with expertise that might be brought to bear on it to have some input. In the case of applied R & D, where many different skills, talents, and kinds of knowledge must be combined to put a new product together, such discussions are highly functional and efficient. This is in distinct contrast to the usual practice in the United States where much decision making takes place in centralized seclusion by executives presumed to be knowledgeable.

The second purpose for the involvement of lower level employees is motivational. Not only is the discussion not merely pro forma, it is designed to enlist the support and approval of the workers themselves, if not the substantive input, from competent people throughout the organization (though see Hattori 1978). Conflicts among workers as to objectives and/or procedures are expected to be resolved through discussion before the decision is made. So important is consensus that in cases where in a group meeting it is not forthcoming, rather than take a vote, the decision is postponed to allow the leader or leaders to meet with dissenters. At a future meeting, only when it is already known that consensus has been reached, is a vote is taken (see Duke 1986, 31–33). This involuted system provides opportunities for input, reinforces the benefits of contributions from many, thus enhancing the value of integrating efforts across the organization, and gives upper management power through a consensual basis for enouraging concerted action. (For a discussion of different forms of participation in decision making, see Cotton et al. 1988 and Yammarino & Naughton 1992.)

There are, of course, negative aspects of the *nemawashi* and *ringisei* system. On occasion, participation may be piecemeal, and consensus may be illusory.

Lower-level employees contribute from the narrow perspective of their decentralized offices. Sometimes consensus can be established only through an ambiguity in the document that renders it virtually useless as a guide to action. And the multiple sign-offs may ''deindividualize'' responsibility for the overall decision: that is, the upper-level managers point to the signatures as evidence that approval had been secured prior to their own. However, a contrary view might suggest that assignment of responsibility to the collectivity is consistent with the face-saving norms of Japan and does force all employees to be conscious of their own responsibilities. (See Flynn 1982, for a fuller discussion.)

The literature abounds with anecdotal reports about how long it takes for the Japanese to come to a decision, but how committed all workers are to that decision once taken (though see discussion of *ringisei* in the Japanese government by Tsuji [1968] showing its constraints on leadership). In America, the lack of early involvement frequently results not only in poorly informed decisions but in desultory worker commitment, if not sabotage. As Sasaki (1981, 69) reports,

the consensus-forming information procedure produces huge amounts of oral and documentary information, but as a result it also produces a merit that is the full participation of the group members in the decision-making process. Once a consensus is gained, the resultant actions are extremely rapid.

The conclusion to be drawn from these very abbreviated observations about Japanese work settings is that the extremely close and harmonious work relations in Japanese organizations create a climate and setting for leadership that is quite different from that in the United States. As has been noted throughout this book, to understand leadership in the Japanese organization, it is necessary to comprehend the culture. As Hofstede found in extensive cross-cultural research on management, the values of different countries impel managers in those countries to account for cultural factors in their behavior. Hofstede found, for example, that four factors accounted for differences in 40 countries: power distance, tolerance for uncertainty, individualism versus collectivism, and masculinity (Hofstede 1980a). These are the products of the culture. Again, the commonality of background and education, family-like closeness of work relationships, normative consensus, and sharing of goals make the tasks of leadership in Japan at once both easier and difficult, and certainly different from this country.

Three implications for the understanding of leadership follow from the decision-making structure and processes. First, the formal leader of the organization can yield much of the executive direction or oversight for decision making to the informal processes and to informal leaders. As Perrow notes, this frees up the leader to be more attentive to cross-boundary relationships, both vertically and horizontally. Second, and not to give too unrealistic and naive a view of this, manifest disagreement is treated as a temporary, resolvable condition, not as irreconcilable conflict. The latter may, of course, exist, but it remains latent primarily because of the social prohibitions against persistent holdouts from majority opinions. (See Chapter 7.) As noted above, harmony (*wa*) looms large as a strong value in Japanese culture. Ask a Japanese person if conflict exists in his organization, and he will say no.

In point of fact, of course, much of the potential conflict involving personalities and values is resolved through the recruitment and socialization processes which ensure a commonality of intrafirm perspectives and through the *nemawashi* process itself, which addresses substantive differences. But a residual level of conflict persists as an undercurrent of discontent that is not articulated, and sometimes is not even conscious in the minds of the workers. As will be shown through the findings from the empirical research reported later (Chapter 16), there are some kinds of leaders who can bring the latent conflict out into the open without destroying the norms of collaboration and consensus-seeking, and there are some who can identify the "holdout" from the consensus as worth supporting because of the innovativeness of the idea.

A third consequence of the shared decision-making processes has to do with the nature of the decision itself. Earlier it was suggested that there was an informal and formal process for making decisions that necessitated significant lower-level involvement. It must be pointed out here, however, that it is important not to assume that the formal leadership is merely a rubber stamp operation. In part this is because of the promotion mechanisms in Japanese organizations referred to above. Further, the processes of *nemawashi* and *ringi* take into account what the superordinate will find acceptable. Hence, the "rule of anticipatory reaction" (Friedrich 1972) is in force. Having lived with that person, the subordinates come to know well and respect the prospective and then actual leader's ideologies, dispositions, and preferences. The system, then, closely conforms to the Weberian criterion for a properly functioning bureaucracy—promotion on the basis of acknowledged expertise.

As is well-known, leadership takes place at all levels of an organization. Leadership behavior at the top, however, is quite different from leadership of a small section. At least it is in Japan, where the functions are distributed differently. In Japan, the formal laboratory leader plays leadership roles quite differently from the section leader. Importantly, both are intimately involved in the lives of the section workers, though in quite different ways. As will be elaborated later, the section leader in Japan is freed from some of the interpersonal role responsibilities that social scientists studying leadership in this country would insist is an essential ingredient of effective leadership. In particular, responsibility for planning and controlling and for initiating behavior (cf. the Ohio State leadership model) is distributed to other than formal leaders in Japanese organizations. The implications of the assignment of such a critical, traditional, formal leadership role to others is significant in comprehending the effectiveness of Japanese leadership. It also has potential far-reaching significance in understanding how leadership in this country is and could be exercised. Before discussing this, however, we must consider in the next chapter the group context in which leadership of research and development is manifested.

**NOTE**

1. Estimates vary. Hamilton and Sanders (1992, 30) say it is only 30 to 40 percent.

# 8

# Small Work Groups in Japan

The setting for this research was the research and development section, comprising six to fifteen persons working in constant face-to-face relationships. Understanding this organizational entity in Japan (the *shudan*) is critical to a comprehension of the nature of effective leadership. For the Japanese, knowledge and wisdom are products of group experience. *Shuchi,* or the wisdom of many, must be assiduously sought (cf. Matsushita 1975, 39). As Pascale and Athos (1981) suggest,

the work group is the basic building block of Japanese organizations. Owing to the central importance of group efforts in their thinking, the Japanese are extremely sensitive to and concerned about group interactions and relationships. They regard group phenomena primarily in terms of morals and emotion rather than role and function. (p. 198)

The Japanese worker regards the work group as a second family with whom he spends far more time than his own. He socializes with them on the job, usually having lunch and snacks with them. Despite popular literature to the contrary, it is not unusual in Japan to see Japanese workers sharing lunch in front of a television set showing the latest soap operas. Afternoon tea may last as much as an hour with similar conviviality. Work often extends until or beyond eight o'clock, whereupon workers frequently go out to dinner together, followed by a stop or two at a favorite pub.

This intimate setting, therefore, must be analyzed as a workplace and as a source of profound life satisfactions and frustrations for the Japanese worker. One of the literatures most directly applicable comes from the research on small group behavior, of which there is a plethora. Let us begin with a description of the general characteristics of groups, since each of these features must be reflected in the analysis of group processes in the Japanese firm. In Hare (1960, 10), some of the elements of groups are outlined:

In addition to the *interaction* of the members, four features of group life typically emerge as the group develops . . . :

1. The members share one or more *motives* or *goals* which determine the direction in which the group will move.
2. The members develop a set of *norms*, which set the boundaries within which interpersonal relations may be established and activity carried on.
3. If interaction continues, a set of *roles* becomes stabilized and the new group becomes differentiated from other groups.
4. A *network of interpersonal attraction* develops on the basis of "likes" and "dislikes" of members for one another.

Bales notes that it is possible to analyze group behavior in terms of form and content. The form consists of communication networks and interaction rates, while content classifies behavior as task or social-emotional in orientation. Independent variables that affect these dimensions of groups are characteristics of the individual, group-level factors, like cohesiveness, and environment-level factors such as organizational rewards (Dore 1973; Lincoln & Kalleberg 1985). The processes in which groups engage can themselves be determinants of performance outcomes, such as quantity, quality, error rates, creativity, turnover, absenteeism (Hackman & Morris 1975; Cummings & Srivastva 1976). In their review of literature and their own research, Hackman and Morris note that no single omnibus theory of group effectiveness has emerged, though a small number are helpful explanators. They also suggest that effectiveness is enhanced through team building to develop group self-management, a concept that has increased in salience in recent years (cf. MacDuffie 1988; Huszczo 1990; Sundstrom, DeMeuse, & Futrell 1990; Cotton 1993) and embraces much of what is found in the Japanese setting. This is not to suggest that Western social scientists have been unaware of the importance of work groups and teams as vital components contributing to organizational effectiveness. Especially since the publication of the research on and theories of "sociotechnical systems" by Trist and Bamforth (1951), considerable research effort has been directed to inquiries into this field. Much of this interest, however, has been directed at improving work design by accounting for the socioemotional character of the complex relationships among members of groups and teams (see, for example, Cohen, Kruse, & Anbar 1982). In this chapter (and book), the concern is more with the subtleties of the leadership dynamics that obtain in groups, particularly with a modification of vertical dyad linkage theory through observation of Japanese groups.

As noted in Chapter 7, partially because of the extreme homogeneity of the Japanese society, and owing to the very careful scrutiny of new hires to organizations to assure similarity or at least potential similarity of values and dispositions to those of current staff, groups in Japanese organizations are highly cohesive, with norms that are low in variance and strongly sanctioned. Conformity, in other words, is highly valued and rewarded, while nonconformity is severely punished. There is reason to believe that the special features of this conformity may be unique to the Japanese (Mann 1980), as will be discussed below. Indeed, *shudanshugi*, or group ideology, is a much-lauded management philosophy in Japan (Murayama 1982b).

Bales (1965, 24) notes that individuals have four choices when faced with norms: conform, change the norms, become or remain a deviant, or exit the group (cf. Hirschman's related notion of *Exit, Voice and Loyalty* 1970). In Japan, the latter two of these are not viable options for most workers. Deviance brings ostracism, one of the most extreme punishments a Japanese can suffer. And since employment in Japan is usually for the life of the worker (though, obviously, there are exceptions to this pattern, particularly in recent years), exit would mean loss of status, if not unemployment. These threats are very real to the Japanese worker and constrain him to work with extraordinary diligence toward group solutions. As Yamagishi (1988) suggests, "members of a group with high exit cost will develop a collectivistic solution, whereas members of a group with low exit cost will fail to develop such a solution." Oddly, the within-organization fluidity of cross-unit movement brings with it many advantages. Since there is much movement in and out of groups in the course of the carefully designed job rotation system, persons both take group information (secrets) with them and are thrust into educating roles in the new groups in which they find themselves (cf. Caraley 1982, 208).

Ensuring compliance of members in groups is exercised in a number of ways (Hechter 1987, 48 ff.), some of which are formal and visible to all, others of which are below the surface. On occasion, social control is openly intentional and coordinated, especially when exercised by formal authorities. Other times it is exerted by members of the group, either by concerted plan or informally, though consensually. It is said in Japan that when superordinates must constrain a subordinate, he is "hit on the head," but when his peers do it, he is "pulled down by the feet" (Yoo 1984). As noted in several previous chapters, the constant surveillance of peers, which is a desideratum for each individual (Shishin 1988), serves to control as well as support behavior. Where peer pressure augments vertical control, it enlarges the "zone of indifference" (cf. Barnard 1938) within which workers unquestioningly accept superordinate authority. That is, perceived (though not actual) discretionary "opportunity" at the individual level is reduced. Workers are more willing to accept others' directives without question. Although innovation in Japanese organizations is highly sought after and rewarded (e.g., the enormous success of Japanese suggestion systems), if the Japanese can be faulted for the alleged lack of willingness to depart significantly rather than incrementally from the status quo, it is likely due to the cultural conditioning that narrows their perceived sphere of influence at the individual level.

This is not to say, of course, that lower levels of employees in organizations do not participate in decisions, nor even recognize their collective right and obligation to do so. As noted in the earlier discussion of *nemawashi* and *ringei*, quite the contrary is the case. The point here is to observe that at the individual level, both the impetus to deviate and the perceived opportunity are mitigated by peer pressures unlike those found in American organizations.

Groups develop a role structure that is invariably differentiated and hierarchical. Task leaders, emotional leaders, and other kinds of leaders emerge to provide known resources and hence sources of stability and efficiency for the group. In effective groups, each member can turn quickly to role players known for their competencies. The role structure may or may not overlap isomorphically with the formal structure of offices. More often than not, in Japanese work organizations, it does not. Formal structures in Japan tend to give formal recognition to seniority as often as merit, but the titled-but-less-effective upper management officials, as noted earlier, may be provided with only the appearance, not the apparatus of power and authority (e.g., prestigious window offices [*mado giwa zoku*] but little responsibility and few duties).

Empirical reports of role-taking behavior in groups reveal that individuals tend to select from among a number of alternative responsibilities. Typically, they include the task functions, group building and maintenance functions, and personal expressions. These are delineated in Exhibit 8.1. These roles can be played by group members who hold either formal roles or occupy informal positions of respect and power.

The behaviors may or may not be leadership roles, depending on the situation and the type of group. Leadership in work groups has been shown to be distributed across various persons. The leader of the work group need not be the formal leader. Redl (1942; cf. Mintzberg 1973) identified ten possible leader-subordinate roles. The leader as:

1. Patriarchal sovereign
2. Leader
3. Tyrant
4. Idol[1]
5. Scapegoat[1]
6. Organizer
7. Seducer
8. Hero
9. Bad influence
10. Good example

Scientific research teams are or can be quite diverse in their social structures. For each type, different kinds of formal and informal leaders emerge. Cohen,

**Exhibit 8.1**
**Individual Role-Taking Behavior in Groups**

### A. TASK FUNCTIONS

1. Defining problems
2. Seeking information
3. Giving information
4. Seeking opinions
5. Giving opinions
6. Testing feasibility

### B. GROUP BUILDING AND MAINTENANCE FUNCTIONS

7. Coordination
8. Mediating-harmonizing
9. Orienting-facilitating
10. Supporting-encouraging
11. Following

### C. INDIVIDUAL FUNCTIONS

12. Blocking
13. Out of field
14. Digressing

*Source:* Dimmock (1987, 95); cf. Benne & Sheats (1948).

Kruse, and Anbar (1982) conceived of four prototypical research team types using two orthogonal dimensions: centralization of control and intellectual/administrative. Against this they hypothesized relative degrees of effectiveness for four different leader roles: nominal, line manager, facilitator, and bridge. As will be shown in Chapter 12 on leadership, what kinds of concrete leadership behaviors are attached to these (and other) characterizations of leadership has been (or can be) identified through research. "Effective" leadership in each of the Redl depictions may or may not require group maintenance functions, again depending on the situation.

For example, one of the most critical determinants of the effectiveness of groups is the degree to which the members are able to assuage their anxiety about their relationships with their superordinates and with one another (Bennis & Shepard 1976). Groups and individuals must deal with this differently. At the group level, all groups must resolve the ambiguity of formal authority and informal power, must come to some consensus about how much obedience and deviance should be permitted, and about how deviations from group expectations about conformity should be managed. There is some disagreement in the literature about the manner of resolution. Slater (1966), for example, argues that as groups form, there is a "revolt" against the leader, usually marked by a specific event—"the 'ganging up' of group members in some sort of hostile attack on the assigned group leader ... (and) the group members' growing independence of, yet identification with, the leader" (p. 3). Slater continues later:

The "vigorous successor" to the group leader is usually the group as a whole. The feeling is that they can only become strong if they destroy and incorporate him while they still believe in his mystical power. (p. 82)

It will be successful as a group insofar as the members are willing to depend on each other rather than on the leader, and this will occur when the group as a whole is perceived strong and able. (p. 83)

Slater goes on to suggest that the process of individual separation from the leader is terrifying. The individual feels "small and impotent. It feels itself a tiny, defenseless speck" (p. 239). But when the group comes to perceive itself as comprising different individuals, each with unique strengths that can contribute to group emotional and external efficacy, the development of the group can proceed with a new and different dynamic. This is certainly the case in Japan where, as Murayama (1982b) notes, the small work group or *shudan* is both an emotional system, which can be translated as the we-group (we-feeling or *nakama ishiki*), and a goal-oriented system. The danger in this ideology, he notes, is when members so subject themselves in the emotional system that they lose their sensitivity to the situational constraints that should drive the goal achievement—the demands of economy, culture, technology, legal, and other systems.

Organizational development theorists argue that team building requires the explicit and open recognition of conflict, especially when it involves disputes about power. The findings of Murnighan and Conlon (1991), however, suggest that in some intense small groups where worker reciprocal interdependencies are high, effectiveness is promoted by implicit, rather than explicit, recognition of the "leader-democracy paradox," that is, the continuous tension between vertical and lateral authority. The Japanese leader's concern with enhancing harmony (*wa*) reflects the prominence of the emotional system and its preservation, even at the cost of effectiveness.

Further, the degree to which agreement about and commitment to organizational goals, policies, and procedures is forthcoming in organizations is a function at least in part of the perception of positive control that members have over those goals. As Smith and Ari (1968) found:

The significant exercise of control by both members and leaders leads to a high degree of identification and involvement in the organization. All organization members are more motivated to develop a set of shared policies and practices, to accept jointly made decisions, and to act on behalf of the organization. The system of high mutual influence which this pattern of control signifies provides an opportunity for members and leaders to reconcile their interests and facilitates an atmosphere of cooperation. This further bolsters common loyalties and promotes shared objectives which are reflected in the wider acceptance of organizational norms. (p. 162)

In groups in Japanese organizations, there appears to be recognition of both of these two principles: the need for perception of control and the need to keep the conflict over control latent. Perhaps the key point here is the question of whether R & D groups, by taking this route, do damage to their capacity to be innovative. Depending on the nature of the research—basic, applied, developmental—where the strength of functional (in contrast to social) interdependencies may be quite different, the authority question may need to be addressed differentially. This issue is discussed at some length in Chapter 16.

At the individual level, each person must determine what action to take in the face of group pressures to conform. At one extreme, one or more members could decide to rebel (either verbally or by action), submit loyally, with varying degrees of effort toward group goals, or withdraw and leave the group (cf. Hirschman 1970). Smith and Berg (1987) refer to these as the three major ambiguities of groups: the paradoxes of belonging, commitment, and speaking. When individuals come together, they generate a variety of potential sources of conflict. New supraindividual goals are created that require collaboration, since insufficient skills and knowledge are available in any one individual. Collectivities tend to fragment or polarize into suboptimizing subgroups. And individuals fear submersing themselves in a group that may obliterate much of their sense of their individuality. As Smith and Berg note, "The simultaneous desire for inclusion and fusion triggers the fear of consumption, absorption, and deindividuation, while the desire to be independent triggers the fear of exclusion, aloneness, and isolation" (p. 66).

As noted earlier, however, socialization in the Japanese society renders the worker virtually void of the fear of deindividuation. Indeed, quite the contrary, the Japanese need to be part of and identify with the group. The structuring of the organization and work group represent uniquely Japanese ways of overcoming the second of the fears—of aloneness and isolation. As will be noted below, however, the absence of the other pole may result in a loss in creative energies that can be manifested in the group.

Typically, according to Bennis and Shepard (1976), the solution to these problems of role differentiation and individual conformity takes place sequentially. As the authority relationship becomes stabilized, lateral problems of interpersonal relationships become more salient. At this point, the informal, differentiated role structure needed to solve group problems suffers through a testing stage until it becomes clear who has the required competencies to perform each group task. As Gibbard (1976) notes, this differentiation serves both positive and negative functions. It is a "defensive and restitutive effort" in that by clarifying who does what, it reduces conflict and confusion. On the other hand, such restrictions both isolate the individual and restrict his opportunities to take on roles that he can perform. Typically, however, and especially in Japan (for reasons noted in the previous chapter, e.g., job rotation and training and group solidarity), once the role structure has been established, thus clarifying sources of respect and power, behavioral deviations from role become more possible. In a healthy group, the "authority of the situation" (Follett 1942) obtains. Expertise and knowledge are brought to bear on problems, regardless of formal role or status. Indeed, as will be seen, in Japan these teams are virtually "self-managed" (Manz & Sims 1987; Fairhurst 1993), with formal leadership assigned an unusual combination of internal and external responsibilities.

As noted above, virtually no Japanese would risk being accused of not carrying his weight in a group effort. In many respects this observation is anomalous. Research has shown that in most groups where persons are not identified for their individual efforts, a phenomenon labeled as "social loafing" or "free riding" frequently occurs (Earley 1989, 1993; Jones 1984; George 1991; Yamagishi 1988; Latane, Williams, & Harkins 1979; Gabrenya, Latane, & Wang 1983). Social loafing is the reduction of personal effort in group settings by individuals who see that because group rather than individual achievement is rewarded, external returns to the individual are not usually reduced when personal effort and commitment are lower than others. The low producer, in other words, hides in the group's higher achievement. Moreover, as groups increase in size, so also does individual effort decline. As Earley notes:

An individual may loaf because he or she assumes that the actions of others will ensure the attainment of the collective good (i.e., from greed) or in anticipation of the loafing of others so as to avoid appearing the "sucker" (i.e., from fear). . . . Thus, social loafing would be affected by both an individual's perceived dispensability and expectations concerning others' intended efforts. (p. 566)

In Japan, this kind of thinking or behavior rarely takes place. It is extremely important for the Japanese worker's psychological well-being that he conceive of himself as making a contribution to his group. The motivation to contribute is accentuated by the nature of the reward structure, where "team" rather than individual rewards are passed out. In contrast, in the United States, many leaders try to take a balanced approach by also rewarding individuals. As Mower and Wilemon (1989) report, however:

The evidence from the field of psychology is very clear, and it derives from hundreds of studies of reward and team achievement. Teams rewarded on a strictly team basis, with everybody sharing equally, almost always outperform teams in which certain persons are rewarded more than others, no matter what the reason. Individualistic or competitive rewards lead to higher team achievement only in the case of teamwork that really isn't teamwork, with no real interdependency of tasks. (pp. 27-28)

The question raised for this research, then, is how "high producer" Japanese workers psychologically handle the perceived inequity of equal allocation? Yamagishi (1988) observes that behaviorally, there is relatively less free riding because individuals in this kind of a culture are group oriented, and there is a system of interpersonal monitoring that enforces sanctions against free riders.

Thus, both individual and group solutions inhibit free riding. However, Deci (1975) and others have found that strong external rewards will frequently reduce internal motivation. A similar argument has often been made for strong external sanctions. Conceivably, in Japan as in the West, some individuals do, in fact, want to free ride. Both free riding and nonconforming, exemplary productivity thus constitute two extremes of deviance. Whereas group solutions to deviant free riding which are functional for the organization have emerged in Japan, no similar group solution has been found for encouraging and supporting deviant, organizationally creative activity. The role of leadership in this area thus becomes crucial, as is detailed in later chapters.

## SELF-MANAGING WORK TEAMS

Groups perform differently depending on the prevailing management philosophy of the organization in which they are immersed. Walton and Hackman (1986; cf. Dore 1973) suggest that there are two prevailing kinds of organizations: control and commitment organizations. Control organizations usually have centralized authority structures, with work designed to minimize the need for decision making among lower-level workers. In commitment-type organizations, on the other hand, the structure is flatter, and "job responsibilities tend to be broad, combining planning and implementation activities. Employees are expected to manage themselves to a considerable extent, making adjustments in what they do or how they do it when circumstances change" (Walton & Hackman 1986). Further, "self-enacting" or "self-managing" teams emerge out of member affiliations and mutual concern and take on responsibilities and power to accomplish organizational goals (Manz & Sims 1987). Such teams are distinctive also in their relative absence of direct, hierarchical, downward-directed commands and in extensive use of discussion methods (Fairhurst 1993). Leaders (or "superleaders" according to Manz and Sims), in their laid-back, low-communicative stance, engender group-centered goal setting, independent problem solving, and self-evaluation.

It is clear that most Japanese organizations are commitment organizations, and that self-enacting teams are the predominant mode by which work gets done. Note how derivative this is of the forms of group self-management described in the earlier chapter on elementary school education. What is critical about this configuration is the modes by which leadership is exercised. As Walton and Hackman note with respect to control organizations:

How do self-enacted groups exercise power in relation to *supervision*? Often the process can be characterized as "mutual boundary setting." Since neither the group nor the supervisor can dictate to the other, there is implicit bargaining over limits. What worker behaviors not countenanced by the formal organization will the supervisor actually tolerate? What supervisory behaviors will the group actually accept? The group and the supervisor tacitly agree that it is in their mutual interest to accommodate each other within certain boundaries rather than for either to escalate the influence tactics available. (p. 179)

The mode in control organizations, in other words, is one of careful bargaining and tacit agreement over what are often conflicting and mutually exclusive goals—workers' and supervisors'.

A very different picture emerges for commitment organizations:

The formal designs of task teams provide for certain leadership functions and member roles, posit decision mechanisms that require negotiation among team members, and provide a means for teams to exercise influence upward in the organization. But not everything can be planned and structured formally, and the *emergence* of additional leadership within teams, and further differentiation of roles, additional forms of peer pressure, and so on appears to be critical in creating a high commitment culture. In the healthy commitment organization, then, the boundaries between organizationally created and self-enacted group phenomena are blurred and difficult to sort out. (Walton & Hackman 1986)

The Japanese have great needs to be part of a group, and many groups resemble families in their structure and interpersonal relationships. The heavy "dependence" of members on one another is not anxiety producing as in the West, but is a source of security, provided there is confidence in those on whom the person is dependent—a confidence born out of the development of relationships similar to those that obtain in the family. (See Chapters 4 and 5.) While the intimacy of the family is limited in groups that are large, many Japanese organizations engender some not-inconsiderable sense of care and concern. The clear counterpart of this is that "outsiders" are different and not to be trusted to the same degree. The projection of outsiders as enemies in turn reinforces internal bonding.

Thus far in this chapter, we have discussed the work group in the Japanese organization rather generally. Perhaps the best description of the details of "the company work group" comes from Rohlen (1975). As he notes, "a key variable in most employees' response to their company is the quality of their face-to-face relations in office or factory groups (usually called *ka*)."

The center of the Japanese worker's life in his organization is his work group. He is assigned to it first, even before knowing what job or jobs he is to perform. The recruitment system brings new employees from common backgrounds and schools, and they join others with those same origins. They become "related" (the use of a family word is intentional) to their peers and to those hired previously, with elders becoming uncles and cousins (Rohlen calls them older brothers). The mentoring relationship across the senior-junior (*sempai-koohai*) ranks noted in earlier chapters reflects this family-centered culture.

Most groups average about twenty workers. Competition within groups is studiously avoided in the open, though there is a constant but underground tension in the early years of employment as younger employees jockey subtlely for recognition and access to positions of responsibility. Outward comity and cooperation, however, are placed at the highest priority level for the group.

Even the physical layout of the office reinforces the norms of the group and, simultaneously, the egalitarian nature of the cohort groups and the hierarchical levels established by age and seniority. Typically, the chief sits slightly to rear of center. All of the desks face each other. The patterns of interaction are functional, permitting frequent conversation, observation of others, and access to levels of authority.

The informal system and its norms must, of course, be supportive of the formal goals and procedures. Rohlen notes further:

An informal circle is the common arrangement for relaxation and fellowship. Group morale and commitment and the intensification of individual friendships are sponsored through activities arranged to reduce the sense of rank, age, and even sex differences. The circle form stresses the fact of common membership. *If the essence of the working order is hierarchy, the essence of the group principle is the circle* (emphasis added). It is not difficult to perceive the interplay of the two in most office activities, for seldom is the pattern strictly linear or circular. Each activity and context calls for slightly different arrangements, and the group finds it quite normal to shift from one to another. One characteristic of vital work groups, in fact, is their frequent but orderly shifts from one arrangement to another, permitting realization of the spectrum of possible official and personal relationships within the group.

The well-remarked system of after-hours socializing reinforces affective connections and provides avenues for circumventing the formality of the daytime hierarchy.

Finally, it is useful to briefly examine the manner in which the individual and the group manage deviance. (This subject is discussed at some length in Chapter 6). From the perspective of the individual, there are few options for indicating a fundamental disagreement with organizational philosophy, goals, policies, strategies, or procedures. Loyalty, not exit or voice, as noted earlier, is the recognized route to external respect and upward mobility, not to mention the preservation of self-respect. Again, inasmuch as Japanese individuality is intimately linked to organizational identity, disassociating oneself from the prevailing directions of the organization constitutes a virtual denial of self or a fragmentation and loss of integrity. Paradoxically, the Japanese, who can tolerate much intellectual ambiguity and conflict in philosophic perspectives, can not simultaneously entertain the idea of the self at least partially separate from the group.

Nevertheless, there are venues for venting dissatisfaction with the group. Rohlen notes that "deviation is most often expressed by withdrawal from participation in the group and with its leader" (p. 193). The individual will choose not to participate in after-hours social activities, will not contribute to meeting discussions, and may consciously brand himself as "different" through associations with more radical organizations outside of his organizational or group setting. Instead of treating such individuals as deviants and punishing them through the usual social sanctions exercised in the United States (e.g., ostracism), in Japan they are considered sympathetically and understandingly as temporarily having regressed to adolescent stages of rebellion which they will outgrow. Elders and peers are very aware of the emotional strain on the individual that outward resistance causes and take care to provide succorance as the person learns to deal with his deviant notions. In many ways, this mode of addressing deviance is similar to the control exercised over medical professionals. Freidson (1975) notes, for example, for physicians,

Essentially, I wish to show that they used both *functional* and *symbolic* criteria for deciding how to respond to rule violations. The functional criteria concerned whether or not sanctions would "do any good"—that is, lead to the rectification or control of undesirable performance or not. To the physicians, sanctions could not be functionally effective if they were not fitted to the physicians' own source of motivation or incentive to perform their work suitably. They rejected the use of sanctions for purely punitive purposes. (pp. 187–188)

This notion of the conception of deviance as regression to less mature mental states is consistent with the group-as-family idea. It also makes patently clear why creative ideas in research and development often fail to receive proper recognition. If the individual who is deviant comes to be seen emotionally as an adolescent child, there is a concomitant ascription of immaturity of ideas. Hence, the new and different are bound up in an affective framework that prevents the Japanese from dealing with the idea separate from the individual.

In the next chapter, we deal with another aspect of the management of deviance in Japanese organizations—the enhancement and suppression of creativity and innovation.

## NOTE

1. Names for these Redl characterizations were added later by Bales. Not all of these will be found in the Japanese organization, however, as will be noted below.

# 9

# Technology, Creativity, and Innovation

## INTRODUCTION

Creativity and innovation refer to different concepts and behaviors, though they are frequently linked and/or confused in the literature (Rickards 1991; Woodman, Sawyer, & Griffin 1993). Creativity more properly has its behavioral referents in either the actions or processes in which individuals or groups engage or the production of solutions to problems and the generation of ideas not previously known to exist. Innovation, on the other hand, has been defined variously. Marquis (1969), for example, makes a distinction between innovation and technological change, the latter a "unit" of the latter. Abernathy and Utterback (1978; cf. Riggs 1984) distinguish between process and product innovation, while Katsuto (1987) suggests process innovation, material innovation, and methodology innovation. A further distinction is frequently made between incremental change and paradigmatic shifts. Innovation conveys the notion of a more systematic incorporation of ideas and solutions into an action mode that builds on technological "processes" or "products" already extant (cf. Moritani 1981). Similarly, Schumpeter (1939) differentiates between "alpha innovations" and "beta innovations." The former are revolutionary in the measure of their practical impact in the marketplace, while the latter make only incremental changes (Barney & Baysinger 1988; cf. Stinchcombe 1990). Innovation thus connotes an economic outcome, either short or long term, while creativity refers to the acts of imagination that generate ideas, concepts, and theories ultimately to be used in innovation.

Perhaps the most crucial component in the management of innovation in Japan lies in the adoption of the concept of *kaizen* or "continuous improvement" (cf. Imai 1986). Contrasted with the Western emphasis on one-time breakthrough innovation (the marketing of total quality management as a "new" technique is not likely to change this), *kaizen* provides an important clue to the nature of Japanese R & D. It reflects the intimately felt connection between individual motivation to create and innovate and long-term organizational success. It permits delays in personal short-term success, since the long-term payoff to the worker is perceived to be forthcoming. In terms of traditional expectancy theories of motivation, both the "instrumentality" and the "valences" are high for the individual—the rewards are seen as likely and are highly valued.

From a systems perspective, innovation at the organizational level is comparable to creativity at the individual level. In both cases, there are departures from structured patterns of thought, expectations, and behavior. Moreover, creativity and innovation are intimately connected. Both are needed for each to succeed. At the organizational level, structural and normative support for innovation will usually provide the context for creativity at the individual level. Graphically, the overlap and interaction may be depicted in Figure 9.1.

When the conditions that support creativity and innovation are not present, one or both suffer. As has been remarked throughout this book, those conditions reflect the values of the culture in which they exist. For example, in Japan, Western methods of scientific inquiry may be seen to clash significantly with Japanese culture (cf. Watanabe 1990). Further, Japanese notions of nature and reality, not to speak of time frames and contemporary socialization, give creativity a different meaning from Western understanding. With respect to innovation, culture has been shown to be a profound influence (Shane 1993). Thus, the differences between Japan and the United States will be manifested in the rates of innovation. It would appear that in Japan, the organizational climate is restrictive of creativity, but supportive of innovation, while in the United States, the reverse is true—the climate is supportive of creativity, but the structure is restrictive of innovation. (There are some hints at changes in this formula. See Tatsuno's discussion of encouragement of significant breakthroughs—*hassoo*). (Tatsuno 1990, chapter 8.) Hence, in Japan, creativity must often be imported from outside, but once identified, it thrives in the organizational climatic and structural support for innovation. On the other hand, in the United States, creative ideas can be produced but will not be able to be readily converted into viable organizational outputs. Technology transfer in the United States is an illustration of this failure. Again, in Figure 9.2, these notions are presented.

## INNOVATION

The literature on organizational innovation also has a long history—too long, and in large part too tangential to the purposes of this study to review here (cf. Van de Ven 1986; Katz 1988; Tushman & Moore 1988; Lawler 1986; West & Farr 1990). Innovation research covers at least two quite distinct domains. One is concerned with within-unit transformations of technology or/and organization;

**Figure 9.1**
**The Relation between Innovation and Creativity in Organizations**

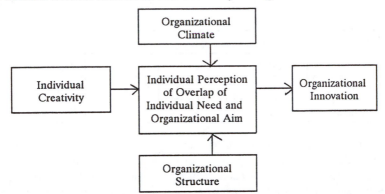

See Woodman, Sawyer, & Griffin (1993) for a slightly different model.

the second with the diffusion of these transformations across units. The latter research looks to the nature, patterning, and causes of adoption (Rogers 1983). A consistent finding that regularly appears, however, is that structural contingencies are brought about by the natures of technology and environment. As Jelinek and Schoonhoven (1990) point out, contemporary wisdom has it that, given uncertain technology and a dynamic, changing environment, organizations with structures and cultures that are ''organic'' rather than ''mechanistic'' better allow the rapid adaptation required.

Deeper analysis of the seminal works describing this hypothesis (especially those originating from the Tavistock research, e.g., Burns & Stalker 1961) by Jelinek and Schoonhoven revealed four characteristics of this supportive framework: (1) ambiguous reporting relationships, with an unclear hierarchy of authority; (2) softly defined job responsibilities; (3) decision making that is consultative and grounded in demonstrated personal expertise rather than being authorized only through a management hierarchy; and (4) interpersonal and interunit communication routes that are lateral as well as vertical.

It is reasonable to suspect that research and development units in Japan would follow the prescription of the last three of these. R & D workers do participate as the work demands it, decision making is consultative, and there is much communication throughout the organization. On the other hand, there are quite clear authority structures, with the *ringei* system described earlier ensuring conformity to it.

Of surprise to Jelinek and Schoonhoven, however, were the findings from their empirical studies of high technology firms showing that there was, in fact, much less uncertainty and ambiguity than would have been predicted. Just as in Japan, structure is used to facilitate efficient connections among workers. They note:

**Figure 9.2**
**Comparisons of Support for Creativity and Innovation in Japan and the United States**

|            | United States |            | Japan      |            |
|------------|---------------|------------|------------|------------|
|            | Creativity    | Innovation | Creativity | Innovation |
| **Climate**   | +          | -          | -          | +          |
| **Structure** | +          | -          | -          | +          |

With explicit reporting relationships, there is little of the predicted ambiguity of reporting relationships, there is little of the predicted ambiguity of organic systems, and none of the wasteful uncertainty about to whom to turn. Structure is actively used to guide employees in the firms, for delimiting responsibilities, identifying connections between positions and people, and insuring that attention is actively allocated to appropriate tasks.

It would appear that as Barney and Baysinger (1988) conclude, "there apparently is no single optimal solution." Structures suitable to pedestrian, incremental innovation are inhospitable to Shumpeterian innovations, and, indeed, even for the latter, there is no one "best way." The so-called "linear model" introduced by Vannevar Bush in 1946 (Bush 1946), which consisted of Research/Development/Production/Distribution, has become outmoded in today's highly competitive setting. An informed group (Japanese Working Group 1986) believes a more appropriate description is an "innovation spiral." Indeed, Bowonder and Miyake (1992) note that the elements in the innovation cycle—the idea recycling (*sairyo*), idea exploration (*tansaku*), idea cultivation (*ikusei*), idea generation (*hasoo*), and idea refinement (*kaisen*) are founded on Japanese values, norms, and practices endemic in Japanese folk arts. *Netsuke*, for example, miniature wood carving, could well have been the origin of Japan's spectacular success at miniaturization in general (cf. Tatsuno 1990, 55).

More particularly, in the innovation process, each "market divergence or specialization is fed back from Distribution to Research, from which new innovation cycles develop." Kline (1985) suggests that innovation is not a "linear process." There are many inputs into the chain, including market competition, R & D breakthroughs, analytic design, early production feedback, and initial user feedback (cf. Branscomb & Kodama 1993). The modes of integrating the variables in the transfer process have also been widely researched (cf. Shrivastava & Souder 1985). Innovation thus includes creativity as well as its integration into some change in a larger system (though see Nystrom 1979, p. 1, for a contrary conceptualization).

Although there has been prolific research on team or group effectiveness (see Chapter 8) and lately on "self-managed" teams (Manz & Sims 1987), a surprisingly small amount of inquiry has been conducted into organizational conditions leading specifically to R & D team effectiveness (Shepard 1956a; Allison 1969; Payne 1990). R & D, of course, constitutes the confluence of creativity and innovation and thus deserves researcher attention. The early and still influential work of Pelz (1967) and Pelz and Andrews (1976) is still most frequently identified as the defining and relevant description of optimum conditions for both creativity and innovation to occur. The work of Thamhain and Wilemon (1977), who gathered data from more than 500 engineers, provides some modicum of updating. Dividing the motivating conditions into "drivers" and "barriers," they found for drivers a number of task and people characteristics, including an orientation to technical success, high need for achievement, innovative and creative interests, concern for quality, high energy, good communication and conflict management, interpersonal trust, and good team spirit. On the other hand, barriers included unclear objectives, inadequate resources, and unconcerned management. Once again confirming both Pelz and Andrews and Jelinek and Schoonhoven, it would appear that the conventional wisdom suggesting the efficacy of a laissez-faire climate and loose structure needs to be seriously reexamined. The Japanese have addressed this anomaly in imaginative ways discussed in earlier chapters. Among them is a leadership format that supports the climate and structure for individual creativity as well as organizational innovation. Zuckerman (1977) describes such settings as "evocative" environments for creativity.

## CREATIVITY

Creativity research borrows from a wide range of intellectual sources played out in various arenas: psychobiological and psychological; group; organizational; and national (cf. Isaksen 1988). Amabile (1983) has suggested that creativity stems from "intrinsic motivation." Based on empirical research she reports that intrinsically motivated people are more creative and that that creativity is facilitated by the absence of controlling events. For the Japanese scientist, then, working under exceptionally heavy constraints, creativity may be inhibited. Amabile (1982) also notes that creativity is inhibited by competition, while Hennessey (1982) suggests that extrinsic rewards also undermine creativity. Other researchers who study the "overjustification" phenomenon (e.g., Kruglanski 1975; Lepper et al. 1973; Deci & Ryan 1985) note that too much external reward may diminish the intrinsic value of the task to the performer.

Some of these studies have a clear Western bias, however. There is an assumption that intrinsic motivation or at least satisfactions result in greater effort and commitment to task and organization goal achievement. In other words, a creative and productive worker is what organizations need for success. The paradox for the West is that providing extrinsic incentives to encourage creativity is very likely to dampen it.

What "intrinsic" means in the context of Japanese culture and the Japanese individual psyche, however, is somewhat uncertain, as noted earlier. There is clearly a merging of intrinsic and extrinsic goals for the Japanese worker. There is, as well, a collectivization of the unconscious. Thus, group goals and the structures and processes to meet them perform the psychological function of stabilizing and orienting individual behavior. If the externalities provided by the organization are overly rigid, so also will be the individual psyche. As Hagen (1962, 119, 143 ff.) notes, authoritarian individuals tend to be high in need for dependence and look to external sources of support for their anxieties. The hierarchical structure of the Japanese organization thus may provide not only a stability but a constraint within which creativity cannot take place. Pelz and Andrews (1976) found that a limited amount of formal constraint on behavior has positive benefits for individual motivation and productivity. However, if the structure of the normative system is clearly too strong (i.e., deviance is heavily and negatively sanctioned), any latent, intrinsic motivation available in creative research activity will be insufficient to invoke that behavior. Thus, the socialization of dependency and the structure supporting it tend to be inhibitory of creativity.

The important point here is to identify the structural and cultural supports for and constraints on creativity (Woodman, Sawyer, & Griffin 1993), including most particularly the antecedent conditions in the culture that do or do not predispose the Japanese worker to be creative, and the effects of various forms of conflict management and leadership on the creative will and process. As Katsuto (1987) notes, "The weakness of Japanese industry is rooted in a weakness in the Japanese education system, and overcoming it implies far-reaching changes in Japanese society." The domain of the research in Japan for this book was limited to creativity in small groups. There have been many studies reporting the structural conditions under which group versus individual problem solving is more effective (March & Simon 1958; Thompson & Tuden 1959). There have also been a considerable number of studies that deal with the internal dynamics of group decision making. As VanGundy (1984) notes, "the dynamics of group functioning often place considerable restraints on a group's ability to reach its potential. For instance, groups can be less efficient than individuals when time is diverted from a task to satisfy social interaction needs or when conflict develops among group members" (p. 7). VanGundy notes further that trained and informed and skilled leaders can materially affect the creative problem-solving process. Further, as Mohr (1969) notes, the ideologies of leaders (e.g., liberalism, activism) strongly influence the frequency of innovation.

A central variable in understanding the problem-solving/creativity process is the nature of the problem to be solved. Clearly, problems that involve many steps to be solved sequentially by different persons, each with a distinctive set of skills or a body of knowledge, are different from problems that demand simultaneous application of potentially creative components without integration. In turn, these problems are different from others that require mixing of disparate ideas into a new form that is more than a sum of the parts. Scientific research ranges across all of these. Indeed, within each of the common subdivisions of basic, applied, and developmental research, there is a diversity of problem types.

Another key variable considered frequently in the creativity literature is the "phase" in which the creativity is expected to take place. Phase refers rather ambiguously to organizational state (e.g., competitive ascendency versus decline) or group conditions (e.g., recency of formation versus long-standing) or individual involvement (e.g., stage of creative process—preparation, incubation, illumination-insight, verification—cf. Nystrom 1979, 39).

Baker et al. (1980) sought to identify how the interaction between structural variables (such as centralization, formalization, incentive system, and so on) and small group behavioral variables (such as leader style, worker interactions, and specificity of work) may enhance or inhibit creativity, both in the individual and group. Among other things, they found that the generation of new ideas was influenced by the perceptions of workers as to the value the organization places on the following:

(a) colleague contact within the laboratory;
(b) colleague contact between the laboratory and the operating divisions;
(c) colleague contact outside the firm either directly through professional activities or indirectly through gatekeepers;
(d) diversity in work assignment;
(e) project-initiating ideas; and
(f) project-related information and communication. (p. 47)

As will be seen, these perceptions are related to the various psychological states necessary to sustain motivation in the Hackman and Oldham framework discussed earlier. More important, perhaps, is the heavy cognitive emphasis in the theory. As noted earlier, "expectancies" play an important part in this schema, whereas in Japan, it is unlikely that these are salient on an individual level. As Hideki (1987) notes:

The peculiarity of the Japanese mode of thinking lies in its complete neglect of complementary alternatives. This we may term Japanese irrationalism. Of course, this is completely foreign to any form of scientific spirit, but it is identical neither with absolutism nor with skepticism. Moreover, it is akin to an optimistic rather than a pessimistic point of view. Nevertheless, it is well known that Japanese mentality is very far from any kind of insensibility. (pp. 54–55)

The Japanese mentality is, in most cases, unfit for abstract thinking and takes interest merely in tangible things. This is the origin of the Japanese excellence in technical art and the fine arts. (p. 56)

In the philosophy of Lao Tzu and Chuang Tsu we notice an element of thought similar to that characterizing science. This recognizes the insensate aspect of Nature, as was symbolized by Lao Tzu's saying, "The law of the universe is insensate without *jen*, for it regards all things as straw dogs," and, moreover, contains an element of the negation of human existence itself. In contrast with this, the Japanese mentality has a regard for ideas having concrete applicability to human living. The indifferent pursuit of the truth, made independently of such implications, did not and cannot appeal to most of the Japanese. (p. 57)

Cutler (1987) reports that in contrast to problem solving in the United States, in Japan problems are not usually broken down or deconstructed for analysis. Problems that do not lend themselves to holistic and intuitive appraisal are simply not addressed.

Finally, it is worth remarking the important research on the propensity toward risk taking in groups contrasted with individual willingness to depart significantly from the norm. The "risky shift" phenomenon observed by a number of researchers (Wallach, Kogan, & Bern 1962) shows that groups tend to make riskier decisions than do individuals, presumably because responsibility for the risk is shared, and blame can be equally distributed (Johnston & Bonoma 1979). One might expect, then, that since so much work in Japanese organizations is group-based, there would be a strong risk-taking propensity. The shift, however, does not occur in Japanese organizations, primarily because of the openness of the system and because individuals identify so closely with the group. That is, in the West a group member can disassociate himself from group failure both practically and psychologically. He can become "simply" another, anonymous member of a group. In Japan, on the other hand, member contributions to groups are widely known among all employees. Further, failures of groups are experienced as personal failures by individuals. An individual's unwillingness to be identified as a failure—via group failure—prevents his shifting to a higher risk-taking stance in collective decision making. Paradoxically, the likelihood of success of a group, with which an individual member might identify, is also not, apparently, a sufficient inducement for him to make a risky shift. While group achievement is highly valued, no one individual is willing to risk being blamed for group failure—hence, is unwilling vociferously to propose a risky decision.

In sum, the manifestation of technology, creativity, and innovation in Japanese research and development laboratories revolves around the complex interaction of formal and informal structures and the culturally implanted psychological dispositions of the Japanese researcher. Creativity, defined as a significant departure from the cognitive paradigm of the field, can take place only in an organizational context (comprising formal rules and informal norms) supportive of such enterprise. The tolerance of the Japanese person for cognitive dissonance, however, rather than the virtue it is in social situations, surrounds the Japanese with a more relaxed, less-than-strenuous need for resolution. "Virtually anything goes" as a norm does not connote support for deviance. Rather, it means that deviance must be viewed as temporary aberrance to be accommodated in mainstream thinking over time.

Before turning to the implications for leadership in this context, we will examine (in the next chapter) how these elements of technology, innovation, and creativity are affected by the overall organization of research and development in Japan, and the support for it by outside agencies like the government.

# 10

# National R & D Policy and the Organization of R & D

While leadership in small work groups is a reflection of interpersonal relations between and among formal and informal workers, it is subject to constraints external to the group. Earlier chapters reported on the cultural influences on the behavior of leaders and followers. Here, the constraints of the formal system are discussed. In particular, the expectations of the external system for R & D output are considered. This chapter takes up the frameworks or contexts of the federal government and the larger organization of which the R & D unit is a part.

Although government relations and academic science in Japan have gone through some turbulent and dramatic struggles for power (Bartholomew 1982, 296–297; Silverman 1982), since the beginning of the Meiji period, the Japanese government has recognized the critical importance of close collaboration between government and industry (Bartholomew 1982). As Sethi, Namiki, and Swanson (1984) note:

The government deliberately set out to create industry in order to modernize Japan, often by building factories and then turning them over to private business. In the process, the government retained a large degree of control over business affairs. (pp. 16–17)

Japan's Ministry of Education, Science and Culture (MOMBUSHO) generally oversees basic research, while other ministries and agencies of the federal government monitor and promote applied and developmental research (Kida 1986, 2). This leaves universities and government research bureaus subject to MOMBUSHO, while corporations are under the jurisdiction of several powerful federal bureaucracies, the Ministry of International Trade and Industry (MITI)—especially its Agency of Industrial Science and Technology—and the Ministry of

Finance, the Ministry of Agriculture, Forestry and Fisheries, the Ministry of Health and Welfare, and the Science and Technology Agency (STA). These latter establish and promote research in science and technology that meets their more specialized needs.

The Japanese government in general engages in what Watanabe, Santoso, and Widayanti (1991) call " 'soft' technologies of public administration,'' whereby visions of the future and ideas for change are ingested through open discussions conducted by various councils such as the Industrial Structure Council and the Industrial Technology Council (Watanabe et al. 1991, 55). Well-versed in long-range strategic planning, the Japanese government has committed itself to financing the growth of sectors of the society that it sees as critical to the economic well-being of the country in the near and far future. Given top priority in MITI's science policy are three areas: technology for inventing new materials, technology that permits extensive use of alternative energy sources, and technology that applies to resolution of social conflict (Turney 1984). R & D in these sectors has tended, therefore, to be securely funded at high levels. In 1993, the Japanese government increased its science and technology budget to $21 billion, an increase of more than 6 percent (Pollack 1993b).

In the last five to ten years, there has been some considerable modification of the traditional Japanese pattern of conducting and financing research and development, as the government has recognized the limitations of the domination of big science by the industrial sector with its more parochial research agendas. As a result, there has been a movement to establish large research laboratories which are associated with the more prominent universities in Japan. The university research sector, while indirectly linked to industrial concerns, has longer time perspectives and broader social outlooks.

In 1959, in recognition of the need to maintain its technological superiority, the Ministerial Council for Science and Technology (CST) was convened to consider the priorities and extent of involvement of the Japanese government in the support of science and technology. Reconstituted in 1980, CST became the primary advisory body to the Japanese Prime Minster on science and technology policy. It determines, in addition, the amount of funds to be made available to the Special Coordination Funds for Promoting Science and Technology, administered by the Science and Technology Agency (STA). Through its Committee on Policy Matters, the CST conducts hearings at which leading experts from ministries and agencies, industry, and education make observations about national needs and appropriate research projects. The government (CST) then selects "target" industries and technological fields with economic promise to support with direct funding, loans, tax incentives, and other guidance and counsel. Funds are distributed by STA, and research productivity is monitored by the subcommittee on Research Evaluation of the Committee on Policy Matters.

There is some debate, however, as to how much power this and other policy-making councils have. Some (e.g., Sethi et al. 1984) assert that the prestigious member composition on these councils constitutes mere pro forma window dressing, with decisions made elsewhere by private, wealthy, power holders, both individuals and industrial groups (*zaibatsu* or *keiretsu*), and international trading firms (*sogoshosha*—cf. McMillan 1985). What is critical about this carefully articulated system is the psychological sense of sustained external support that both leaders and followers find for their work.

Nevertheless, there is now emerging in Japan a belief that the strong, centralized control of the R & D enterprise may have reached its limit in efficiency. The Japanese are certainly not complacent about their success. Recently, national leaders and the Japanese scientific community as well as science policy officials in government circles have expressed concerns that there are problems with the funding, organzation, and management of research and development and its articulation with technological development. It is increasingly being said that much of the industrial effectiveness in Japan has come from applying theory originated in other countries. Despite heavy investments by the government, basic research is alleged to be inadequately attended to. Furthermore, in the severe recession times of the early 1990s, R & D expenditures in the corporate sector were substantially cut back (Pollack 1993b).

The viability of both traditional structure and processes in the Japanese industrial sector is thus called into question (Kagano, Nonaka, Sakakibara, & Okumura 1983–84; Ohmae 1985) as is the ability of the system to be technologically creative as well as adaptive in the increasingly competitive world markets. Since Japan is so dependent on those markets, the issue is a serious one. More specifically, the question is raised as to whether the Japanese ''groupism'' (Befu 1980; Ouchi 1981) and the associated structural and processual support systems noted earlier (e.g., bottom-up—*ringei*—decision making, free and extensive information flow laterally and vertically, nonspecialized career paths, job rotation, group evaluation, job security for life), while promoting harmony and communal spirit, prevent the individual growth and development, creativity, and motivation which may be needed for organizational effectiveness in the new international markets (Christopher 1983; but see Marugama, Mouer & Sugimoto 1983; Shimada 1985).

Despite the Japanese government commitment to R & D, it is only in the last fifteen years that investments in R & D as a percent of GNP have approached the levels of other highly industrialized nations (e.g., the United States and the former West Germany). Although Japan increased its investment in R & D by 600 percent from 1965 to 1985, in R & D expenditures per R & D employee, it ranks lowest among the United States, the United Kingdom, West Germany, and France—while in nondefense spending for R & D, it ranks higher (Slaughter & Utterback 1990). In part, this has resulted from an increase in corporate spending on R & D to offset or reverse Japan's dependency on basic research and technological innovations imported from the West. The implications of the recognition for self-sufficiency create new strains on the leadership of R & D laboratories, which have been accustomed to long-term support and tolerance of slow progress. Japanese leaders who have been brought up in the ''old'' system are finding themselves pressured to behave in ways they find quite unfamiliar and with which they are still uncomfortable.

The pattern in the United States is obviously quite different (OSTP, The White House; OSTP 1985). Coles (1984) reports that there are about 755 laboratories in the federal laboratory system with a budget that consumes over a third of the national R & D budget, allegedly diverting funds away from industry and university research centers. While this splitting of resources may have been functional in earlier times, serious questions have been raised about the effects on the productivity and effectiveness of both education and industry (Anderson 1984). Although universities are a more formidable participant in the conduct of research in the United States, it is not at all clear that management of research in these institutions is by any means exemplary. Critics question the probability of sustained U.S. competitiveness (Fusfeld 1986; Turney 1984) especially beyond the year 2000.

Science policy in the United States is also overseen by a variety of relatively uncoordinated federal agencies (Nichols 1992, 75). These include the president's office, to which report the National Security Council, the Economic Policy Council, the Domestic Policy Council, and the Council of Advisors for Science and Technology. The operating arm of these agencies (except the last) is the Office of Science and Technology Policy which is charged with responsibility for developing a coherent execution of the oftentimes disparate directives. The Federal Coordinating Council on Science, Engineering and Technology manages this activity. The sum and substance of this formal configuration of concerned agencies is the not-so-subtle communication to the R & D establishment of the need to compete independently for funds and to demonstrate effectiveness in the short run if that funding is to be sustained. And the implications for leadership of R & D are of a quite different nature from those in Japan.

The much lamented, excessively short-term orientations of managers, lack of concern for high quality, labor-management separation, and high worker turnover, among many other organizational problems, have been widely discussed. Certainly, there is much reason to believe that the viability of the R & D enterprise in this country will require some rather dramatic new thinking about leadership and organizational conditions in the laboratories, both in the educational and industrial domains. While empirical research on these matters in the United States is certainly not a new subject (see, for example, Likert 1961; Pelz & Andrews 1975; Thamhain & Gemmill 1974; Thamhain & Wilemon 1977), it has not been extensive in the Japanese setting.

American and Japanese governments have long been aware of the intimate relationship between technology and innovation and the continuing prosperity and growth of the economic sectors of their countries (see, for example, Kahn & Pepper's *The Japanese Challenge* (1980) and Masanori Moritani's *Japanese Technology*, 1982; Johnson 1983). Much of the literature on technology is concerned with "technology transfer"—with the structures, personnel systems, and communication mechanisms needed to identify new products and to facilitate their concretization and subsequent development and movement through the organization in efficient and effective ways. (See, for example, Shrivastava & Souder 1985; Kono 1984; Hayashi 1990.) If Sputnik was the impetus in the United States to embark on an ambitious program of research on space travel, the domination by Japan of so many domestic consumer product fields has forced a recognition of the need for a similar reappraisal if the United States is to compete at all in world markets.

## TECHNOLOGY

Technology has been variously defined, but the most common understanding of the term is that it refers to both the tools and material of production and the knowledge associated with their manufacture and use (cf. Perrow 1970). Others (e.g., Woodward 1965) include organizational design or production modes, such as unit or small-batch, mass or large-batch production, or long-run production processes. Still others (e.g., Thompson 1967) identify different types of technology—for example, long-linked, mediating, or intensive—referring to the different kinds of linkages and dependencies among units engaged in the production of goods and services. Research and development quite obviously is related to technology in that economic progress requires new technologies that fit into products considered relevant to and needed in contemporary society. Of necessity, knowledge precedes the creation and utilization of the tools and the design of an organization to maximize the productivity of technology (cf. Ellul 1964). Research and development to produce that knowledge is thus critical to the economic progress of production units individually in producing units and collectively on a national basis (National Governors' Association and The Conference Board 1987). Technologies as ingredients in the design of organizations also are informed by research and development, since new knowledge and production techniques involve the construction of efficient flows of knowledge and material across organizational subunit boundaries, as well as the redesign of those subunits better to facilitate that process.

While many industries engage in research and development, it is useful to concentrate on those currently labeled "high technology," since the professionals who occupy key roles there are usually on the leading edge of new developments in their fields. High-tech industries usually have a larger percentage of engineers and scientists in their employ than do organizations in other fields. They also spend more on R & D and produce goods and services that are technologically sophisticated. Such industries exist in market environments that can vary from simple, placid, and stable to others that are changing with a dramatically rapid intensity. An inquiry into the leadership and management processes that are effective for high-tech firms must account for pressures that leaders encounter—both the internal expectations that professionals have for their work environments and the environmental contingencies outside of the R & D group and outside of the institution.

Westney and Sakakibara (1986) report that large Japanese firms in high-technology industries have two competitive strengths vis-à-vis U.S. firms: (1) they have found out how to be efficient in the technology transfer mechanism (moving quickly from R & D to market); and (2) they have developed highly sophisticated environmental scanning mechanisms that rapidly bring information about global technology back into the firm. (The Japan Information Center for Science and Technology, also heavily funded by the government, facilitates their efforts.) Indeed, whereas only a short time ago Japan's reputation was for swift technological copying or/and minor modification of innovations founded in other parts of the world, today there is a new recognition that in the area of applications and development of R & D, Japan is a leader, working at the frontiers of knowledge, especially in robotics, computers, materials science and engineering, and biotechnology (Westney 1994; Sakakibara 1988).

## RESEARCH AND DEVELOPMENT IN HIGH-TECH INDUSTRIES

David Drew (1985) trenchantly observes that the R & D sociocultural work environment is subtle and difficult to manage. He notes: ''Scientific research has become a complex system incorporating psychodynamic, interpersonal, institutional, and economic factors. Consequently, the effective use of management techniques assumes great importance in determining scientific success'' (p. 5). Drew also notes that the knowledge base about the management of science is insufficiently developed, seriously impeding the exploration of scientific frontiers.

Most R & D relies on an experimentally validated base of knowledge. The sharing of technological knowledge within and across units (and nations), however, has become a subject of considerable social science research. Within organizations, managers are anxious to determine how best to integrate the producers of the technological knowledge with the producers of the tools, and ultimately with the users of those tools. Indeed, the goals and directions for research on new technologies originate not only within the firms but with market managers/researchers who anticipate market needs for products that involve new technology. It has been well remarked that Japan has been exceptionally successful in articulating the connections among R & D, engineering, production, and marketing departments. Westney and Sakakibara (1986), for example, report that

One of the most striking differences between the U.S. and the Japanese firms was that U.S. development and design groups were much less closely linked to manufacturing than their Japanese counterparts, at all levels. . . .

In the Japanese firms, half the research budget is allocated directly to the central R & D lab, and half is allocated through the business divisions, which can use their funding either to carry out development activities within their own facilities or to commission specific research projects from the central labs. (cf. Bergen & Miyajima 1986; Hayes & Wheelwright 1979)

They note further that rather than create arbitrary liaison agents as in the United States, the Japanese move people throughout the organization, thus providing generalists who can do their own coordination.

In the last decade, the Japanese government has recognized the potential value of large-scale laboratory research uninhibited by the constraints of the profit-making sector and has attempted to establish large laboratories in universities (Hara 1982). These units usually operate outside of the usual governance frame-work of the Japanese universities. Indeed, the most well-known and successful of these efforts is the collaborative ventures between government-sponsored but university-run laboratories, Tsukuba University, and an increasing number of corporations in the industrial park growing up around the university.

The government, in addition, has set up its own highly respected scientific laboratories, mostly under the sponsorship and administration of the Japanese Ministry of Trade and Industry (MITI) and with the recommendation and guid-ance of the Council for Science and Technology (Japan's highest official policy-making body in the area of science). Some of the government laboratories coexist with those at Tsukuba University. Others are placed around the country. For the research for this book, data were collected from a number of exemplary government laboratories under the aegis of the Research Development Corpo-ration of Japan (JRDC). JRDC launched a multilaboratory project called ERATO or Exploratory Research for Advanced Technology focusing on basic research and led by scientists of national repute.

## RESTRUCTURING R & D AT THE ORGANIZATIONAL LEVEL

To move into more basic areas of research Japanese firms have begun to restructure the organization of R & D. Central research laboratories conduct basic research, while new product development is carried out in the decentralized plants where the products are being manufactured. About half of the research funding budget goes to the central R & D lab, while the remainder is distributed to the plants. There is a close linkage between the central labs and the plants, with transfer of research projects from the basic to applied area taking place with regularity. This is facilitated by the personnel job rotation system which ensures that there is familiarity across locations, not only with agendas and procedures but with the research workers themselves.

Most large Japanese organizations organize their R & D functions similarly. Research on most product lines is decentralized to the location where the product is being produced, but there remains a central laboratory where basic research, some cross-divisional research, and long-range planning is conducted. The following organization charts of Hitachi (Exhibit 10.1a) and of Matsushita (Exhibit 10.1b) are typical.

It might be expected that high-tech industries have found ways to organize themselves to accommodate the fast pace of change and to encourage rapid invention to market transitions. The literature on organizational innovation also has a long history—too long, and in large part too tangential to the purposes of this study to review here (cf. Kornhauser 1962; Pelz & Andrews 1976; Katz 1988; Tushman & Moore 1988; Lawler 1986). A consistent finding that regularly appears, however, is the contingencies brought about by the natures of technology and environment. As Schoonhoven and Jelinek (1990) point out, contemporary wisdom has it that, given uncertain technology and environment, an "organic" type of organization, rather than a mechanistic one, would best allow the rapid adaptation required. Deeper analysis of the seminal works describing this hypothesis (especially those originating from the Tavistock research, e.g., Burns & Stalker 1961) by Schoonhoven and Jelinek revealed four characteristics: "(1) ambiguous reporting relationships, with an unclear hierarchy; (2) unclear job responsibilities; (3) decision making is consultative and based on task expertise rather than being centralized in the management hierarchy; and (4) communication patterns are lateral as well as vertical.

Of surprise to the authors were the findings from their empirical studies of high-technology firms:

With explicit reporting relationships, there is little of the predicted ambiguity of reporting relationships, there is little of the predicted ambiguity of organic systems, and none of the wasteful uncertainty about to whom to turn. Structure is actively used to guide employees in the firms, for delimiting responsibilities, identifying connections between positions and people, and insuring that attention is actively allocated to appropriate tasks.

Clearly this is in contrast to the Japanese mode of organization and communication.

## TECHNOLOGY AND INFORMATION DISSEMINATION

Private sector firms in an open market society are traditionally and understandably reluctant to share technological knowledge with competitors. Nations, too, carefully guard technological and scientific secrets that will damage their competitive positions. In Japan, as will be seen, policies have been instituted that mitigate these self-interested and protectionist policies. The government, for example, has mandated and generously supported with funds the collaboration of selected companies whose productivity is deemed central to the country's long-term interests. As Sato (1985) points out,

These selected firms jointly cooperate to produce new technologies or new innovations. The advantage of the cooperation of the selected firms lies in the fact that they can

**Exhibit 10.1a**
**Sample R & D Organizational Structure—A. Hitachi Corporation**

| Chairman of the Board |
| --- |

| President |
| --- |

| Executive Vice President | Technical Administration Dept. | Corporate R & D Coordination Dept. | Production Engineering Dept. |
| --- | --- | --- | --- |

| LABORATORIES | BUSINESS GROUPS |
| --- | --- |
| - Central Research Lab.<br><br>- Hitachi Research Lab.<br><br>- Mechanical Engineering Research Lab.<br><br>- Energy Research Lab.<br><br>- Production Engineering Research<br><br>- Systems Development Lab.<br><br>- Microelectronics Products Development Lab.<br><br>- Advanced Research Lab. | - Divisional Laboratories<br>  Consumer Products Research Center<br>  Design Center<br>  Device Development Center<br><br><br>- Divisions<br>  Works<br>    Development & Design Dept.<br>    Manufacturing Engineering Dept. |

*Source:* Industrial Research Institute (1986).

exploit economies of scale and increasing returns. . . . A good example of this kind of cooperative effort is the development of the so-called fifth generation computers.

The government has also wisely provided extensive funding for the gathering and ultimate dissemination of scientific information. The Japan Information Center for Science and Technology is the most visible evidence of Japan's recognition of the importance of global scanning and of making available to its scholars and researchers information published in many languages, especially English.

This somewhat simplistic description of the open communication norms and processes breaks down, however, when research activity itself is disaggregated into the basic, applied, and developmental categories.[1]

Workers engaged in basic science R & D serve a dual constituency: their immediate employers and the scientific community at large. While the norm of secrecy is strong in the former, the norm of openness and disclosure is equally strong in the latter. Scientific discoveries are welcomed and lauded in academic

**Exhibit 10.1b**
**Matsushita Electric Industrial Co., Ltd.**

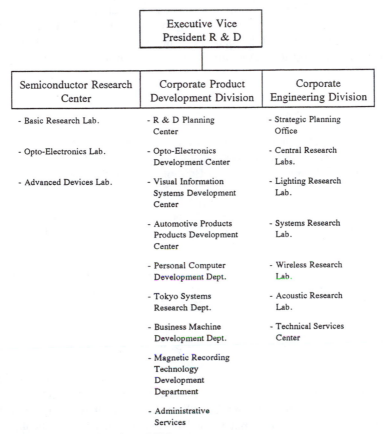

Source: Industrial Research Institute (1986).

and professional science. In Japan, therefore, the individual researcher suffers a considerable degree of role conflict. To be sure, fame accruing to an individual researcher in a firm is seen by colleagues who strongly associate with the firm as a group or firm achievement. The individualized attention to the scientist who makes the breakthrough, however, calls attention to his individuality in a way that violates cultural norms.

## RESEARCH AND DEVELOPMENT IN HIGHER EDUCATION

In addition to its enculturation and training functions (e.g., undergraduate and graduate education), higher education in many developed countries also functions as a producer of new knowledge to be used both in science and industry and in the continuing advancement of the general culture. As noted above, some considerable part of the knowledge production role of universities in Japan is shared by a powerful and well-supported system of research in the industrial sector. Research and development units in business and industry bear the major burden of invention and adaptation of new ideas and products, leaving more of the responsibility for basic research to the educational sector. Central government support of industrial research at both the basic and applied level is maintained at high levels and is distributed in sophisticated ways designed to stimulate and support R & D in areas deemed central to the nation's long-term interests.

### University R & D in Japan

Despite some recognition (even in Meiji and Taishoo years) of the need for a research establishment in universities, the efforts and results were largely unsuccessful and continue so today. As Bartholomew (1989) notes:

Universities were founded, laboratories built, and academic societies established; but the researcher role remained vaguely defined, inchoate, and surrounded by hostile forces. (pp. 82–83)

By the end of the nineteenth century the Japanese scientific and technical community had entered a new steady state, with support generated but at minimal levels. Facilities were inadequate, budgets insecure, and expectations low. (p. 111)

There are approximately 800 universities in Japan (Ryooichi 1985). A little more than 5 percent are classified as pure "research universities"—the others being doctorate or other degree granting (Tominaga 1984). Just as in the United States, research is carried out within the faculties and graduate schools of the universities, in research institutes funded by the universities, in research institutes attached to universities but funded by outside agencies, particularly the federal government, and in in-house institutes of the government. In 1983, there were 406,000 full-time researchers in Japan, with about 170,000 in university-affiliated facilities (MOMBUSHO 1984).

Research in Japanese universities tends to be conducted primarily by individual faculty members organized in units (called *koza*) with no more than three full-time faculty and associated graduate and support staff. Little or no "big science" takes place within Japanese universities, and few significant breakthroughs are made at universities. The pattern is one in which university graduates with talent seldom stay on at universities to receive their doctorates. Rather, they move directly to R & D laboratories in the largest and most prestigious corporations they can find, where they are trained by the corporate staff to conduct research in the prescribed modes preferred at the corporation. (Indeed, the common practice is for dissertations to be prepared at corporate R & D centers, subsequently to be submitted to universities where, without coursework or continuous faculty oversight, the doctorate is usually conferred.)

## Organization of University Research and Teaching

Research and teaching within universities in Japan are organized in two ways, depending on the type of university. Seven universities are designated as imperial universities, and their organization differs significantly from the remaining institutions. To the seven, Tsukuba University and Hiroshima University may be added, as they are quite similar. It is necessary, therefore, to discuss each group separately. In the imperial universities, the *gakubu* is the largest organizational unit. The next lower unit is the *gakka*, which corresponds roughly to the department in the United States university. Thus, for example, there might be a department of engineering technology, civil engineering, and so on. The head of the *gakka* is called a *kakka shunin* and is elected by the faculty in his unit. Each *gakka* is comprised of five to ten research units or *words*. All undergraduate and graduate education in Japan is built around the *koza*. That is, there are no courses offered by the department or by a separate graduate school. Each *koza* comprises two or three faculty, with only one in each rank—full professor, associate professor, or assistant professor (sometimes called a *joshu*). The number of *koza* with three faculty has been diminishing recently, due to several factors. Demographic projections show less need for faculty in universities. Further, the quality of faculty in universities has been diminishing of late. Weak departments tend to hire weak replacements for retired faculty. Since the administration has no power over the *koza* or department, it can not interfere with this process. As the *koza* become less reputable, the public and government have less and less confidence in them and seek other kinds of educational systems to produce the desired research and teaching.

Students in the *koza* study with the faculty and do their research for or with them. Students with the most longevity are frequently not paid and serve in various teaching and research roles. Graduate students have no distribution requirements. In the late 1970s, MOMBUSHO ruled that universities should not formally require certain courses. It was only necessary that the courses be offered. No formal curriculum exists. Science courses, however, appear to be somewhat more structured because of the sequential nature of the subject matter.

Imperial universities have both *koza* and research institutes. In the *koza*, faculty do virtually no research. Only some faculty are selected to be part of the research institutes. Money for research goes directly to the research institute and to the chair of the *koza*. The *koza* gives part of its income back to the university for overhead (the exact percentage subject to negotiation between the senior professor and university officials, with relative power being the deciding factor). The associate professor in the *koza* receives some proportion of the available research funds—usually not too different an amount from what the full professor receives. (For a fuller description, see Ushiogi 1993, 317–321.) Again, this is subject to negotiation and power considerations. Some *koza* are quite harmonious, while others are fraught with power struggles.

Since there are at most only three professors per *koza* and at most ten *koza* per *gakka*, the maximum number of faculty in a *gakka* or department is thirty. More commonly, it is about ten to twenty. There is often a grouping of *koza* into what would correspond to departments in the United States. These departments have names similar to our professional schools, though they do not teach subject matter as professional preparation. For example, what Americans call the College of Arts and Sciences (or a similar name) does not exist as such in Japan. Instead, just as with the professional schools, its subjects are divided into autonomous departments. Thus, there is a department of literature, economics, and so on. In all of the departments, all of the subjects may be offered, regardless of the fact that they are offered elsewhere. The department of education, for example, offers courses in law and economics, while the department of literature also offers these courses.

Students choose to study in the particular departments based on the reputations of the faculty. Graduates of the departments or/and groups of *koza* do not become professionals. They are more likely to become white-collar workers (in Japan, "salarymen"). As the reputation of the faculty members in a *koza* grows, and more and more students are well placed in the corporations, it becomes easier for the subsequent generation of students to become placed. Graduates of the *koza* like to hire people from their own alma maters, since, in part, their education and training is similar and thus more easily accommodated and molded to the corporate image.

As virtually all decisions are decentralized to the *koza*, however, the *gakka* as a decision-making or social unit exists largely as a formal structure only, without significant function. The life of the research operation centers at the *koza* level. It is here that both faculty and students look for their social and intellectual satisfactions and seek security and protection. The system works very much on a mentor/disciple basis. There is, as a result, much imitation of the mentor by the students, and it is sometimes—indeed, frequently—possible to assume that if one has discussed a matter with any member of a faculty member's former students, one will have received all the information available from the group as a whole, including the mentor himself. Hence, for national universities, the leadership for research is keyed to personnel matters. The full professor has no control over the salaries in his unit, and little or no funds to allocate to students for their research. The "best" leadership in the *koza* system, then, is conducted by persons who have the ability to select highly talented and self-motivated individuals.

This is not to say, of course, that the internal management of the *koza* can be ignored. Just as leadership roles are distributed in a research institute, so also in the *koza*, different individuals may take on different leadership responsibilities. The full professor is formally the *kacho* or leader, while the associate professor is the *kocho hosa* or second in command. If the unit has only two professors, the *kocho hosa* will also be the *nyobo yaku* (wife role) or informally designated assistant to handle the administrative detail. If the unit has three professors, the assistant professor (*joshu*) most often takes on the role of *nyobo yaku*, especially with respect to the graduate students. Further, one of the graduate students will act in the role vis-à-vis the undergraduate students. It seems to be the case that no *nyobo yaku* can also play the role of "mother" in the research unit, since the "dirty work" required to protect the *kacho*'s reputation and image may demand that some unpleasant responsibilities be carried out. Hence, the workers' need for security and belongingness is attended to by the *kacho* himself, who often looks out for each worker's personal welfare (e.g., marriage arrangements, loans, housing). In sum, while in the Japanese family, the woman can play the roles of both wife and mother, in the Japanese organization, these roles are divided. While the division of task responsibilities within *informal* groups has long been known (cf. Bales 1965), and differentiation of formal roles is the sine qua non of bureaucracy, in the Japanese system, the formal and informal are combined. The important informal succorance responsibilities are thus preserved for the formal leader to carry out by the introduction of an intermediary who can relieve the formal leader of the conflicting roles of evaluator and supporter.

The *koza* system has been severely criticized for its rather static structure. The pattern of seniority, the protection of small domains of academic inquiry, and the funding mechanisms which avoid internal university control (i.e., externally administered salaries and research funds) all combine to constrain faculty, especially ambitious and inventive ones, to more or less "safe" or at least small research. According to Amano (1979), the Japanese government has determined that the *koza* system is so entrenched that big science must be conducted elsewhere, and it has begun to fund large laboratories outside of the university setting. These laboratories are considering offering their own higher degrees. Indeed, in many cases in Japan, the most talented undergraduate students, upon graduation, move to the corporate sector where they are permitted to complete a dissertation. Despite the fact that they have taken no classes at the university, if a university faculty approves their dissertation, they may receive a degree from that institution. The majority of doctoral degrees in Japan are received in this way.

Private universities in Japan do not operate on the *koza* system. Instead, a research unit is established independent of the teaching unit. This research unit is comprised of some but not necessarily all of the faculty from the teaching units. Its head is sometimes called a *dai koza* or "big chair," signifying the operation of a multi-*koza* or multidisciplinary research unit.

It is useful, finally, to comment on the nature of the graduate degree in Japanese higher education. In Japan, relatively few Ph.D.s are awarded in the social sciences and humanities, and those that are are usually given to faculty in their older years as an honorific. One reason for the small number of doctoral degrees awarded is that the master's coursework is extremely rigorous. The recipient of a master's degree, it is said, has the equivalent of a Ph.D. in America. In contrast to the undergraduate sphere, some coursework is required (about 30 credits over two years) and there is a somewhat more structured curriculum. This situation may change soon, however, since there is a new, heavy emphasis on internationalization of higher education in Japan. The hope is to encourage many foreign students to come to Japan to study. With the very demanding master's degree programs and a significant language barrier, however, most foreign students are discouraged from coming to Japan and seek the degree elsewhere. MOMBUSHO, as a result, has been urging the universities to relax their standards. These generalizations do not apply unequivocally. In the sciences, where the Ph.D. is more frequently sought, it is increasingly given the respect it has in the United States.

## IMPLICATIONS FOR LEADERSHIP OF R & D

Research and development in Japan is clearly set in a national context that rewards certain kinds of productivity and ignores others. MITI's efforts to develop Silicon Valley-like "technopolises" in 26 cities and "regional research core programs" throughout the country (Tatsuno 1990, 94 ff.) reflects its sensitivity to the necessity for external support of research scientists that permits the tolerance for both deviance and error that daring, risk-taking enterprises require. Whether the tradition of centralized control in Japan will be relaxed in its evaluative component remains to be seen.

## NOTE

1. Although the conventional classification of R & D is into basic, applied, and developmental, the U.S. Department of Defense finds this too simplistic. Its categorization includes: (1) fundamental research; (2) exploratory development; (3) advanced development; (4) engineering development; and (5) operational systems development.

# IV

# Organizational Determinants of Motivation: Conflict Management Modes and Leadership

# 11

# Conflict and Conflict Management

We turn, in the next two chapters, from a presentation of the complexities of the sociocultural background for the study to a discussion of the key independent variables and their interaction in the conceptual framework. More particularly, the next several sections are concerned with the nature of conflict and leadership in Japan and in Japanese organizations.

Understanding how organizations deal with conflict depends in part on how conflict is defined (cf. Kolb & Putnam 1992). This, in turn, is contingent in part on some assumptions deeply rooted in national cultures. The Japanese appear to deny the existence of conflict in their organizations. Yet observers of organizations in Japan report behaviors quite similar to those that U.S. researchers describe as conflict interactions and conflict resolutions when observed in this country. What accounts for this anomaly? Is it merely semantic? Does *denial* of conflict mean the same thing in both countries? Or perhaps the denial of conflict has some function in terms of the organizational efficiency, effectiveness, or comity for which the Japanese have earned high marks. Or, it may have some utility in terms of personal psychological adjustment or satisfaction among employees.

Since conflict is a key independent variable in the conceptual framework for this research, it is important to understand how it is used in this book. This chapter will examine conflict in Japan—its meaning, its associated behaviors, and its management from both Japanese and Western perspectives. The chapter begins with a general introduction to the manifestations of conflict in Japanese society and organizations. It is literally impossible for most non-Japanese people to appreciate fully what conflict in Japan means. As noted in earlier chapters, the culture is complex and subtle and has a very long history whose components have influenced contemporary society in so many different ways (Reischauer

1988, 1–120). Indeed, conflict itself in Japanese history has undergone cyclical changes in levels of cultural legitimation, particularly in the early twentieth century—the late Meiji-Taishoo eras (Najita 1982). It continues to change, even today, as political uncertainty continues seemingly without end.

The formal and informal obeisance to authority today is a product at least of a long social history of semimilitaristic structure and to a complex of religious beliefs, for example, Confucianism's philosophic respect for those in senior positions, Shintoism's terseness of expression, and Buddhism's distrust of oral language (among other things). What follows, therefore, is only a partial view of an exceedingly complex phenomenon, even for native Japanese scholars.

The material below is organized to reflect what seem to be several predominant approaches to conflict in Japan that can only partially be compared with Western practices. As Befu (1990) notes with respect to possible explanatory models of conflict in Japan, "a catholic attitude toward various models is the most profitable approach, rather than to insist on one and only one model at the exclusion of all others" (p. 236). The approach here focuses somewhat on the apparent "denial" of conflict in Japan and some of its components: anticipation, engagement, tolerance, and consensus formation. To understand denial, it is set first in the context of other conditions that are basic to Japanese culture and organizations, some of which were discussed in earlier chapters: a cultural predisposition to harmony and cohesiveness, different orientations toward persons inside and outside of groups, the nature of organizational goals, the organizational structure, and manner of conflict resolution.

This more general section is followed in the chapter by an extended review of the literature on conflict. Since the subject has been widely considered and heavily researched, it is necessary to clarify fully the various domains in which the idea has been employed conceptually in the literature in order to extract the features that were employed in this research. As will be seen, for example, the idea of denial of conflict has been explored in a variety of different contexts, and it is necessary to consider these contexts themselves before discussing the subject of conflict denial. The plan of the chapter, then, is to consider in turn the nature of conflict in Japanese context, the conceptual foundations of that conflict, including discussions of various dimensions of conflict, and the meanings of conflict denial. The chapter concludes with a consideration of conflict in R & D settings. The findings from the empirical data and implications of the latter for the management of R & D professionals appear in later chapters.


## HARMONY/COHESIVENESS AND CONFLICT DENIAL
## IN JAPAN

As is well-known, the strain toward stability, community, and concord is omnipresent in Japan. Harmony (*wa*) is viewed as absolutely critical to the well-being of the state and, indeed, to the psychological health of its citizens (Nakamura 1987). As Simmel (1955, 65) notes more generally about social systems:

The more narrowly unified the group, the more can the hostility among its members have quite opposite consequences. On the one hand, the group, precisely because of its intimacy, can stand inner antagonisms without breaking apart, since the strength of the synthetic forces can cope with that of their antitheses. On the other hand, a group whose very principle is a considerable unity and feeling of belongingness is to this extent particularly threatened by every inner conflict.

Thus, manifest conflict, occasioned by clearcut deviations either in ideology or behavior from the expectations of the members of a system, must be considered illegitimate. The Western means of controlling deviance is usually to call attention to it and to put constraints on the perpetrator. In Japan, on the other hand, there are normative/cultural imperatives *not* to identify openly any individual as deviant. Not only is such recognition embarrassing to the individual, but its public nature violates the alleged unity and stability of the group. Hence, "real" departures from norms must be dealt with in other ways—in short, through what will be identified here as "denial" (especially anticipation and quiet tolerance).

It is the strain for harmony that predisposes the Japanese workers to label cognitive and affective dissension not, as in the West, negatively as dysfunctional conflict, but as a temporary and productive stimulus to problem solving (Krauss, Rohlen, & Steinhoff 1984). If workers can assume or be socialized to believe there is agreement on the long-term goals of the organization and that members are committed to achieving them (the "professional" model of Pfeffer, cited above), then disagreements arise largely in connection with *means* to accomplish goals. The importance of maintaining the myth of goal consensus is critical to the notion of conflict denial.

Organizations in Japan undergo both centripetal and centrifugal forces in the experience of conflict. Workers are socialized to tolerate *more* conflict precisely because of their high levels of group solidarity (cf. Durkheim 1933). There arises a collective and individual confidence in the ability of the group as a whole to survive temporary discord. However, since the members value that solidarity so much, when it is threatened by conflict, strong efforts are taken to anticipate deviance and to forestall it. This is not to say that no interpersonal strife is present in Japanese organizations (cf. Simmel's distinction between competition and rivalry—Simmel 1955, p 70).

## INTERNAL/EXTERNAL ORIENTATIONS AND CONFLICT DENIAL

The system's need to remain productive and adaptive to external conditions creates still another important norm in Japan: *uchi-soto* (Ishida 1984), the clear distinctions between insiders and outsiders. Here, too, the very real, though latent positive functions of conflict denial can be seen.

As described in Chapter 6, every Japanese person feels an extremely powerful psychic need to be a part of a group that has bonds approaching familial character. Indeed, being excluded from the group (*mura hachibu*) has historical roots in the serious consequences of ostracism in Japanese village culture (Kikuchi 1951). Indeed, many if not most groups in Japanese organizations resemble families in their structures and interpersonal relationships. The heavy "dependence" of group members on one another is not, however, anxiety producing, as in the West, but is a source of security—provided there is confidence in those on whom the person is dependent—a confidence born out of close relationships.

While the intimacy of the family in a group is limited by group size, many large Japanese organizations engender some not inconsiderable sense of care and concern. "Outsiders" from the organizational family are believed to be different and hence not to be trusted to the same degree. The projection of outsiders as enemies, in turn, reinforces the internal bonding.

As in Western organizations, furthermore, the Japanese manufacture not only their products but their myths about their environments (Weick 1977). The myths include strong prejudices and perceptions of external threat, which in turn engender a "wagon-circling" unification of organizational members to ward off the threat. While such processes are functional in the short run, the internal dynamics of a continual defensive posture can be deleterious. There are several reasons.

First, as Coser (1956, 103) notes, "Groups engaged in continued struggle with the outside tend to be intolerant within. They are unlikely to tolerate more than limited departures from the group unity." Second, external adaptiveness potentially disrupts internal efficiency. (This is classic Chester Barnard. See, for example, Barnard 1938, 85 ff.) The continual adaptation of the organization to external contingencies and the corresponding changes in internal goals results in an organizational condition that would ordinarily upset the stability and certainty needed for internal communication and efficient interaction.

The fact that the Japanese have been so adept at scanning their environments and seizing opportunities in it is in part a result of the efficiency with which they deal with conflict within their organizations. Through an elaborate set of processes and structural conditions, starting with recruitment (from a highly homogeneous neophyte worker pool) and socialization, and proceeding through job enrichment, job enlargement, job rotation, and extensive participation in decision making, the Japanese have so stabilized the internal mechanisms of control and decision making that more time and effort can be devoted to external circumstances. This is not, interestingly, a simple "organic" versus "mechanistic" distinction. The special combination of role ambiguity and hierarchical structure in the Japanese organization renders it peculiarly adaptive.

In other words, the Japanese are able to adapt more quickly and effectively to external demands because the work force has a built-in readiness to anticipate conflicts and make necessary structural and interpersonal changes within the organization at a rapid rate and without significant organizational disruption. In still other words (cf. Parsons 1951), the Japanese have developed highly sophisticated methods for attending to the organization's needs for integration and latency among workers, leaving workers free to attend productively to cross-boundary matters of adaptation and goal attainment.

## ORGANIZATIONAL GOALS AND CONFLICT DENIAL

In Japan, because of extremely high levels of idiographic homogeneity at the cultural and organizational levels, goal consensus is more likely to be present or assumed to be so. Hence, disagreements center more on means than ends. Were the temporary ''disputes'' (cf. Kolb & Putnam 1992) raised to the seemingly irreconcilable level of ''conflict,'' there would be a shift away from the objective of serving organizational ends and an open recognition of the apparently greater potential benefits that might accrue to each party by virtue of the distribution of resources to accomplish the means.

The difference between the two systems lies in the assumptions of goal congruence noted above. In smaller organizations, the *Gemeinschaft* characteristics will render the culture more homogeneous (Toennies 1957), while in larger places there will be a breakdown by subunit (in educational institutions, by college, department, discipline, and even physical location of offices), as *Gesellschaft* phenomena manifest themselves. In the Japanese organization, the worker is oriented toward the organization as a whole. Hence, differences are more likely to occur interpersonally than between units. In the American organization, differences arise between units and between individuals.

## INTERPERSONAL COMMUNICATION AND DENIAL

The Japanese have another cultural disposition against *explicit* disagreement or refusal. The phenomenon is captured in the Japanese distinction between *omote* and *ura* (Lebra 1984). It is extremely rare for a Japanese person to express open disagreement or to refuse to comply with a request, even when circumstances beyond the control of the person make it necessary. The prevailing mode of dealing with this apparent difference between two parties is either to remain silent or to change the subject. This form of conflict avoidance is understood by both parties and directs each to seek a solution that is acceptable to both. Clearly, one solution is for the first person tactfully to withdraw the request. Indeed, because denial implies a commitment to consensus, some Japanese will feel guilt at finding themselves in such a situation (on rare occasions even seeking solace in suicide). Essentially, this is a displacement or reorienting of aggressiveness toward the self (Lebra 1984).

## ORGANIZATIONAL STRUCTURE AND CONFLICT DENIAL

There is a consensus among most scholars that virtually all systems (individuals, groups, organizations, nations) engaged in conflict are attempting to maximize values that are in scarce supply, or are perceived to be (Himes 1980, 124). The main values that are usually in short supply are "power," "status," and "resources." That is, as individuals and subsystems evolve, these values and their strengths tend to shift. Some attempted redress of perceived deficiencies is always in process. In Japan, however, the carefully articulated and openly manifested social relationships in organizations render these scarce resources not as readily amenable to redistribution. The system allocates them in ways perceived by participants to be bureaucratically rational (in the Weberian sense), hence, less assailable. While individual Japanese may harbor inner thoughts of higher status or may covet more power, the lack of systemic availability of the resources forces him both to accept the lack of opportunity for conflict and ultimately to deny its existence. In Japan, then, conflict is denied partially not because workers do not have differences, but because the differences are seen to be beyond the control of disputing participants in any controversy. In the helpful conceptualization of Thomas noted earlier, the "joint outcome space" is conceived in integrative rather than distributive terms. The "pie" can be enlarged rather than merely divided. (This is considered further below in the discussion of cooperative versus competitive conflict management.)

Another reason for some degree of conflict disavowal is the Japanese reliance on the relative permanence of status hierarchies. Conflict, both vertical and horizontal, threatens the legitimacy of those hierarchies. Differences between leader and subordinate quite obviously raise questions as to the purity of the bureaucracy. In Weberian terms, hierarchies are ideally formed on the basis of technical competency and seniority (the former, then the latter). This is certainly the case in Japan. Thus, a questioning of hierarchy is a threat to the legitimacy of the authority system, as, of course, it would be in any culture. However, in Japan, the authority system as manifested in clearly demarcated statuses is a key to the stability of relationships.

A further complication in the explanation of conflict in Japan is introduced through the concept of leadership, about which much more will be said in the next chapter. Recent research has shown that the nature of the leadership style exercised is a function of the perceived interdependence of goals among workers. Since leaders in hierarchical settings are expressly mandated to resolve conflicts among lower-level employees, in situations where workers share goals and the desire to cooperate in the achievement of them, the exercise of leadership can mitigate most proclivities toward conflict. As Tjosvold (1989) notes,

superiors and subordinates expected mutual assistance, exchanged resources, and developed confidence and liking. . . . Managers in cooperation, compared to competition and independence, used collaborative rather than coercive influence, gave assistance when requested, and responded to the specific problem of the subordinate appropriately.

The Japanese structuring of the roles in the design of the organization further reduces potential conflict. In other cultures, there can be several different kinds of interdependence among workers or groups. In the classic Thompson (1967) typology, as noted above, it can be sequential, reciprocal, or pooled. In Japan, however, most interdependence is both perceived and conceived as reciprocal. That is, members of organizations (including university research and development laboratories) tend to see colleagues in reciprocal relationships over a long period of time. Reciprocity as a norm in Japan has a much more powerful impact on relationships among workers, as each person recognizes that benefits to others in the short run are also benefits to themselves and that benefits received are the result of benefits tendered to others earlier.

Clearly, in the context of a highly homogeneous Japanese R & D setting, where workers are carefully recruited and selected for their compatibility with the organization's goals and style of work and where new workers are intensively socialized and institutionalized, the cooperation fostered in other settings and enhanced through cultural norms is exceptionally strong. The styles of leadership that follow, not unexpectedly, take their cue from this outlook, with leaders tending to be highly supportive.

Manifest vertical conflict implies a lack of confidence in leadership. As Gamson (1968) notes, in the presence of neutral or alienated lower participants in an organization, the assumption is that management and worker goals are divergent. Moreover, the tactic of upward influence is through the exercise of ''inducements'' or ''constraints.'' Since contrary assumptions obtain in Japanese organizations (i.e., high confidence in leadership), the tactic of both upward and downward influence is through persuasion.

Manifest lateral conflict also raises questions of status legitimacy. While intense rivalry among peers is common, it is expressed soto voce. Conflict revealed as open competition would threaten the egalitarian condition of peer groups.

It would appear, then, that where systems are integrated on the basis of work-related matters, the above resources are forced into the background. Conflict becomes controversy over organizational priorities, policies, strategies, and tactics without the protagonists becoming as personally invested in them.

## CONFLICT AND COMPETITION

Not only are there substantive differences among workers in Japanese organizations, some of which can be labeled as goal or process conflict, but there is also suppressed competition. Here, instead of differences over ends and means, the conflict is over rights to rewards. Most of the time, in Japan conflict takes the form of striving for supremacy of formal position rather than for recognition of individual merit through various other types of formal organizational rewards.

Demonstrated merit in a meritocracy is clearly different from demonstrated merit in a social system that holds back explicit recognition of it for individuals. In the former, the game is a zero-sum or distributive one; in the latter, it is formally a collaborative or integrative one. In actuality, the collaboration may conceal a latent competition. As Simmel (1955, 64) notes, organic solidarity protects the group against overt, intragroup conflict. The dilemma of tight norms which suppress conflict is that they also suppress individuality and the potential for creativity. When competition is legitimate, so is individuality. When competition is allowed to go unprotected by organic solidarity, the collaboration needed for group productivity is lacking.

The answer in part lies in the forms by which recognition for achievement is accorded. More and different kinds of rewards for a diversity of achievements give dignity to each person. Importantly, the roles played by group members in support of others' achievements are given equal weight. This is different from having each person lose his identity to the group and relying on group achievement for ego satisfaction. One of the functions of leadership of research and development units is the balancing and adjudication of these competing demands—the centrifugal forces of individual achievement and the centripetal pull of satisfaction from group solidarity and group achievement. This is certainly not a new notion (cf. Argyris 1987) but it is especially salient in R & D.

## THE PSYCHOLOGY OF JAPANESE COGNITION

Despite the normal reticence and need to conciliate, the modes of communication and their extensiveness in Japan make miscommunication less likely. Although the language itself and the styles of interaction lend themselves to subtlety, the contrary practice of extensive discussion of *substantive* matters mitigates misunderstandings. The prominence of the practicalities and exigencies of the work thus, in Japan as in the United States, subordinate the affective conditions of work groups. Conflict as feeling remains latent and dysfunctional. Since creativity and innovation are results in part of individual commitment to personal investment in deviance, the suppression of these feelings results also in a suppression of the ideas associated with them.

Under usual conditions, it might be expected that the looseness in role definition in Japan would make role ambiguity more likely. The diffuseness of the roles is not, however, perceived by Japanese workers as a cause of ambiguity for two reasons. First, through cultural conditioning, the Japanese come to accept potentially conflicting ideologies or/and authoritative directives as normal. They are able to entertain without cognitive dissonance perspectives that to others seem contradictory.

For example, most Japanese are able to practice Eastern and Western religions simultaneously, despite incompatible assumptions and philosophic beliefs of the religions. Personal or intrapsychic role conflict does not, therefore, manifest itself as frequently. Similarly, temporary or even long-standing differences between persons or parts of the organization can be accepted as natural. Note that this does not mean that the Japanese necessarily "tolerate" opposing views, though they do that also in other circumstances. It means that they frequently do not recognize the opposition as requiring resolution. Hence, "denial" of conflict becomes easier, or more functional.

## CONCEPTUALIZATIONS OF CONFLICT

Having thus considered the practices of conflict denial in Japan, it is necessary now to reflect on them more theoretically. Considerations of the complex phenomena of conflict in organizations tend to be divided into sociological, processual, structural, and personnel approaches. Sociologists, for example, have examined the subject from different perspectives over time, with at least three broad approaches having been emphasized historically: traditional, behavioral, and interactionist (Robbins 1974). The first, prominent in the late nineteenth century through the middle 1940s, emphasized the destructiveness of conflict, and, therefore, the importance of its elimination from social systems. After World War II, a shift in the conceptualization of conflict occurred. While the emphasis on dysfunctions continued, there was a growing recognition of its inevitability. Some writers, indeed, recognized some of the positive latent functions that conflict serves. Despite the recognition of its apparent ineradicable presence, however, the behavioralists continued to attempt to explore possibilities for the resolution of conflict.

In more recent years, an interactionist perspective has gained acceptance. This conceptualization suggests that conflict is inevitable, but that some forms may be useful. It suggests that there are some positive functions of conflict in organizations and takes the logical next step of recommending the stimulation of appropriate conflicts while seeking to prevent, resolve, or suppress others. The "management" of conflict, rather than the elimination of conflict today underlies most current theoretical thinking and research (cf. Himes 1980; Brown 1983; Rahim 1986; Bisno 1988; Borisoff & Victor 1989).

As will be seen below, however, in some cultures, particularly the Japanese, the approach to conflict follows none of these models. Rather, conflict is paradoxically anticipated and accepted, yet denied, as noted earlier. It is necessary here to define and distinguish among several levels of individual and group awareness and acknowledgment of conflict, as well as the consequences of each (cf. Moses 1989). This deconstruction will be seen as useful for understanding differences between the terms as used in this country and in Japan. There are six critical questions that can be asked about organizational conflict. These move from the level of individual cognition to individual behavior. Different answers to the questions reflect the working conditions of culture, norms, technology, and structure. In other words, under different conditions, workers will have different answers. The questions are:

1. Do real and important differences in beliefs about methods[1] exist among workers?
2. Are workers conscious of the differences?
3. Do workers openly acknowledge the differences?
4. Are the differences manifested in behavior that inhibits effective decision making?
5. How do workers feel about the probability of conflict resolution?
6. What actions are taken to deal with the various combinations of the above?

The interactions among the answers to these questions are graphically displayed for easier understanding in Exhibit 11.1.

Let us discuss the answers to these questions for research and development. First, in Japanese organizations, as any organization, there are controversies over method. Depending on whether the research orientation is basic or applied, these differences will be more pronounced. As pointed out earlier, basic research typically is conducted more by individuals than by teams, as in applied research. Applied research requires more interpersonal interaction and more involvement of persons with different skills, perspectives, and orientations. Because of the greater sensitivity to others of workers in Japan, differences among workers will be apparent to them. Thus, the answer to the first two questions of the above six is that differences exist and that individual workers *are* aware of them.

As to the third question, whether the differences are openly acknowledged, the answer is "no." Of course, in all organizations where work is not repetitive, differences will arise and must be reconciled. Indeed, it is the expectation of the workers that there will be differences. Where those differences are important, however, the cost of public acknowledgment to the Japanese worker is usually not worth chancing. Calling attention to group disharmony both violates critical bases of individual security in the group's comity and longevity and calls additional attention to the person who raises the issue as a fomenter of disharmony. So workers often refuse to acknowledge openly that position differences even exist. The reaction frequently is to deal with the problem somewhat less rationally. That is, workers will either move back up to step number 2 and not let differences enter their consciousness or will rationalize them away as insignificant. "There is no conflict in this organization," a worker might say and genuinely feel that there are no serious disagreements between him and his co-workers.

The behavioral results of this step emerge in question number 4: either the work can be impeded, or the required decisions can be made in other ways. On the one hand, disavowal of differences means refusal to accept the premise that acknowledged differences in position can be reconciled. In this case, workers may recognize differences, but deny that they are so serious as to be irreconcilable. "I would prefer that we follow policy 'A' rather than 'B' as advocated by several other workers in this group, but I am sure we can work out our differences," a worker who denies conflict might say. Hence, it is possible for either or both conditions to exist in any institution. For example, whereas in the

Exhibit 11.1
## Organizational Conflict

**Differences Exist (1)**

**Real**

| Personal Awareness — Yes (2) | | | | | | | | Personal Awareness — No | | | | | | | |
|---|---|---|---|---|---|---|---|---|---|---|---|---|---|---|---|
| Open Acknowledgment (3) | | | | Public Disavowal | | | | Open Acknowledgment | | | | Public Disavowal | | | |
| D-Making Impaired(4) | | D-Making Not Impaired | | D-Making Impaired | | D-Making Not Impaired | | D-Making Impaired | | D-Making Not Impaired | | D-Making Impaired | | D-Making Not Impaired | |
| Rec. Yes | Rec. No (5) | Rec. Yes | Rec. No | Rec. Yes | Rec. No | Rec. Yes | Rec. No | Rec. Yes | Rec. No | Rec. Yes | Rec. No | Rec. Yes | Rec. No | Rec. Yes | Rec. No |
| CM | CM | CM | CM | CM | CM | CM | CM | CM | CM | CM | CM | CM | CM | CM | CM |
| Y N | Y N | Y N | Y N | Y N | Y N | Y N | Y N | Y N | Y N | Y N | Y N | Y N | Y N | Y N | Y N |

(Numbers in parentheses refer to the in-text questions).

West, disputants will on occasion conceptualize their positions as irreconcilable and resort to various management techniques ranging from "disavowal" that the differences exist to "compromise" to "coalition formation" and "domination exercises." These techniques have been captured in the Western instrument used for the empirical phases of this research—the Thomas-Kilmann MODE instrument, which is discussed in Chapter 11.

Given this apparent anomaly in Japanese organizations, it is useful to consider parts of the prevailing Western interactionist models of conflict that may help explain the phenomenon, including the origins of conflict, its structural components, its course of action, and its effects (Thomas 1976). Each of these constitutes a presumably exhaustive set of points of management intervention for the purpose of improvement or change. *Sources* of conflict are antecedent conditions that lead to opposing forces that appear to require resolution. Conflict as *structure* (really a subset of sources) directs observers to the more static conditions of social systems. Here, the focus is on the underlying conditions which shape conflict behavior—goals, interdependence, authority, and power relationships that may be responsible for the emergence of conflict. Conflict as a *process* is conceived as a dynamic sequence of events which transpire episodically, with different temporal points inviting different kinds of actions. The *effects* of conflict describe the results for the parties involved and for the stakeholders in the parties' well-being. Since, as noted earlier, the "management of conflict" rather than its elimination is the prevailing view in the conflict literature today, different investigators, both theoretical and practical, have concerned themselves with modes of intervention at these various junctures.

Before discussing conflict in these terms—origins, structure, process, or effects—it is useful to establish the various social settings in which these terms can be applied. Although the primary domain for consideration in this book is the group or/and organization, a broader systems orientation recognizes the inevitable crossovers across system levels. As noted below, there are at least five overlapping levels in which conflict can exist (Rahim 1986; Azar & Burton 1986; Bisno 1988, 28 ff.; Hellriegel, Slocum, & Woodman 1989, 446–473) (see Exhibit 11.2).

Regardless of the system in which conflict takes place, each of the four component intervention foci (again, origins, structure, process, and effects) can be identified. To understand the conceptualizations of conflict in any setting, however, it is most helpful to consider some notions that apply to them all. Some theorists, for example, are interested in understanding conflict in terms of its function or dysfunction to the system in which it exists. A long-standing debate in the sociological literature, for example, is concerned with the conceptualization of "deviance" and the means of its social control. (In psychology, the comparable phenomenon is the psychosomatic departure from personality stability and the means by which ego-centered forces enter into a conflict over control of behavior.) Socially or personally unacceptable behavior may be viewed in a number of ways. It may be considered as a "departure" from the

**Exhibit 11.2**
**Conflict System Levels**

| Focal System | Kind of Conflict | Examples |
|---|---|---|
| Person | Intra-Personal | Psychic disorders; schizophrenia |
| Dyad | Interpersonal | Between individuals |
| Group | Intragroup | Within a group |
| Organization | Intraorganizational | Between groups; between individuals from different groups |
| Social system | Interorganizational, international | Between different organizations, nations |

stasis that a social system has established, with control intended to return the system to the status-quo ante (Parsons 1949). Or, as more recent conceptions have it, it may be conceived ecologically, as a response to conditions within and outside of the system which move the system in directions that may lead to its continued survival or its demise (Coser 1956), obviously in a different system/environment relationship than before.

The question, in other words, is whether conflict evokes controlling or adapting forces. As will be seen below, beliefs about the answer are relevant to the question of reactions to conflict. A university, for example, that is constrained by its leadership philosophy to see conflict or even potential conflict as needing strict monitoring will probably not find its research and development activities on the forefront of new discoveries. Another university, whose perspective is to see conflict as functionally adaptive, will see researchers' "deviance" as not requiring social control. Clearly, other norms and conditions constrain researcher behavior in this case.

## THE ORIGINS OF CONFLICT IN ORGANIZATIONS

Organizational conflict has its origins in many places. The local particulars in part determine the sequence of the conflict cycle and the modes of conflict resolution. Most observers point to the trends in industrialized societies toward greater division of labor, complexity, and specialization as the prime sources of conflict. As Selznick (1949) points out, the division of labor results in worker identification with local goals and the motivation to optimize goal achievement at the local level. Absent sufficient macroorganizational goal promulgation (cf. Selznick 1957) and socialization and without adequate integrating devices (Lawrence & Lorsch 1967), and in the presence of scarcity of resources and/or external threat, interunit conflict is likely to manifest itself.

A useful model for this perspective comes from the work of Jeffrey Pfeffer (1977; cf. Mintzberg 1983). Pfeffer describes four types of organizations differentiated not only on the grounds of goal consensus, but also means consensus (i.e., agreement or disagreement on the technology to be used—cf. Perrow's [1986] typology of technology for another useful diagnostic complication). To this Pfeffer adds a dimension of "centralization." The four organizations generated by this two-by-two matrix are noted in Exhibit 11.3 below. Note that the origins of conflict according to this model lie in the different perspectives and aims of organizational participants in each of the quadrants.

For example, March and Simon (1958, 129 ff.) observe that there are two predominant forms of conflict resolution: "analytic" and "bargaining," each of these divided respectively into two parts: problem solving and persuasion and bargaining and politics. When there is agreement on system goals or there are assumptions that the parties can reach agreement on those goals, disagreements between parties revolve around the reaching of consensus as to tactical, pragmatic issues. The assumption is that integrative rather than distributive (e.g., zero-sum) solutions can be reached. On the other hand, when there is disagreement about goals, conflict processes involve the aggregation of relative power advantages by each party such that one can gain more of the available, disputed goods in question.

The origins of conflict, then, can be said to lie in part in the degree of consensus on goals. As will be seen, assumptions about goals and the conditions of their acceptance in Japanese organizations give ample validity to this position. However, the downside aspect of goal congruence is the absence of sufficient divergence to stimulate new thought. It may be that in the presence of close harmony, structural devices to ensure adequate cross-boundary signal stimuli must be established. The opposite may also be true: In a community of cosmopolitan professionals like university R & D personnel, structural and other mechanisms to ensure sufficient levels of goal congruence must be established. This is not to suggest that outside contacts be closed off, but rather to indicate that additional means of binding cosmopolitans to internal needs are required.

Another contingency that explains the origins of conflict is the degree and nature of interdependence between units that moderates the levels of conflict that may emerge (cf. Thompson 1960). Thus, for example, units that are sequentially or reciprocally interdependent to high degrees are more likely to be in conflict than those that are less dependent on one another or/and are in a pooled relationship, especially when some performance evaluation criteria favor some units over others (Aldrich 1979). Once again, in Japan, carefully structured interdependencies give this observation strong validity, while the pattern of isolated activity for U.S. university researchers (particularly in the area of basic research) is just the opposite.

A final insight on the origins of conflict is revealed through an examination of the structure of authority relationships. Status, authority, power, and leadership are expressed in both formal and informal ways in organizations. The

**Exhibit 11.3**
**Organizational Types**

| | | Degree of Centralization of Authority | |
|---|---|---|---|
| | | Low | High |
| Degree of Consensus on Goals and Technology | High Certainty | Professional Model | Bureaucratic Model |
| | Low Uncertainty | Political/Coalition Model | Centralized Model |

*Source:* Adapted from Pfeffer (1977, 240).

legitimacy of autonomy and self-control in work situations varies according to the belief patterns by which status differences are in line with both cultural and organizational expectations. Where authority exceeds cultural and organizational expectations, and/or power undermines it, conflict over rights of control over work are likely to emerge. Where too much distance separates the upper from lower echelons, communications dysfunctions tend to disrupt the relationships (Borisoff & Victor 1989, 155). Cultural variations on power distance legitimacy abound (Hofstede 1980a; Adler & Doktor 1986), as do differences within cultures in the extent of their deviation from mean cultural expectation. In some cultures, for example, there is less room for departure from the norm than in others. As will be seen below, excesses may be denied in some cultures, while in others, they will be more tolerated. In research and development, of course, departures from paradigmatic thinking need to have more than mere protection from collegial obloquy. These deviations must be encouraged and lauded. Here the Japanese have not been as successful, particularly in the basic research areas.

Structures that are maladaptive in organizational or job design are another source of conflict. For example, tall or flat hierarchies, narrow or wide spans of control, functional rather than product or matrix forms of organization, and specialized versus broadly defined roles all contribute to the formation of conflict (Katz & Kahn 1978; Thompson 1960; 1967; Hackman & Oldham 1980).

## CONFLICT AS A PROCESS

Approaches to the conceptualization of conflict as a process are also helpful in understanding the functions of conflict denial in Japan. Thomas (1976; cf. Pondy 1967; Walton 1969) has identified five stages in a conflict episode: frustration, conceptualization, behavior, interaction, and outcomes.

Thomas suggests that frustration is the perception that another party is responsible for one's own failure to satisfy needs, desires, or objectives, or to carry out some behavior. The experience of frustration is brought about by such things as disagreements, denial of requests, insults, interference with roles, and so on. Usually, these frustrations are founded in problems with either means or ends (i.e., difficulties encountered in the standard decision-making mechanisms or persistent absence of rewards for task accomplishment) (March & Simon 1958, 112). So, the starting point in the conflict episode is with a felt uneasiness or unhappiness with some organizational situation. As will be seen later, it is possible that both conflict recognition and denial can take place at this stage— indeed, it does in the Japanese setting.

The second stage for Thomas is conceptualization. At this point the person or subunit experiencing conflict seeks to define the possible action alternatives and their outcomes. More specifically, the person in the conflict assesses the primary concerns of the parties in dispute and the realistic possibilities of so- lution. Thomas's graphic representation of the ''joint outcome space'' alterna- tives is helpful in conceiving of conflict resolution as some distribution of available desired outcomes among the disputants, the range for each party being none, some, or all. (Conceptualization may also include two additional possi- bilities: there is *no* solution or it is impossible to conceive of a solution, though the parties agree that there may be one.) Here once again, the very mode of conceiving of the possible outcomes may lead to conflict denial versus dis- avowal. For example, if the outcomes of a frustrating situation are seen as re- sulting in an expansion of the outcomes beyond those given in the situation, instead of a ''conflict,'' the situation may become a goal jointly sought by the parties (see below).

The third stage in the conflict episode, as conceived by Thomas, is behavior. It is comprised, in turn, of three components: orientation, strategic objectives, and tactics. The orientation of parties toward conflict (really a prebehavior dis- position), like the joint outcome space above, can be understood as a continuum of desire ranging from an interest in having all of the rewards for oneself, to sharing them, to letting the opposing party have them all. Thomas suggests that these alternative orientations can be arrayed in a two-by-two matrix, with one dimension measuring the assertiveness of a party in satisfying the party's own concerns, and the other measuring the strength of the willingness of a party to cooperate with the other party in satisfying that party's concerns. Five concep- tually (though not necessarily statistically) distinct positions are identified in Exhibit 11.4.

The competitive position, representing a highly assertive posture with respect to party's own concerns and an uncooperative stance toward the other, indicates a desire to win at the other's expense—to dominate win-lose power struggles. An accommodative orientation would be comprised of a strong desire to co- operate with the other, with no need to satisfy one's own concerns. Similar descriptions can be made of the other points in the matrix. (The substages of strategy and tactics temporarily are put aside here.) A fuller description of these conflict management styles follows:

**Variables in the Conflict Management Framework**

1. *Competing*. The leader's behavior in this mode is toward pursuing his own concerns at the expense of others. This is a power-oriented mode.

2. *Accommodating*. Under this mode, the leader neglects his own concerns to satisfy the concerns of others. He usually obeys another person's orders when he prefers not to. He yields in most cases.

3. *Avoiding*. The behavior of this kind of leader does not address conflict. The leader does not immediately pursue either his own concerns or those of the other person.

4. *Collaborating*. Here the leader is both assertive and cooperative. The leader attempts to work with the other person to find some solution which fully satisfies the concerns of both parties.

5. *Compromising*. This is a mid-point mode, between collaborating and accommodating. It represents behavior in which the leader tries to find some expedient, mutually acceptable solution which partially (but not fully) satisfies both parties.

What is critical about this phase in the conflict episode is that in contrast to conceptualization, which is a cognitive appreciation of possibilities, behavior takes into account a concrete other and enters into the calculation an affective component. Once again, as will be seen, cultural conditioning orients the Japanese toward the cooperative side of the matrix. It also forces the Japanese away from self-assertiveness. Contribution to the good of others is an extremely strong norm in all organizations in Japan. As well, it is an internalized ethic. Hence, it is necessary to free oneself of any feelings of aggressiveness in pursuit of one's own goals, especially at the expense of others.

Thomas introduces two additional contingencies that modify the orientation that a party takes in a conflict episode. These are the personal stake a party has in the outcome and the degree of congruence between the parties' interests. Clearly, if there is little perceived to be of value in "winning" a contested issue, the party is more likely to be oriented toward accommodation or avoiding. Similarly, if there is considerable overlap in the interests of the parties, there will be more of a tendency to be oriented toward collaboration—the gain of the other being also in the interests of one's self.

Why this is relevant to conflict denial in Japan is fairly evident. Since there is great homogeneity in the country and a high degree of identification with organizational goals, parties in any dispute are almost invariably impelled to invest themselves in others. Add to this a widespread commitment to lifetime employment in one organization, and it is easy to see why cooperation and collaboration are the most likely behavior orientations in Japan. A contrasting perspective can be found in U.S. R & D units, where mobility across universities and in and out of industry makes loyalty and commitment problematic.

Next, Thomas introduces us to the interaction phase. Here the focus is on the dynamics of escalation and deescalation during negotiations. In the light of the assumptions of this paper with respect to conflict anticipation and denial, this part of the theory has less relevance to the issues at hand.

**Exhibit 11.4**
**Orientation toward Conflict Behavior**

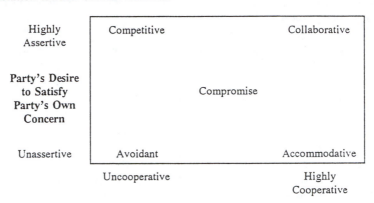

Party's Desire to Satisfy Other's Concern

*Source:* Adapted from Thomas (1976, 900).

The final stage in the conflict episode, according to Thomas, is outcomes. In the terms introduced above, we can reconceive this as either the management or conflict or the resolution of conflict.

## THE MANAGEMENT OF CONFLICT

As noted earlier, this topic constitutes virtually a completely separate branch of the research literature dealing with conflict. It is concerned with normative conditions that may lead to more organizationally effective management (Himes 1980; Brown 1983; Rahim 1986; Bisno 1988). However, since conflict in the contemporary view is now seen as either constructive or destructive, most academic observers of the conflict process agree that some forms of conflict at some level of intensity can be healthy for the organization, while others may not (Brown 1983, 8). Further, some forms of conflict resolution result in organizationally functional outcomes, while others do not. Deutsch (1987) identifies four typical problems that arise when conflict takes a "psychological" course: avoidance, premature resolution, excessive involvement, and rigidification. Avoidance, while sometimes useful, often keeps opposing forces from engaging in useful, constructive conflict resolution. (More on this below.) Premature or excessive intervention from upper-level authorities can prevent organizational learning from taking place among participants in a conflict dispute. In this case, "the conflicting parties come to an agreement before they have adequately explored the issues involved in their conflict" (Deutsch 1987, 39). Here a party in the dispute may find it psychologically necessary to make controversial issues manifest out of fear that those issues, if unattended, may be resolved in ways that are detrimental to the party.

Last is Deutsch's fourth pathology—rigidification. As this may, indeed, be quite characteristic of the Japanese approach to conflict and its resolution, it is well to consider it here carefully. Rigidification can result in an irrational holding on to old positions and a group-think mentality that closes off participants to new solutions. Deutsch suggests that when individuals become anxious about conflict they:

start to have a kind of tunnel vision with regard to the issues in conflict. They see only a limited range of possibilities for resolving the conflict. They lose their creative potential for conceiving a range of options which might make the conflict a constructive experience in which both sides might profit. Rigidification and tunnel vision are often associated with excessive anxiety. (1987, 40)

Bisno (1988, 31 ff.) notes other dysfunctional reactions to conflict: misattributions and displacement/scapegoating.

## Cooperative versus Competitive Conflict Management

Deutsch's most useful contribution to the theory of conflict may be his classification of the phenomenon into constructive and destructive forms and his description of the conditions that lead to each. Allowing for its obviousness, Deutsch (1973) suggests that a desire for cooperation generally engenders constructive resolutions, while competition frequently leads to destructive conflict. This notion is similar to Thomas's (1976) conceptualization of integrative and distributive conflict resolution. Cooperation, Thomas suggests, will more likely lead to conflict resolution that increases the resources available to both parties, while distributive conflict resolution forces a division of the ''pie'' in a zero-sum mode.

Deutsch suggests that the reason that the cooperative versus competitive orientations lead to the different ends lies in the kinds of communication processes that are necessitated. Not unexpectedly, when people have a desire to cooperate, they are more willing to be open, free in their interactions with one another, and to be attentive to one another's needs, since there is confidence that through persuasion rather than force, a common solution can be found. Under the contrary conditions of competition, parties in the exchange have less confidence in the power of persuasion (cf. the conceptualizations of Gamson 1968, on the hierarchical relationships under conditions of trust and alternative forms of influence), and resort to secrecy, deception, and power—the bargaining rather than the analytic framework of March and Simon. As has been detailed in previous chapters, the Japanese culture—particularly through family and school life—so strongly bends the individual in group settings toward cooperation that the probabilities of constructive conflict resolution are greatly enhanced. Indeed, the denial of conflict as defined earlier is in some ways the cognitive prerequisite of the cooperation norm. To reiterate, suggesting that conflict is irreconcilable would be to admit to the failure of a cherished national value.

It is necessary to make clear at this point that there is a difference between the concepts of "conflict denial" and "conflict avoidance" noted in the Deutsch typology. (Recall that Deutsch uses the term "denial" in the sense that "disavowal" is employed in this chapter, namely, the insistence that conflict does not exist.) For Deutsch, conflict avoidance means not only disavowing the existence of conflict, but a "shying away from dealing with the issues in conflict." Here, the parties in a dispute will acknowledge to themselves that the conflict exists, but will permit it to lie latent, below surface levels. The elaborate mechanisms needed to carry on the subterfuge of no conflict are, according to Deutsch, debilitating in terms of psychic costs, resulting in various neurotic behaviors—defense mechanisms, identification with the aggressor, rationalization, and so on.

Conflict in Japan is not, however, avoided or denied, in Deutsch's conceptualization, or disavowed, in the sense used here. Rather, conflict is anticipated, engaged, mediated, displaced, and turned inward. The denial of irreconcilability of resolution in Japan helps to explain why the psychic costs of conflict *avoidance* are themselves avoided. As Lebra (1984, 42 ff.) notes:

conflict management in Japan does not necessarily mean resolution. Management can involve procrastination, aggravation of conflict, or introduction of a new phase of conflict. The culturally available techniques for management at the interpersonal level . . . may be characterized as non-confrontational.

## CONFLICT RESOLUTION MECHANISMS

It is necessary to return briefly to Deutsch's observations about conflict resolution at this point. With regard to his conceptualization of premature resolution, the Japanese denial of conflict avoids this trap. The elaborate and time-consuming processes of *nemawashi* and *ringei*, in addition to their manifest positive function of preventing decisions from being made prematurely and without input from all potential contributors, also represent in part a latent need to keep conflict "under the table." These procedures basically describe a participatory decision-making process in which workers at all levels are involved in consensus-forming discussions and official sign-offs. In an odd way, then, while the Japanese are reluctant to admit to conflict, they have developed an elaborate mechanism that keeps the parties in disputational posture for extended periods of time. The reasons this apparent organizational contradiction does not fall into a conflict condition must lie, therefore, in the manner in which the decision-making process is carried out. The Japanese are committed to extensive involvement in decision making. Hence, conflict denial, as defined here, means accepting the legitimacy of the system and acknowledging its efficacy. Given the Japanese antipathy to calling attention to individual differences, it is usually not likely that the Japanese worker risks either dropping out of the discussions or resorting to other conflict management techniques that are likely to be distributive rather than integrative.

Deutsch's concept of rigidification, on the other hand, does speak to one of the deficiencies in the Japanese system. It seems clear that the individual Japanese person's concern for not standing out from the group results in the closing off of possibilities for creative solutions that may not have prospects for easy adoption among colleagues. The Japanese are more likely to "satisfice" than "optimize." Again, using the March and Simon (1958, 140–141) framework, they select the first available solution to a problem, rather than search extensively for the optimum solution. Behavior patterns of this nature will probably result in units missing out on new discoveries. At another university, whose perspective is to see conflict as functionally adaptive, researchers' "deviance" will be seen as not requiring social control. Clearly, other norms and conditions constrain researcher behavior in this case, as will be shown below.

All systems, of course, move cyclically between stability and change, the more successful ones achieving the necessary balance and timing to keep the system alive and healthy. During different phases in a system's history, different degrees of departure from the norms of the system are viewed as illegitimate and hence in need of attention. As Himes (1980) notes,

conflicts may be defined as legitimate when they are required, endorsed, or permitted by the universalistic norms of an inclusive social system, for instance, that of a society or a community. Terms like non-violence, protest, struggle, and defensive war reveal popular perception of this fact. The property of legitimacy may be attributed to both the ends and the means of conflict. (p. 18)

Since strong norms for cooperation tend to smother conflict appearances, sustained problem solving through satisficing will be tolerated during periods of rapid change. Perhaps more important, however, while internal "satisficing" may address internal needs for comity, such solutions may not meet external needs for high-quality, competitive products. These externally imposed stimuli serve to reopen the issues but at a higher level of discussion. As Dewey noted, the resolved conflict becomes "warrantable" knowledge, usable as a base on which more sophisticated problems can be situated and analyzed.

Still another mode of dealing with conflict is through mediation. It is frequently the case in Japan that parties in disagreement will ask a third person to attend meetings between the two disputants. The ostensible pretext is just that the third person is a friend of one of the parties who happens to be around. In reality, the third person is expected to adjudicate the differences by careful rephrasing of the positions into formats acceptable to each. Each party can express his unique perspective to the third party rather than engage in a head-to-head expression that evokes blatantly the nature of the differences. This recourse to a third party is not conceptualized as a mode of conflict resolution by the parties in a disagreement, however, again because the conflict has not yet been permitted to rise openly to the level of irreconcilable disagreement.

The organizational structures and climate for productive research in the United States and in Japan differ in some significant ways, but are quite similar in others. The fostering of individual creativity among research scientists requires working conditions that match the special circumstances of R & D (Marcson 1960; Pelz & Andrews 1976; Pelz 1978; House, Filley, & Kerr 1971; Little 1984; Lee, Fisher, & Yau 1986; Aoki 1986; Kidder 1981). As noted earlier, important differences obtain, depending on whether the research being conducted is basic, applied, or developmental. There is a range of necessary interdependence among workers across these categories, with basic research requiring far fewer connections with other researchers than the other two categories.

Structural and processual differences in the nature of conflict also differ across these categories. Exhibit 11.5 below reflects the differences in disavowal and denial that seem to depend on the technology of creative research in each category. The exhibit suggests that applied research usually evokes means-oriented conflict, since there is more intra- and intergroup interaction. Basic research, on the other hand, tends to be more the result of ends-oriented conflict, as individuals must demonstrate the validity of their studies in the context of the overall objectives of the organization and in competition with other projects. In both cases, in Japan, conflict is disavowed. For applied research it is also denied, and the denial is veridical. Researchers believe that their conflict with collaborators can be resolved. For basic research, the denial is pro forma only. Japanese basic researchers tend to "eat" their frustrations. As noted in earlier chapters, the person who puts forth creative ideas that are deviant will tend to withdraw into the anonymity of the crowd rather than continue to press for acceptance.

The typical structures for research and development in Japan better serve the applied and developmental areas. Involvement of workers from different phases of the R & D process (the technology transfer phenomenon)—from research, engineering, development, mass production, marketing—serves to mitigate the conflicts that arise. Although more people are in the process, they all come to "own" the final product, and see *its* success, rather than their personal achievement, as significant and meaningful (cf. Hackman & Oldham 1980). As noted above, job rotation and other personnel development procedures lead also to collaborative conflict management. Having worked with so many others throughout the organization makes it easier for individuals to obtain information and makes it difficult to pass on a product with poor workmanship to others with whom one has an affiliative investment. Finally, the lengthy processes of *ringei* and *nemawashi* described earlier also build confidence in the possibilities of conflict resolution and hence lead to conflict denial—to the denial that conflict is irreconcilable.

In sum, different cultures tend to make different normative assumptions about the social acceptability of the ends and means of conflict. Some cultures view conflict per se as a negative condition, basically disruptive, and something that

**Exhibit 11.5**
**The Relation of Conflict Source and Management Process to Worker Responses in Research and Development Organizations**

| | | Conflict Source | Conflict Mgmt. Process | Worker Response | |
|---|---|---|---|---|---|
| | | | | Disavowal | Denial |
| R & D Focus | Applied | Means Conflict | Collaborative | No | Yes (Real) |
| | Basic | Ends Conflict | Competitive | No | Yes (Pro Forma) |

should be disposed of quickly (cf. the critical theory perspectives of Dahrendorf [1969] and Harris [1981]). In other cultures, the tendency is to see conflict as a normal, expected condition with positive features, thus legitimating a variety of manifest conflict management activities. A third position looks at conflict as positive or negative, depending on the particulars. Each of these positions carries with it procedural baggage that dictates the ways in which conflict is approached and managed. For example, as Nadler, Nadler, and Broome (1985) noted, while Americans tend to value compromise highly, others refrain from it.

The Japanese, on the other hand, bring positions to the bargaining table that have been worked out through a detailed process of consensus-reaching, and they are not normally prepared to compromise without going back through this process. (p. 95)

While the finer tuning of the Japanese culture as a whole would make one think that conflicts would be more frequently perceived and manifested, the Japanese have had a long history of successful internal conflict management which has generated a remarkably stable system with a high degree of comity. The resolution mechanisms that Deutsch identifies, both functional and dysfunctional, are all present in Japanese society, so that ostensible stability and calm come at some collective psychic cost. Nevertheless, the success of the mechanisms has enabled conflict denial, as defined here, to be a viable cognitive option for most Japanese, including those in R & D centers. The functions of conflict denial for the Japanese R & D manager permit the Japanese an optimism about problem solving that makes it possible for them to be highly successful researchers in the applied and developmental domains. It permits them to engage in lengthy discussions that aim at total consensus because they have a record of success at that process. Integrative, rather than distributive solutions to conflict are more possible in the Japanese R & D setting because conflict is denied.

Thus, if conflict is seen to have a positive function, then refusal to recognize it may have detrimental consequences. Since the early 1980s, the Japanese have become models for organizational success (notwithstanding recessionary constraints on productivity). It is clear that denial, as differentiated from disavowal, may actually preserve the positive aspects of conflict while dampening the negative. On the whole then, conflict denial has a highly salubrious effect on Japanese R & D. In the next chapter, the critical influence of leadership in dealing with both open and concealed conflict will be considered.

## NOTE

1. For the moment, we deal here with ''means-oriented differences, rather than disagreements of a more fundamental nature about organizational goals and/or policies. In Japan, the latter are less likely to occur because of recruitment and socialization procedures.

# 12

# Leadership

The history of leadership research and writing reveals a continuing tergiversation among researchers—from a belief that leadership is a significant predictor of group or organizational effectiveness to one that gives more credit to other factors in the immediate or distant surround (Thomas 1988). Complications, contradictions, and conflicts in the understanding of leadership that have emerged as empirical studies over some time have revealed new relevant variables and new relationships among them (cf. House & Singh 1987; Wakabayashi 1987). Among these, for example, are the interactions between leader personality and/or behavior style and such contingencies as organizational culture/climate (Bennis 1984; Chemers 1984; Blake & Mouton 1964); external environments and power (Pfeffer & Salancik 1978; Mintzberg 1983); organizational design, particularly bureaucratic elements (Perrow 1986); technology (Barrow 1977); management assumptions about human nature (Selznick 1957; McGregor 1960); group or organizational size (Blau 1964); worker goals (House 1971; Locke & Latham 1990; Yukl 1989); worker capacities and maturity, individually and collectively (Hersey & Blanchard 1969; Graen, Scandura, & Graen 1986; Meindl 1993); industry (Etzioni 1961); substitutes for leadership (Kerr & Jermier 1978); and organizational life cycle stage (Cameron & Whetten 1984; Baliga & Hunt 1988; Bess 1988). To understand the dynamics of leadership in Japan as interpreted in this book, it will be necessary to set it in the context of these theories. A brief recapitulation precedes a more substantive discussion of the Japanese condition.

## LEADERSHIP THEORIES REVIEWED

A review of virtually any contemporary organizational theory or management textbook will reveal the documentation of the shift in orientation and focus of leadership studies. In brief, initially, research on leadership was influenced by those who saw large-scale social movements seemingly dominated by "great men." The history of well-known and documented charismatic leadership among demagogues, politicians, and religious revivalists, particularly as they exercised their powers in great crowds, directed studies to the character of the personalities of the leader (Graumann 1986). With the advent of group psychology, and new interest in organizational dynamics, there came a shift in attention to the dynamics of small group leadership (Lewin, Lippitt, & White 1939; Bales 1950; Shartle 1956; Ghiselli 1966). Further, as Graumann notes, new foci for study emerged: "from emphasis on theory to emphasis on research, from unidirectional to interactional or reciprocal conceptions, from individual-centered approaches to individual X group or person X situation conceptions" (p. 3). It was with the recognition of the importance of Kurt Lewin's work that attention in the academic community began to shift away from the examination of the intrinsic essence of leadership phenomena to an interest in the exploration of the nature of relationships among leadership variables and other variables that appear to have some consistency over time (Graumann 1986, 85). With Bales' concentration on the group and the roles group members play came a recognition of the impact of interpersonal relationships in groups on group dynamics (Bales 1953; cf. Parsons 1951, 135 ff.). The shift in focus to the group became more reasonable in the light of decision-making modes arising out of a more democratic ethos and the realization of the pragmatics of widespread participation in a technologically sophisticated age. It became apparent that Weberian principles of ideally functioning bureaucracies were not appropriate under certain contingencies, particularly rapidly changing, complex organizational environments. The shift also reflected the continuing bifurcation in the social sciences between psychology and sociology, as each emphasized different sides of the phenomenon without adequately linking them.

## SHARING OF LEADERSHIP RESPONSIBILITY

The more behavioral approach to the study of leadership recently receiving renewed attention has its derivation in part in the Ohio State University studies of leader *behavior* (rather than in either leader characteristics or environmental contingencies). Such redirection calls attention to leadership activities per se, rather than to the characteristics of the people who perform them. Hackman and Walton (1986), for example, argue for a "functional" approach to leadership. As they note, "The critical leadership functions for a task-performing team in an organization are *those activities that contribute to the establishment and maintenance of favorable performance conditions*" (emphasis in original). It is necessary, say these authors, to understand all of the needs of the group in order to portray the various functions that leaders must perform. This seems to mirror the functionalist approach to understanding social systems at the macro level, perhaps most famously expostulated by Parsons (1951; cf. Sashkin 1987) in his functional prerequisites schema (AGIL). The Parsonian prerequisites are adaptation, goal attainment, integration, and latency. Arrayed in a two-by-two table, one dimension reflects the internal/external orientation and the other the instrumental/consummatory orientation. Leadership, conceivably, must attend to these four functions if the system—that is, work group—is to be effective (cf. Trice & Beyer 1991). As Turquet (1976) notes, however, such roles may be incompatible:

Open-system groups are involved not only in an internal/external world of differentiation but also in an internal-world differentiation, in the setting up of the internal processes of intake, conversion, and output. Such internal processes help in turn to strengthen the boundary between the internal and external worlds and thereby to support the exercise of the leadership function of boundary control. The complication for leaders is that, like the psychoanalytic model of the ego, it has to be Janus-like, looking both internally and externally, becoming both the participant and observer. If the leader allows himself to become an observer gliding above the fray as a nonparticipant, he will deprive himself of knowledge of certain vital aspects of the group's activities. Hence, he will lose much of his evidence about the state of the group and especially the group's expectations with regard to his leadership. Indeed, there will be times when the only evidence available to him as to the state of the group's health will be his own personal experience of the group, what he feels the group is doing to him, and how he feels the group inside himself. Equally, of course, total immersion or loss of self in the group is destructive to leadership as a boundary function. It follows, too, that leadership has to act as a projection receptacle and to bear being used. (p. 352)

There is now relative agreement that clear evidence exists supporting the Balesian proposition that leadership is not the responsibility of one person in a group. Early studies of small groups (e.g., Bales 1953; 1965) reveal the distribution of roles over many persons. The organizational leadership literature at the macro level, however, seems not to have given much attention to this phenomenon (though see Rost 1991). Foster (1989) actually suggests that leadership:

is not a function of position but rather represents a conjunction of ideas where leadership is shared and transferred between leaders and followers, each only a temporary designation. Indeed, history will identify an individual as the leader, but in reality the job is one in which various members of the community contribute. Leaders and followers become interchangeable. (p. 49)

In recent years, there has arisen yet another "alleged" paradigm shift in the conceptualization of leadership. The transition has been described as a movement away from "transactional" leadership (Hollander & Julian 1970) to "transformational" leadership (Bennis & Nanus 1985). The former, according to Bass (1985; cf. March & Simon 1958 on "inducements and contributions"),

1. Recognizes what it is we want to get from our work and tries to see that we get what we want if our performance warrants it.

2. Exchanges rewards and promises of reward for our effort.

3. Is responsive to our immediate self-interests if they can be met by our getting the work done. (p. 7)

In contrast, the transformational leader leads:

1. By raising our level of awareness, our level of consciousness about the importance and value of designated outcomes, and ways of reaching them.

2. By getting us to transcend our own self-interest for the sake of the team, organization, or larger polity.

3. By altering our need level on Maslow's (or Alderfer's) hierarchy or expanding our portfolio of needs and wants. (p. 20)

While these prototypical aims and activities of the two types of leaders probably differentiate between effective and ineffective leaders in the long run, the approaches appear to place an excessive emphasis on the role of the formal leader *absent* the context in which that leader performs. In other words, it is essentially a revisionist perspective on the "great man" theory.

In point of fact, leadership responsibilities across the Parsonian or Jungian groupings can be (and are in Japan) widely shared both formally and informally. In contrast to transformational theories of leadership, which assert that leadership necessarily requires for subordinates a cognitive shift in ideology, a corporate identification and an increase in group-centered motivation, leadership in Japan involves many different kinds of responsibilities, not all of which are transformational. To a large degree, the very concept of transformational leadership is meaningless in Japanese organizations. Transformational leaders induce followers "to transcend personal self-interest for the betterment of the group or organization" (Keller 1992; cf. Bass 1985). However, since in Japan, workers' identity is already closely identified with the group or organization, such efforts by formal leaders would be redundant. There are, in fact, "substitutes for leadership" (Kerr & Jermier 1978) in the form of culture and socialization that perform these transformational activities. Thus, perhaps the most profound of leadership domains is shifted from a one-on-one hortatory effort on the part of the leader to the management of an organizational culture that substitutes for the individualized effort.

As will be discussed later, the recognition of the diversity of roles and role-takers in Japanese organizations reflects the Japanese division of family life into inside and outside dimensions, *uchi* and *soto* (Ishida 1984) remarked earlier, and the assignment of responsibility for instrumental and consummatory leadership to various family members. The conceptualizations of Kilmann and Herden which framed the research for this book embody these same inside-outside considerations.

## CANONICAL LEADERSHIP

Modern leadership theory has attempted to explain the variance in group effectiveness by analyzing separately the roles, dispositions, and behavior of *either* the formal or the informal leader vis-à-vis individual members of a group, particularly in the light of a variety of internal and external contingencies. Relatively little rigorous research attention has been paid, except by anecdotal report, to the conceptualization of leadership exercised by function across *multiple* formal and informal leaders and group members both individually and collectively. As Meindl (1993) notes,

Leaders and followers are creations that, for the most part, describe the informal aspects of their relationship; subordination describes their formal aspects. Leadership is an overlay that followers place onto an otherwise formally defined hierarchical relationship with the supervisor. The emergence of leadership, then, implies more than subordination: It represents an enrichment in the conceptualization of the relationship.

In the conceptual model for this book, the approach to leadership bridges the gap between the great man theories, which presume that transactional or charismatic transformational characteristics in leaders provide the prime impulse for change, motivation, and satisfaction, and both role theory and situational leadership (cf. Heine 1963). Role theory places leadership behavior within the constraints of externally imposed sent roles (namely, Goffman 1959), while situational leadership suggests that necessary and appropriate leadership behavior emerges informally within the group, not externally. This renders leadership as only one of many influences generated by a great many organizational variables (cf. Goodman, Ravlin, & Schminke 1990; Smith et al. 1994).

This is especially true in Japan. For the Japanese worker, leadership responsibilities are considerably more dispersed than in the United States. Indeed, as noted earlier, leadership has an entirely different meaning for the Japanese. Chie Nakane observes that in Japanese, there is no word signifying "leadership."

In the Japanese organizational setting, the needs for satisfaction of internal/external–instrumental/gratificatory prerequisites are conceived as roles to be played by different players. Since in Japan, however, the group is so closely knit and cohesive, the aggregation of individuals in a group actually comprises not a congeries of separate persons so much as a single entity, with a singular identity, collective ego, and set of affective dispositions. While to be sure, anthropomorphising an organization has its limits (Kets de Vries, to the contrary notwithstanding; cf. Nutt 1989), the conception of the organization in this way helps to explain more fully the leadership phenomenon, at least as practiced in Japan. The functions of leadership are carried out collectively. The ego is differentiated for formal distribution of roles, then integrated through harmonizing of the disparate parts. The distribution of leadership roles, as played out across both formal and informal organization, roughly corresponds to the rational and emotional parts of the psyche.

It is not only the leader, therefore, who is responsible for organizational success, but those other persons who fill the formal leader's gaps. As Sasaki (1981) notes:

Generally speaking, Japanese firms do not have individual leadership but group leadership. What is very important here is how individual "followership" is transformed into group leadership and through what organizational process individual passiveness is changed into collective activeness. (p. 65)

Moreover, it is the "fit" among the persons filling the leadership roles that is responsible for good, overall leadership. It is necessary both that all the requisite roles are filled, that they are filled well, and that the "chemistry" between or among the role incumbents, both formal and informal, permits the roles to be played with little conflict and/or easy conflict management. As Becker (1960) notes, "side bets" are placed with co-workers that stabilize the network of roles.

Some of this thinking is reflected in the work of H. Peter Dachler (1984), who urges a "refocussing of leadership from a social systems perspective of management." Dachler notes:

It is the central thesis here that the concepts of leadership and management are not crucially tied to given individuals who have been assigned such roles. Furthermore, what is being led or managed are not individuals, nor individual-productivity-related behaviors and attitudes; what is being led or managed are, instead, collectivities and social systems—very complex ones at that. (p. 102)

Dachler's point is that the focus of leadership should be the group and its dynamics, not the usual vertical dyadic linkages (VDL) found in many contemporary leadership theories (cf. Graen & Scandura 1987), however modified they may be by situational and other contingencies. This fundamental distinction is mirrored in the work of von Cranach (1986), who points out that leadership is the "allocation of important group action functions to certain positions in the group structure." Moreover, the fit among individual workers within the group, among formal leaders in that group, and across the two sets by individuals is what accounts for effectiveness. Thus a "canonical" conceptualization is necessary.

Since part of the very essence of Japan is the group, to see leadership as a simple or even complex transaction between hierarchically spaced individuals is to ignore a fundamental fact of Japanese (and probably all) organizations. All relationships in Japanese formal organizations are dominated by extremely fine status differentiations (*kata-gaki*) among workers. As discussed in Chapter 8 (cf.

Nakane 1988a), there are three main categories of relationships that the worker sees: *sempai* or seniors; *koohai* or juniors; and *dooryoo*, referring to colleagues of the same rank. The latter are further differentiated by distinctions according to age, year, or entry or graduation from school or colleges.

Nakane, on the other hand, sees much more importance in the role of the formal leader. She notes (Nakane 1988a): "He is both the holder of legitimate status and the outstanding personality, able to synthesize the members and suppress antagonisms among them. Even though a leader's absence from his men is only temporary, it may give rise to increased antagonisms among them." Thus, the preservation of harmony (*wa*) seems to be a central responsibility of the formal, hierarchical leaders, since it can not be managed by members of the *dooryoo*, who are in competition with one another for personal upward mobility. This suggests a more general observation that the distribution of leadership roles across members of the section is constrained not only by the availability of talent and skill, but by the interpersonal dynamics of the group itself. Certain roles *must* be played by certain persons regardless of their intellectual or other capabilities (or lack thereof) because harmony is so critical to group functioning. That is, the hierarchy of goals of the group gives priority to the preservation of the group *qua* group, even to the detriment of achievement. In Parsons' terms, latency and integration are superordinate prerequisites to goal attainment and adaptation. Leadership roles are distributed, then, first in accordance with internal, then as external considerations dictate. This prioritizing tends to force a distribution of the leadership roles that takes account of the incompatibility of the primary and secondary influence tactics. That the Japanese have been so extraordinarily successful in being externally adaptive suggests that the formal leader's release from the responsibility for internal stability allows him the broad and open perspective that cross-boundary activities permit. Further, the frequent rotation of workers across units is itself a means of attending to the adaptive and goal attainment prerequisites.

The underlying conceptualization for the research in this book relies heavily on a symbolic, interactionist perspective. It takes its starting point not from the framework of the roles of single persons (e.g., the formal leader) vis-à-vis the group, but the relationships among individuals in a group to each other and to the group. The tradition of "vertical dyad linkage research" (VDL) (Dansereau, Graen, & Haga 1983; Graen & Cashman 1975), in turn, derived from the larger framework of "social exchange theory" (Blau 1964; Homans 1958; Thibaut & Kelley 1959; Jacobs 1974; Hollander 1979), seems too narrow to provide parsimonious explanation of leadership effectiveness. This study does accept as legitimate and useful the past research showing (1) the dyadic connections between individuals (e.g., formal leader and subordinate), and (2) the relationships between individuals and the group as a whole (e.g., formal leader or informal leader and the membership of the group), particularly as each relationship plays some part in serving the functions of the group.

For example, different members of the group serve different leadership functions as the needs of the group demand. This study extends the conceptual framework by combining the two prior approaches. It looks first at the needs of the group, then at combinations of individuals, formal and informal, inside and outside, who serve those needs. In other words, this research abandons the quest for packages of individual traits and organizational contingencies that might be "matched" in order to foster group effectiveness in favor of an analysis of *collective* traits among a number of individuals as those *aggregated* traits may constitute the grounds for effective leadership. Hypothetically, only when a leadership team is symbiotically efficient *and* when the collective characteristics of the individuals making up the leadership group are matched against organizational contingencies will leadership be effective. Thus, sociometric analysis of the group is required to determine clusters of persons who display leadership roles. The diagram in Exhibit 12.1 illustrates.

The research adds one more element to the leadership equation. While there is much evidence in the literature of the effects of chief executive officers on the culture of the organization as a whole (Selznick 1957; Bass 1985), little research has been conducted on the leadership functions played by persons outside of the group. Officers higher or adjacent in the organizational hierarchy often have important relationships not only with the leaders of a group but with their subordinates. Once again, in this research the relationship itself is considered in terms of its *joint* effect on the group's functioning. That is, the dyadic or triadic relationships between outside persons and members of the group are examined first, prior to exploring the one-on-one or one-on-group relationships and effects.

Workers in this setting are involved in a number of relationships, both among themselves and with their leaders. On the assumption that different members of the group, especially the formal leaders, play different leadership roles vis-à-vis the workers, some of the potential relationships that might exist for a B Group worker are displayed in Exhibit 12.2.

## THE ORGANIZATION AS FAMILY AND THE LEADERSHIP OF FAMILIES

Culture plays a crucial role in the manifestations of leadership. As noted in Chapter 5, early conditioning in family life in Japan as well as in the United States predisposes the individual to expect and find satisfactions in work organizations that are similar to the family experience.

While the patterns of family relationships are changing somewhat in both countries, in Japan they are more stable and enduring than in the United States. How leadership roles are played out in organizations, then, invites an analysis using the family background as guide. Bennett and Ishino (1963, 34), among others, have remarked on the utility of this mode of inquiry, suggesting that the family as metaphor for organizational analysis is revealed in four ways: "(1) hierarchical relations between members, of which the father-son is the most

**Exhibit 12.1**
**Sample Primary Leader Relationships with and among Workers**

Dyadic Relationships

M and $WB_1$
SB and $WB_1$
ASB and $WB_1$
IL-B and $WB_1$
SA and $WB_1$
$TA_5$ and $WB_1$
$TA_1$ and $WB_1$

Leader-Group Relationships

M and SA, AS-A, $WA_1$, $WA_2$, etc.
IL-A and M, SA, $WA_1$, $WA_2$, etc.

Intra-Group Dyadic and Multiple Relationships

$WA_1$ and $WA_2$
$WA_2$ and $WA_3$, $WA_4$

Intra and Extra-Group Dyadic and Multiple Relationships

AS-A and AS-B, $WB_4$
SA and $WB_1$, $TA_5$

important; (2) emphasis on personal loyalty in terms of specified and reciprocal rights and duties, constituting obligatory patterns of *noblesse oblige*; (3) development of a body of ritual observances of these reciprocities; (4) development of a system of contractual arrangements between such groups, modeled on familial relationships.''

As was pointed out earlier, the Japanese organization is a surrogate family for working male adults, providing continuity of basic need satisfaction. The family, then, by virtue of its multiple and different personal relationships, serves to explain well how the organization's need for the Parsonian prerequisites of ''integration'' and ''pattern maintenance and tension reduction'' are met.

In childhood, for example, the mother sets up a dependency relationship with her children such that, absent a surrogate mother at work, the Japanese employee will experience great anxiety. So also, the father in the Japanese family plays roles of disciplinarian and role model, among others. Equally important, he displays a style of interaction and control that profoundly affects the expectations of leadership by the worker in the employment situation. Taking the place of brothers in the family are employees in the same cohort group who are more or less equal (*doryoo*), though other marks of higher or lower status such as age, just as in the family, invariably create distinctions. Thus, the conditioning that began in childhood (see Chapters 4 and 5) continues in the organization

**Exhibit 12.2**
**Hypothetical Relationships among Supervisors and Subordinates**

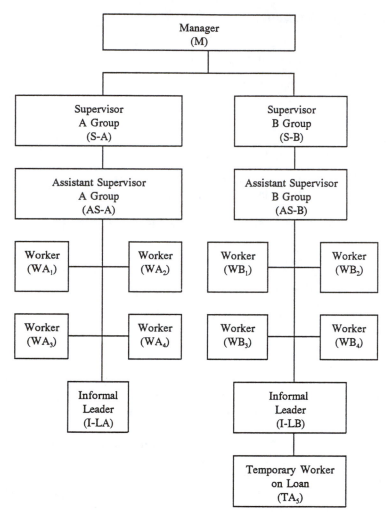

Note the similarities between this scheme and the discussion of the Hitachi small group organization in Davidson (1984).

where the Japanese worker is led to expect a continuation of the familial roles to which he is accustomed. Organizational leadership roles that address individual affect/emotion in others, rather than individual, group, or organizational productivity, are played out, therefore, in ways that allay anxieties and satisfy the most elemental needs of the Japanese worker. In contrast to the American worker, whose independence is greater and whose ego for many reasons is not so closely bound to organizational success, the Japanese worker's orientation toward his leader demands additional leader behaviors.[1] This is not, of course, to say that American leaders do not play father and mother roles in their organizations, especially in ones that are small and paternalistic. It is, however, to suggest that these role behaviors are subdued and usually subordinated to other expected behaviors in the American setting. Though the Ohio State studies may have distinguished between consideration and initiating structure and found empirical evidence that they both exist, the image of Western leadership connotes much more of the latter. Leadership generally conveys a machismo ideal of strong, assertive, even oppressive, behavior with short-term, pragmatic desired outcomes, usually relating to the financial bottom line. Indeed, even when "consideration" is the behavior, it is applauded more when the "leader" initiates it. Though Blau (1964, 70) observes that American managers frequently employ "strategic leniency" in exercising leadership, leading to the misapprehension of the leader as ineffectively utilizing his authority, in point of fact, this mode of behavior is still an aggressive posture. The flexibility in enforcement of the rules is a requisite mode of social interaction between leader and led that establishes and maintains the leader's authority. As will be seen, social interactions of a quite different sort enable the Japanese leader to exert considerable leadership influence. Matsushita (1975) notes, the leader who produces *shuchi* (the wisdom of many) "must be the one who can listen to the greatest number of opinions, and he must keep his own viewpoint while he thinks out good ways of offering opinions to the group or of putting their opinions together" (p. 43).

When the authority of the father and the succorance of the mother in the Japanese family are examined in their manifestations in the Japanese organization, an apparently anomalous phenomenon is revealed. Japanese workers *appear* to have wrested much of the authority for decisions from the formal leader qua father. And much of the responsibility for care and consideration seems to have been shifted from the formal organization to members of the peer group. Coincidentally, Knowles and Saxberg (1971, 140 ff.) suggest that family roles (at least in the United States) are changing such that "subordinates" (i.e., children) have come to have a much more powerful role in decision making. Further, the informal organization of the family has always reflected the individual capacity and capability of its various members, the demands of various situations, and the mutual arrangements and agreements for the proper functioning and survival of the family unit and the support of its individual members. Thus, the intelligent wife and mother has probably always exercised leadership far beyond the rights provided her by law. Similarly, sons and daughters who have been endowed with superior intellects or provided with the opportunity for advanced education assume leadership in particular instances (pp. 141–142).

In point of fact, both of these observations are misleading. While certainly not always the case in earlier times (Befu 1980), the Japanese company today continues to accept and exercise ultimate responsibility for both productivity and care of the employees, though the roles are shared both hierarchically and laterally. That is, though there is an appearance of organizational democracy, and unionization seems on occasion to be powerful, workers in Japan have not taken on more leadership roles, nor more power, than heretofore. The structure of the shared decision-making model attends manifestly to the adaptation and goal attainment prerequisites, and in latent form to the integration and pattern maintenance and tension reduction roles. The structure of the organizational values and formal hierarchy does the reverse, through its paternalism dealing manifestly with internal prerequisites and in latent form to external concerns.

"Paternalism" as a concept, especially when applied to leadership in Japan, has come under some skeptical criticism, largely because of the ambiguity or/ and multiplicity of its meanings. McGown (1980) suggests seven major characteristics of paternalism that can be used to explore the concept in the Japanese organization:

1. Obligations of the organization are more than simple payment of wages.

2. Employees normatively agree to be dependent on the organization. They willingly engage in the relationship.

3. There is an expectation of a quid pro quo exchange of loyalty in exchange for caring by the organization.

4. Employer and employee see their interests as common.

5. External agents (e.g., unions) to mediate the relationship are not necessary.

6. The organization provides most or all of the services required by the employee.

7. It is an ideology that is adapted to serve management's long-term interests: it does not exist for its own sake.

A major difficulty in understanding the application of paternal modes of leadership lies in reconciling it with bureaucratic principles of control that appear to prevail (cf. Hamilton & Sanders 1992, 10ff). Paternalism in its face-to-face applications relies on particularistic interpersonal relationships, whereas bureaucracy is based on universalistic application of rules. The unraveling of this conundrum in Japan stems from the worker's complete identification with the organization, such that aid to another worker is conceived of (and felt as) aid to self. (For one classic definition of the cathectic aspects of "identification," see Parsons & Shils 1951.) Moreover, inasmuch as involvement in decision making is so completely decentralized in Japanese organizations, responsibility (both real and perceived) is shared among many. So also is blame for failure and its concomitant, the application of negative sanctions. In short, the formal leader, qua father, in Japan, has little of the formal "authority" of the father, but much of the psychological power of the father figure. Indeed, as in Freudian psychology, the transference of identity from mother to father (in the West, at least) is accompanied by the developing sense in the child of a capacity to master reality, that is, to make decisions for himself (cf. Freud 1989). While in the West, the feeling of competition with the father that arises in the child eventually results in an increase in freedom of the child from the parent as he "has to repress, renounce, or sublimate (his) impulses in response to the leadership of his parents" (Hill 1984), such change does not for the most part take place in Japan. The adult Japanese carries with him into maturity a residue of respect for and fear of the father which he transfers to his organizational leaders. Importantly, however, although the latter possess but are generally reluctant to exercise negative sanctions openly, their hold over workers must rely almost exclusively on charismatic influence processes. These are fiercely supported by peer norms that hold to the importance of respect for authority. That is, fear of peer disapproval, more than formal authority, engenders obedience among subordinates. In addition, the resentment of and/or alienation from the leader that is found among American workers for whom the power asymmetry is onerous and counter to egalitarian norms is absent in Japan. More on this later.

## TRANSACTIONAL ANALYSIS AND JAPANESE MANAGEMENT

While there have been some cautions expressed about the dangers of overusing the family as a metaphor for understanding the dynamics of interpersonal relationships in Japanese organizations, as has been shown, there are some quite compelling reasons to do so. In the first place, as reported in Chapter 3, there can be no argument that the Japanese culture as a whole is strongly rooted in the traditions of family life (cf. Hsu 1975). As in other cultures, the young Japanese is imprinted early with patterns of interaction in the family. In the Japanese setting, however, these relationships are less subject to idiosyncratic or individual family interpretation. The rules are well-known and immutable. The young Japanese person comes not only to obey them, but to see them as a source of predictability and stability in his life. In some other cultures, of course, as young persons move through adolescence and early adulthood, there is a pattern of rebellion against both the rules and the individuals exercising them. Indeed, it is claimed that the rebellion is functional for the freeing of the individuality that lies latent in each person. In recent years, the emergence of "adolescence" as a distinct stage of growth has had to be recognized by observers of Japanese youth, as changing patterns of behavior reveal underlying proclivities to become separate from parents.

Nevertheless, in Japan, because of the characteristic need for "dependence" severely imprinted in early years (see previous chapters and Doi 1973), it is important for the Japanese worker to continue the interpersonal style and, indeed, pattern of relationships established so firmly in childhood.[2] Hence, it is critical that his organization create surrogate parents or parent roles. Whereas prior to the Meiji Restoration, the vast majority of organizations were family owned and staffed with family members, with the industrial revolution and modernization period, larger and more bureaucratic organizations evolved. Despite this, the Japanese organization continued its historical reliance on family roles, though in different economic sectors the roles are played out somewhat differently (Bennett & Ishino 1963). Thus, in the organization today will be found the equivalents of father, mother, uncles and aunts, grandparents, and elder and younger siblings. There are unwritten rules guiding his relationship to each of these roles. Hsu (1975, 125) describes this as a "controlled diffuseness rather than unfettered diffuseness."

[A]lthough the scope of Japanese life patterns (including language) is wide and full of incongruities, the actual tasks for various individuals are extremely specific, and very clearly designed and executed. There is no evidence of diffuseness in them.

This is not to say, of course, that the playing of the roles is invariant across individuals, that is, that every act is as prescribed as a tea ceremony. It is to indicate, however, that at the formal level of interaction in the Japanese firm, the role relationships are powerfully communicated, though with utmost subtlety. Violations of the order of interaction are sanctioned negatively, though since the early imprinting is so strong, the Japanese are often able to walk through the role playing without consciousness of the need to fulfill expectations. They do not "play" the role; they act existentially. Their behavior and behavior predispositions based on role preparation are isomorphic.

To understand the dynamics of the leadership process, then, it is important to see how it is carried out within the context of family-like role relationships. As has been stressed throughout this book, the leadership role is distributed widely across many persons in the Japanese organization. The relationships of various leaders to followers or groups of each take two forms—one a dyadic, the other person-to-group. In the first instance, individuals establish over time the roles they occupy vis-à-vis one another and act out those roles as they carry out their organizational duties. In the second instance, the leader relates not only to each individual, but to the group as a whole, much as the Japanese teacher in elementary and secondary schools more frequently than not establishes a relationship between herself and the pupils as a whole, rather than between herself and each individual. Further, as there are multiple leaders in Japanese organizations, multiple patterns of relationships emerge. This flexibility or fluidity of pattern further permits the adoption by different persons of the leader roles required for the satisfaction of the functional prerequisites noted in the Parsons/Kilmann and Herden theory. As Tyler (1993) and Tyler and Lind (1992) note, a group-generated need for authority emerges in most groups in response to individual needs for status in the group. The latter is accorded by the leader's behavior toward each member. When leadership in the group is shared, this translates into a search for the security of known group status from others within the group.

Dyadic relationships in Japanese groups vary combinatorily and canonically with the number of role relationships possible—primarily husband/wife, mother/son, father/son, brother/brother, and secondarily grandfather/son (cf. Hsu 1965, 88 ff.). To understand the various relationships, it is helpful to invoke parts of the theory of Eric Berne (see his *Transactional Analysis in Psychotherapy,* 1961, particularly as informed by Mitroff's integration of the theory with the Jungian typology (see Mitroff 1983; Chapter 5). It is most important to note here that while the theory of interpersonal relationships that Berne developed was intended as a tool for clinical diagnosis of individuals, the theory is being used here to unravel the complexities of *role* relationships as they exist in the Japanese firm. In other words, the emphasis here is on categories of relationships among roles, not on people playing those roles.

In the context of research and development groups, the complexity of these relationships is reflected in the stylistic variations among research scientists, for example, zealot, initiator, diagnostician, scholar, artificer, esthetician, methodologist, and independent (Gough & Woodworth 1960).

A cautionary note is necessary here. Some might argue that the Japanese individual lacks ego strength and that genetically Japanese people are less emotional. In point of fact, however, both are far from true. The Japanese have just as intense particularistic drives, needs for achievement, pleasures in accomplishment, disappointments in failure, as well as all-embracing *Weltanschauung* and/or angst. The difference between American and Japanese egos is that the latter are engaged with the larger organization. For the Japanese person, there is less difference between his own ego and that of his organization personified (cf. Aron et al. 1991). He identifies with it and with its workers. A sense of the common suffuses the organization. The Japanese person is often unable to differentiate himself from the organization as a whole and from others in it, insofar as organizational matters are concerned (cf. Borland 1988).

As Berne notes, each person retains in the adult psyche three ego states that represent "real people who now exist or who once existed" (1961, 32). These states are Parent, Adult, and Child. Moreover, Berne states:

1. That every grown-up individual was once a child.

2. That every human being with sufficient functioning brain-tissue is potentially capable of adequate reality testing.

3. That every individual who survives into adult life has had either functioning parents or someone in loco parentis.


Each individual installs one or more of these ego states in each interaction with another. Since the other party independently also invokes an ego state, there is a "transaction" between the individuals. While each state may be utilized by any individual, it is common for one to be dominant, another recessive, and the third seldom employed. In Western society, Berne asserts, one of the states may be captive of the others, preventing healthy utilization of the others in appropriate situations. Thus, a Parent may so dominate one person's psyche that he can not act out a childlike role when circumstances call for it.

Berne suggests that each of the three psychic states comprises two forms. One form of The Parental ego state, for example, is manifested usually in a "prejudicial" form—essentially a set of attitudes and behaviors which express prohibitions to actions of others. The second is a "nurturing" form, manifested as sympathy for others. The behaviors accompanying these states can be either culturally syntonic or culturally dystonic, that is, can corroborate and be corroborated by the culture (here, read organizational norms *and* national culture)—or the reverse, that is, can be disconfirmed by them. In the Japanese organization, the formal leader qua Parent/father (*buchoo* or *oyabun hada*) is almost invariably in a nurturing rather than prejudicial form, whether the leader is in a dyadic relationship or is dealing with the group as a whole (cf. Smith 1983, 60 ff.). Indeed, as noted earlier, in the light of the emerging "transformative leader" conceptualizations (e.g., Bass 1985), the paternalism of the Japanese formal leader can be read as parent-child relationships but with the leader seen as symbolically coincident with the organization as a whole. The formal leader, that is, communicates the paternalism of the organization and reinforces the subordinate's commitment to the group, that is, beyond the personal, egocentric level.

It should not be understood that the formal leader always acts as Parent. Bergen (1990), for example, suggests that different elements of Parent, Adult, and Child emerge depending on the levels of maturity of the subordinates encountered (e.g., over the Hersey-Blanchard [1988] cycle). In the "telling" phase, for example, the leader subordinate can be characterized as a P-C transaction. Certainly, the Japanese will on occasion have psychic clashes among the ego states. This is only to suggest that the function of leaders vis-à-vis the other individuals or the group is most efficiently performed when the leader acts out his Parent role in its appropriate form, that is, that form that is supported by the culture and that allows the subordinate to respond in a "complementary" way. Pascale and Athos (1981 216 ff.) note that the manner of interaction between individuals follows the *sempai-kohai* structure. But it is often the case that the leader will astutely ascertain his subordinates' strengths and, by revealing his own weaknesses, invite those subordinates' strengths to be utilized in the leadership role. Indeed, the role of the delegating leader in the Hersey-Blanchard model presupposes a Western type of maturity among subordinates that does not exist in Japan. There is never complete delegation, though it may appear to exist. Japanese leaders are often admired for behaviors that are outwardly meek and tractable (*sunao*), since that attitude is necessary to elicit the latent wisdom of the group (*shuchi*). The *sunao* mind includes love and openness, with a desire to seek truth (Matsushita 1975, 43 ff.).

The role of Parent in its "prejudicial" form rests primarily with the second in command (*nyobu yaku*) and with the peer group. (For a Western view of this symbiotic relationship, see Krantz 1989, on the "managerial couple.") That is, the sanctioning component is split away from the formal leader so that he personally and on behalf of the organization can be more nurturant. The *nyobu yaku* is not merely a specialized role (*semmon shoku*), but rather has more general skills, some of a management nature, others more interpersonal. He is chosen by the *buchoo* in consultation with the peers of the *buchoo*, rather than being "elected" by workers. Though the *nyobu yaku* is translated loosely as "wife role," in this case the appellation refers to the more mechanical details of management rather than to the softer ministrations of mother to child. These latter are handled by the *buchoo* himself. Both *buchoo* and *nyobu yaku*, then, are outside of the task group but provide important leadership roles with respect both to the group as a whole and to each worker. Their activities run the range of internal and external requirements, but the existence of the *nyobu yaku* frees up the *buchoo* not only to perform the leadership rather than management roles but to spend more time and give more attention to concerns beyond the borders of the group.

## LEADERSHIP COMMUNICATION STYLES

If leadership comprises many roles and is spread across many persons, the question arises as to whether and how the behaviors in the leadership episodes are different. If the history of the Ohio State studies tells us anything, it is that there are important behavioral differences in manifested leadership (leaving aside for the moment the question of effectiveness). Personality trait theory also reveals that subtleties of leadership behavior exist. For example, there is reason to believe that Fiedler's findings of differences in behavior across high and low LPC leaders are real. The premise of the research for this book, as outlined in Chapter 2 explicating the conceptual framework, is that leadership traits are manifested in distinctive behaviors, and that these trait/behavior combinations can, along with conflict management modes, account for differences in subordinate motivation, productivity, and satisfaction.

It is helpful, therefore, to return at this point to a discussion of the viability of trait theory and to the special ways in which in Japan leadership traits may be carried out in behavior. Beginning with a discussion of personality traits, the argument will be made that the trait of "charismatic" leadership exists in Japan but that its behavioral manifestations differ significantly from the behavior so labeled in American organizations. For example, whereas in this country, charisma (in the Weberian sense) is usually associated with leadership demonstrated in rather dramatic organizational change, in Japan charismatic leadership prevails over the more stable daily decisions of organizational life. It does not shift, as Weber suggested, to other forms of organizational authority, nor is it seen as "a necessary antidote to the increasing bureaucratization of society" (Hunt 1984). The view here is undergirded with the perspective of "symbolic interactionism" (cf. Cooley 1909, 1983; Mead 1934) as the foundation of the expression of Japanese leadership. Thus, to use the words of Sonja Hunt (1984), one can view leadership as the "processes of transaction, interaction, and negotiation as moves in a perpetual drama which defines, confirms, and maintains for both audience and participants the conventions of the social world." The Japanese leader creates and maintains a reality for the worker that sustains and confirms his view of his organization. Since the leader is the personification of that organization, the leader and the organization are joined. Both leader and organization blend the characteristics of familial roles and express those roles in interactions with workers that perpetuate the shared perceived reality. Moreover, as attribution theorists point out, the follower has an implicit view of what kinds of behaviors are appropriate to the leadership roles to be played (cf. Calder

1977). The path to desired goals, to borrow yet another theoretical paradigm (cf. Locke & Latham 1990) is constrained by the subordinate's set of acceptable, legitimate leadership behaviors. As will be seen, disrupting this mutual reinforcement of leader and follower in order to achieve creative change, either in organization or R & D product innovation, thus becomes supremely difficult.

As noted earlier, leaders are groomed in early career, and the best are selected by superiors but with the complete endorsement of peers. Thus, there are personal traits or characteristics that appear to be desirable in leaders. As these become evident in the course of the early career, would-be leaders are promoted.

It was noted above that leadership responsibilities are spread across many individuals and across the group as a whole. Thus, it may be assumed that many leaders have many interpersonal relationships, both with fellow leaders and with followers, and that followers have many relationships, both with leaders and with co-workers who are followers (cf. Rost 1991, 109–112). Also, it may be assumed that followers also assume the role of Parent or Child when the occasion demands it (cf. Podsakoff 1982).

At this point, let us consider only the dyadic relationship between leader and follower, recognizing (with Rost) that the dyadic focus should not be construed to represent the entirety of the influence process of leadership. The general role of follower in a dyadic hierarchical relationship (as differentiated from his decision-making role vis-à-vis his own peers or subordinates) is dominated in the Japanese firm by the Child ego state. As Berne notes, these "feelings, attitudes and behavior patterns . . . are relics of the individual's own childhood" (1961, 77). Further:

The Child is exhibited in one of two forms. The *adapted* Child is manifested by behavior which is inferentially under the dominance of the Parental influence, such as compliance or withdrawal. The *natural* child is manifested by autonomous forms of behavior such as rebelliousness or self-indulgence.

The Japanese worker, in his hierarchical relationships, tends most often to assume the ego state of the adapted Child. Indeed, as was pointed out earlier, it is a major concern of Japanese firms that the natural Child is repressed, with a concomitant reduction in creativity.

The general role of peer is manifested in Japanese firms through the role of Adult. For Berne, it is the function of the Adult to process information that can be most efficiently used by the individual. As Bennett (1976) notes: "The Adult ego state . . . functions like a computer. It is used for processing data, estimating probabilities, and making decisions as a basis for action." Whereas the Parent is rigid and judgmental, enforcing the standards of others, and the prelogical Child reacts on the basis of distorted archaic sentiments, the Adult computes present-time information into decisions (p. 21). The fact that the worker acts out his Parent and Child interactions in hierarchical relationships frees both him and his superordinate to pursue their Adult roles through peers. Thus, the extended time spent in *nemawashi* and the *ringei* system are tied not only to the workers' needs to maintain the coherence and integrity and esprit of the group (*wa*), but are related to the Adult role prescribed for peer relationships in the Japanese firm.

The family manifested in the Japanese firm is reflected in the concept of *iemoto*. As described by Hsu (1975), *iemoto* refers to hierarchical arrangements that are institutionalized to achieve a set of common objectives. The central characteristic of *iemoto* is the master-disciple relationship. Hsu (1975, 63) notes that the relationship is one of teacher to learner. The leader in Japan, then, sees his role at least in part as supportive and developmental, rather than directive. As noted earlier, it is manifested in extremely subtle behaviors:

The central core of teaching is *haragei* (literally, abdomen technique) through which the disciple learns not by receiving explicit instructions but by unconscious imitation of the master. The instruction is often secretive and frequently given orally so that the position of the master retains its superiority and mystery. (Hsu 1975, 63)

And:

The master's obligation to promote the disciple professionally and the disciple's obligation to serve the master faithfully are mutual. This "return value relationship" (*taika ankei*) is a very real relationship and cannot be dissolved. These mutual obligations, like the obligation between fathers and sons, are not quantifiable and there are therefore no limits, though the master will not, of course, make extra-legal demands on the disciples. (Hsu 1975, 64)

Further discussion of these subtle communications will be considered later, but first, it is necessary to reflect on the place of personality and charisma in leadership in Japan.

## PERSONALITY AND CHARISMA

Since the subordinates in the Japanese R & D setting are homogeneous by virtue of common Japanese ancestry and acculturation and because of the careful recruitment policies and procedures of each firm, contingency approaches to leadership which suggest that leader behavior must be modified to be appropriate to the needs of the situation need not be considered. To take issue somewhat with the situationist perspective on leadership, the "situation" in Japan is more constant, or at least highly predictable (cf. Schneider 1990). What affects group or organizational productivity and innovation, then, is more likely to come from the initiative of the leader—or as has been maintained throughout this book—from multiple leaders. Since leadership is spread across both functions and persons, there are opportunities for different kinds of personalities to occupy the varying posts. Job rotation across posts, of course, assumes that the individual is adaptive and not dominated by personality constraints that make him better at one position than another. In Japan, however, such rotation results more in maintaining and enhancing group solidarity, commitment, and improved access to and sharing of information than in the betterment of leadership.

Different leader behaviors are required, then, to meet the needs of the varying leader roles to be played. Different personality dispositions, further, will permit those roles to be played to maximum advantage and will better facilitate the acting out of the complementary follower roles. Idiosyncratic leader behavior which is either too far afield or too long in duration will exceed the idiosyncrasy credits (Hollander 1979) that the leader has acquired. In Japan, idiosyncrasy credits are limited by the strong constraints on deviant behavior and by the proscriptions against persistent, individualistic activity that violates social norms or accepted practice. Hence, the leader whose ideas are, indeed, unusual must find ways to express those ideas in extremely subtle ways. Anomalous as it seems, personality itself is a fundamental constituent of leadership in a Japanese society whose culture degrades its expression! Hence, the leadership responsibilities that call for paternal or maternal behaviors in support of group or individual maintenance or enhancement are easier for the Japanese leader to play. These activities can be modeled on traditional family role behavior.

By now it is commonplace for observers of the evolution of leadership literature (e.g., Weiss & Adler 1990; Hunt 1991, 106–107) to remark that Stogdill's famous denigration (later partially recanted) of the utility of personality traits in leadership theory overemphasized the "situation." The return to personality as a source of explanation for effective leadership promises to bring new insights into the sources of the complicated behaviors that comprise leadership.[3] As noted above, in Japan, where the internal organizational "situation" is usually relatively stable and where individualistic expression is suppressed, an examination of personality traits will reveal important clues to the more subtle aspects of leadership (Monson, Hesley, & Chernick 1982). These subtleties are useful to analyze, since even in the presence of situational mediators, as in the United States, they speak to the expression of leadership. Thus, for purposes of explanation here, the use of personality as a variable in this study looks to the "direct effects" on relevant dependent variables, ignoring (if admittedly somewhat oversimplifying) other approaches to research design—mechanistic interaction, reciprocal effects, and dynamic, and so on.

The construct of personality can be defined in a number of ways. As Weiss and Adler (1990) note: "Personality traits come in all sizes and shapes. Some relate to cognitive styles, some relate to motivational principles. Some constructs in use are well developed. Others are poorly conceptualized." Here, it is broadly employed to connote a persistent disposition over different conditions to behave in ways that can be reasonably predictable by outside observers (notwithstanding the methodological difficulties of measuring what is "predictable"). That is, personality as used here means the mental trait or set of traits that appear(s) to be the source of behavior that others in the role set can count on with some degree of certainty. As will be seen in later chapters that report on the empirical data from Japan, there are a surprising number of clusters of traits of leaders that differ from those found in this country. These lead further to behaviors that are also different.

Personality theory as embodied in current studies of leadership, either as a trait or a behavior, utilizes an adjacent or overlapping concept—"charisma." And while no effort was made directly to measure charisma or its behavioral concomitants in Japan, because of its importance in the literature today, a discussion here will be illuminating.

As Trice and Beyer (1991) note, a crucial issue in the examination of the place of charisma in leadership is how to separate its unique qualities from other personality characteristics. This issue becomes even more complicated in a cross-cultural context, since what is charismatic in the United States may not be charismatic elsewhere, and the reverse.

It is impossible, of course, to consider charisma without giving proper recognition to the foundational interpretations of Max Weber (1947). Weber saw charisma as a form of authority, a mode of inducing compliance among followers. In contrast to traditional authority, which has its basis in subordinates' beliefs in the legitimacy of inherited status and rights, and to rational-legal authority, which stems from the belief of employees in the rights of status and command accruing to offices in an organizational hierarchy, charismatic authority engenders obeisance and obedience through the willingness of subordinates to suspend their judgment and to identify with the goals and projected rewards of a person who may or may not be formally vested with either of the first two bases of authority. Weber viewed charismatic authority as transitory, at best overlapping with its possessor, and subject to encroachments from institutionalization of rules and procedures of the systems that the charismatic person invites, however unintentionally (Trice and Beyer 1991).

The traits of charisma are varied and for the most part still under heavy empirical review. Schwartz (1983), for example, suggests that George Washington's retiring leadership style could hardly be called charismatic in the terms usually used to define it. It is important to note, however, that presidential charisma exercised in a political arena is quite different from the face-to-face charisma considered in this study. House, Spangler, and Woycke (1991), for example, in discussing presidential charisma, define it as ''the ability of a leader to exercise diffuse and intense influence over the beliefs, values, behavior, and performance of others through his or her own behavior, beliefs, and personal example.'' Here, we consider not distant, a personal, political or routinized charisma but ''pure'' charisma that must be earned and rearned through continual face-to-face interaction. It is this relationship, at the dyadic level, that involves both leader and led in a psychological exchange. Graen and Scandura (1987) suggest that this process requires that both leader and follower offer and withdraw emotional investments as the relationship changes and matures. In contrast with the pattern in the United States where CEOs spend time with subordinates in short spurts, in Japan, the interpersonal interactions are of significant lengths (Doktor 1990), allowing the emotional investments to be nurtured and to mature.

## INFLUENCE AS LEADERSHIP

Accepting the hypothesis above that leadership roles are widely distributed, and that leaders with different personalities occupy those roles, there still remains some question about the actual behavior exercised by the various role incumbents. The concept of leadership in Western society is commonly thought to be an "influence" process—an effective leader being one who is best able to affect the goal choices and commitment to them of subordinates—even, by the way, if that means a continuation of goals, methods, and decision processes that have been successful in the past. The object of influence is both cognitive and affective, depending, in part, on which organizational prerequisite is being addressed. For example, tension reduction organizational needs manifested in individuals call for more leader attention to affective goals. As will be seen, in Japan, the leadership traits and behaviors associated with each functional prerequisite are quite different.

Influence can be wielded in many ways, ranging from physical coercion to inducements to subtle, if not subliminal, persuasion (Gamson 1968). Donohue (1985) explains various interactions between leader and follower that include the following: distance work, coherence or sense-making work, and structuring work, each of which has important effects on control, trust, and intimacy of the subordinate group. Perceptions and interpretations of these and the exchange of emotional investments noted above enter both consciously and unconsciously into the decision-making options of leaders and subordinates.

Effective leaders, then, have both the capacity and the desire to make a difference in the lives of their subordinates. They want to control behaviors in ways that appear to the leader to be related to the leader's own goals (cf. Locke & Latham 1990), even, to be sure, if those very goals are to empower subordinates to maximize their autonomy and/or satisfaction. What is not entirely clear, despite many years of extensive research, are the special modes by which influence or control is expressed for the purpose of affecting subordinate, peer, or superordinate cognition and affect.

Before going on, it will be useful to summarize the several theoretical perspectives expostulated above to explain leadership in Japan:

1. Leadership is distributed among many participants.

2. Some of these participants may be outside of the formal organization.

3. Some of the participants may be formally vested with leadership responsibility; others act informally.

4. Leadership is exercised in many directions—upward, laterally, and downward.

5. Leadership is addressed both *to* individuals and collectivities of individuals *by* both individuals and collectivities of individuals.

6. Leadership responsibilities may be directed toward internal conditions or across boundaries.

7. Leadership attention is paid to a variety of organizational functions—indeed, must be paid to the exhaustive set of organizational prerequisites, including adaptation, goal attainment, integration and latency (AGIL).

8. The influence behaviors of leadership are aimed at both cognitive and affective change.

9. Leaders adopt a truth-seeking, receptive persona to elicit information and wisdom
   from the group.

These principles appear to be especially valid when one looks at leadership
cross-culturally. By way of introduction of this complication, it may be pointed
out that control of another person's behavior in a Western sense makes the
important assumption that there are, indeed, two separate people whose egos are
in some way different from, yet related to one another. On the other hand, in
Eastern settings such as Japan, an assumption is often made that in working
relationships, both parties to a relationship may become one (cf. Buber 1970).
As Weisz, Rothbaum, and Blackburn (1984) note, the method of control exerted
can best be understood in terms of important cultural differences. Westerners,
they point out, tend to see themselves as individuals who can shape their own
lives through assertive behavior, which they call "primary control" (cf. Thomas
& Kilmann 1974). Those who can not or do not exert such control are labeled,
often derogatively, as passive or helpless in Western society. Thus, organizational conflict is born at least in part of the clash of individuals over the power
to control their own and others' lives, with elites typically winning out. Prior
and anticipatory socialization further passify the worker (Argyris 1957; Seligman 1991) into yielding authority and responsibility to upper echelons. Thus,
"leaders" in Western society gradually come to see themselves as having the
potential, if not the responsibility, to control others, while followers tend to
believe that others can and should control their lives.

Weisz, Rothbaum, and Blackburn suggest that the same behavior in Japanese
society calls for an alternative explanation because of the cultural context. As
they note: "In secondary control, individuals attempt to align themselves with
existing realities, leaving them unchanged but exerting control over their personal psychological impact." The evidence reviewed by Rothbaum et al. (1982)
indicates that on some occasions people really do relinquish control, but on
many other occasions, people pursue control. Sometimes they try to gain primary
control by being assertive or aggressive in an effort to enhance their individualism and autonomy. But at other times, they strive for secondary control, accepting as inevitable such organizational realities as hierarchy, power, and
disagreeable working conditions. By doing so, in effect they are *gaining* internal,
emotional rather than external control over their lives. Perhaps most important,
this psychological acceptance of the inevitable provides the Japanese with a
sense of certainty and continuity. Indeed, the structure of Japanese society and,
in microcosm, business organizations, replaces the anxiety of indeterminism
with the stability of predictability (cf. Dewey 1929). The tranquility of inner
acceptance, especially when culturally reinforced, is easier to deal with than
either oppression or ambiguity. The cost, however, may be a loss in the personal
risk taking and creativity necessary for collective advancement. The gain to the
individual may be the loss of the group of externally validated worth.

Two consequences follow for the understanding of leadership generally, and especially in Japanese society. First, secondary control is practiced by both leaders and followers. That is, the leader and the led yield to one another and to the "system" and join together psychologically to identify organizational goals—in terms both of group achievement and group pattern maintenance and tension reduction—as mutually desirable. As Katovich (1987) notes, interactants initially engage in transactions that utilize "instrumental identities," that allow a smooth flow of interaction based on mutual interpretations and habits of relationships of the past. The interactants also employ "categorical identities" that take advantage of ascriptive labels to define the context of the situated action. The nature of the exchanges then proceeds in ways that allow interactants to "program their futures so as to construct a structure to their transactions. This enables them to make sense of their activity as directed toward some common goal or set of goals. Interactants then share these futures as they announce and coordinate identities and resolve their transactions."

The imagined or real and the internalized or revealed congruence of these enacted futures determines whether the interaction is terminated or placed on hold, pending further clarification. It is in this context of some degree of ambiguity that leadership takes place. The practice of "influence" by leaders, then, becomes a marginal move away from the collective oneness. Too great a deviation from the apparent consensus is a threat to that oneness (cf. Hollander's "idiosyncrasy credit" notions). As a result, influence is sometimes exerted through "back door" primary control (Kojima 1984)—through extremely subtle means that ensure the image of status quo maintenance or enhancement but are really attempts at primary, not secondary control.

The subtlety of the expression of influence and the measurement of intention often make it difficult to see which of the forms is intended. Japanese society as a whole and Japanese organizations in particular are suffused with ambiguity while at the same time marked by social and economic structural certainties. As contradictory as that may appear, it is characteristic of the Japanese that both can be accepted, though not without some difficulty. Whereas in the United States ambiguity is often associated with uncertainty, anxiety, and wasted energy (Baum 1985), in Japan, such is not usually the case. As Frost (1987) notes, there is an "ingrained vagueness" in Japan engendering much nonverbal communication which, as will be seen, is quite functional. Frost continues: "As one might expect in a culture that values intuition and sensitivity to human feeling, communication between individuals is characterized by ambiguous language, nonverbal signals, and silence" (p. 86). In many ways, Frost further reports, Japanese communication styles might be considered by Western observers as "feminine" in sensibility (p. 88). Although in the United States highly successful women chief executives are often indistinguishable from men (since to achieve that position, they were called upon to exhibit male leadership characteristics), there is a tendency, at least by self-report, to engage in a more interpersonally interactive style of leadership (Rosener 1990, though see also Adler 1988). Bass (1991) also notes that women tend to engage more in "transactional leadership"—involving subordinates in a redirection and recommitment of energies. Nonverbal communication seems to be the sine qua non of leadership behavior in Japan, regardless of the person who performs it or the function being served by it.

## NONVERBAL COMMUNICATION

Communication skills in management have long been the subject of management development programs. Typically, these involve rather pedestrian notions about clarity and directness of communication and sensitivity to the receiver. Relatively little attention has been paid to nonverbal forms of communication by leaders rather than managers, and still less has been reported about the communication of charisma.

It has been estimated that "between 60 and 65 percent of the meaning in a social situation is communicated nonverbally" (Burgoon 1985). Though not all will be discussed, the following are some classes of nonverbal behavior that may be said to exist (Burgoon 1985):

1. Kinesics—observable bodily movements
2. Vocalics—sounds other than words
3. Physical appearance—manipulable features, such as dress
4. Haptics—touch
5. Proxemics—interpersonal distance and spacing
6. Chronemics—uses of time
7. Artifacts—environmental features

Since, by one estimate, nonverbal kinesthetic activity can be coded into 700,000 physical signs (Pei 1965), an analysis of the total communication modes used by Japanese leaders in different contexts for different purposes (prerequisites) is impractical. The analysis is further complicated by the problem of interpreting the communication within cultural paradigms. As Ekman and Friesen (1969; 1971) suggest, there are norms in every culture limiting the nature and extent of choice of communication modes (though there apparently are also universally recognized modes or "display rules" of expression) (see Ekman 1973, on facial expression; Goffman 1959). Beliefs about what is and what is not socially permissible/demonstrable constrains communication behavior. For example, wives of Samurai warriors smiled, rather than wept at their husbands' funerals, reflecting, perhaps, both the expected social disapprobation about public displays of grief and the nobility of heroic death (Oster 1989). Matsumoto (1989) reports that cultural differences measured in terms of Hofstede's (1980a; 1983) variables of power distance and individualism are revealed in displays of emotion. In cultures where power asymmetries are great and individualism is low (i.e., much as in bureaucracies with collectivity orientations), communication of negative emotions threatens group solidarity and interpersonal social structure. On the other hand, cultures low in power distance and high in individualism may sanction the communication of these emotions more, as they relate to individual freedom to express and perceive negative emotions.

In explicating the nature of leader-worker and leader-group relationships in small groups in Japan, it is necessary to examine the relationships in their dyadic and nondyadic forms. Further, it is important to be clear on the power dynamic that is operative. Hence, as will be seen, the communication is different, depending on whether the relationship is perceived to be symmetric or asymmetric. As pointed out in Chapter 3, the Japanese are extremely status/power oriented. Barnlund (1975, 162) observes that, "In Japan, nearly all interaction takes place within an elaborate and vertically oriented social structure." The verbal language reflects this, as does the nonverbal communication. The formal status of the senior member in a relationship calls for certain kinds of linguistic and body posture deference by the junior, even if the former is not literally more powerful. In a study of body postures in Japanese communicating dyads by Kudoh and Matsumoto (1985; cf. Bond & Shiraishi 1974), the authors found that the logic of the factors (groups) signifying related bodily postures was similar to that found in the United States. However, there was a spareness and simplicity of expression indicated in the Japanese sample. Kudoh and Matsumoto note:

Within cultures whose members rely on vertical relationships for the maintenance of bonds between people, clues associated with status and power rather than the nonverbal clues concerning like-dislike are more heavily relied on, which contributes to the simplicity of those postures.

These findings lend support for the notion that many of the postures that people adopt in normal human interaction can carry information about not only the emotional state of but also the relationship between the interactants.

But it is not simply the historical relationship alone that determines the interpersonal behavior. While "status signs" (Mazur 1985) call for deferent or dominant behavior, so also does demonstrated competence to facilitate the accomplishment of group goals (Ridgeway 1987). In a culture like Japan's where promotion is carefully regulated by bureaucratic principles of measured and recognized competence (cf. Wakabayashi, Graen, Graen, & Graen 1988; though see Pollack 1993a), it is likely that the latter will predominate in affecting nonverbal behavior (cf. Borland 1988).

It is in the context of the ambiguity of power in a decentralized decision-making system that the expectations of the leader (be he superior or subordinate) must be conveyed. For example, the locus of real (not pro forma), final, decision-making authority lies somewhere between the titular leader and the group. The directions that the discussions take during the *nemawashi* phase, however, follow from the efficacy of the leader in conveying with utmost subtlety the output desiderata in his own mind. "Openness" of communication, long a lauded characteristic of growing and developing, humanistic organizations in the United States (cf. Pelz 1952), would be frowned upon in Japanese firms. Indeed, silence, however ambiguous, is much preferred to the clear expression of emotion during an episode of disagreement. Japan is known as a *kotoagesenu kuni*—a nation where people refrain from speaking. Uno and Rosenthal (1972) note that in part this predisposition has its origins in both Buddhism and Confucianism, the first in placing high value on quiet and tacit communication and the second on refraining from speaking in the presence of people of higher status. Lebra (1984) notes that despite its ambiguity,

Japanese are so used to silence that they may see nothing wrong in it; silence could be taken as a sign of sincerity, *enryo* (social reserve), acquiescence, or even compliance, as when children are told not to talk back.

While to be sure, conflicting opinions can be explored (see previous chapter), feelings about those opinions and/or the other person are usually withheld, except perhaps when interpersonal communication codes change in different situations, for example, the formal work versus the after-work social setting. Feelings of the leader, on the other hand, *must* be conveyed, else by definition leadership as influence can not be effectuated. It is the subtlety of that conveyance that is distinctively Japanese. Importantly, it is critical that followers be alert to that subtlety. Uno and Rosenthal (1972) note that the "Japanese have developed the ability to read what others are thinking through delicate nuances in facial expression."

Of what is this subtlety comprised? According to Bond, Nakazato, and Shiraishi (1975), sensitivity to three personality characteristics is cross-culturally evident. These characteristics are extroversion, agreeableness, and conscientiousness. However, in their study of a Japanese sample, "extroversion" dominates. They conclude that such a finding makes much sense because in Japan's "vertical" society, relative status is all important and "the most salient behavioral indicator of a person's relative status in Japan is his (or occasionally her) level of extroversion. It is the role of the higher-status person in a given situation to assume the initiative and to direct the interaction." While this personality trait would seem to violate the requirement for subtle, more laid-back, or even meek postures, as noted earlier, the additional extroversion of higher-status people is marginal, probably imperceptible to Western eyes. As will be seen in Chapters 14 and 15, revealing the findings from the empirical phase of this study, extroversion was, indeed, a characteristic of some, but not all leaders.

Another characteristic of the Japanese personality that is critical to observe in leadership behaviors is "self-effacement." It is virtually universal for most Japanese in conversations with peers to ascribe less to their accomplishments than they rightfully could demand. They express considerable modesty and apologize in advance for appearing to call attention to their achievements. Such behavior, however, is not as evident in interpersonal relationships among persons of unequal status, including leader-follower conditions. As Johnson, Marsella, and Johnson (1974) point out:

For those who understand the Japanese cultural meaning for these attitudes, a neat balancing occurs whereby the status and accomplishments of persons *can* be established in subtle and indirect ways. However, for persons outside the culture, the *enryo* behaviors may mistakenly be interpreted as exaggerated politeness, false modesty, unusual silence, even obsequiousness.

There still remains the question of how extroversion, as well as other leadership behaviors, are communicated. Few, if any empirical investigations of this have been conducted in Japan. Bond and Shiraishi (1974) looked at nonverbal communication between high and equal status subjects using a number of indices: eye contact, pauses between speech, total speaking time, average response latency, physical self-manipulations, gestures, torso shifts, and smiles, but found relatively few differences for males on these measures. Nevertheless, Johnson, Marsella, and Johnson (1974) suggest that because the Japanese are more sensitive to nonverbal cues, emotion can be conveyed, even when there is silence. "Paraverbal" accompaniments to language, they note, allow for a considerable amount of communication, especially in dyads or small familiar groups. Borland (1988) calls this "empathic sensing," helped by the homogeneity of Japan, and transcending American modes of communicating.

To return to the family metaphor, Conger, Kanungo and Associates (1988) note that "Followers may endow their leaders with the same magic powers and omniscience they attributed in childhood to parents or other significant figures" (p. 244). Fitzpatrick and Badzinski (1985) note that this faith in leaders permits messages to be "broadly characterized as support and control messages." This downward Parent-Child mode is countered by a different set of responses and initiations from the subordinate (qua child in this case) which moderate the superordinate communication modes (cf. Kipnis, Schmidt, & Wilkinson 1980; Porter, Allen, & Angle 1991). In sum, formal superordinate communication to subordinates in small groups such as research and development units in Japan is functionally ambiguous. The communication medium is "cool" in McLuhan's terms (McLuhan 1964). It forces the listener to participate actively in the communication process, rather than passively receive it. Subtle expressions of extroversion as hints of content importance can be discerned by subordinates who have been enculturated to the listening style and who have worked with the formal leader for the duration of his or their tenure on the job.

To conclude, we return to the subject of charisma. The complications of Japanese decision-making structures (e.g., *ringei*) should not lead to a conclusion that Japanese leaders are mere figureheads, confirming what subordinates have decided apparently independently. There are many reasons that followers in Japanese organizations are induced to take action that complies with their understanding of the formal leader's wishes (Bird 1992). As noted earlier, the pattern of socialization in childhood and schooling breeds a long-standing awe of authority. As Conger, Kanungo and Associates (1988) note, "Followers may endow their leaders with the same magic powers and omniscience they attributed in childhood to parents or other significant figures" (p. 244). The elevation of a person to leadership status in an organization is based on desirable qualities perceived by peers and superiors. These include not only the ability to adjudicate among conflicting ideas by sensing and evoking a consensus, but the capacity to imagine beyond the group and to convey the substance of that imagination without its appearing idiosyncratic (Nanus 1992).

In addition, Japan has a long history of infatuation with heroes and, paradoxically, antiheroes. The hero model constitutes an unachievable role model for organizational leadership. As Saito (1985) remarks, the essential "trait" possessed by these heroes is *makoto*—sincerity. It denotes "purity of mind and motive, and a rejection of self-serving objectives. It despises pragmatic ways of thinking and doing. It is moral fastidiousness." Citing Ivan Morris's work, *The Nobility of Failure*, Saito suggests that the "true" Japanese hero is a poignant loser—one who fails, but fails gracefully and "sincerely." The Japanese leader, however, is not a hero but a conduit, a link between subordinates and superiors, between outside and inside, between the ideal and the real. His charisma and idiosyncracy credits allow him to "lead" in the sense of personifying the ideals of the organization, even as they may be emerging from across boundaries or within the group. These traits of imagination and subdued reticence are difficult to manifest in service of organizational efficiency and effectiveness. As will be seen in later chapters that reveal the data on actual behavior of R & D leaders in Japan, there are a variety of modes by which leadership is expressed.

But first the methods by which those data were collected must be described. The following chapter takes up this topic.

## NOTES

1. Needless to say, the converse is also true. In America, leaders play roles not needed in Japan.

2. This is not to say that there is no adolescent rebellion in Japan. In point of fact, in recent years there is evidence of significant changes in attitudes and values of teenagers.

3. Though not an unimportant issue, the question of the stability of personality across situations is begged here. The controversy may be pursued at least in part through Bem & Allen 1974; Ajzen & Fishbein 1973, 1980; Sarasan 1975; Epstein 1979; Kenrick & Stringfield 1980; Veroff 1983; Mischel 1983; McCrae & Costa 1984; Miller & Grush 1988; Rowe 1987; Kenrick & Funder 1988.

# V

# Findings from Empirical Research in Japan

# 13

# Methods of Research

Understanding the nature of leadership in Japan is a difficult task for any researcher, but especially a foreigner. As noted earlier, the ascription of inscrutability to the East, however hackneyed, is not without some considerable validity. It is important, therefore, for the research methods employed to be sensitive to cross-cultural dimensions and biases and to recognize the natural resistance of the subjects to investigation.

For the inquiry reported here the empirical methods were both qualitative and quantitative. They included general observations of the culture through immersion in a year-long residential stay and subsequent extended visits, colloquies with Japanese colleagues about the research, studying the Japanese language, interviews with Japanese workers and with leaders of the scientific community in government, university and corporate circles, and extensive reviews of the manuscript by Japanese colleagues and friends. In addition, a lengthy questionnaire in Japanese was administered to a large sample of R & D leaders and workers. The findings and conclusions drawn from the research have been used not so much to explain relationships among critical organizational variables in the Japanese setting as an heuristic tool to provide insights that may be considered for possible utilization in the West.

It is important to be explicit in the description of the methods used so that readers will have confidence in the validity and reliability of the findings. The methods of social science were assiduously pursued. This chapter provides an overview of the methods, including: the operationalization of the variables, the nature of and mode of selection of the sample, the response rates and biases, and the data analysis procedures.

## SURVEY METHODS

The unit of analysis for the study was the R & D laboratory "section," defined as a subunit of 15 to 40 workers. This choice was dictated by the need to circumscribe the research to cover "face-to-face" leadership, rather than the more distant leadership that might be tapped by examining laboratory leadership at the top. Scientific research and development laboratories in selected industrial, governmental, and university organizations in the three countries were chosen.

Collection of data in a foreign country constitutes an especially difficult task, not only because of translation issues, but because of subtle cultural biases such as honesty or social desirability in responses. For example, whereas in the United States, it is possible to select a random sample from a population and to survey that sample by securing names and addresses from some reliable source, such may not be the case abroad. In the first place, directories of institutions are organized in different ways from the Western tradition. Even with the help of skilled translators, it is often only by trial and error that the nonnative researcher (and sometimes the indigenous social scientist) can discover the criteria for inclusion or exclusion of names from a directory to be used for sampling.

The objectives of the research dictated the selection of a survey research population constrained by several variables. First, the economic sector of the laboratory (government, university, or corporate) had to be differentiated on the grounds that the subcultural differences among these types might require different kinds of leadership. Second, the type of industry (iron and steel, chemicals, transportation, and electrical) was chosen for the current varying economic circumstances in which the industries exist. It was reasoned, for example, that industries in decline, steady state, or ascent might benefit from different kinds of R & D leaders (as, for example, if the research in the industry requires incremental versus breakthrough advances).

A third cut in the sampling was a division of research and development units into basic, applied, and developmental foci. Though the sample was not stratified on this dimension, questions in the survey instrument were designed to make the necessary discrimination.

Still another criterion used in the sampling was suggested by the desire to obtain a model or prototypical, high-performing group against which the other surveyed laboratories or groups of laboratories could be measured. Such a category was identified in the special funding provided by MITI (Japan's federal agency concerned with national scientific industrial productivity). Nine nationally known, individual, scientific researchers had been asked to set up and lead newly founded R & D laboratories without the usual sponsor control over objectives and methods. They were given large grants to carry out their research with relatively greater autonomy than at other government-funded labs. A sampling of sections within these laboratories was conducted to provide the model data.

Because of the relative unfamiliarity of Japanese workers with survey research

methods, some greater assurance of cooperation in responding to the questionnaire was needed. Accordingly, in-person contacts were made with six selected,
large organizations, and arrangements were made to enlist the direct support of
the directors of their R & D laboratories. The six were:

**Corporate**

Mitsubishi Metals

Mitsubishi Electric

Nissan Motors

Nippon Steel

**Government**

Agency for Industrial Science and Technology

**Quasi-government**

National Telephone and Telegraph (newly converted from a public to a private organization)


Directories of R & D laboratories were used to select names of laboratories
in each of the above-noted three sectors. The initial sample comprised 180 laboratories in each (not including the above grouping). A size criterion cutoff was
chosen to standardize the population. Each laboratory, furthermore, was required
to have at least one section of 15 to 40 workers—the unit of analysis for the
study.


### Questionnaire Administration

Names of the section leaders were not available in the directories, partly
because in Japan there is a strong pattern of frequent job rotation and partly, as
in America, because directories tend not to be updated regularly. More important, section heads tended to be relatively low in the hierarchy and were seldom
listed.

Partly because of this condition, it was decided to send the survey to the
laboratory director himself with instructions to redistribute the questionnaires.
This decision was made also in the light of the power of hierarchical authority
in Japan. It was reasoned that when an addressed sample member received it
from the director of the laboratory, he would be more likely to respond than if
he received it in the mail. Furthermore, since the bottom-up, decision-making
patterns in Japanese organizations demanded lengthy discussions on whether or
not to participate, the prior approval by the superior prevented lengthy delays.
In sum, not only did individual workers feel compelled to respond, but the
pattern of extensive group participation in decisions concerning individual responses was somewhat vitiated.

The data were collected through questionnaires distributed first to directors
of laboratories, then sequentially to unit heads and their workers. The directors

of the laboratories were asked (in Japanese translation) to select two sections to which sets of questionnaires were to be delivered. The instructions also asked them to make the selection on the following grounds: One section should, in the opinion of the director, be headed by an exemplary person whose effectiveness had been demonstrated in previous R & D success; the other section leader was to be a "less than maximally effective" one. The two sections were to be chosen on the basis of the director's judgment of the "best" and "worst" of his sections (the wording was more subtle than this). The purpose of this "quality" division was to allow examination of the leadership characteristics of the best and worst sections as conceived from the perspective of the laboratory leader. The quality dichotomization was also dictated in part by the difficulty of obtaining externally valid criteria of section effectiveness. That is, there is some looseness in the connection between the overall success of a larger organization and the success of its R & D operation, other factors than R & D having the decided potential for influencing organizational success. In point of fact, subsequent comparisons between "quality" levels on most of the variables of the study did not prove to be revealing.

Both of the two section leaders who received the packages of questionnaires were given two tasks: (1) to fill out questionnaires designed for themselves as section leaders; and (2) to distribute to six of their workers another type of questionnaire designed for the latter. Special instructions were included to prevent the section leader from distributing the questionnaires to workers thought to have unusually favorable or deviant attitudes toward the leader or the laboratory. All of the questionnaires were accompanied by stamped, self-addressed envelopes that ensured their delivery to the National Institute for Research Advancement, a prominent, well-respected Japanese "think tank" in the Tokyo area (which also, incidentally, offered its imprimatur for the study in the cover letters).

To reiterate, the overall *director* of the laboratory was sent a letter (in Japanese) outlining the research objectives and design. Accompanying the letter was a short questionnaire asking about the characteristics of his laboratory as a whole. He was given, in addition, two packages of questionnaires for further distribution to workers in two of the sections under his control. Each of the two section leaders, in addition, was given a questionnaire to complete by himself and was given seven copies of another questionnaire to be distributed to six of his section workers (one extra questionnaire for misplaced copies, if any). The six workers were chosen on the basis of a simplified randomization procedure that minimized personalistic bias on the part of the section head (thus avoiding his selection of workers who were known to be favorably, or, for that matter, unfavorably, disposed toward the section or organization).

**Variables of the Study**

The design of the research utilized three conceptualizations of organizational phenomena which had never been combined: the studies of leadership utilizing the Jungian psychology that Kilmann and Herden (1976) had originated; the identification of alternative modes of conflict resolution that Kilmann and Thomas (1977) developed; and the "job characteristics" theory originated by Hackman and Oldham (1976).

The three independent variables were operationalized as follows: (1) *Leadership style*, measured by the Myers-Briggs Type Indicator (MBTI) (Myers 1962; McCaulley 1981; Kilmann & Herden 1976); (2) *Conflict management style*, measured by the Thomas-Kilmann "MODE" instrument; and (3) *Managerial attitudes* critical in personnel areas, measured through some original scales developed for this research. The dependent variable of primary interest is *motivation*, which is tested through the administration of the Hackman and Oldham Job Diagnostic Survey (which provides, in addition, measures of perceived "job characteristics" conducive or deleterious to motivation). Other dependent variables include satisfaction, commitment, and risk-taking propensity.

## Instrumentation

Standardized instruments with published valid and reliable translations were selected as the major medium of data collection in the Japanese survey. Choosing well-tested Western questionnaire instruments that had been professionally translated mitigated many potential problems of researcher cultural naivete or bias which might have occurred through other, more qualitative research methods. All of the English-language questionnaires were translated into Japanese, then back-translated to assure at least minimal validity, subject to empirical testing and other validation techniques. While there is still some controversy over instrument translations (Deutscher 1968), properly chosen instruments can produce the data needed for cross-cultural comparisons (see Triandis 1972, especially pages 35–57; also Brislin, Lonner, & Thorndike 1973). To the standardized instruments were added a number of variables especially relevant to cross-cultural study, as well as a range of demographic and controlling variables. All were subjected to the usual statistical scrutiny for reliability and validity.

## Data Analysis

For purposes of data analysis in this paper, the leader variable scores were attached in a computer system file to the scores of *each* of his workers (regardless of the number of workers who returned the questionnaires). Thus, instead of averaging for each leader his workers' scores, as many matches of leader-worker were made as resulted from the data collection. The unit of analysis for the study is thus the leader, not the section.

## Research Questions

The central concerns of the study were identified earlier in the chapter on the conceptual framework (Chapter 2). These concerns are reiterated below.

## Leadership Style

1. What are the psychological characteristics of effective academic and industrial research leaders? While simple analysis of leadership traits has been generally discredited, the use of the MBTI can result in new findings which reflect contingencies where certain traits may be more successful. For example, concerns for internal efficiency or effectiveness may, under certain conditions, have to be subordinated to market share or social responsibility pressures.

2. What kinds of leadership types exist in different laboratory organizations (university, corporation, government institutes) and in different fields (e.g., electronics, iron and steel, chemicals, and transportation)?

## Conflict Management Modes

3. What styles of conflict management predominate in effective and ineffective leaders? The use of the Thomas-Kilmann MODE instrument may reveal distinctive approaches to conflict resolution (e.g., accommodative, competitive, compromising, avoiding, or collaborating) which, in turn, reveal culture-bound and/or specialized academic/industrial dispositions. Which approaches lead to organizational effectiveness in Japan and in the nonprofit versus profit sectors of interest?

4. What are the various modes through which interpersonal conflict (in many forms) is productively resolved—and how do these differ over types of laboratory organizations and fields?

## Managerial Attitudes

5. *Control of Work.* In different kinds of laboratories, what is the manager's attitude toward worker versus management control over choice of projects and project methods?

6. *Focus of Rewards.* To what extent does the laboratory leader emphasize individual or group achievement?

7. *Norms of Information Flow.* Are workers encouraged by management to share discoveries freely or to keep them secret?

8. *Social Status.* Does management practice a hierarchy of status relationships, or is the pattern more egalitarian?

9. *Nature of Sanctions.* Are positive or negative sanctions typically applied by managers?

10. *Risk Taking.* Are workers encouraged to take risks in their research or to work on projects with more certain outcomes?

## Controlling or Ancillary Variables

### Research Orientation

11. When an R & D organization emphasizes basic, applied, or developmental research, what kinds of leaders and conflict management are the most effective?

### Field and Economic Conditions of the Market

12. To what extent and in what way do industries in declining, steady state, or expanding markets differ in R & D leadership? What differences exist among organizations in the fields of electronics, iron and steel, chemicals, and transportation, the fields chosen for analysis.

### Laboratory Age/Research Project Stage

13. What is the relationship between R & D management style and the age of the laboratory and stage of development of a project?

### Demographic Characteristics of Leaders

14. How are age, education, and employment history related to R & D management style?

## Dependent Variables

### Motivation, Satisfaction, Commitment, Risk taking

15. What levels and types of worker motivation and satisfaction exist, how much commitment to the organization and its goals is there, and to what extent are workers willing to take risks in their research endeavors?

16. What is the impact of leader characteristics defined by the three independent variables on subordinate motivation and creativity?

17. Are there specific combinations of psychological characteristics of leaders, group conflict management styles, and managerial attitudes which produce departments which are reputed to be more successful than others and which also promote subordinate satisfactions?

18. Under what conditions is individual motivation enhanced or inhibited (e.g., when "efficiency" is the leadership orientation and "collaborating" the conflict management mode—or is some other combination appropriate)?

19. Are there differences in the fit between the above independent and dependent variables across the sectors of interest—corporations, government institutes, and universities? Does successful conflict management in universities, for example, require different modes than in corporations or government institutes?

20. Is a laboratory orientation toward basic, applied, or developmental research related to the nature of the leadership and conflict management found in there?

21. How do market forces (e.g., perceived availability of funding for research in key areas) affect the variables of interest? In a declining field, for example, are certain kinds of leadership and conflict management more effective?

22. As projects near completion, is a different kind of leadership required than for projects just beginning or at the midpoint?

A schematic diagram outlining the multivariate relationships among these variables was presented in Chapter 2.

### Response Rate

Including both random and nonrandom samples, a total of 160 questionnaires was received from section leaders, and 796 questionnaires were received from R & D workers. No follow-up letters could be written to elicit a greater response, as in Japan such an overture would be construed as an insult. That is, it must be assumed that the request was received and attended to. Calling attention to a "failure" to respond, or even hinting that the questionnaires may have been overlooked would be to cause a loss of "face" and would not only have been ineffective but would have embarrassed the agency sponsoring the research.

### Response Bias

Data collection is a significant problem in any cross-cultural research. In this case, the nature of the nonresponse bias can only be estimated. When responses were not received from workers, at least three possible sources of the nonresponse were possible. For example, it could be (1) that a decision had been made by the director not to cooperate, (2) that the section head had so decided, or (3) that the workers had made individual decisions. In point of fact, there were a number of instances where the section head sent his questionnaire back but no worker questionnaires were received, and there were other occasions where at least one worker returned his questionnaire, but none was received from the section head. There were very few times that the full complement of six workers *and* unit head returned their questionnaires. Since the concern of the study was with the correlations between leader and worker characteristics, only cases where there was a match of at least one worker for the leader were used in the analysis. As will be discussed later, because of the great homogeneity of the Japanese population, bias may not be as significant as otherwise might be the case.

## INSTRUMENT VALIDITY AND RELIABILITY

With the exception of three items from the Judging-Perception dimension of the MBTI (omitted because of space limitations), all of the questionnaire items in the English-language version were utilized in the translated instruments. As noted earlier, each instrument was translated into Japanese and then back-translated to establish validity. Data from each questionnaire were entered into a computer and verified in Japan and then transferred to tape for transport to the United States. Here they were prepared for analysis at NYU's computer facility. After the usual data cleaning, factor analyses were performed to determine whether the preexisting theoretical concepts and instrumentation from the Western literature held up with Japanese data. In particular, the MBTI, the Thomas-Kilmann MODE, and the Hackman-Oldham JDS questions were subjected independently to principal components factor analyses with rotations (varimax, oblimin, quartimax). The results of this analysis revealed, not surprisingly, that the reliability and validity of the United States instruments were only partially confirmed. Since some testing of the hypotheses for purposes of cross-cultural comparison was intended, the constructs of the original test instruments were examined for validity. The characteristics of the scales created by the items in the factor analysis of each of the variables are described in the remainder of this chapter, with the results of the use of the validated scales reported later in the findings chapters.

## VALIDATION OF THE LEADERSHIP SCALES

The first of the scales to be examined for validity is the Japanese version of the Myers-Briggs Type Indicator, adapted here to measure leadership characteristics. As reported in Chapter 12, trait theory in the study of leadership has been experiencing somewhat of a resurgence of interest. As various contingencies have been explored empirically in conjunction with traits, new insights into the dynamics of the interactions between traits and those contingencies have been uncovered. In this book, one of the empirical findings that emerged is that multiple leaders exist in social settings in Japan (and doubtless elsewhere) and that there are temporary, emerging, and long-standing relationships not only between one leader and his followers but between each of the leaders and his followers and among the leaders as a group and the followers as a group. Hence, the leadership relationships can best be seen as canonical.

The examination of leadership in Japan necessitated an examination of the traits of the Japanese leaders who hold formal positions as well as those of persons who, in the Mary Parker Follett schema, become leaders according to the "law of the situation," that is, as the situation demands their involvement qua leaders. In this book, only the first of these is considered: the formal leader behaviors. This section looks at the traits of those formal leaders as they emerged from the factor analysis of the translated MBTI instrument.[1]

As a first step in the analysis of the data, then, an attempt was made to determine the degree to which the English-language MBTI scales were valid for a Japanese sample. While a factor analysis of the data revealed some similarities, there were some significant differences, as noted in Exhibit 13.1.

While these reliabilities are acceptable, they are rather low. The enlarged set of variables, however, may provide sufficient diagnostic power to suggest that further refinement by Japanese psychometrists may be worthwhile. For example, the English version of the MBTI suggests that Thinking/Feeling is one dimension and Sensation/Intuition another, resulting in the four personality types. For this Japanese sample, however, two separate factors for each dimension emerged from the factor analysis of the questionnaire items comprising the scales. In each case, the factors with similar-appearing face validity were virtually uncorrelated, but the signs of the factor loadings were opposite. For example, the three items in the first Sensation/Intuition factor loaded heavily on the sensation side (i.e, were positively weighted), while the second Sensation/Intuition factor was loaded on the intuition side—the inference being that two subgroups from

**Exhibit 13.1**
**Scale Names and Reliabilities for the Japanese MBTI**

| Name | No. Items | Reliability (alpha level) |
|---|---|---|
| Extroversion/Introversion I | 5 | .70 |
| Feeling/Thinking | 4 | .69 |
| Intuition/Sensation | 3 | .68 |
| Thinking/Feeling | 3 | .66 |
| Sensation/Intuition | 4 | .70 |
| Extroversion/Introversion II | 2 | .53 |
| Extroversion/Introversion III | 2 | .58 |
| Judging/Perception | 2 | .49 |

this sample answered differently. In the first stage of the analysis, only the first Thinking/Feeling dimension (Eigen value = 4.1) and the first Intuition/Sensation dimension (Eigen value = 2.7) were used, as these tended to be most closely correlated with the dependent variables. Additional research will be necessary to determine the reasons for the multidimensionality of the two dimensions in the Japanese setting, but the first two dimensions alone, as will be seen, are sufficiently diagnostic for a first look.

To establish the four leader types suggested in the Thomas-Kilmann typology, each dimension (information accessing mode and information processing mode) was divided into high and low categories, with a fifth category established as a "mixed" leadership style. The score cutoffs used to create the categories are indicated in Exhibit 13.2.

Clearly, the division of the scale scores into these categories is arbitrary, not criterion referenced, and thus does not reveal anything about the reality of the leader dispositions. All that can be said is that the subjects who fall into one or another section are higher or lower or different from the others. It is not possible at this point to draw comparisons with scores of leaders in the United States who may have taken the MBTI. For example, the lowest Japanese score on F/T may be higher than the highest U.S. score. Further investigation of the psychometrics of the U.S. MBTI is planned, and a testing of the Japanese version in a U.S. setting will be conducted in order eventually to make the cross-cultural comparisons.

The factor analysis was used a second time for the purpose of determining the face validity of the factors without the constraint of the Kilmann-Thomas conceptualizations underpinning the instrument and with the addition of items from the Introversion/Extroversion and Judgment/Perception dimensions. Eight factors emerged. These factors or scales constitute a useful spread of preferences, dispositions, and behaviors for analyzing leader behavior. In contrast to the

**Exhibit 13.2**
**Cutoffs of Scale Scores for MBTI Categories**

Intuition/Sensation Range

|  | | 3 | 4 | 5,6 |
|---|---|---|---|---|
| | 8 | NF | | SF |
| Feeling/Thinking Range | 7 | | Mixed | |
| | 4,5,6 | NT | | ST |

Kilmann-Thomas bivariate split into information input and information processing categories, the data here seem to reflect another two categories: (1) dispositions to behave in social situations; and (2) preferences for certain types of
mental acts. That is, whereas in the Kilmann-Thomas/Jungian MBTI conceptualization, there are two dimensions, each measured on continuous scales (i.e.,
sensation versus intuition and thinking versus feeling), in this new analysis of
the items, the two ends of each continuum often fell out as separate dimensions,
lending themselves to different interpretations of the meanings. These new categories or dimensions on face validity fall into two classes: behaviors and dis-
positions/attitudes:

**Leadership Interpersonal Behavior Scales**

   Factor #2 Intimacy versus Relationships

   Factor #3 Gentility versus Firm-mindedness

   Factor #5 Introvert versus Extrovert

   Factor #8 Consideration versus Reasonableness

**Leadership Disposition/Attitude Scales**

   Factor #1 Practicality versus Unconventionality

   Factor #2 Rationality versus Affect

   Factor #6 Extemporaneity versus Premeditation

   Factor #7 Ideational versus Literal

A second-order factoring of these eight factor scores, however, in point of
fact produced three, not two, categories. These categories address three distinct
qualities on which leaders can vary. The first seems to be a quality of "mind"—
the ability to apply rational principles to problem solving. The second is concerned with the quality of "relationships"—both the sharing of information and
the expression of feelings. And the third deals with a quality of "goal orientation"—pragmatic contrasted with unconventional risk taking. These three may
be the quintessential elements that distinguish different kinds of leaders in Japanese research and development (and perhaps leaders in all organizations). The
three categories are not used as measures in summary form, however, in order

to utilize the diagnostic possibilities of the scales that comprise them. The breakdown of the three categories is as follows:

**Qualities of Mind**

Gentility-Firm-mindedness

Rationality-Affect

Consideration-Reasonableness

**Interpersonal Relationships**

Intimacy-Relationship

Introvert-Extrovert

**Social Conformity Disposition**

Practicality-Unconventionality

Extemporaneity-Premeditation

Ideational-Literal

The tripartite division of these measures suggests a particularly useful diagnostic for analyzing leadership. Incontrovertibly, depending on contingencies, leadership demands certain mental characteristics, for example, toughmindedness (cf. James 1975), intelligence, emotionality, caring. Leadership, again under alternative circumstances, requires expressiveness, openness, or reserved behavior. Finally, leadership in different cases is expected to demonstrate divergent or conventional dispositions or attitudes. Ellen Frost (1987), citing Sarison, suggests that the Japanese outlook is essentially "practical and intuitive rather than intellectually rigorous" (p. 89). They "shun or downplay reason and logic in the Western sense." Whether Japanese leaders manifest these qualities and whether they can be measured by the scales remains to be seen.

The eight factors and the items comprising them are noted in Exhibit 13.3. Thirty-two of the 42 items from the MBTI array in the questionnaire were aggregated in the eight factors that emerged. A analysis of the omitted eight yielded no meaningful additional factors. A calculation of the correlations of the omitted items with the scales revealed no significant correlations. The eight factors accounted for 60.2 percent of the variance in the retained items.

The reliabilities of some of the scales created from the factor analysis are sometimes lower than desirable, but the scales are utilized here because diagnostically they reveal potentially interesting differences among R & D leaders. With further refinement (this was the first time such a psychometric enterprise was assayed using the MBTI on leaders in Japan), it is conceivable that the factors/scales will be stronger.

It should be noted that the MBTI items are bipolar, forced choice in nature. Respondents may firmly choose one answer over another, or, equally likely, may reject one answer in favor of the other. That is, their choices over the range of items in the questionnaire may be a combination of preferences for some and

**Exhibit 13.3**
**Renamed Factors Derived from the Factor Analysis**

Factor #1 — Practicality-Unconventionality

This factor reflects a leader's orientation toward practical, down to earth matters in contrast with an orientation toward the creative or imaginative matters.

| Question Number | Code Name | Factor Loading | Abbreviated Item | Original MBTI Concept |
|---|---|---|---|---|
| 10 | JCOMPAT | .64 | Realistic vs Imaginative * | Sensation |
| 19 | JASSOC | -.66 | New Ideas vs Feet on the Ground | Sensation |
| | JNGO4 | -.79 | Imaginative vs Matter of Fact | Sensation |
| | JNG10 | -.62 | Create vs Make | Sensation |
| | JNG16 | -.46 | Fascinating vs Sensible | Sensation |

* Item reversed in scoring

Standardized Item Alpha = .73
Low Factor Score = Unconventionality; High Score = Practicality

rejections of others, thus rendering interpretation of the meanings of groups of strongly loaded items in the factor analysis somewhat problematic. In the cases described below, the name which appears first (of the two in the dichotomous name designation) represents the more easily comprehended meaning of the polar opposites. The second name is in some cases recognizable from the face validity of the items, but in others is the "logically" rather than empirically derived opposite. In these latter cases, it seemed to be more meaningful to label the scale with the name of the construct whose face validity was more evident. Indeed, there are two pairs of scales (1 and 7 and 4 and 8) where the two "opposites" seem to overlap. This occurred when the English-language scale broke into two in the Japanese version and when the positive sides may have been quite different, while the negative sides appeared to be the same.

Further information about the scales is revealed by interscale correlations, means, and standard deviations, as in Exhibits 13.4 and 13.5. Note that there are only four correlations above .35, suggesting the diagnostic utility of the scales. The higher correlations are not unexpected, given the face validity of the scales. For example, the two scales using the extroversion items from the MBTI (Intimacy-Relationships and Introvert-Extrovert) are correlated at a level of .45. Similarly, Consideration-Reasonableness and Gentility-Firm-mindedness are correlated at a level of .35; Rationality-Affect and Ideational-Literal at .34; and

**Exhibit 13.3** (continued)

### Factor #2 — Intimacy-Sociability

Leaders high in intimacy tend to be somewhat out of the flow of information, preferring more to converse with close friends. Those who are high in sociability prefer more to keep abreast of news and to be involved with many individuals. (Note contrast with Factor 5 which deals more with the mode of expression rather than the type of relationship).

| Question Number | Code Name | Factor Loading | Abbreviated Item | Original MBTI Concept |
|---|---|---|---|---|
| 6 | JAWARE | .65 | Newsy vs last to hear | Extroversion |
| 8 | JFRENDS | .67 | Broad friendships vs deep friends | Extroversion |
| 14 | JDISCUS | .76 | Talk easily to many vs certain few | Extroversion |
| 17 | JMTGS | .50 | Introduce others vs be introduced | Extroversion |
| | JNG01 | .51 | Facts vs Ideas | Sensation |

Standardized Item Alpha = .68
Low Factor Score = Intimacy; High Factor Score = Relationship

### Factor #3 — Gentility-Firm-mindedness

This factor appears to reflect a firm or uncompromising disposition contrasted with warm-hearted consideration.

| Question Number | Code Name | Factor Loading | Abbreviated Item | Original MBTI Concept |
|---|---|---|---|---|
| | JNG12 | -.77 | Gentle vs firm | Thinking |
| | JNG17 | .60 | Firm vs warmhearted | Thinking |
| | JNG201 | .43 | Foresight vs compassion | Thinking |
| | JNG21 | .68 | Hard vs Soft | Thinking |

Standardized Item Alpha = .63
Low Factor Score = Firm-mindedness; High Factor Score = Gentility

**Exhibit 13.3 (continued)**

## Factor #4 — Rationality-Affect

This factor differentiates between leaders who are disposed to relate to information received with reason versus feeling.

| Question Number | Code Name | Factor Loading | Abbreviated Item | Original MBTI Concept |
|---|---|---|---|---|
| 4 | JHEART | .70 | Heart vs head | Feeling |
| 12 | JFLTHNK | .63 | Feeling vs reason | Feeling |
| 18 | JSNTMNT | .63 | Sentiment vs logic | Feeling |
|  | JNG18 | .58 | Feeling vs thinking | Feeling |

Standardized Item Alpha = .67
Low Factor Score = Affect; High Factor Score = Rationality

## Factor #5 — Introversion-Extroversion

R & D leaders can be distinguished on the basis of their willingness to display their emotion rather than keeping their feelings to themselves.

| Question Number | Code Name | Factor Loading | Abbreviated Item | Original MBTI Concept |
|---|---|---|---|---|
| 3 | JSOCIAL | .46 | Mixer vs quiet | Extroversion |
| 20 | JINTRST | .51 | Open to others vs closed | Extroversion |
| 21 | JFEELNG | .81 | Show feeling vs keep to self | Extroversion |
|  | JNG08 | -.47 | Reserved vs talkative* | Extroversion |

\* Item reversed in scoring

Standardized Item Alpha = .67
Low Factor Score = Extrovert; High Factor Score = Introvert

**Exhibit 13.3 (continued)**

### Factor #6 — Extemporaneity-Premeditation

Leadership of research and development sometimes calls for careful planning at the expense of spontaneity; sometimes the reverse. This scale differentiates among leaders who prefer to act extemporaneously compared with others who like to premeditate their activities.

| Question Number | Code Name | Factor Loading | Abbreviated Item | Original MBTI Concept |
|---|---|---|---|---|
| 1 | JPLAN | .58 | Plan vs just go | Judging |
| 7 | JORGANIZ | .45 | Organize vs ad hoc | Judging |
|  | JSTRTUR | .69 | Act according to plan vs play by ear | Judging |
|  | JNG06 | .40 | Peacemaker vs judge | Feeling |

Standardized Item Alpha = .43 (Note: the low alpha here is probably due to the omission from the questionnaire instrument of some of the MBTI items in the judging scale. In the original Kilmann conceptualization, judging is not a variable. Some judging items were included in the research for general interest, and they proved, as indicated here, to be of potential interest for diagnostic purposes).

Low Factor Score = Premeditation; High Factor Score = Extemporaneity

Exhibit 13.3 (continued)

### Factor #7 — Ideational-Literal

In contrast to Factor #1, which is concerned with the new and different constrasted with the conventional, this factor differentiates leaders who are theoretical in their thinking versus literal. Note that both factors use Sensation-designated items from the MBTI.

| Question Number | Code Name | Factor Loading | Abbreviated Item | Original MBTI Concept |
|---|---|---|---|---|
| 2 | JTEACH | .68 | Rather teach facts vs theory | Sensation |
| 13 | JREAD | -.63 | Read odd/original vs exact meaning* | Sensation |
|  | JNG13 | .41 | Certainty vs theory | Sensation |

* Item reversed in scoring

Standardized Item Alpha = .49
Low Factor Score = Literal; High Factor Score = Ideational

### Factor #8 — Consideration-Reasonableness

This factor, like Factor 4, is composed from the MBTI "feeling" items. In constrast to Factor 4, which in the Jungian framework, reflects a leader's preference for processing information once absorbed, this factor is split out as an attitudinal or behavioral preference for dealing not with information, but with people.

| Question Number | Code Name | Factor Loading | Abbreviated Item | Original MBTI Concept |
|---|---|---|---|---|
|  | JNG03 | -.73 | Convincing vs touching | Feeling |
|  | JNG09 | -.35 | Analyze vs sympathize | Feeling |
|  | JNG15 | -.39 | Justice vs mercy | Feeling |

Standardized Item Alpha = .45

Low Factor Score = Reasonableness; High Factor Score = Consideration

**Exhibit 13.4**
**Scale Intercorrelations**

**Scale Correlation Matrix**

| Scale Name | PU | IR | GF | RA | IE | EP | IL | CR |
|---|---|---|---|---|---|---|---|---|
| Practicality-Unconventionality | 1.00 | .24 | .03 | -.15 | .23 | .01 | -.22 | .17 |
| Intimacy-Relationships | .24 | 1.00 | -.02 | .06 | .45 | .22 | .13 | -.09 |
| Gentility-Firm-mindedness | .03 | -.02 | 1.00 | -.29 | .05 | .01 | -.17 | .32 |
| Rationality-Affect | -.15 | .06 | -.29 | 1.00 | .14 | .09 | .34 | -.34 |
| Introversion-Extroversion | .23 | .45 | .05 | .14 | 1.00 | .12 | .11 | .03 |
| Extemporaneity-Premeditation | .01 | .22 | .01 | .09 | .12 | 1.00 | .17 | .09 |
| Ideational-Literal | -.22 | .13 | -.17 | .34 | .11 | .17 | 1.00 | -.24 |
| Consideration-Reasonableness | .12 | .02 | .35 | -.36 | .07 | .11 | -.26 | 1.00 |

Rationality-Affect and Consideration-Reasonableness at a negative .36. Presumably these correlations can be further reduced with additional psychometric testing.

There is some evidence of skewness in the data. This finding, in fact, forced some of the analysis to be performed with only parts of the data, as noted later in Part V dealing with the findings. In Exhibit 13.6, the distributions for each scale are noted.

In a final check on the validity of the scales derived from the factors, the stability of the factor structure was tested. The sample was divided into two groups comprising first, government, universities, and ERATO; and second, the corporate sector, including NTT. While no formal statistical comparison of the factor structures was attempted, it is fair to say that the single structure described above may not be stable across all of the sample groups. First of all, in each case, a six-factor, rather than eight-factor solution emerged. Some of the factors contained similar items to the overall factor structure, but others pulled in items that had been omitted in the full-sample factor analysis. It is clear that additional work must be performed to develop an underlying structure that can be applied validly to all groups.

**Exhibit 13.5**
**Mean Scores on the Scales for Leaders**

| Scale Name | N | Mean[*] | Standard Deviation |
|---|---|---|---|
| Practicality-Unconventionality | 150 | 6.43 | 1.55 |
| Intimacy-Relationships | 150 | 6.61 | 1.57 |
| Gentility-Firm-mindedness | 150 | 6.17 | 1.29 |
| Rationality-Affect | 150 | 6.83 | 1.33 |
| Introvert-Extrovert | 150 | 6.29 | 1.43 |
| Extemporaneity-Premeditation | 150 | 5.23 | 1.15 |
| Ideational-Literal | 149 | 4.17 | 1.03 |
| Consideration-Reasonableness | 150 | 4.22 | 1.04 |

[*] Sums of scale scores were converted to Z Scores in order to compare scales with different numbers of items.

## PSYCHOMETRICS OF THE CONFLICT MANAGEMENT SCALES

With respect to the second key independent variable, conflict management modes, the categories of the Thomas-Kilmann MODE instrument also broke down somewhat in the Japanese testing (though as with the MBTI, the dimensions are interestingly diagnostic and potentially reflective of cultural differences).

Attempts to measure conflict empirically have increased in recent years, particularly as the conceptualizations of the idea have proliferated (see, for example, London & Howat 1978; Zammuto, London, & Rowland 1979; Howat & London 1980; Rahim 1983a; 1983b). For this research, the instrument designed by Thomas and Kilmann (1974) was chosen. According to the Thomas-Kilmann theory (derived in part from the earlier work of Blake and Mouton and from Thomas's conceptualization noted above), individuals will express a preference for resolving differences with others through one of five means (actually, through one dominant, one secondary mode): accommodation, avoidance, compromise, competition, or collaboration. These five modes, in turn, are the resultant of the motivational vector formed by the joining of two personality characteristics or attitudes: the need to be assertive in service of one's own needs

**Exhibit 13.6**
**Frequency Distributions for Eight Factor/Scales**

| Scale Name | Value | Frequency | Percent[*] |
|---|---|---|---|
| Practicality-Unconventionality | | | |
| | 2 | 1 | 1 |
| | 5 | 52 | 35 |
| | 6 | 38 | 25 |
| | 7 | 25 | 17 |
| | 8 | 15 | 10 |
| | 9 | 10 | 7 |
| | 10 | 9 | 6 |
| Total | | 150 | 101 |
| | | | |
| Intimacy-Relationships | | | |
| | 1 | 1 | 1 |
| | 3 | 1 | 1 |
| | 5 | 41 | 27 |
| | 6 | 34 | 23 |
| | 7 | 34 | 23 |
| | 8 | 17 | 11 |
| | 9 | 15 | 10 |
| | 10 | 7 | 5 |
| Total | | 150 | 102 |
| | | | |
| Gentility-Firm-mindedness | | | |
| | 1 | 1 | 1 |
| | 4 | 17 | 11 |
| | 5 | 27 | 18 |
| | 6 | 34 | 23 |
| | 7 | 51 | 34 |
| | 8 | 20 | 13 |
| Total | | 150 | 100 |
| | | | |
| Rationality-Affect | | | |
| | 2 | 1 | 1 |
| | 4 | 9 | 6 |
| | 5 | 17 | 11 |
| | 6 | 25 | 17 |
| | 7 | 31 | 21 |
| | 8 | 66 | 44 |
| | - | 1 | Missing |
| Total | | 150 | 100 |

[*] Figures may not add to 100% due to rounding.

**Exhibit 13.6 (continued)**

Introversion-Extroversion

| | | |
|---|---|---|
| 1 | 1 | 1 |
| 3 | 1 | 1 |
| 4 | 44 | 29 |
| 5 | 45 | 30 |
| 6 | 38 | 25 |
| 7 | 17 | 11 |
| 8 | 4 | 3 |
| Total | 150 | 98 |

Extemporaneity-Premeditation

| | | |
|---|---|---|
| 1 | 1 | 1 |
| 3 | 1 | 1 |
| 4 | 44 | 29 |
| 5 | 45 | 30 |
| 6 | 38 | 25 |
| 7 | 17 | 11 |
| 8 | 4 | 3 |
| Total | 150 | 100 |

Ideational-Literal

| | | |
|---|---|---|
| 2 | 1 | 1 |
| 3 | 48 | 32 |
| 4 | 42 | 28 |
| 5 | 41 | 27 |
| 6 | 17 | 11 |
| - | 1 | Missing |
| Total | 150 | 99 |

Consideration-Reasonableness

| | | |
|---|---|---|
| 2 | 1 | 1 |
| 3 | 43 | 29 |
| 4 | 49 | 33 |
| 5 | 36 | 24 |
| 6 | 21 | 14 |
| Total | 150 | 100 |

and the need to be attentive to the needs of others. Thus, a person who is strongly assertive in service of his or her own aims and is not dispositionally inclined to care about others is likely to engage in highly competitive conflict management behavior. On the other hand, a person who is highly assertive but also attentive to others' concerns will be more collaborative in his conflict management behavior, tending to use nonzero sum, integrative means to resolve differences.

By invoking constructs of personality as the driving forces predisposing individuals to resolve conflicts in various ways, Thomas and Kilmann make assumptions about the relative strength and persistence of personality across different situations, a subject of some considerable debate in the literature (cf. Bem & Allen 1974; Veroff 1983; McCrae & Costa 1984) and of special interest in the Japanese setting because the culture creates pressure to be more adaptive than persistent. Although Thomas and Kilmann allege that the modes of resolution actually are influenced by *both* personality and situation (cf. Womack 1988), it is unclear what proportion is attributable to each. As will be seen, because of the differences in cultures, particularly in the inner- and other-directedness discussed in earlier chapters, this ambiguity directly affects the interpretation of the findings from comparative research.

The Thomas-Kilmann "MODE" instrument comprises 30 forced-choice, dichotomous items, set in an ipsative format, that is, respondent choices of one item or set of items result in an increase in one conflict management preferred mode score matched by a corresponding reduction in the others. The scales have been validated and tested for reliability with fair-to-good success with American subjects (Thomas & Kilmann 1978; Kilmann & Thomas 1977; though see the serious critical review by Womack 1988). For this research, the MODE was translated into Japanese and back-translated to assure validity.

As noted earlier, the data were coded and recorded on tape in Japan, transported to the United States, then entered into a university computer mainframe for analysis. The initial objective of the research was to examine the distribution of Japanese R & D managers across the five conflict management styles and to compare these figures with those obtained in the United States. It was necessary first, however, to determine the construct validity of the Japanese version and the degree of its comparability to the English-language version. A factor analysis of the Japanese data was conducted for this purpose. Despite criticisms of the use of factor analysis for ipsative measures (Jackson & Alwin 1980; Saville & Willson 1991; Cornwell & Dunlap 1994), the exploratory nature of the study in the Japanese setting seemed to warrant such an inquiry.

Initial results show a dramatic departure from the factor structure reported by the publishers of the American version, thus preventing valid cross-cultural comparisons of mean use by laboratory leaders of the various conflict management modes. Factors unique to the Japanese sample were, however, identified and named.

## FINDINGS FROM THE FACTOR ANALYSIS

The factor analysis produced some interesting and potentially useful scales. The following are the names of the eight factors that were produced in the factor analysis.

|                        | Eigen Value | Percent of Variance Explained |
|------------------------|-------------|-------------------------------|
| 1. Avoid Assertiveness | 4.9         | 16.2                          |

| | | |
|---|---|---|
| 2. Self-Assertiveness | 2.3 | 7.8 |
| 3. Collaborate | 2.0 | 6.7 |
| 4. Avoid Tension/Controversy | 1.6 | 5.2 |
| 5. Avoid Responsibility | 1.5 | 4.9 |
| 6. Not Compromise | 1.3 | 4.4 |
| 7. Compromise | 1.3 | 4.4 |
| 8. Not Avoid | 1.3 | 4.2 |

Cumulative 53.8

The composition of each of these scales appears in Exhibit 13.7. The factor analysis was computed using a principal components approach with various rotational strategies, including varimax, equamax, quartimax, and oblimin. The structure did not vary across these strategies, however. The figures reported above are for the varimax procedure. Variations in the constraints on the number of factors produced resulted in these factors as constituting the most interpretable set. The eight factors appear to reflect four pairs of polar opposites: assertiveness/nonassertiveness; collaboration/noncollaboration; avoidance/nonavoidance; and compromise/noncompromise. (Missing from the Thomas-Kilmann MODE framework is a pairing of accommodation/nonaccommodation, attesting, in part perhaps, to the lack of consistent commitment to or rejection of a totally cooperative attitude on the part of the sample respondents.) Several features of these findings are worth noting. First, Japanese respondents to the instrument perceive more nuances in the questions than Western respondents. Whereas the latter concentrate on the part of the stem that positively reflects their personalities, the Japanese also strongly take into account the stem they are *rejecting*. Hence, Westerners' scores may be arrayed from high to low on each of the five scales, but the Japanese responses include not only the preferred responses but those rejected. Thus, for example, on the competitiveness dimension, some of the Japanese respondents appear to be indicating that they must be able to reject the assertiveness aspects of the items. Others, on the other hand, need to indicate that they are, indeed, competitive. It is possible, therefore, for Japanese R & D managers to be self-rated as both highly competitive and highly noncompetitive, since the rejected items for the "compete" scale are different from the chosen items for the noncompete scale, and, conversely, the rejected items for the noncompete scale are different from the chosen items for the compete scale. (Although the Varimax rotation theoretically should have produced orthogonal dimensions, in actual practice, there are often correlations across the scales.)

While these findings appear somewhat similar to the conceptualization of Herzberg, who dichotomized satisfaction into two separate scales measuring satisfaction (from low to high) and dissatisfaction (from low to high), the dichotomization is conceptually and theoretically quite different. For Herzberg, a

**Exhibit 13.7**
**Factor Structure of the Thomas-Kilmann MODE Instrument (Japanese Translation, 1989)**

Factor I — Avoid Assertiveness

Japanese R & D leaders who score high on this scale desire to avoid aggressive pursuit of their own ends vis-à-vis others.

| Question Number | Factor[1] Loading | Original Thomas-Kilmann Item Category | Abbreviated Item |
|---|---|---|---|
| 9 | 68 | Avoid | I feel differences are not always worth worrying about. |
|  |  | **Compete** | I make some effort to get my way. |
| 13 | 57 | Compromise | I propose a middle ground. |
|  |  | **Compete** | I press to get my points made. |
| 14 | 73 | Collaborate | I tell the other person my ideas and ask his. |
|  |  | **Compete** | I try to show the other person the merits of my position. |
| 16 | 60 | Accommodate | I try not to hurt the other's feelings. |
|  |  | **Compete** | I try to convince the other person of the merits of my position. |
| 22 | 66 | Compromise | I try to find a position that is intermediate between his and mine. |
|  |  | **Compete** | I assert my wishes. |
| 25 | -65 | **Compete** | I try to show the other person the logic and benefits of my position. |
|  |  | Accommodate | In approaching negotiations, I try to be considerate of the other person's wishes. |

1. Decimals and signs omitted. The original T-K category names are noted for reference, with bold type signifying the items whose face validity was considerd in the naming of the factor. For this particular factor, the cluster of items on which there were high loadings made no sense. However, all of the paired opposites of the loaded items were classified as "Compete" in the T-K typology. The factor can thus be interpreted as a *rejection* of "competition," rather than a preference for any of the loaded items.

**Exhibit 13.7 (continued)**

Factor II — Self-Assertiveness

This factor reflects the Japanese R & D manager's predisposition to be competitive in interpersonal relationships.

| Question Number | Factor Loading | Original Thomas-Kilmann Item Category | Abbreviated Item |
|---|---|---|---|
| 3 | 69 | Compete | I am usually firm in pursuing my goals. |
| | | Accommodate | I might try to soothe the other's feelings and preserve our relationship. |
| 10 | 70 | Compete | I am firm in pursuing my goals. |
| | | Compromise | I try to find a compromise solution. |
| 17 | 73 | Compete | I am usually firm in pursuing my goals. |
| | | Avoid | I try to do what is necessary to avoid useless tensions. |

**Factor III — Collaborate**

Leaders scoring high on this factor prefer collaborating over the other conflict management modes.

| Question Number | Factor Loading | Original Thomas-Kilmann Item Category | Abbreviated Item |
|---|---|---|---|
| 8 | -68 | Compete | I am usually firm in pursuing my goals. |
| | | Collaborate | I attempt to get all concerns and issues immediately out in the open. |
| 11 | 70 | Collaborate | I attempt to get all concerns and issues immediately out in the open. |
| | | Accommodate | I might try to soothe the other's feelings and preserve our relationship. |
| 19 | 76 | Collaborate | I attempt to get all concerns and issues immediately out in the open. |

**Exhibit 13.7 (continued)**

| | | | |
|---|---|---|---|
| | | Avoid | I try to postpone the issue until I have had some time to think it over. |

### Factor IV — Avoid Tensions/Controversy

This abbreviated scale (which must be fleshed out for further empirical investigations) connotes a predilection not to become involved in controversy. (See Factor V also)

| Question Number | Factor* Loading | Original Thomas-Kilmann Item Category | Abbreviated Item |
|---|---|---|---|
| 27 | 77 | Avoid | I sometimes avoid taking positions that would create controversy. |
| | | Accommodate | If it makes the other people happy, I might let them maintain their views. |
| 5 | -59 | Collaborate | I consistently seek the other's help in working out a solution. |
| | | Avoid | I try to do what is necessary to avoid useless tensions. |

### Factor V — Avoid Responsibility

In some contrast to Factor IV, where avoidance of controversy characterized the attitude or disposition, here, managers who score high on this short scale prefer to avoid accepting responsibility.

| Question Number | Factor* Loading | Original Thomas-Kilmann Item Category | Abbreviated Item |
|---|---|---|---|
| 1 | 67 | Avoid | There are times when I let others take responsibility for solving the problem. |
| | | Accommodate | Rather than negotiate the things on which we disagree, I try to stress the things upon which we agree. |
| 23 | -65 | Collaborate | I am very often concerned with satisfying all our wishes. |
| | | Avoid | There are times when I let others take responsibility for solving the problem. |

## Exhibit 13.7 (continued)

### Factor VI — Not Compromise

With this factor, as with the first, managers who score high are not selecting any particular conflict management mode so much as they are expressing a preference not to engage in compromise.

| Question Number | Factor* Loading | Original Thomas-Kilmann Item Category | Abbreviated Item |
|---|---|---|---|
| 12 | 52 | Avoid | I sometimes avoid taking positions which would create controversy. |
|  |  | Compromise | I will let the other person have some of his positions if he lets me have some of mine. |
| 18 | 75 | Accommodate | If it makes the other person happy, I might let him maintain his views. |
|  |  | Compromise | I will let the other person have some of his positions if he lets me have some of mine. |
| 20 | 52 | Collaborate | I attempt to immediately work through our differences. |
|  |  | Compromise | I try to find a fair combination of gains and losses for both of us. |

### Factor VII — Compromise

This factor rather straightforwardly taps managerial preference for compromise.

| Question Number | Factor* Loading | Original Thomas-Kilmann Item Category | Abbreviated Item |
|---|---|---|---|
| 2 | 47 | Compromise | I try to find a compromise solution. |
|  |  | Collaborate | I attempt to deal with all of his and my concerns. |
| 24 | 63 | Accommodate | If the other person's position seems very important to him, I would try to meet his wishes. |
|  |  | Compromise | I try to get the other person to settle for a compromise. |
| 26 | 63 | Compromise | I propose a middle ground. |
|  |  | Collaborate | I am nearly always concerned with satisfying all our wishes. |

**Exhibit 13.7 (continued)**

### Factor VIII — Not Avoid

Managers who score high on Factor VIII are expressing their predilections not to avoid conflict.

| Question Number | Factor* Loading | Original Thomas-Kilmann Item Category | Abbreviated Item |
|---|---|---|---|
| 7 | -62 | Avoid | I try to postpone the issue until I have had some time to think it over. |
| | | Compromise | I give up some points in exchange for others. |
| 15 | 56 | Accommodate | I might try to sooth the other's feelings and preserve our relationship. |
| | | Avoid | I try to do what is necessary to avoid tensions. |

worker could be simultaneously satisfied and dissatisfied, though with respect to different features of the organizational environment. In the case of the conflict management scales developed herein, while it could be also argued (as with Herzberg) that any one manager could score high on each pole of the pairs, particularly if the issue or question shifts, it is more likely that the pairs veridically reflect subtle differences across managers in their preferred interaction modes. For example, different managers in Japan may indeed be more or less assertive, but they may also vary in the degree to which they seek to avoid being assertive. Similarly, there is a range of collaborativeness and non-collaborativeness; of avoiding and rejecting avoidance; and of compromising and not compromising.

In sum, rather than four scales with continuous values from high to low, for Japanese managers there are eight, with the negative sides revealing strong preferences for *not* doing something, rather than a weak or low preference in favor of doing something. The complex and ambiguous nature of the Japanese psyche is thus here reflected in the positive "force" of diffidence or deference given by managers to certain behaviors which in other cultures would be viewed as simply low value for that particular personality variable. As will be noted later, it is the set of traits of a negative or "refraining" nature that distinguishes between leaders and nonleaders in research and development laboratories.

The ways in which this array of conflict management preferences differs from the American one reveals much about the meaning of conflict denial in Japan. Recall first that the items developed by Thomas and Kilmann for the American instrument represent behaviors intended to reflect one of the five modes of conflict management: compete, accommodate, compromise, avoid, or collaborate. These modes, in turn, reflect two ''personality'' dimensions: assertiveness and cooperativeness. For the Japanese respondent, however, these dimensions are culture-biased. First of all, as noted earlier, assertiveness in Japan is manifested in a much more subtle and indirect way than is expressed in the items as written in English (and as translated for this research). As a result, when faced with a choice between any of the high-assertiveness items (compete or collaborate) and items from any of the other conflict management modes, the Japanese respondent will almost invariably choose the latter, even if the stated behavior does not really reveal his preference. Hence, the first factor is virtually not interpretable through the face validity of the items which loaded on it. However, when examining the alternatives from which the respondent had to choose, it is clear that collectively they constitute a nonassertiveness disposition.

Second, as noted above, the importance the Japanese place on the group and on group harmony makes it difficult for them to imagine themselves as having characteristics which are invariant across situations. Without a specified group, person, and particular situation, Japanese respondents find it difficult to conceive of how they would act and so are hard-pressed to respond to any questionnaire item that asks them to do so. This is not to say that the Japanese do not have distinctive personalities. It is only to say that different aspects of the personality are manifested over time and situations. ''Personality,'' in other words, is not just a complex of predispositions to behave; it is a set of complexes, each of which is called into action when the situation is appropriate. (Note the related Japanese concept of *shugyo*—the transfer of knowledge, skills, and behavior patterns from one situation to another [Hasagawa 1986, 115].) In terms of theories of symbolic interaction, the dyadic framework for action is created by the partners in the interaction, and the behavior represents one of the personality complexes in the repertoires of each partner.

Looked at from the perspective of canonical leadership theory, each leader or potential leader, in interaction with colleagues, subordinates, or superordinates, invokes those aspects of personality as are appropriate to the situation. In the short run, faced with a conflict situation in which expression of certain parts of his personality would not be functional for the group, the Japanese manager will refrain from manifesting it. This would seem to invalidate Fiedler's conclusions for U.S. leaders, namely, that situational contingencies demand changes in the situation (not the leader behavior which is relatively intransigent for any one individual) in order for the organization to be effective. Westerners tend to believe that their psychological makeup is a consistent, coherent set of predispositions to behave similarly almost regardless of situational constraints.

Although, of course, all but the completely naive would admit that short-run contingencies sometimes demand restraint of certain personality traits, Western managers will be more likely to assert that over time, they act consistently toward workers, irrespective of the situation. Indeed, it is virtually a mark of virtue in the Western world to be able to claim an enduring, even predictable personality—departures being labeled as weak, duplicitous, or giving-in to others with stronger personalities. Japanese managers, in contrast to those in this country, are apparently able to be more flexible and adaptive to the situation, and without social stigma. Although the situations in Japan may appear to be less variable to Westerners (because of the perceived homogeneity of the society to outsiders), in point of fact, there is great variation, however subtle it may be. Just as some cultures are able to perceive quarter- or even eighth-tone differences in pitch that Western music listeners can not discern, so also, the Japanese make finer distinctions in situational contingencies than do Americans. Hence, even if the variance seems to Westerners not as wide, to the Japanese it is, and the culture-induced sensitivity of the Japanese both permits and constrains the manager to make necessary adaptations in ways that American managers are not disposed, nor trained to make.

As a result of these subtleties, there is considerable "noise" in the Japanese data from the translated MODE questionnaire. Respondents were forced to make assumptions about the situation, and, since these assumptions may have been different for different respondents, there is much added variance in the data. Despite these reservations about the instrument, the scales (at least some of them) and the format may be worth saving and developing further. The scales noted above seem to have some face validity and could be fleshed out with further items in subsequent testing.

## VALIDATION OF THE JOB DESCRIPTION SURVEY

As with the MBTI and the Thomas-Kilmann MODE instruments, validation of the instrument measuring the dependent variables of the study—worker attitudes—was performed through a series of factor analyses, using a principal axis procedure (Harmon 1976) with various rotations and extraction delimitations. For these data a Quartimax rotation produced the most meaningful and interpretable factors. Thirteen factors in the Hackman and Oldham model accounted for 53.3 percent of the variance (see Exhibit 13.8).

The initial factor analysis produced a strong single factor plus a number of secondary factors. The items with high loadings on the first factor in the analysis were then segregated and subjected to a second-order factor analysis. The result was a breakdown of the first factor into three clearly identifiable subfactors (labeled in the exhibits 1A, 1B and 1C), thus increasing the number of factors or scales to thirteen in number. These are listed in Exhibit 13.9, organized somewhat arbitrarily in groupings suggested by the face validity of the scales. Nine of the scales appear to be what Hackman and Oldham would call "job characteristics." The other four are hypothetical resultants of the values of those job characteristics. The descriptions of each of the scales and their reliabilities are noted in Exhibit 13.9.

Interpretation of the meaning of this factor structure using the Japanese sample is not easily accomplished, owing in part to the alleged instability of the

**Exhibit 13.8**
**Thirteen Factors Emerging from the Job Description Questionnaire (Japanese Version, 1989)**

I.  Job Characteristics

    A.  Worker Interactions and Relationships
        1.  Work/Task Interdependence
        2.  Cooperativeness/Collegiality

    B.  Clarity or Ambiguity of the Work
        3.  Clarity of Job Content
        4.  Feedback Adequacy

    C.  Work Demands and Characteristics
        5.  Workload
        6.  Work Diversity
        7.  Control Over Task
        8.  Adequacy of Tools and Equipment

    D.  Psychological Relevance to Work
        9.  Job Meaningfulness/Significance

II.  Outcome Variables

    A.  Relationship to Organization
        1.  Organizational Identification and Pride
        2.  Organizational Commitment

    B.  Relationship to Self
        3.  Personal Satisfaction
        4.  Self-Esteem

factor structure in the English-language version as well. As the Dunham, Aldag, and Brief study (1977) reported, the Hackman and Oldham conceptualization of a five-factor solution for the job characteristics appeared to be validated in only two of twenty samples reported in the research literature (cf. Fried & Ferris 1986). Other purported limitations of the instrumentation include the ''common method variance'' resulting from using respondents to report both the nature of the characteristics as well as their dependent satisfactions (cf. Algera 1990). In combination with the extraordinary intertwining in Japan of social/interpersonal nuances with all organizational actions and interactions, the attribution of ''reality'' to the job characteristics themselves must be suspect. What these factors seem to indicate, consequently, follows more closely the Salancik and Pfeffer (1978) suggestion that the job characteristics are perceptual, not [necessarily] ''real'' (cf. Algera 1990). Fortunately, such an intepretation does not invalidate the insights to be gained from the findings. How Japanese scientists view their work environments can be better understood as comprising the complex of the thirteen factors that emerged from this research. The impact of these perceptual

**Exhibit 13.9**

**Factor Structure of the Job Description Questionnaire (Japanese Version, 1989)**

### Factor 1A — ORGANIZATIONAL IDENTIFICATION AND PRIDE

| Question Number (and Page)[2] | | Code Name | Factor Loading[1] | Abbreviated Item |
|---|---|---|---|---|
| 2 | (7) | QUITPROP | .67 | Low quit propensity |
| 1 | (8) | WORKHRDER | .67 | Work harder |
| 2 | (8) | NICEPLCE | .77 | Nice place to work |
| 3 | (8) | IDENTIFY (R) | -.58 | Don't identify with org'n |
| 4 | (8) | ROTHRD | .57 | If rotate, will work hard |
| 5 | (8) | AGREEMGT | .64 | Agree with management |
| 6 | (8) | ORGPRIDE | .75 | Pride in organization |
| 9 | (8) | CLIMATE | .68 | Favorable climate |
| 11 | (8) | SATSCHCE | .81 | Satisfied with choice |
| 12 | (8) | QUITLT (R) | -.70 | Would quit |
| 15 | (9) | BESTWORK | .76 | Do best work |
| 16 | (9) | MISTAKE (R) | -.73 | Mistake to join here |

R= Item reversed in scoring

Standardized Item Alpha= .90
Low Factor Score= Low organizational identification and pride

### Factor 1B — PERSONAL SATISFACTION

| Question Number (and Page) | | Code Name | Factor Loading | Abbreviated Item |
|---|---|---|---|---|
| 18 | (9) | SATSGENL | .53 | Satisfaction general |
| 22 | (9) | SATSROLE | .46 | Role satisfaction |
| 1-3 | (7) | SATSWORK | .36 | Satisfaction with work |
| 1 | (5) | SATSFTOT | .39 | Total satisfaction |

Standardized Item Alpha= .88
Low Factor Score= Low satisfaction

### Factor 1C — ORGANIZATIONAL COMMITMENT

| Question Number (and Page) | | Code Name | Factor Loading | Abbreviated Item |
|---|---|---|---|---|
| 7 | (8) | XFERWORK | -.53 | Would xsfer for better work |
| 8 | (8) | XFERPAY | -.35 | Would xsfer for better pay |

1. The loadings noted in the Exhibit are those that appeared in the original factor analysis, not in the refactoring of the first factor.
2. Page numbers refer to Japanese version of the questionnaire.

**Exhibit 13.9 (continued)**

| 10 | (8) | QUITFRNG | -.47 | Would quit for more fringes |
|----|-----|----------|------|------------------------------|

Standardized Item Alpha= .78
Low Factor Score= Low organizational commitment

### Factor 2 — WORK TASK INTERDEPENDENCE

| Question Number (and Page) | | Code Name | Factor Loading | Abbreviated Item |
|----|-----|----------|------|------------------------------|
| 2  | (5)  | CWRKLINK     | .44  | My work affects others |
| 6  | (5)  | WKPEOPLE     | .64  | Must work closely w/others |
| 11 | (6)  | INDEPEND (R) | -.50 | Can work even if others don't |
| 6  | (10) | WORKLINK     | .60  | Others depend on my work |
| 12 | (10) | PERFEFCT     | .53  | Other persons affected |
| 17 | (11) | WORKPACE     | .78  | Other's pace affects mine |
| 20 | (11) | OTHERQUAL    | .73  | Other's quality affects mine |
| 22 | (11) | LINKSREQ     | .64  | Must talk and coordinate |
| 23 | (11) | JOBEFFECT    | .50  | Job can affect many others |
| 27 | (11) | COOPNECY     | .70  | Job requires cooperation |

Standardized Item Alpha= .88
Low Factor Score= Low interdependence

### Factor 3 — WORK DIVERSITY

| Question Number (and Page) | | Code Name | Factor Loading | Abbreviated Item |
|----|-----|----------|------|------------------------------|
| 3  | (5)  | JOBVARY      | .44  | Variety in Job |
| 10 | (10) | OPPTYCRAT    | .66  | Opp'ty to be creative |
| 18 | (11) | HIGHSKIL     | .50  | Use complex skills |
| 19 | (11) | WORKSIMPL (R) | -.46 | Use simple skills |
| 28 | (11) | CHLNGEOK     | .58  | Able to challenge |

Standardized Item Alpha= .73
Low Factor Score= Low diversity

### Factor 4 — CONTROL OVER TASK

| Question Number (and Page) | | Code Name | Factor Loading | Abbreviated Item |
|----|-----|----------|------|------------------------------|
| 7  | (6)  | AUTONOMY     | .58  | Degree of autonomy |
| 12 | (6)  | COMPLJOB     | .64  | Do whole piece of work |
| 3  | (10) | WORKAUTY     | .60  | Can decide by self |
| 16 | (11) | WORKDONE     | .62  | Opp'ty to finish work |
| 24 | (11) | JOBIDENTY (R) | -.48 | Job not begin to end |

Standardized Item Alpha= .76
Low Factor Score= Low Control

**Exhibit 13.9 (continued)**

### Factor 5 — SELF-ESTEEM

| Question Number (and Page) | | Code Name | Factor Loading | Abbreviated Item |
|---|---|---|---|---|
| 17 | (9) | OPINIONUP | .63 | Opinion up if good job |
| 19 | (9) | SATSPERF | .63 | Satisf. w/own performance |
| 21 | (9) | FEELPERF | .58 | Sad if bad performance |
| 23 | (9) | PERFEEL (R) | -.60 | Perf. not affect feelings |

Standardized Item Alpha= .74
Low Factor Score= Low self-esteem

### Factor 6 — EXTERNAL FEEDBACK ADEQUACY

| Question Number (and Page) | | Code Name | Factor Loading | Abbreviated Item |
|---|---|---|---|---|
| 10 | (6) | OTHRFDBK | .70 | Info. from mgrs/co-workers |
| 13 | (10) | FDBKOTHR | .59 | Superv./colleagues advise |
| 25 | (11) | NOFDBACK (R) | -.78 | No superv./colleagues advise |

Standardized Item Alpha= .78
Low Factor Score= Little feedback

### Factor 7 — COOPERATIVENESS/COLLEGIALITY

| Question Number (and Page) | | Code Name | Factor Loading | Abbreviated Item |
|---|---|---|---|---|
| 9 | (6) | COOPROV | .51 | Cooperation from others |
| 1-1 | (7) | SATSCOLG | .60 | Satisfaction w/colleagues |
| 1-4 | (7) | SATSLEDR | .41 | Satisfaction w/leader |
| 7 | (10) | CCPEASY | .40 | Cooperation when needed |

Standardized Item Alpha= .70
Low Factor Score= Little cooperation

### Factor 8 — WORKLOAD

| Question Number (and Page) | | Code Name | Factor Loading | Abbreviated Item |
|---|---|---|---|---|
| 1 | (10) | WORKOVLD | .77 | Difficult to do all work |
| 9 | (10) | WORKQUANT (R) | -.70 | Work quantity not burden |
| 11 | (10) | LINKDFCLT | .45 | Too much to coordinate |

Standardized Item Alpha= .73
Low Factor Score= Little work overload

**Exhibit 13.9 (continued)**

### Factor 9 — ADEQUACY OF TOOLS AND EQUIPMENT

| Question Number (and Page) | | Code Name | Factor Loading | Abbreviated Item |
|---|---|---|---|---|
| 5 | (5) | TOOLPROV | .74 | Tools & machines provided |
| 14 | (10) | MACHTOOL | .86 | Machines & tools provided |

Standardized Item Alpha= .85
Low Factor Score= Few tools and machines provided

### Factor 10 — JOB CONTENT CLARITY

| Question Number (and Page) | | Code Name | Factor Loading | Abbreviated Item |
|---|---|---|---|---|
| 4 | (5) | JOBFDBK | .63 | Job itself feeds back |
| 2 | (10) | WORKFDBK | .49 | Can assess job success |
| 5 | (10) | CLRCNTNT | .46 | Assignments clear |
| 26 | (11) | FDBKUNEC | .47 | No need for feedback |

Standardized Item Alpha= .66
Low Factor Score= Job content is unclear

### Factor 11 — JOB MEANINGFULNESS/SIGNIFICANCE

| Question Number (and Page) | | Code Name | Factor Loading | Abbreviated Item |
|---|---|---|---|---|
| 8 | (6) | JOBSIGNF | .63 | Significance of job |
| 8 | (10) | JOBVALUE (R) | -.60 | Low job imp. in org'n |
| 23 | (11) | JOBEFFCT | .49 | Job affects others |

Standardized Item Alpha= .79
Low Factor Score= Low job meaningfulness/significance

frameworks on their work motivation and productivity can be instructive in explaining the success of Japanese R & D in general. As Glick, Jenkins, and Gupta (1986) note, although there is still much work needed on method effects in the use of the JDS, valid predictions are possible. They note:

Social information processing has its theoretical roots in social comparison theory and thus provides a better explanation of individuals' affective responses. On the other hand, the job characteristics approach, which has its roots in expectancy theory, serves better in predicting more behavior-oriented responses like motivation, effort, and performance.

## SUMMARY

To recapitulate, translations of three English-language questionnaires were employed in the research. Not unexpectedly, cross-cultural validity could not be established for any of them. The two cultures, Japan and the United States, differ significantly in so many ways that the meanings connoted by the conceptualizations and their operationalizations in English were quite differently interpreted by the Japanese. While at some future time, it may be interesting, possible, and useful to compare responses across the two nations using instruments psychometrically validated for comparable use instruments, for the instruments used herein and for the purposes of the study direct comparisons cannot be made.

The data and instrument analysis, nevertheless, have considerable value. By themselves, they reveal much about how organizational conditions are perceived by workers in Japanese organizations. As noted in this chapter, for example, the nature of the personality variable "assertiveness" in conflict management must be seen in its cultural context—the Japanese being unable or unwilling to consider themselves as assertive and unable or unwilling to indicate probable actions in the absence of the concreteness of specific situations.

The development of new variables and scales to measure them will be seen in the findings (Chapters 14–16) to be of significant value in sorting out the relationships among independent and dependent variables. In point of fact, the conceptual framework that guided the research is not vitiated by the change in instrumentation. Broadly, the independent variables of leadership and conflict management, now newly defined and measured, can be expected to have impacts on worker motivation, satisfaction, and productivity. This, indeed, is the subject of the next chapter.

## NOTE

1. The questionnaire in both English and Japanese forms may be obtained from the author.

# 14

# Leadership by Japanese
# R & D Managers

## INTRODUCTION

The number of findings from the analysis of the questionnaires and interviews are many and diverse. In general, the plan of presentation follows the sequence of the research questions presented in the methods chapter. Along with the data, interpretations are offered, drawing on the observations in earlier chapters. This chapter begins with an analysis of some basic demographic characteristics and attitudes of R & D leaders, particularly as these may differ across the three kinds of settings: corporations, universities, and government laboratories. (These categories were expanded later to include subcategories that proved to be revealing of special differences within the major sectors.)

This section is followed with a discussion of leadership traits found in the sample. Since the Myers-Briggs Type Indicator was the basic data-collection instrument used for the research, it is necessary first to show how the results reflect a uniquely Japanese set of traits. As will be noted, inspection of the data as they were reorganized through computer-assisted analysis revealed a need to reconstitute and relabel the major factors. With the new constructs, it was possible to find eight clusters of different kinds of leaders whose characteristics were maximally differentiated from one another. In other words, Japanese leadership is not a monolithic concept; there are a number of different types of leaders. As will also be noted, different types of leaders seem to prevail across the different settings in which the research was conducted.

In the next section, a similar presentation is offered, this time using the data from the Thomas-Kilmann Conflict MODE instrument. Here again, the scores on this instrument were factor analyzed. Once more, the validity of the Western interpretation is called into question. The discussion in this section explains how adjustments in the interpretation of the data are required to reflect the Japanese condition. An analysis of the predominant conflict management styles of Japanese R & D managers follows, using these revised factors and constructs. The section concludes with an analysis of the differences across types of R & D laboratories.

The third section of the chapter examines the dependent variables in the study—worker attitudes and satisfactions, as measured by the modified Job Description Survey administered to the laboratory workers associated with the leaders whose answers were reported above. Here the results of the computer-assisted manipulation of the scales of the JDS are shown, and the differences between the English-language and Japanese-language versions are discussed. Again, the differences among corporate, university, and government labs are shown.

The next part of the chapter draws together the results of the analysis of the relationships between the self-reported leader traits and conflict management modes and the reported satisfactions of their workers, again across the settings.

Finally, the interpretations of the open-ended parts of the questionnaire are presented and analyzed.

## STRUCTURAL CHARACTERISTICS OF LABORATORY SECTIONS

Since research and development in Japan is carried out in different organizational settings, some effort in this study was made to determine the important structural and processual differences across these work places. Some significant differences among these types of laboratories exist. The data are presented in Exhibit 14.1.

First, because of the nature of the organizational control structure, university laboratories tend to be smaller, with fewer workers, smaller administrative staffs, and fewer research projects under way. On average, there are 26 professional research workers (including engineers) in the section. Corporations and government labs average about 30, while universities have only 11. The units are administered by a staff of about seven, again, with far fewer in universities and far more at NTT. Government institutes report that they begin approximately seventeen projects each year; universities only seven. Because of their emphasis on applied research and their bottom-line orientation, corporations tend to terminate projects sooner than the other types of labs; minimum project lengths average thirteen months compared with approximately twenty for the other types, ERATO being the exception at the upper limit. Government laboratories, on the other hand, concentrate most on applied research and tend to be willing to continue a research project for a longer period of time (as much as a quarter longer than universities and a third longer than corporations: a maximum of 69 months for government institutes compared with 53 for universities and only 49 for corporations.

**Exhibit 14.1**
**Section and Section Leader Characteristics[1]**

| | Grand Mean | Std. Dev. | $C^2$ | $U^2$ | $G^2$ | $NTT^2$ | $ERATO^2$ |
|---|---|---|---|---|---|---|---|
| **A. Section Characteristics** | | | | | | | |
| 1. Number of professional reseach workers per section. | 26 | 20 | 30 | 11 | 28 | 24 | 30 |
| 2. Administrative staff size per section. | 7 | 9 | 7 | 2 | 7 | 13 | 5 |
| 3. Number of research projects (with at least one full-time worker) begun in unit this year. | 14 | 17 | 14 | 7 | 17 | 9 | 10 |
| 4. Minimum project length (months). | 17 | 14 | 13 | 19 | 21 | 20 | 27 |
| 5. Maximum project length (months). | 57 | 25 | 49 | 53 | 69 | 63 | 66 |
| **B. Section Leader Characteristics** | | | | | | | |
| 6. Age (years). | 51 | 6 | 47 | 53 | 54 | 42 | 57 |
| 7. Number of years served as director of this work unit. | 4 | 5 | 3 | 7 | 3 | 2 | 10[3] |

**C. Research Emphasis**

| 8. Research emphasis. | | % Section | | Goal | Emphasis | |
|---|---|---|---|---|---|---|
| | Basic | 10 | 54 | 21 | 40 | 38 |
| | Applied | 40 | 33 | 52 | NA | NA |
| | Developmental | 50 | 13 | 27 | NA | NA |

[1] Note: The statistical procedure used to analyze differences among groups was Analysis of Variance. To avoid cluttering the table, the presence of statistically significant differences between the groups is indicated with an asterisk after the variable, rather than between groups. Results of post hoc Scheffe tests are available on request.

[2] Key: C=Corporation      U=University      G=Government      N=NTT
E=ERATO

[3] This figure is anomalous because of the unusual circumstances by which ERATO managers were chosen.

As might be expected, corporations concentrate most on developmental research (50% of budgeted funds), universities on basic research (54%), and government institutes on applied research (52%).

## DEMOGRAPHIC CHARACTERISTICS OF SECTION LEADERS

The average age of the section leader in the corporation is 47, in the university, 53, and in the government institutes, 54 (see Exhibit 14.1). At NTT the leaders were quite a bit younger (42), while at ERATO, they were significantly older (57).

University section leaders tend to have held their positions for much longer than leaders in other types of organizations, doubtless owing to the relative infrequency of changes in jobs compared to corporate and government laboratories. The average time as leader for university section leaders was 7.1 years versus a relatively short 3.5 years in the other two laboratory types. NTT leaders had the shortest tenure (2.8 years), while at the ERATO labs, section leaders were kept on for an average of 10 years (though this is an artifact of the MITI commitment to the leaders rather than the labs alone). Corporate laboratories have younger section leaders because corporate R & D is rapidly expanding, and there are opportunities for upward intrainstitutional mobility within the laboratories. In addition, there is increasing recognition of the great need for young leadership, especially in scientific domains.

## PATTERNS OF INTERNAL AND CROSS-BOUNDARY COMMUNICATION

As noted in Exhibit 14.2, the average time spent in meeting with staff other than their own researchers was 37 percent, with NTT tending to restrict communications more to internal matters, while NTT managers were more frequently connected to the outside world.

The understandable need in the corporate sector to maintain secrecy about discoveries may inhibit frequent outside contact on business-related matters (cf. Nagi & Corwin 1972, pp 276 ff.). On the other hand, one would have expected that in universities, the tradition of cosmopolitanism as well as the relatively small academic community would lend itself to a more open and fluid cross-institutional communication pattern. It appears, however, that university R & D leaders are no more cosmopolitan than in corporations or government institutes.

## MANAGEMENT PHILOSOPHIES

Among the questions asked of section leaders were 31 that dealt with various aspects of leadership and administrative philosophy. The questions measured six key categories: (1) degree of worker control of their own work; (2) emphasis

**Exhibit 14.2**
**Cross-Boundary Communications by Leaders**

| In the last full month, percent of time spent in meeting (by telephone or in person) with personnel other than own researchers and staff. | % Time Outside of Own Organization | | | | | | |
|---|---|---|---|---|---|---|---|
| | Grand Mean | Std. Dev. | C | U | G | NTT | ERATO |
| | 37 | NA | 39 | 37 | 33 | 20 | 61 |

on group versus individual rewards; (3) freedom of information exchange; (4) formality/informality of interpersonal interactions; (5) assumptions about worker motivation; and (6) risk-taking propensity. In each question, the raw data given represent means and standard deviation scores on a scale of "very strong disagreement" (1) to "very strong agreement" (7). The data are indicated in various exhibits. Differences across the major types of research laboratories in the sample are provided.

## INDIVIDUAL VERSUS MANAGEMENT CONTROL OVER WORK

Individual choice in R & D is critical to the creative process. Too much monitoring and/or control will stifle impulses to explore unconventional ideas and projects. On the other hand, managerial oversight is necessary in order to keep costs at reasonable levels and to rein in overzealous or stubborn researchers whose ideas have run their course without promising results. Given the widespread practice of extensive participation in decision making in Japanese organizations in general, these managerial attitudes toward the distribution of authority are interestingly different. The results are discussed for the sample as a whole as well as in terms of differences across types of organizations (see Exhibit 14.3).

From the data collected from these R & D section leaders, it can be concluded that R & D section leaders appear to be moderately favorably disposed to letting workers select the type of research they wish to work on (M = 5.4), but not to choose the materials and procedures they need (M = 2.8). Perhaps this is perceived as a managerial, not research prerogative. Whether workers should be responsible for setting the pace of the work is not clear in the view of these leaders, some agreeing, others disagreeing. Similar ambiguity surrounds the question of setting standards of quality. The mean (3.8) reflects neither strong agreement nor disagreement. Of special interest, however, is the particularly low mean at NTT (2.8) compared with the high mean (4.6) at ERATO. It is possible that the older, more experienced, longer-tenured and more famous managers at ERATO are less willing to yield this authority to workers.

**Exhibit 14.3**
**R & D Managers' Attitudes toward Control of Work**

| | Grand Mean[1] | Standard Dev. | C | U | G | NTT | ERATO |
|---|---|---|---|---|---|---|---|
| 11. Workers should have a considerable voice in the choice of project on which they work. | | | | | | | |
| Mean Agreement | 5.4 | 1.4 | 5.5 | 5.6 | 5.7 | 5.5 | 5.8 |
| 12. Workers should not be able to choose the materials and procedures used in the project. | | | | | | | |
| Mean Agreement | 2.8 | 1.4 | 2.8 | 2.8 | 2.8 | 2.6 | 3.3 |
| 13. Workers should be permitted to set the pace of their work. | | | | | | | |
| Mean Agreement | 4.7 | 1.5 | 4.8 | 4.8 | 4.7 | 4.5 | 4.5 |
| 14. Workers should **not** be allowed to set the standards of quality for the work they are doing. | | | | | | | |
| Mean Agreement | 3.8 | 1.7 | 3.6 | 4.2 | 4.2 | 2.8 | 4.6 |
| 15. Workers should have the responsibility for evaluating the results of their research. | | | | | | | |
| Mean Agreement | 5.6 | 1.4 | 5.7 | 5.8 | 5.5 | 6.0 | 5.8 |

1. Respondents were asked to use a scale of 1–7, with 1 being "very strongly disagree" and 7 being "very strongly agree." Because of the small sample sizes of managers in the university, NTT and ERATO groups, with some exceptions, differences in means did not reach statistical significance.

In each of these cases, then, while there is no clear-cut evidence to suggest differences across R & D units with respect to control of R & D work, there is an indication that for all types of organizations, managers keep tight control of methods and do not decentralize quality control. The picture may be clouded by the "social desirability" of the answers—section leaders preferring to give an answer that would appear more acceptable than to give their *honne*, that is, conveying the impression of more worker discretion than is actually the case. In some institutions, section leaders (following the unique, prevailing philosophy of the larger organization of which the laboratory is a part) say they would permit greater freedom in all matters, while in other institutions, management takes a firmer hand in controlling the work. The solid, entrenched, and wide-spread practice of significant worker participation and input into decision making is not reflected in the recognition of these leaders to yield control over worker autonomy, procedures, and standards.

## INDIVIDUAL VERSUS GROUP REWARDS

Another series of questions was concerned with the manager's attitudes to-ward explicit and open recognition of any one individual rather subordinating the individual and recognizing the achievements of the group as a whole. As noted in earlier chapters, the requirement for individual creativity in research and development conflicts with the Japanese proscription against the public, personal self-aggrandizement which accrues to authors of successful break-throughs. How section leaders balance these competing demands was, therefore, an interesting question. Exhibit 14.4 reveals their responses.

This set of answers reveals again some ambivalence among these section leaders as to the proper balance between individual and group efforts. There is high agreement ($M = 6.5$) that outside public acclaim for group achievement should be made known to all workers. On the other hand, these managers believe that external acclaim for individual accomplishments should not be passed on ($M = 2.4$), nor should workers expect it ($M = 2.4$). The contrast between NTT and ERATO reflects somewhat different positions on this topic.

There is moderate agreement ($M = 4.7$) that individuals conducting research and development should concentrate on group versus individual projects. Asked the converse—whether individuals should concentrate on their own versus group efforts—these managers moderately demurred ($M = 3.3$). Clearly, there are times when individual workers should be permitted to pursue their own line of inquiry, regardless of the directions desired by the group. There are other times when individual effort must be sacrificed to common goals. In the light of earlier chapters, it is not surprising that section leaders tend to be somewhat biased in the direction of emphasizing group goals, perhaps to the detriment of potential individual achievement and individual satisfaction. On the other hand, one might have expected an even stronger endorsement of group efforts. It is probable that these are questions not usually asked of Japanese managers who, like most managers everywhere, act without serious reflection on the values they hold.

## MANAGER ASSUMPTIONS ABOUT WORKER MOTIVATION

In considerable contrast to prevailing attitudes and practice in American R & D laboratories (see, for example, Tracy Kidder's revelations in *The Soul of a New Machine*, 1981), Japanese managers appear to be firmly in the Theory X camp (McGregor 1960). They believe that the major source of motivation of research-ers is fear of failing, *not* the promise of success ($M = 2.6$). They are in

**Exhibit 14.4**
**Leader Attitudes, Individual versus Group Rewards**

| | Grand Mean[1] | Standard Dev. | Corp | Univ. | Govt | NTT | ERATO |
|---|---|---|---|---|---|---|---|
| 16. Workers should be told about outside acclaim for group achievements. | 6.5 | 1.6 | 7.0 | 6.5 | 6.3 | 6.8 | 6.1 |
| 17. Workers should be told about outside acclaim for **individual** achievements.· | 2.4 | 1.6 | 2.0 | 2.8 | 2.8 | 1.3 | 3.4 |
| 18. Workers should expect public recognition for their creative achievements. | 2.4 | 1.5 | 2.1 | 2.5 | 2.8 | 2.0 | 1.8 |
| 19. People should seek satisfaction from working in a group rather than on their own. | 4.7 | 1.3 | 4.1 | 4.9 | 4.9 | 4.3 | 3.9 |
| 20. Workers should concentrate on individual projects rather than contribute to group efforts. | 3.3 | 1.4 | 3.1 | 3.8 | 3.1 | 3.4 | 4.8 |

moderate agreement that workers should be made to fear the negative consequences of their mistakes (M = 5.3), should be made aware of penalties for failure (M = 5.3), and should be immediately penalized for poor performance (M = 5.4). In contrast, and inexplicably, these respondents also believe strongly that supervisors should provide positive incentives instead of threats (Exhibit 14.5).

The responses to this section on assumptions about worker motivation are especially telling in their reflection of the normative burdens of the group success ethic. Something in the Japanese culture manifested in the workplace makes Japanese managers skeptical of the possibility of intrinsic motivation. The early childhood negation of individual ego and the absence of rewards for that ego force the manager realistically to appraise each individual as incapable of sus-

**Exhibit 14.5**
**Leader Assumptions about Worker Motivation**

|  | Grand Mean | Standard Dev. | Corp | Univ. | Govt | NTT | ERATO |
|---|---|---|---|---|---|---|---|
| 21. Most workers are motivated by promise of success rather than fear of failure. | 2.6 | 1.4 | 2.5 | 2.6 | 2.9 | 3.4 | 2.0 |
| 22. Workers should be immediately penalized for poor performance. | 5.4 | 1.3 | 5.4 | 4.7 | 5.4 | 5.6 | 5.5 |
| 23. Supervisors should provide positive incentives instead of threats. | 6.5 | 0.7 | 6.5 | 6.2 | 6.6 | 6.8 | 6.5 |
| 24. Supervisors should make workers aware of penalties for failure. | 5.3 | 1.7 | 5.4 | 5.6 | 5.0 | 4.6 | 6.0 |
| 25. Workers should be made to fear negative consequences of their mistakes. | 5.3 | 1.6 | 5.1 | 5.3 | 5.7 | 4.9 | 4.9 |

tained motivation based on the anticipation of personal success. In terms of classical expectancy theory, managers in Japanese R & D feel that workers do not believe they can perform the task, do not believe that rewards will follow from successful performance, and do not care about the rewards that are available (though there is no evidence of the latter). The dominance of the group and the fears of group disapprobation are thus enhanced by downward pressures from the Japanese manager in the form of threatened negative.

## MANAGER ATTITUDES TOWARD DISSEMINATION OF RESEARCH RESULTS

Despite concerns at the corporate level that organizational secrets may be revealed, two other organizational values appear to override them. One is a cardinal norm of the scientific research world, namely, that new scientific knowledge cannot be "owned" and must be shared. Further, the norm suggests that continued progress in science requires exchange of information for validation.

Finally, workers in science are entitled personally to the accolades of their colleagues in the profession. Although these norms are perhaps more relevant in basic/theoretical laboratories, they carry over to the applied and developmental areas.

The second value has its roots in the homogeneity of the Japanese society. While science is carried out in thousands of laboratories in different settings (government, corporate, university), there is a sense of *one* scientific community. Hence, "disclosure" is not a violation of rules of secrecy but a routine sharing of progress in service of the common good. Exhibit 14.6 reveals the accommodations that R & D managers in Japan make to the conflicting norms of secrecy and disclosure.

Section leaders in the these R & D groups do not agree that their workers should be restricted in their discussions of research findings with workers from other institutions (M = 1.9). Indeed, they should be allowed to present papers at professional conferences about work in progress (M = 5.3). On the other hand, they are somewhat ambivalent about the next step in the usual dissemination sequence—publication. The mean agreement/disagreement is 4.5, with a fairly substantial variance, showing some differences on this item. They would prefer on the whole to see a very long time elapsing between research discovery and submission of a manuscript to a journal or book publisher (M = 5.1), suggesting some recognition of the needs to keep discoveries quiet until they can be exploited. Most of the respondents disagreed that management should not be involved in the determination of when and where new discoveries may be released to the outside public (M = 2.5).

From these data, it would appear that Japanese R & D managers have some mixed feelings about freedom of communication. Not unexpectedly, they want to keep control of the process in their own hands, but they also recognize the need of workers to exchange ideas with others. It is highly likely that R & D managers suffer some considerable internal conflict over this issue, since as former researchers they can empathize with their subordinates, but as managers, they must attend to the long-range objectives of the organizational entity as a whole, which demand restraint from immediate dissemination. It is also probable that this ambivalence is passed on to subordinates as a mixed message. Absent the promise of personal reward through professional recognition, it may be that the motivation of researchers to be productive is reduced.

## MANAGER BELIEFS ABOUT FORMALITY/INFORMALITY IN COMMUNICATION AND REWARDS

As noted in some detail in previous chapters, interpersonal relations in Japan are constrained by a long and rich history and tradition, particularly with regard to formal and informal hierarchical relationships. In an attempt to see how managers of R & D units upheld or violated these norms and values, questions were asked about the status distinctions among workers and the manifestations of

**Exhibit 14.6**
**Manager Attitudes toward Freedom of Communication for Researchers**

|  | Grand Mean[*] | Standard Dev. | Corp | Univ. | Govt | NTT | ERATO |
|---|---|---|---|---|---|---|---|
| 26. People should have little freedom to discuss their research findings with workers from other institutions. | | | | | | | |
| Mean Agreement | 1.9 | 1.2 | 2.4 | 1.6 | 1.9 | 1.9 | 2.3 |
| 27. Workers should be free to publish the results of their research. | | | | | | | |
| Mean Agreement | 4.5 | 1.8 | 4.0 | 5.9 | 5.1 | 3.9 | 4.6 |
| 28. Workers should be allowed to present papers at professional conferences about work in progress. | | | | | | | |
| Mean Agreement | 5.3 | 1.5 | 4.4 | 6.1 | 5.6 | 5.9 | 4.9 |
| 29. A very long time should elapse between research discovery and submission of a manuscript to a journal or book publisher. | | | | | | | |
| Mean Agreement | 5.1 | 1.4 | 4.8 | 5.5 | 5.4 | 4.8 | 5.4 |
| 30. Management should **not** be involved in the determination of when and where new discoveries may be released to the outside public. | | | | | | | |
| Mean Agreement | 2.5 | 1.6 | 1.9 | 2.0 | 2.5 | 2.5 | 2.0 |

those distinctions in terms of allocation of privileges and the formality of forms of address.

As will be noted in Exhibit 14.7, these managers take the position that privileges should not be allocated to certain individuals, thus appearing to reflect the absence in Japanese organizations of the Western-type distinctions between bosses and workers (namely, the usual common occupation of large office spaces by workers and supervisors as noted in Chapter 8). There was less concurrence among managers in their attitudes toward the use of formal job titles to apportion privileges (M = 4.7). Job titles, furthermore, do not automatically call for differences in styles of interaction or verbal communication (M = 4.9), according to the managers.

It is difficult to interpret the meaning of this finding. It may be that managers normatively believe in free and easy communication in order to facilitate both information exchange among workers and decision making. As in working teams in America, bosses often become partners in the research enterprise except where critical financial decisions are made. Interactions in most work-related situations are easy and open. In Japan, on the other hand, while similar informal modes are operative on the research floor, especially in group settings, in one-to-one interactions, formal titles and proper, polite (teinei) language is called for. Whether this bifurcation of interaction protocols is disruptive of the research process is worthy of speculation.

Consensus also does not emerge when leaders are asked whether job seniority or age should *not* be used as a basis for distributing special privileges (M = 4.4). Considering the Japanese reverence for age and the usual practice of using seniority as a basis of allocating respect in the organization, the lack of agreement on this matter is puzzling. While singling individuals out for unusual attributes calls unwanted attention to them, for the Japanese, age and seniority are socially legitimate media for the expression of differences. As with other variables, the data for this one do not reveal a bimodal distribution (the variance is relatively low), leading to the conclusion that respondents simply were neither in agreement nor disagreement on this issue.

With regard to one of the most important of perquisites in R & D, authorship of publications, there *was* disagreement among the managers that the section chief should always be listed first as the author of an article written by a member of his organization (M = 2.1). This is somewhat surprising, since it is very common practice in Japan for subordinates to write most or all of the articles or reports but for the section head to be listed as first author (with the others, often many, appearing below). Perhaps for this sample, there is some recognition of the motivational damage this may do to the true authors.

## THE NATURE OF RISK

It seems patently evident that work of R & D section workers can be strongly influenced by the support the leader gives to experimentation and risk taking

**Exhibit 14.7**
**Importance of Title and Status**

| | Grand Mean | Standard Dev. | Corp | Univ. | Govt | NTT | ERATO |
|---|---|---|---|---|---|---|---|
| 31. Certain workers should be allocated non-work related privileges (such as nearby parking spaces and larger offices). | | | | | | | |
| Mean Agreement | 2.8 | 1.8 | 3.0 | 3.4 | 2.4 | 2.4 | 3.0 |
| 32. Formal job titles should not be used as a basis for allocating privileges and perquisites to the group. | | | | | | | |
| Mean Agreement | 4.7 | 1.7 | 4.2 | 5.3 | 4.8 | 4.6 | 5.4 |
| 33. Job seniority or age should not be used as a basis for distributing special privileges. | | | | | | | |
| Mean Agreement | 4.4 | 1.7 | 4.2 | 4.6 | 3.8 | 5.1 | 5.3 |
| 34. All workers, regardless of job title, should be allowed to determine unit policy related to working conditions (space, heat, recreational facilities, etc). | | | | | | | |
| Mean Agreement | 5.2 | 1.7 | 5.3 | 5.4 | 5.1 | 4.4 | 6.0 |
| 35. Little emphasis should be placed on job titles in the manner of interaction and verbal address among workers. | | | | | | | |
| Mean Agreement | 4.9 | 1.8 | 5.0 | 4.2 | 5.0 | 5.1 | 5.6 |

**Exhibit 14.7 (continued)**

Grand Standard Corp Univ. Govt NTT ERATO
Mean     Dev.

36. The section chief or
    unit leader should
    always be listed
    first as the author
    of an article written
    by a member of his
    organization.

Mean Agreement   2.1        1.3   2.2    2.3   2.0   1.8         2.1

that goes beyond conventional thinking. Absent vigorous endorsement of creative thinking and the taking of chances (abetted, of course, with adequate resources), workers will spend time on "safe" projects. The data in Exhibit 14.8
reveal managerial attitudes toward various aspects of risk in R & D.

Leaders of R & D sections strongly supported the notion of risk taking in
research ($M = 6.2$) (university section leaders were somewhat less than others,
$M = 5.3$). They agreed somewhat less enthusiastically that substantial amounts
of time could be put into work where the likelihood of success was unknown
($M = 5.6$) and that they should even be rewarded for creative experiments that
ultimately were not successful ($M = 5.4$). Similar moderate endorsement came
in the form of their disagreement with the statement that workers should *not*
attempt to depart from appropriate methods and procedures ($M = 3.8$) and
should not attempt to depart from ideas and/or theories known to be valid ($M
= 3.8$). To summarize, managerial attitudes on risk taking in R & D appear to
be moderately supportive. In some senses, this is not surprising. One would
hardly expect total, unmitigated endorsement of risk taking in all of its radical
forms. Perhaps noteworthy is the lack of significant differences between the
profit-making and non–profit-making sectors. It would have been reasonable to
assume that corporate section leaders would be somewhat more cautious, given
both cost containment, bottom-line constraints, and shorter project lengths.

## DIFFERENCES BETWEEN SECTIONS RATED HIGH OR
## LOW QUALITY

Part of this study was concerned with differences in management attitudes
and techniques as practiced by leaders of laboratory sections rated by the overall
director of the laboratory as "highest quality" contrasted with something less
than highest quality.[1] Although relatively few differences across types of laboratory were revealed, there were several interesting findings within each category. The discussion below, consequently, takes up each type of laboratory
separately.[2]

**Exhibit 14.8**
**Propensity toward Risk Taking**

| | Grand Mean | Standard Dev. | Corp | Univ. | Govt | NTT | ERATO |
|---|---|---|---|---|---|---|---|
| 37. Workers should be strongly encouraged to take risks in their work. | | | | | | | |
| Mean Agreement | 6.2 | 1.2 | 6.3 | 5.3 | 6.3 | 6.5 | 6.9 |
| 38. Workers should make investments of substantial time in work with unknown likelihood of success. | | | | | | | |
| Mean Agreement | 5.7 | 1.2 | 5.5 | 5.8 | 5.6 | 6.5 | 6.3 |
| 39. Workers should be rewarded for creative experiments which are not ultimately successful. | | | | | | | |
| Mean Agreement | 5.4 | 1.3 | 5.2 | 5.7 | 5.5 | NA | NA |
| 40. Workers should **not** attempt to depart from methods and procedures known to be appropriate. | | | | | | | |
| Mean Agreement | 3.7 | 1.6 | 3.8 | 3.8 | 3.9 | 3.0 | 2.9 |
| 41. Workers should not attempt to depart from ideas and/or theories known to be valid. | | | | | | | |
| Mean Agreement | 3.8 | 1.6 | 4.0 | 3.4 | 3.8 | 3.5 | 3.0 |

### High- and Low-Quality Corporate Laboratories

The corporate laboratories are discussed first. High-quality laboratory sections tend to have younger section leaders, and these leaders have worked at fewer other institutions than the one at which they are presently employed. Sections in high-quality corporate labs are smaller. Partly as a result, there are fewer research projects begun each year. Projects deemed to be unsuccessful in high-quality laboratories are terminated sooner, while promising projects are extended longer in high-quality laboratories. This capacity of the leader or/and group to make discriminating judgments about project promise is thus critical to high-quality productivity.

The higher the quality of the corporate laboratory, the less likely it is to engage in basic research. Thus, R & D units that depart from the strength of R & D in the corporate sector, namely, applied and developmental research, tend to be lower in quality. Surprisingly, high-quality corporate laboratories apply for fewer patents each year than do lower-quality corporate laboratories, perhaps because of their smaller size. Thus, large size, per se, is a potentially misleading desideratum for successful research and development.

There is some evidence in the findings that corporate R & D leader philosophies are relatively restrictive. Leaders in high-quality corporate laboratories tend somewhat more to agree that workers should not be able to choose the materials and procedures used in the project on which they are working.

Further, high-quality section leaders report more agreement that people should have little freedom to discuss research findings with workers from other institutions (probably in recognition of the need to preserve corporate secrets). On the other hand, high-quality leaders tend more to believe that workers should be free to publish the results of their research, partly, one might suppose, because the corporate name becomes more visible. It may also be that these leaders are more sensitive to the need for individual recognition.

Within the corporate sector, there is a clear trend in *high*-quality corporate laboratory sections for leaders to have more egalitarian values than do their counterparts in lower-quality sections. For example, high-quality section leaders more than low-quality section leaders tend more to believe that privileges should not be allocated to certain workers, that formal job titles should not be used as a basis for allocating privileges and perquisites, that job seniority or age should not be a basis for distributing special privileges, and that leaders should not always be first authors of published articles. These are values based on achievement, not ascription, and may contribute to an overall normative commitment to high quality (and the converse, to a lack of respect for low quality).

### High- and Low-Quality Government Laboratories

A conservatism prevails in the leaders of high-quality government laboratories as well. While they are more willing than low-quality section leaders to overlook poor performance on a particular job, in high-quality sections, leaders believe workers should not attempt to depart from ideas and/or theories known to be valid. Perhaps this conforms with the above notion that group rather than individual frames of reference are more salient in high-quality government laboratories.

In government laboratories, furthermore, sections rated as high quality tend to let projects continue for longer periods than do low-quality sections, according to their leaders. Also, in high-quality sections, the emphasis is somewhat more on basic research than on applied research or developmental research—this despite the predominant emphasis in general of government R & D on applied projects. One might reason that this research emphasis results from the greater stability over long periods of time of government funding for successful units, but section leaders in high-quality government laboratories are actually more pessimistic about future funding than are those in low-quality sections.[3]

High-quality government laboratory sections (in contrast to high-quality corporate laboratory sections) tend to apply for more patents than in low-quality sections. Why this is so cannot be determined from the data.

Just as in the corporate laboratories, high-quality government laboratory section leaders believe more strongly than in low-quality sections that individual workers should not expect to be publicly recognized for creative achievements. High quality, or at least reputation for it, is more likely, then, even when individual creative achievements do not receive attention. High-quality laboratory leaders tend more to value group rather than individual recognition for high achievement. Thus, a somewhat stronger, group-centered ideology seems to be associated with higher quality. This is not to suggest that a greater decentralization of authority and decision making takes place in high-quality sections. Indeed, high-quality government laboratory section leaders tend to agree more strongly than do low-quality leaders on the standards of quality for the work they are doing.

Low-quality government laboratory leaders more than high-quality leaders, on the other hand, believe that management should be involved in the determination of when and where new discoveries may be released to the outside public. Hence, control over information seems to be associated with lower-quality laboratory performance for government labs.

Interestingly, while government laboratory sections are not different on the whole from corporate laboratories in their emphasis on hierarchical rather than egalitarian norms, there are differences in attitudes of leaders across quality levels. While in the corporate sector, high quality seems to be associated with more egalitarian attitudes, in the government laboratories, high-quality leaders tend to be more hierarchical or bureaucratic. High-quality government laboratory leaders tend to *dis*agree more strongly that workers should be allowed to determine unit policy and that little emphasis should be placed on job titles in interpersonal relations. On the other hand, just as in corporate laboratories, the higher-quality section leaders tend to believe that the section chief or unit leader need not always be listed as first author of a published article.

High-quality government laboratory section leaders, too, are "theory X" people. They more strongly agree than low-quality leaders that most of their workers are motivated more by fear of failure than by promise of success and its rewards. On the other hand, what may account for the success in high-quality laboratories is the leader agreement that workers should not be made to fear negative consequences for their mistakes.

Like corporate leaders, high-quality government laboratory leaders tend to agree more than low-quality leaders that workers should not attempt to depart from ideas and/or theories known to be valid.

### High- and Low-Quality University Laboratories

In the university laboratories represented in this study, there were no significant differences between leaders in high- and low-quality laboratory sections.

## SUMMARY OF ATTITUDES OF R & D LEADERS

In sum, there are quite a few remarkable differences in the characteristics of the leaders across the different types of R & D organizations. The above data point to larger corporate labs with shorter-term project lengths, government labs that are oriented toward applied work and work on projects for longer periods than the others. The specialization of function is particularly noteworthy, with more than 50 percent of funding being directed to different aims. Universities seem more dedicated to basic research; government institutes to applied research; and corporations to developmental research. Because of the unique employment and job rotation systems, laboratory leaders tend to stay in office longer in universities. There is much higher turnover in government institutes and corporations, with the shortest tenure at NTT and the longest at ERATO.

Cross-unit boundary communication by laboratory directors averages about 37 percent of time spent for all the groups. The directors at NTT spend more of their time internally, while more than 60 percent of the ERATO managers' time on average is spent in communications with other than their own staff.

R & D managers in all settings appear to keep tight control over worker methods—one reason, perhaps, for the lack of creativity and experimentation. There is little sense that R & D workers in Japan are treated like the autonomous professionals that one finds in the United States. Managers appear to believe in the necessity for continual assessment of, if not close direction of research activities. Relatedly, managers in Japan seem to have a "theory X" philosophy of human nature (see McGregor 1960). They believe that left alone, workers will *not* take responsibility for their work nor devote necessary time and energy to it. This philosophy is generated in part by their own socialization experiences, for example, being watched and observed in school and feeling the need to be monitored. While they personally believe in the importance of group goals and the effectiveness of group pressure to be committed to organizational welfare, they apparently do not believe that workers individually or collectively can be trusted to sustain their commitment and high-quality standards. Somewhat surprisingly and inexplicably, the strength of their support for group efforts is not as high as one might expect. Thus, the typical R & D leader philosophy of human nature as well as his appraisal of worker psychology leads him to retain control over critical decisions in his subordinates' lives—decisions that are central to creative R & D.

Not only are means to achievement controlled, but so are the sources of external satisfaction. Confirming the values and norms of the society at large, Japanese R & D leaders in general clearly would suppress the internal visibility of externally validated, individual achievement. The credit for achievement thus gravitates to the group as a whole, in part, once again, vitiating the strength of the intrinsic satisfaction of individual achievement. On the other hand, there is moderate agreement that workers should be allowed to present papers at professional conferences. The contrast with the lack of support for visible individual achievement in cosmopolitan circles can be partially explained by understanding that individuals in those circles are seen primarily as organizational representatives, not individual entrepreneurs. Hence, achievement made public outside (but not inside) brings glory to the institution as a whole, but preserves the integrity of the unit or institution.

Finally, in comparing high- and low-quality R & D units, there appears to be some evidence of greater equality of status and opportunity in higher-quality laboratories. In some ways this can be explained through the greater allegiance given to achievement than ascription in scientific communities. It is not possible to determine, however, whether the greater accomplishments of the workers in high-quality laboratories leads to less concern for formal hierarchical symbols or the opposite—the more relaxed climate leads to greater achievement. In any case, the evidence here is that they are paired.

## MANAGERIAL TRAITS IN R & D

Having considered some general characteristics of managerial attitudes of R & D leaders in Japan, it is now possible to explore in some detail the results of application of the various theories used in the research. In particular, what follows is an examination of the relationships between managerial traits and worker attitudes. This is done in several ways. The first uses the fourfold typology of Kilmann and Herden to see how each of the leader types is distributed across the different kinds of organizations and how each of these types is related to the worker attitudes measured by the revised categories in the Job Description Survey. The second takes the revised set of traits derived from the MBTI, rather than the fourfold typology of Kilmann and Herden, and looks at the relationships of leader traits to the scales in the Job Description Survey. Two methods of analysis are used here: one, a straightforward correlational analysis; the second, a look at different leader characteristics (again revised from the MBTI) as perceived by workers self-classified as high and low scorers on the JDS.

A further analysis is then presented revealing how the leadership traits (conceived this time according to the factored MBTI scores rather than Kilmann and Herden) differ across different organizational types: universities, government institutes, and corporations. Yet another form of study presents the results of a "cluster analysis" of the traits and the identification of eight distinctive leader types that are variously distributed in the laboratories studied.

## LEADER TRAITS IN DIFFERENT KINDS OF R & D ORGANIZATIONS

In this section, the distribution of leader traits as measured by the Kilmann and Herden typology (Jungian and Parsonian) is examined across the different kinds of organizations: government institutes, universities, and corporations (and, in addition, in NTT and ERATO). Recall from the chapter on Methods that according to the Kilmann and Herden approach, hypothetically there are four leadership functions to be served, matching the four functional prerequisites that Parsons posits. In the Kilmann and Herden theory, each of these prerequisites demands a different set of leadership traits. As Mitroff (1983, 56 ff.) notes, it is likely that NTs will predominate in successful R & D organizations. In the empirical phase of this research, the MBTI was utilized to identify the traits of R & D section leaders in Japan. Exhibit 14.9 reveals the distribution of leader types across the different kinds of organizations in the sample.[4]

For the sample as a whole, the data show that the percentage of NTs is not significantly greater than SFs or STs, but is greater than NFs. Conversely, it is more meaningful to report that NFs are underrepresented in the entire sample. That is, among R & D section leaders, intuitive/feeling types are fewer in number. Later, we will consider whether such an underrepresentation disadvantages the R & D effort in Japan.

For example, it is worth noting that for laboratories in every kind of organization, there are leaders of all four types, although there are somewhat fewer Intuition-Feeling (NF) types (18%) for the total group. Within each kind of organization, the distributions are not highly skewed. Government labs seem to have slightly fewer NFs represented (14%), corporations have fewer NTs, and universities are dominated by NTs. The other categories have too small numbers in each category to draw conclusions, except to note that no one type seems to dominate. Later, we will see the relationships between leader type and effectiveness in each kind of organization.

The finding of fewer NFs in government labs is somewhat anomalous. It might be expected that government agencies as a whole have a public service orientation with an objective of improving the lives of people. Large, broadscale decisions of this nature would call for an NF leader. Why government R & D laboratories seem to have fewer of these is not clear. Conceivably, those who hire the laboratory directors are themselves NFs and seek complementary

**Exhibit 14.9**
**Types of Leaders in Different Kinds of Organizations by Number and Percentage**
**of Total in Organization Kind**

Kind of Organization

| | | Government | Universities | Corporations | NTT | ERATO | Total |
|---|---|---|---|---|---|---|---|
| | SF | 9 | 5 | 15 | 1 | 3 | 33 |
| | | (26) | (29) | (31) | (20) | (50) | (30) |
| | ST | 10 | 1 | 12 | 2 | 1 | 26 |
| Leader | | (28) | (6) | (25) | (40) | (17) | (23) |
| Type | | | | | | | |
| | NF | 5 | 2 | 12 | 0 | 1 | 20 |
| | | (14) | (12) | (25) | (0) | (17) | (18) |
| | NT | 11 | 9 | 9 | 2 | 1 | 32 |
| | | (31) | (53) | (19) | (40) | (17) | (29) |
| | | | | | | Total | 111[1] |
| | | | | | | | (100) |

(Numbers in parentheses are percentages. Column totals may not equal 100% because of rounding.)

1. Total N of 111 is less than the sample of 150 leaders because definitions of leader types omitted leaders with "mixed" traits.

research leaders. Or, experience may have shown that NFs as R & D leaders are less successful.

That 53 percent of the university laboratory directors are NTs is less surprising, or at least more easily explained. Long-range, basic research of the kind in which universities engage demands an intuitive-type, "grand theory" person, yet one who can think through the theory skillfully. An NT would make sense in this context.

Similarly, the smaller percentage of NTs in corporations also appears sensible. Practical, applied research requires market-oriented (people-sensitive) leaders who are flexible and adaptive. The more rapid turnover of projects in corporations may rule out NTs who want to concentrate on long-term, theoretical objectives.

## DIFFERENCES IN RELATIONSHIPS OF LEADER TYPES TO WORKER ATTITUDES ACROSS TYPES OF LABORATORIES

This section builds on the above findings concerning the distribution of leader types across different kinds of organizations. For this analysis, the data were separated first into the three major sample categories: universities, corporations, and government institutes. The resulting small cell sizes and nonnormal distributions enabled an analysis only of a portion of the data, namely, of the relationships between leader traits and scores on the revised Job Description Survey that fell at a point significantly below the mean (equal to or below one standard deviation). In other words, a matrix of the responses given to the JDS by workers in the three different kinds of organizations was created. A skewed distribution was revealed, with sufficient cell sizes only when the *negative* JDS scores were considered. That is, for each of the dependent variables, the numbers of workers answering in each answer category permitted a classification in leader traits cells of sufficient size only when workers whose responses were well below the mean (equal to or more than 1 ½ standard deviations). The remaining responses distributed themselves too sparsely to permit cells of sufficient size when the data were further classified by leader type. Differences across the three sectors (government, university, and corporation), therefore, are reported for each dependent variable (e.g., job satisfaction) as it is related to the four different types of leaders: NT, ST, NF, SF. A summary chart (Exhibit 14.10) revealing the findings for all thirteen variables is shown and discussed first. This is followed by a consideration of some of the variables separately.

A brief explanatory note of caution is in order here. By observing the differences among laboratories in worker-reported attitudes, the inference should not be drawn that a particular leader type is necessarily "bad." Rather, the conclusion should be drawn that leaders with these predispositions either choose not to or are not able to give adequate time and attention to leadership responsibilities that the group, organization, and circumstance demand. Inherent in this analysis, then, is the "fit" or "contingency" notion now prevalent in leadership theory (however, those contingencies may be extraordinarily different in another culture) which suggests that as organizations move through their life cycles, different kinds of leaders may be more effective. Such also, hypothetically, is the case with R & D organizations.

Exhibit 14.10 displays the overall relationships between psychological type of leader and the thirteen worker variables. For each economic sector, government, university, and corporation, the trait of the leaders with the lowest and highest reported frequency (in the *negative* ranges only) on the JDS dependent variable is given.

In the following separate analyses, the relationships between leader types and some of the thirteen variables comprising the modified JDS, controlling for type of laboratory (university, government, or corporation) are examined. First, the dependent variables are considered, then the job conditions and psychological states.

## LEADER TYPES AND ASSOCIATED ORGANIZATIONAL CONDITIONS

There is both a consistency across variables *within* the three sectors and a great disparity *across* them. For example, in government R & D laboratory sections, it appears that, without exception, when SF types are leaders, there are strong, negative responses reported by workers. Not only do the independent

**Exhibit 14.10**
**Leader Types with Highest and Lowest Frequencies Reported by Workers in the Low Score Range[1] on Each Dependent Variable—Classified by Economic Sector**

| | Government | | University | | Corporation | |
|---|---|---|---|---|---|---|
| | Highest | Lowest | Highest | Lowest | Highest | Lowest |

**Variables**

**I. Job Characteristics**

**A. Worker Interactions and Relationships**

| | | Government | | University | | Corporation | |
|---|---|---|---|---|---|---|---|
| 1. | Work/Task Interdependence | SF | NT | M,SF | ST | ST,NT | M,NF |
| 2. | Cooperativeness/ Collegiality | SF | NF | M | ST | ST | M |

**B. Clarity or Ambiguity of Work**

| | | | | | | | |
|---|---|---|---|---|---|---|---|
| 3. | Job Content Clarity | SF | NT,NF | SF | ST | NT,ST | M,NF |
| 4. | Feedback Adequacy | SF | NT | M | ST | SF | NF |

**C. Work Demands and Characteristics**

| | | | | | | | |
|---|---|---|---|---|---|---|---|
| 5. | Work Load | SF | NF,NT | M | ST | ST,NT | M,NF |
| 6. | Work Diversity | SF | NF,NT | M,SF | ST | NT,ST | M,NF |
| 7. | Control Over Task | SF | NT,NF | M | ST | ST,NT | M,NF |
| 8. | Adequacy of tools, equipment | SF | NT | M | ST | ST | M,NF |

**D. Psychological Relevance to Work**

| | | | | | | | |
|---|---|---|---|---|---|---|---|
| 9. | Job Meaningfulness/ Significance | SF | NT,NT | M, SF | NT | NT | M,SF |

**II. Outcomes**

**A. Relationship to Organization**

| | | | | | | | |
|---|---|---|---|---|---|---|---|
| 1. | Organizational Identification | SF | NT,NF | M | ST | ST | M,NF |
| 2. | Organizational Commitment | SF | NF | M | ST | NT,ST | M,NF |

**B. Relationship to Self**

| | | | | | | | |
|---|---|---|---|---|---|---|---|
| 3. | Personal Satisfaction | SF | NT,NF | NF | ST | ST,NT | M |
| 4. | Self-esteem | SF | NT,NF | M | ST | ST,NT | M,NF |

1. One and one-half standard deviations or less below the mean on each modified JDS variable.

variables in the Hackman-Oldham framework have lower mean scores in the presence of SFs, but so do the dependent variables (e.g., commitment to the organization and satisfaction with work variety). A clear-cut case also exists for the pattern of leader types that is most closely associated with *fewer* reports by workers of negative effects. Intuition types as leaders, especially NTs, are more frequently associated with fewer workers expressing negative attitudes. That is, leaders having an intuitive input preference and a thinking style tend to be associated with *less* worker-negative affect.

A completely different picture appears for universities and corporations. In the former, mixed-type leaders are least desirable, while STs appear more favorable, producing the fewest number of workers with negative attitudes. In corporations, almost a totally opposite finding occurs, with STs being least desirable and Ms and NFs the most.

It is perhaps easiest to analyze these patterns if the assumptions of the Hackman-Oldham model are accepted here. That is, it would follow that when job conditions do not produce desired psychological states, end-result variables will also be negative. It is useful, consequently, to start the separate analysis of the thirteen variables with the dependent side of the Hackman-Oldham model, then trace backward the sources of influence on those variables.

In Exhibit 14.11, the data showing the relationships between the five MBTI types and the first dependent variable, "satisfaction with and commitment to the organization," are given.

Of immediate noteworthiness in this exhibit is the overall difference in the distribution of the five types. In the government sector, the SF-type leader in Japan appears to have the most deleterious effects on satisfaction and commitment to the organization. Thirty-five percent of the workers in government laboratories with SF leaders reported scores of one standard deviation or more below the mean, while for the university, it is the leader with no predominant type—the mixed leader (29%) which has the highest negative rankings. In corporations, negative effects are most highly correlated with NT or ST type leaders (30%, 31%).

It is not surprising that in the government sector, which is primarily concerned with the enhancement of the general welfare, a leader whose personality disposition (NF) "matches" that need produces the least undesirable effect on workers (fewer workers reporting dissatisfaction). NFs are concerned with social welfare in a broad general sense, certainly the prime manifest objective of government R & D laboratories. Looked at from the other side, the sensation/feeling-oriented leaders (SF) in government labs seem to have the most unfortunate effect.

There are several reasons why this apparent compatibility may produce the desired results. First, perhaps the long-term, outside orientation of leaders with NF dispositions is theoretically of potential benefit to a nonprofit organization seeking to identify and solve scientific problems for the good of the society. The Japanese government is a forceful and effective presence in Japanese so-

**Exhibit 14.11**
**Leader Type and Worker Attitude by Type of Laboratory**

**Variable #1 — Satisfaction with and Commitment to the Organization**

(Frequencies — % by column)

|       | Government | University | Corporation | Total |
|-------|-----------|-----------|-------------|-------|
| N     | 81        | 34        | 76          | 191   |
| NF    | 11        | 24        | 13          | 14    |
| SF    | 35        | 24        | 17          | 26    |
| NT    | 11        | 18        | 30          | 20    |
| ST    | 19        | 6         | 28          | 20    |
| Mixed | 25        | 29        | 12          | 20    |
| Total |           |           |             | 100%  |

Chi square= 25.29
D.F.= 8
Significance= .0014

ciety. It is responsive to the corporate sector which dominates the R & D field, while at the same time taking the initiative for filling perceived gaps. Workers will, therefore, in all likelihood tend to see their leaders as compatible with the goals and objectives of the larger organization to which they belong.

The NF leader is also suitable for the day-to-day requirements of R & D administration in the laboratory. Japanese co-workers identify with fierce loyalty with their organizations, and their organizations respond with a filial-type concern and caring which is intense and continuous. For the most part this organizational response is peer dominated. That is, the Japanese worker submerges himself primarily in his immediate group and finds succor in their support. There is, to be sure, a certain kind of leader-worker interaction in every group. However, the "leader" in this case is more frequently a person of higher position and status, usually the department chairman or laboratory director, depending on the size of the units and organization. Indeed, as noted in Chapter 5, the Japanese organization qua "family" reinforces family-type roles such as father, mother, and sibling, though these family roles must be understood as they are conceived and enacted in a distinctive Japanese culture.

The sensation/feeling leader (SF), on the other hand, deals in the minutiae of interpersonal relations. This special orientation may be ill-suited to the needs of government R & D workers whose autonomy is critical to effective functioning. Here again, it should be noted that autonomy in Japan is group centered, not individual centered. That is, the group needs, and is given, great discretionary power, thus obviating the need for close supervision by a formal leader. Too, as discussed below, group, rather than individual, tendering of "consideration" (in the leadership jargon) is the norm in Japan, except for special circumstances where personal problems are attended to by persons outside of the immediate formal work group, but within the organization.

An apparent reversal of logic takes place in the corporate sector where the "thinking" types (NT and ST), hypothetically highly beneficial to corporate efficiency, are least effective. To speculate, perhaps in corporate laboratories, with their heavy emphasis on practical matters and their short-term perspective, workers' feelings are less attended to. Note that the feeling dimension is missing from the NTs and STs. In corporation labs, compared with government and universities, the number of projects underway at any one time is fewer, the time on projects is shorter, there are more and different people from other organizational functions, the leaders are younger, and turnover of leadership is higher. These conditions may engender an anxiety about changing group relations that may be exacerbated by the production and efficiency orientations of leaders. Note that Ms and NFs have the least unfortunate effects on workers in government labs, indicating perhaps that a balanced leader orientation is especially important.

Further, as with the government sector, the external orientation of the leader may also be potentially beneficial. Corporate success in Japan is measured not in profitability but in financial stability or security, realized in part through steady growth and large size. Hence, even at the section level, the leader who can forward the goals of section, lab, and company will be more likely to engender feelings of satisfaction and commitment.

Let us now turn to the independent variables in the Hackman and Oldham model. First to be discussed is "work or task interdependence." Again, there are significant differences across the laboratories as revealed in Exhibit 14.12.

Different kinds of leaders are associated with different patterns of worker interdependence. For example, in the government sample, the least interdependence (most autonomy) was associated with a SF type leader (35%). For universities, it was the mixed leader (29%), while in corporations the ST or NT (32%, 31%) type leaders had this effect. More interdependence in universities, on the other hand, was associated with STs (7%), while in government labs it was NTs (10%), and in corporations, NFs or Mixed leaders (10%, 11%). Recasting these rank orderings into chart form reveals some rather dramatic differences as noted in Exhibit 14.13 (which is a subset of Exhibit 14.12).

It is quite difficult to explain the corporate data findings. It would be reasonable to assume that pragmatic concerns for efficiency and effectiveness would lead to the employment of Thinking types in order to structure the interactions more collaboratively, especially to foster the technology transfer process. In Japan, there is a much greater integration of functional areas (marketing, engineering, production, and R & D) than in the United States, thus necessitating more interdependence among workers. Yet, Thinking types in this research are found to be associated with most worker autonomy. The finding reported earlier that Thinking types also are associated with less satisfaction with and commit-

**Exhibit 14.12**
**Leader Type and Worker Attitude by Type of Laboratory**

Variable #2 — Work/Task Interdependence

(Frequencies — % by column)[1]

|       | Government | University | Corporation | Total |
|-------|:----------:|:----------:|:-----------:|:-----:|
| NF    | 13         | 23         | 10          | 13    |
| SF    | 35         | 26         | 17          | 26    |
| NT    | 10         | 16         | 31          | 20    |
| ST    | 22         | 7          | 32          | 23    |
| Mixed | 20         | 29         | 11          | 18    |
| Total | 100%       | 101%       | 101%        | 101%  |
| N     | 79         | 31         | 82          | 192   |

Chi square = 27.71
D.F. = 8
Significance = .0005

1. Note: the way that the data are calculated makes the reporting grammatically difficult. A high percentage means that there were more workers scoring in the lower range for the variable (greater than −1 S.D.) with leaders of this type.

ment to the organization makes this finding of greater autonomy even more anomalous. It may be that it is the *failure* of the ST and NT leader to create tight bonds of interdependence in the face of corporate needs for that interdependence that creates the dissatisfaction. That is, if R & D workers in corporate labs require close collaboration with others, and, if as reported here, that collaboration—or at least interdependence—is not forthcoming, there may be some degree of dissatisfaction.

Alternatively, it could be that the frequent job rotation system in Japan and the highly collaborative interactions across functional boundaries make ST and NT leaders appear superfluous, especially to workers already committed to the goals of corporate growth and efficiency. (As will be seen later, satisfaction with work variety and challenge is also lowest for NTs and STs.)

This conclusion is confounded somewhat in the light of the data for university laboratories where STs are associated with worker perceptions of most interdependence/least autonomy (in direct contrast to the perceptions in corporations). Since STs also are related to highest satisfaction and commitment to organization (or, more correctly, with least detriment to satisfaction and commitment), it is possible to interpret the internal efficiency orientation of the ST leader in university labs as providing more structure in the somewhat more anarchic setting, thus giving workers a greater sense of coherence and focus within the laboratory. The ST leader can reduce the Japanese worker's sense of

**Exhibit 14.13**
**Impact of Leader Types on Interdependence by Organizational Type**

| Worker Perception | Government | University | Corporation |
|---|---|---|---|
| More interdependence (less autonomy) | NT (10%) | ST (7%) | NF,M |
| Less interdependence (more autonomy) | SF (35%) | M,SF (29%; 26%) | ST,NT (32%; 31%) |

isolation occasioned through his greater autonomy by giving him a more ordered environment in which to work. These speculations would seem to confirm the "fit" hypotheses laid out earlier. To reiterate, the optimum leader mediates successfully between external pressures to adapt and internal pressures to satisfy the workers. In the corporate setting, STs are related to highest worker interdependence, but only moderately to overall satisfaction and commitment, while in the university these same types are related to more autonomy and higher satisfaction and commitment.

Worker satisfaction with work variety was examined next. The data are given in Exhibit 14.14.

Again with this variable, it is useful to identify types of leaders who have most and least pernicious influence. NF-type leaders seem to be least effective in government and university labs (38% and 27%), as seen by the number of workers dissatisfied with their work variety and challenge. In the corporate sector, it is NTs (30%), followed by STs (28%). Least detrimental are the sensation types in government (NF, 10%; NT, 11%), STs (7%) in universities, and mixed or NFs (12%; 13%) in corporations.

It is understandable that in the government sector, section leaders with concerns for public welfare are most effective, as noted earlier. Socialization processes in Japan are extreme and effective. Japanese work enterprises are "total organizations" in Goffman's terms. Hence, workers in the organizations can be expected almost completely to have adopted the requisite values and to have made them their own. The leader of the organization, in this case the scientific laboratory section, is the personification of those values and the one with whom workers identify (and the one whom they helped to have chosen as their leader). This similarity of values of worker and leader may in fact contribute to the sense of satisfaction of the workers.

Once again, as noted above, the posture of the NF leader is toward the outside—toward the fulfillment of organizational objectives vis-à-vis the general public (or, perhaps less romantically, of his section within the organization that constitutes its environment). That is, the section sees its role as providing for the good and welfare of the system external to it, in this case the organization as a whole. Further, NF-type leaders are likely to be engaged in external rela-

**Exhibit 14.14**
**Leader Type and Worker Attitude by Type of Laboratory**

Variable #3 — Satisfaction with Work Variety and Challenge

(Percent of column totals)

|  | Government | University | Corporation | Total |
|---|---|---|---|---|
| NF | 10 | 23 | 13 | 13 |
| SF | 38 | 27 | 18 | 28 |
| NT | 11 | 17 | 30 | 20 |
| ST | 22 | 7 | 28 | 22 |
| Mixed | 19 | 27 | 12 | 17 |
| Total | 100% | 101% | 101% | 100% |
| N | 79 | 30 | 87 | 196 |

Chi square= 23.73
D.F.= 8
Significance= .0025

tions more than internal, thus (by benign neglect, perhaps) allowing more worker autonomy and hence satisfaction with variety and challenge.

A similar argument might be made for the corporate sector where NTs and STs are least likely to produce workers who are satisfied with work variety and challenge. It is conceivable that in the more turbulent external and internal corporate world, with its rapid personnel rotation policies, NTs who look primarily *outside* the boundaries of the organization tend to neglect the individual needs of workers for work variety and challenge. In this case, because of the different context, the neglect is not benign. STs, on the other hand, may be overly concerned with efficiency which requires more specialization. The latter, in turn, is inversely correlated with the generalization and challenge forthcoming from working on many different jobs. Alternatively, it could be that under the press of short-term corporate goals, accentuated by the leader, work variety and challenge for workers *exceeds* the optimum amount.

The more favorable impact of NTs in the university sector speaks to the felicitous effects of the apparent "mismatch" of leader type to organizational type, that is, the alleged need of the organization for a leader whose dispositions suit the current internal and external conditions. NTs tend to be concerned with external conditions, growth, market share, and resource acquisition. Japanese university laboratories with NT leaders have successful entrepreneurs—leaders who are able to attract new resources and make a name for the university. For workers accustomed to the snail's pace of university growth, these leaders may be able to provide just the variety and challenge they have been looking for.

## DIFFERENCES IN REVISED JDS SCORES ACROSS KINDS OF ORGANIZATIONS

It is clear from the above that there are many interesting differences in the leader characteristics across the different settings for research and development. The characteristics described above are borrowed from the Kilmann and Herden typology. Before proceeding with another analysis of the differences in leaders across these settings, this time using the revised MBTI scale scores, it will be useful to consider the differences in the values of the dependent variables, also across these groups. That is, in this section, we will outline the ways in which scores on the revised JDS differ in corporate, government, and university R & D laboratories.

The first approach to this analysis is to provide an item-by-item analysis of the differences. In Exhibit 14.15, the results of one-way analyses of variance are presented for each item. Where appropriate, the results of post-hoc tests (in this case, Scheffé contrasts) for group differences are also provided. The means are rank ordered according to government unit scores.

Perhaps most remarkable about these data is the relative similarity of responses across the kinds of organizations. While there are a fairly large number of statistically significant differences, the magnitude of the differences is generally not great. In short, R & D workers in the different kinds of organizations generally feel similarly about their jobs, themselves, and their organizations.

A second observation is that the levels of satisfaction and ratings of supportive conditions are quite high. Most of the workers are generally satisfied with their own performance, with the job, with their colleagues, and with their organization. It is a nice place to work, they do their best work, are committed to it, feel bad when they perform poorly, and take pride in their organization and hope it will continue to develop. On the negative side, at least some report a fairly high level of work overload, competing role demands, and low payoff for risky work.

There are, however, some differences across the kinds of organization. For example, university researchers appear to be most satisfied and free. They express more satisfaction with their own performance, they feel freer to challenge authority, they experience less work overload and hence, find less often that it impedes coordination with others. Research workers in corporations also differ in several ways. From these data, they seem to be more interdependent than researchers in the other two groups. Co-worker links are more often required, close cooperation is needed, and work suffers when other workers' pace is inadequate. Much of this is not surprising, given the more applied and developmental nature of the research in corporations that involves more team rather than individual effort.

Finally, government researchers express less agreement than in the other two groups with the statement that engagement in risky enterprises is rewarded when successful. This may be due in part to the more limited reward variance in a

## Exhibit 14.15
## Differences in Worker Attitudes across Types of Organizational Laboratories

Means[1]

| Variable Name | Gov't | Univ. | Corp. | F Ratio | F Probability | Differing Groups (Scheffé .05 level) |
|---|---|---|---|---|---|---|
| Hope Org'n Will Development | 6.0 | 6.1 | 6.0 | 0.2 | NS | |
| Job Enhances Self-Opinion | 5.8 | 6.0 | 5.9 | 3.1 | .0476 | — |
| Satisf. w/Own Performance | 5.8 | 6.2 | 5.9 | 4.2 | .0155 | G/U |
| No Need for Feedback | 5.7 | 5.9 | 5.6 | 5.3 | .0052 | U/C |
| Creativity Opportunity | 5.7 | 6.1 | 5.5 | 8.2 | .0003 | G/U;U/C |
| Feedback from Job Itself | 5.6 | 5.7 | 5.6 | 0.4 | NS | |
| High Skill Utilized | 5.6 | 6.0 | 5.5 | 7.1 | .0009 | G/U;U/C |
| Feedback from Work | 5.6 | 5.7 | 5.5 | 1.5 | NS | |
| Assigned Work Umambiguous | 5.6 | 5.8 | 5.5 | 2.8 | NS | |
| Independence | 5.5 | 5.9 | 5.3 | 8.2 | .0003 | G/U;U/C |
| General Satisfaction | 5.5 | 5.7 | 5.3 | 3.9 | .0200 | U/C |
| Autonomy | 5.4 | 5.5 | 5.4 | 0.4 | NS | |
| OK to Challenge Authority | 5.4 | 6.0 | 5.3 | 8.8 | .0002 | G/U;U/C |
| Opp'ty to Finish Work | 5.4 | 5.4 | 5.2 | 1.7 | NS | |
| Work w/people | 5.3 | 5.2 | 5.5 | 2.1 | NS | |
| Satisf. w/Kind of Work | 5.2 | 5.5 | 5.1 | 3.8 | .0237 | U/C |
| Own Bad Work Makes Me Sad | 5.2 | 5.3 | 5.5 | 2.7 | NS | |
| Job Variety | 5.1 | 5.2 | 5.0 | 0.9 | NS | |
| Can Do Complete Job | 5.0 | 5.4 | 5.0 | 2.6 | NS | |
| Work Overload | 5.0 | 4.3 | 5.0 | 8.7 | .0002 | G/U;U/C |
| Job Satisfaction | 4.9 | 5.3 | 4.9 | 3.1 | .0457 | - |
| Adequate Information | 4.9 | 5.4 | 4.8 | 7.0 | .0009 | |
| Satisfaction w/Work Itself | 4.9 | 5.3 | 4.8 | 4.3 | .0141 | U/C |
| Co-worker Quality Import. | 4.9 | 5.0 | 5.1 | 1.9 | NS | |
| Own Perf. Affects Dept. | 4.8 | 4.9 | 5.2 | 4.3 | .0144 | G/C |
| Satisfaction w/Org'n | 4.8 | 4.7 | 4.7 | 0.4 | NS | |
| Others Provide Cooperation | 4.8 | 4.8 | 5.0 | 1.3 | NS | |
| Job Significance | 4.8 | 5.1 | 5.1 | 4.3 | .0140 | G/C |
| Tools and Machines OK | 4.8 | 5.0 | 5.0 | 1.3 | NS | |
| Would Transfer for OK Work | 4.7 | 4.9 | 4.7 | 0.5 | NS | |
| Do Best Work Here | 4.7 | 4.6 | 4.6 | 0.4 | NS | |
| Pride in Organization | 4.7 | 4.7 | 4.6 | 0.2 | NS | |
| Would Work Harder | 4.6 | 4.9 | 4.8 | 2.7 | NS | |
| Nice Place to Work | 4.6 | 4.6 | 4.5 | 0.8 | NS | |
| Ease of Cooperation | 4.6 | 4.7 | 4.9 | 4.7 | .0093 | G/C |
| Machines and Tools OK | 4.6 | 4.7 | 4.8 | 1.1 | NS | |
| Co-worker Links Required | 4.6 | 4.1 | 5.0 | 14.2 | .0000 | G/C;U/C |

1. Questionnaire response categories permitted answers on a scale of 1–7. A mean of 4.0, then, represents the midpoint on the scale. N's vary as follows: Government 233–234, Universities 86–89, Corporations 371–373.

**Exhibit 14.15 (continued)**

Means[1]

| | Gov't | Univ. | Corp. | F Ratio | F Probability | Differing Groups (Scheffé .05 level) |
|---|---|---|---|---|---|---|
| Would Exit If Bad Treatment | 4.6 | 4.6 | 4.6 | 0.1 | NS | |
| Workload Impedes Coordin. | 4.5 | 4.0 | 4.6 | 7.5 | .0006 | G/U;U/C |
| Odd Treatment of Employees | 4.5 | 4.4 | 4.3 | 2.1 | NS | |
| Satisfaction w/Colleagues | 4.5 | 4.9 | 4.7 | 2.2 | NS | |
| Close Cooperation Needed | 4.4 | 4.2 | 4.8 | 8.0 | .0004 | G/C;U/C |
| Impact of Other's Quality | 4.3 | 4.3 | 4.5 | 1.0 | NS | |
| Work Centrality | 4.2 | 4.5 | 4.7 | 6.9 | .0011 | G/C |
| Role Overload | 4.2 | 4.1 | 4.3 | 1.6 | NS | |
| Job Affects Many Others | 4.2 | 4.3 | 4.8 | 16.3 | .0000 | G/C;U/C |
| Satisfaction w/Promotions | 4.2 | 4.2 | 4.1 | 0.2 | NS | |
| No Feedback from Others | 4.1 | 4.1 | 3.9 | 2.0 | NS | |
| Other's Pace Inadequate | 4.1 | 3.8 | 4.5 | 6.9 | .0010 | G/C;U/C |
| Good Atmosphere | 4.1 | 4.2 | 4.4 | 3.9 | .0216 | G/C |
| Would Transfer for Pay | 4.1 | 4.2 | 4.3 | 2.1 | NS | |
| Satisfaction w/Leader | 3.8 | 4.0 | 4.2 | 5.3 | .0053 | G/C |
| Agree w/Management | 3.8 | 4.2 | 4.0 | 3.2 | .0417 | G/U |
| Feedback from Others OK | 3.8 | 3.8 | 4.1 | 3.3 | .0363 | — |
| Identify w/Organization | 3.7 | 3.8 | 3.6 | 0.5 | NS | |
| Feedback from Others | 3.7 | 3.9 | 3.8 | 0.3 | NS | |
| Bad to Stay Here Forever | 3.6 | 3.6 | 3.5 | 1.1 | NS | |
| Interdependence | 3.6 | 3.8 | 3.1 | 8.2 | .0003 | G/C;U/C |
| Feel Lost at Work at Times | 3.6 | 3.2 | 3.7 | 2.7 | NS | |
| Quit Propensity | 3.5 | 3.5 | 3.5 | 0.0 | NS | |
| Satisfaction w/Pay | 3.4 | 3.0 | 3.3 | 2.6 | NS | |
| Work Quanity Not Burden | 3.3 | 3.5 | 3.2 | 1.1 | NS | |
| If Rotate, Will Work Hard | 3.3 | 3.2 | 3.3 | 0.2 | NS | |
| Think About Quitting | 2.8 | 2.6 | 3.1 | 3.9 | .0213 | U/C |
| No Beginning-to-End Tasks | 2.8 | 3.0 | 2.9 | 0.9 | NS | |
| Org'n Rates Job Low | 2.8 | 2.7 | 2.8 | 0.3 | NS | |
| Mistake to Come Here | 2.7 | 2.8 | 2.9 | 1.9 | NS | |
| When Success, Risk Pays | 2.6 | 3.0 | 3.3 | 12.3 | .0000 | G/C |
| Work & Feelings Unrelated | 2.6 | 2.6 | 2.4 | 0.9 | NS | |
| Work Is Simple | 2.0 | 1.8 | 1.9 | 1.0 | NS | |

government bureau. Again, it must be pointed out, however, that for the most part there is relatively little difference across the organizations when the data are examined on an item-by-item basis.

## CLUSTER ANALYSIS

We turn now to an alternative way of grouping the laboratory leaders. Another computer-assisted manipulation of the MBTI adjusted scales was conducted. As noted above, eight scales resulted from the factor analysis of the MBTI items. The scale scores from the sample of 150 leaders (actually, there were 148, since two ''outlyers'' were eliminated) were subjected to a ''multidimensional scaling cluster analysis.'' An attempt was made to find ''clusters'' of R & D section

**Exhibit 14.16**
**Differences in Traits across Clusters[1]**

|  | F Ratio | F Probability |
|---|---|---|
| Practicality-Unconventionality | 38.00 | < .0000 |
| Intimacy-Relationships | 20.12 | < .0000 |
| Gentility-Firm-mindedness | 10.71 | < .0000 |
| Rationality-Affect | 25.63 | < .0000 |
| Introversion-Extroversion | 28.42 | < .0000 |
| Extemporaneity-Premeditation | 8.28 | < .0000 |
| Ideational-Literal | 6.02 | < .0000 |
| Consideration-Reasonableness | 6.42 | < .0000 |

1. Post-hoc Scheffé tests showed that at least two clusters differed from one another on each trait and that for most traits, there were differences across more than half of the clusters. (Data available on request).

leaders whose characteristics on the eight attitude/personality scales of the adjusted MBTI were most similar to one another. Using a procedure suggested by Davison (1983), eight clusters of R & D leaders with similar psychological orientations were identified. Following this, an analysis was conducted of differences in mean MBTI scores by R & D leader cluster type on each of the adjusted MBTI traits. In summary form, a one-way analysis of variance produced the F ratios and probabilities for each scale given in Exhibit 14.16.

It was then necessary to characterize for each cluster the predominant traits of the leaders who comprised them. It would then be possible to see the ways in which leader traits in each of the eight clusters were related to the worker attitudes as measured by the revised JDS.

The characterization of the prototypical leader traits for each cluster was based on the mean scores for each of the adjusted MBTI scales. In accordance with the thinking of the originators of the Myers-Briggs Type Indicator who, following Jung, found that there were predominant and passive traits, a decision was made to concentrate on the scores for each cluster that deviated from the grand mean for the sample—again, the whole 148 leaders. Hence, leader characteristics for a cluster were calculated by assessing the degree to which the mean for each scale score for the cluster deviated from the mean scale score for the entire group. That is, the leader in a cluster could be said to have a distinctively unique characteristic if their scores were significantly different from the rest of the leaders on that scale. More specifically, if it was found that the mean for a trait in a cluster was +/− 15 percent from the grand mean, the trait was labeled as a meaningful quality of that cluster.

No allowance was made, however, for the rank ordering of scale scores *within* a cluster. In other words, the trait with the highest mean for the cluster did not necessarily mean that the trait was uniquely characteristic of the leaders in the cluster if, indeed, for all clusters the same trait was highest. Thus, the "personality" of the leaders in a cluster was considered a function of the outstanding (read deviant

**Exhibit 14.17**
**Overview of Leader Clusters and Their Characteristics**

| Cluster Name[1] | N | Dominant Characteristics |
|---|---|---|
| Gregory | 19 | Extroversion, Sociability, Unconventionality |
| Fido | 8 | Literal, Extemporaneity, Intimacy |
| Mouse | 14 | Practicality, Introversion, Affect |
| Nurse | 23 | Gentility, Affect, Consideration |
| Popeye | 39 | Sociability, Unconventionality |
| Salaryman | 5 | Intimacy, Firmness, Practicality |
| Carl Sagan | 15 | Extroversion, Rationality |
| Genius | 8 | Unconventionality, Intimacy, Ideational, Introversion |

1. Names are intended to be mnemonics to help Westerners recall the clusters. No negative connotations about Japanese leaders in general are intended. (For a list of negative, American managerial archetypes derived from the MBTI, see Benfari 1991, 57–60. For a set of leader roles identified in four prototypical scientific research teams, see Cohen, Kruse, & Anbar 1982).

from grand mean) traits. Perhaps more plainly, as an example, since the trait ''consideration-reasonableness'' had the lowest grand mean of all of the eight traits, for most of the respondents in *all* of the clusters, their mean scores on this trait were below their mean scores on other traits. However, there was a within-trait variance even on the lowest scored traits, such as consideration-reasonableness. Again, it was the deviance from the trait grand mean (regardless of the rank of that mean in any respondent's total scores) that was the basis of the attribution of a distinctive characteristic to the person or cluster. Only if the mean for cluster was 15 percent deviant from the grand mean for the trait was it adopted as a cluster trait, regardless of its rank order within a cluster. While it is probably the case that latent or less powerful traits affect the behavioral manifestations of the stronger traits, in the interests of personnel policy analysis, only the dominant traits are identified here, that is, those which may be more easily identified regardless of the lesser traits that may accompany them.

Not unexpectedly, given the clustering constraints of the multiple hierarchical clustering, the eight clusters were found to be quite different on the various traits. The names and characteristics of the traits are listed in Exhibits 14.17 and 14.18.

## THE RELATIONSHIP OF LEADER CLUSTERS TO WORKER ATTITUDES

Having identified significantly different clusters, it becomes possible to determine whether and how these different types of R & D leaders affect their

**Exhibit 14.18**
**Psychological Dispositions of Leader "Clusters"**

Cluster 1

Name:   Gregory (Gregarious)
N = 19
Dominant Characteristics: Extroversion, Sociability, Unconventionality

This type of leader has relationships with many workers and is able to reveal his feelings easily.   He tends to grab onto original and new ideas (perhaps those generated by others), but as he is not very practical, putting them into practice in R & D labs is probably better left to others.

Statistics:

| Scale Name | Standardized Scale Score | Deviation from Scale Grand Mean | > 15% Deviation |
|---|---|---|---|
| **Grand Mean Deviation** | | | |
| Introversion-Extroversion | 4.7 | -1.8 | -38% |
| Intimacy-Sociability | 5.7 | -1.6 | -28% |
| Practicality-Unconventionality | 5.4 | -1.6 | -30% |
| Consideration-Reasonableness | 4.5 | +.4 | |
| Gentility-Firm-mindedness | 6.3 | +.3 | |
| Extemporaneity-Premeditation | 5.8 | +.3 | |
| Ideational-Literal | 4.0 | -.2 | |
| Rationality-Affect | 7.0 | 0.0 | |
| Cluster Mean of all Scales | 5.4 | | |

workers' attitudes and behavior. Pursuant to that question, an analysis of the scores of the workers on each of the revised JDS scales across the different clusters of leaders was performed.

On seven of the thirteen dependent (worker) variables there were statistically significant differences across the leader clusters. That is, for seven of the revised JDS variables, an analysis of variance revealed that worker scores were different from one another when the scores were grouped by leader cluster. These data are summarized in Exhibit 14.19, which also provides a rank ordering from high to low of the Leader Cluster mean scores on each of the worker variables.

Exhibit 14.19 seems to reveal some additional characteristics of Japanese R & D leadership and their relationships to worker attitudes, regardless of the particular location of the laboratory within organizational types. Perhaps most remarkable is the finding that no one type of leader predominates. With the exception of Fido, who heads the list for Cooperation and Adequacy of Tools and Equipment (both with marginally significant F probabilities), and Nurse, who is lowest in impact on five of the seven JDS variables, the leader types with strongest effects are different for each of the worker variables. The three

**Exhibit 14.18 (continued)**

**Cluster 2**

Name:   Fido (Fidelity/Doggedness)
N=8
Dominant Characteristics: Literal, Extemporaneity, Firm-mindedness

This type of leader has relatively little imagination and creativity, preferring to attend literally to the day-to-day realities of R & D activities. Not a careful planner, he, nevertheless, tends to be rather rigid in his opinions. This combination of traits may make Fido a not particularly effective R & D team leader, except perhaps on well-planned long-term projects.

Statistics:

| Scale Name | Standardized Scale Score | Deviation from Scale Grand Mean | >15% Deviation |
|---|---|---|---|
| **Grand Mean Deviation** | | | |
| Introversion-Extroversion | 4.1 | -1.9 | -46% |
| Intimacy-Sociability | 7.3 | +1.8 | +25% |
| Practicality-Unconventionality | 8.4 | +1.1 | |
| Consideration-Reasonableness | 5.1 | -.9 | -18% |
| Gentility-Firm-mindedness | 6.3 | -.7 | |
| Extemporaneity-Premeditation | 7.5 | +.5 | |
| Ideational-Literal | 3.6 | -.5 | |
| Rationality-Affect | <u>6.4</u> | -.1 | |
| Cluster Mean of all Scales | 6.0 | | |

leader types highest in the rank orders are Fido, Scrooge, and Partner. While there is some overlap in their personality characteristics, they are distinctly different in many respects. Fido and Scrooge have few friends, while Partner has many. Partner and Scrooge share Unconventionality as a characteristic.

In many respects this finding is not surprising. As noted earlier, leadership responsibilities in Japanese organizations tend to be spread over many individuals. Moreover, as organizational needs change during different phases, different types of leaders are required and, in the Japanese flexible system, can fill in as required. In the design of this study, the original plan was to examine the face-to-face relationships between the formal leader of the R & D section of 15 to 40 workers. It was hypothesized that this intimate daily interaction must be critical to the effectiveness of the R & D operation. And, indeed, it is. But it would be naive to believe that all of the variance in R & D effectiveness can be accounted for by the formal section leader, nor even, perhaps, that a great deal of it can. In point of fact, different kinds of leadership are not only distributed across the leaders in the study but over the section workers themselves, over the assistant formal leader, the informal leader, the *nyobo yaku* or "wife role" (described in Chapter 5), the leader at the next level in the hierarchy, and

**Exhibit 14.18 (continued)**

Cluster 3

Name:  Mouse
N=14
Dominant Characteristics: Practicality, Introversion, Affect, Consideration

The "Mouse" leader is oriented toward practical matters in R & D, with his feet firmly on the ground and with a realistic, matter-of-fact approach to problem solving. He tends to deal with problems with his heart rather than his head; however, Mouse is not an initiator and will probably not be particularly effective in situations where workers come to him with practical or personal frustrations in their research.

Statistics:

| Scale Name | Standardized Scale Score | Deviation from Scale Grand Mean | >15% Deviation |
|---|---|---|---|
| **Grand Mean Deviation** | | | |
| Practicality-Unconventionality | 9.3 | +2.3 | +25% |
| Introversion-Extroversion | 7.9 | +1.4 | +18% |
| Rationality-Affect | 6.1 | -.9 | -15% |
| Consideration-Reasonableness | 4.9 | +.8 | +16% |
| Gentility-Firm-mindedness | 6.6 | +.6 | |
| Ideational-Literal | 3.7 | -.5 | |
| Intimacy-Sociability | 7.2 | +.1 | |
| Extemporaneity-Premeditation | 5.5 | 0.0 | |
| Cluster Mean of all Scales | 6.4 | | |

leaders farther up in the organizations. Often these roles overlap (Sasaki 1981, 74–76), but not as often as they might in other cultures.

As noted above, Japanese workers are completely exposed to each other in their behaviors. The formal section leader does not hide in a private office, but works in the open among his men. The Japanese worker has been brought up to expect observation from others and is, as a matter of fact, disturbed when he is not observed. He needs to be watched in order to be sure that his contribution to the good and welfare of the group is appreciated.

As noted in the previous chapter, however, there is a widespread assumption among both workers and managers that each individual may not carry out his assignment conscientiously if he is not observed. This is a "Theory X" assumption that is applied in the McGregor sense to individuals, but in Japan *not* to the collectivity. In the framework of Hersey and Blanchard (1988), it would appear that managers act on the assumption that workers as a group are fully "mature"—with abilities and dispositions to effectively make rational decisions in the interests of the organization. Effective leadership would call for a "del-

**Exhibit 14.18 (continued)**

**Cluster 4**

Name:   Nurse
N=23
Dominant Characteristics: Gentility, Affect, Consideration, Literal, Premeditation

The Nurse leader cares deeply about other people and takes on a very warm-hearted, compassionate, approach to working one-on-one with others. Nurse tends also to respond literally, rather than creatively, to problems presented. This kind of R & D leader will attend sensitively to the nurturing needs of his subordinates.

Statistics:

| Scale Name | Standardized Scale Score | Deviation from Scale Grand Mean | >15% Deviation |
|---|---|---|---|
| **Grand Mean Deviation** | | | |
| Gentility-Firm-mindedness | 7.4 | +1.4 | +19% |
| Rationality-Affect | 5.2 | -1.8 | -34% |
| Consideration-Reasonableness | 4.9 | +.9 | +18% |
| Ideational-Literal | 3.5 | -.8 | -23% |
| Extemporaneity-Premeditation | 4.8 | -.7 | -15% |
| Intimacy-Sociability | 6.6 | -.7 | |
| Practicality-Unconventionality | 6.5 | -.5 | |
| Introversion-Extroversion | 6.0 | -.5 | |
| Cluster Mean of all Scales | 5.6 | | |

egating'' style, and, indeed, such delegation is invariably forthcoming. While the consideration or succoring functions of leadership are partially retained by the formal leader, as are some (but by no means all) of the initiating structure responsibilities, the evaluation and control functions devolve on the workers themselves and are exercised by different individuals as the situation demands and by the group as a whole via "ambient" normative stimuli (cf. Hackman 1976).

There are, of course, some deviant workers in Japan who work at less than their optimum capacity, but the assumption is that the group itself will police them. The formal leader *can* leave his workers to themselves partly because the norm is that he *will* leave them to do their own self-supervision. The formal manager, qua manager (not person), therefore becomes largely invisible—a characteristic that fits into the Japanese psychology that abjures any obvious attention paid to any one individual, unless the formal role specifically calls for it. This is not to say that the R & D manager abandons the group. It is only to say that it becomes the group's responsibility to initiate much of the behavior related both to solving problems that have arisen in the group and to setting goals and priorities and the procedures for achieving them.

It is useful to give an illustration of why no one leader type fits all the needs

**Exhibit 14.18 (continued)**

Cluster 5

Name:   Popeye (Pop-ideas)
N=39
Dominant Characteristics: Sociability, Unconventionality

The Popeye leader has a vivid imagination, frequently coming up with creative and original ideas.  He likes to work with a wide range of friends.  He differs from Gregory, however, in that Gregory is an extrovert, while Popeye is not distinguished this trait.  It is likely that this kind of R & D leader will be a source of new ideas to be widely shared with his workers.

Statistics:

| Scale Name | Standardized Scale Score | Deviation from Scale Grand Mean | >15% Deviation |
|---|---|---|---|
| **Grand Mean Deviation** | | | |
| Intimacy-Sociability | 5.8 | -1.5 | |
| Practicality-Unconventionality | 5.7 | -1.3 | |
| Extemporaneity-Premeditation | 5.0 | -.5 | |
| Rationality-Affect | 7.5 | +.5 | |
| Introversion-Extroversion | 7.0 | +.5 | |
| Ideational-Literal | 4.5 | +.3 | |
| Consideration-Reasonableness | 3.9 | -.2 | |
| Gentility-Firm-mindedness | 6.0 | 0.0 | |
| Cluster Mean of all Scales | 5.7 | | |

of all the workers. Much responsibility in Japanese R & D (indeed in most Japanese organizations) falls to the group, even for the initiation of critical matters. This is functional and dysfunctional at the same time. In basic research laboratories, for example, where workers are not as interdependent and where coordination among workers is not as necessary, leaving to the collectivity the generation of new ideas, policies and procedures may do little harm provided there is adequate attention to the norms of initiation at the individual level. That is, each individual worker must understand that there is a forum for his new ideas in the structured relationship between him and the section leader.

For the applied and developmental laboratory, on the other hand, leaving the initiation of activity to workers may not be as productive as it might, even if all workers are highly motivated. First of all, while it is clear that holding meetings is a well-respected and expected activity, workers in these laboratories have different specializations. The sense of necessity for a meeting will therefore arise only when a problem occurs because workers from different specializations attending to a particular problem can not individually solve the problem. Further, the concrete problem focus of the meeting circumscribes the arena for discussion. It is only in the presence of a person whose perspectives are broader than

**Exhibit 14.18 (continued)**

### Cluster 6

Name:  Salaryman
N=5
Dominant Characteristics: Intimacy, Firm-mindedness, Practicality, Literal

Because of the relatively small sample size, there are only five members of this cluster.  The leader type is perhaps the most unusual of the lot, deviating more significantly from the others on many of the scales.  The Salaryman restricts his friendships to a small number.   He is often rather uncompromising in his perspectives, which also lean more toward practical matters and predictable outcomes.   One might expect this kind of person, as an R & D leader, to be somewhat limited in sensitivity to others and rather closed to new ideas.

Statistics:

| Scale Name | Standardized Scale Score | Deviation from Scale Grand Mean | >15% Deviation |
|---|---|---|---|
| **Grand Mean Deviation** | | | |
| Intimacy-Sociability | 9.2 | +1.9 | +21% |
| Gentility-Firm-mindedness | 4.4 | -1.6 | -36% |
| Practicality-Unconventionality | 8.4 | +1.4 | +17% |
| Rationality-Affect | 7.8 | +.8 | |
| Introversion-Extroversion | 7.2 | +.7 | |
| Extemporaneity-Premeditation | 4.8 | -.7 | |
| Ideational-Literal | 3.8 | -.6 | -16% |
| Consideration-Reasonableness | 3.6 | -.5 | |
| Cluster Mean of all Scales | 6.2 | | |

the particular problem at hand that worker minds can be brought to bear on issues that are critical to longer-term and/or deeper research questions. While the extensive job rotation in Japanese organizations does broaden perspectives, one of the most important functions of the formal leader in a self-disciplining unit is cross-boundary, rather than supervisory. Hence, there is more of a need for leader-initiated action in applied labs where new ideas must be introduced. On the other hand, where efficient technology transfer requires a frequent and ad hoc assembly of "strangers," yet a different kind of leader is required. The identification of the variety of leader types (noted in Exhibit 14.9) that operate in Japanese R & D sections demonstrates the flexibility of the system to accommodate different kinds of formal leaders through the extensive delegation of leadership functions to the workers themselves.

Returning to the discussion of the leader types that have more effect on worker attitudes, it would seem that under certain conditions, a "Fido" would be necessary. Fido, it will be recalled, is adaptable but firm in his opinions. One

**Exhibit 14.18 (continued)**

Cluster 7

Name:   Carl Sagan
N = 15
Dominant Characteristics: Extroversion, Reasonableness

Like the Cornell astronomer, Carl Sagan leaders combine analytic abilities and dispositions with an extroverted nature that allows them to communicate their ideas with enthusiasm, convincing others of their validity. This kind of R & D leader will do well in external relations in the scientific community, explaining clearly the laboratory's activities and accomplishments.

Statistics:

| Scale Name | Standardized Scale Score | Deviation from Scale Grand Mean | >15% Deviation |
|---|---|---|---|
| Grand Mean Deviation | | | |
| Introversion-Extroversion | 5.2 | -1.3 | -25% |
| Rationality-Affect | 7.0 | +.7 | |
| Extemporaneity-Premeditation | 4.9 | -.6 | |
| Ideational-Literal | 4.8 | +.6 | |
| Consideration-Reasonableness | 3.5 | -.6 | -17% |
| Intimacy-Sociability | 6.8 | -.5 | |
| Gentility-Firm-mindedness | 5.6 | -.4 | |
| Practicality-Unconventionality | 7.2 | +.2 | |
| Cluster Mean of all Scales | 5.7 | | |

can imagine a research situation in which suggestions can easily be made to Fido, who will review them with his small circle of colleagues, then argue strongly for them. Scrooge might be needed in another situation, particularly one requiring new ideas. Partner fits into still another situation, one requiring a wider involvement of people.

## DIFFERENCES IN LEADERSHIP TRAITS ACROSS ORGANIZATIONAL KINDS

In the chapter on methods preceding this one, the empirically MBTI-derived, adjusted leadership scales were presented. In this section, data on the distribution of leadership traits across different kinds of organizations are presented. Recall that the eight traits that emerged from the factor analysis capture what may be the essence of alternative forms of leadership required in different situations. The eight are:

**Qualities of Mind**
Gentility-Firm-mindedness

**Exhibit 14.18 (continued)**

### Cluster 8

Name:   Genius
N=8
Dominant Characteristics: Unconventionality, Intimacy, Ideational

Geniuses are intuitive in their thinking, often with odd or original ideas. They tend to keep to themselves, having only a relatively small group of friends. This kind of R & D leader will respond well to off-beat ideas, probably developing many himself. He will be effective as a leader as a creative researcher role model, rather than as a communicator either within or across laboratory boundaries.

Statistics:

| Scale Name | Standardized Scale Score | Deviation from Scale Grand Mean | >15% Deviation |
|---|---|---|---|
| **Grand Mean Deviation** | | | |
| Practicality-Unconventionality | 5.1 | -1.9 | -37% |
| Intimacy-Sociability | 8.8 | +1.5 | +17% |
| Ideational-Literal | 5.3 | +1.1 | +21% |
| Introversion-Extroversion | 7.5 | +1.0 | |
| Gentility-Firm-mindedness | 6.8 | -.8 | |
| Rationality-Affect | 7.4 | +.4 | |
| Extemporaneity-Premeditation | 5.5 | 0.0 | |
| Consideration-Reasonableness | 4.1 | 0.0 | |
| Cluster Mean of all Scales | 6.3 | | |

Rationality-Affect

Consideration-Reasonableness

**Interpersonal Relationships**

Intimacy-Relationship

Introversion-Extroversion

**Social Conformity Predisposition**

Practicality-Unconventionality

Extemporaneity-Premeditation

Ideational-Literal

To assess the degree to which there were significant differences in these traits across the different types of organizations comprising the sample for this study, an analysis of the mean scores on the traits for each of the organizational types was conducted. The objective was to determine whether different leadership styles predominated in the alternative kinds of R & D organizations. Exhibit 14.20 reveals the findings.

**Exhibit 14.19**
**Rank Order of Means of Leader Clusters on Worker Variables**

| Worker Variable[1] | Order of Cluster Mean Scores | F Probability |
|---|---|---|
| Satisfaction | Scrooge, Mouse, Gregory, Popeye, Carl Sagan, Fido, Team Player, Nurse | .0449[2] |
| Work Diversity | Popeye, Fido, Mouse, Scrooge, Gregory, Team Player, Carl Sagan, Nurse | .0005 |
| | Scheffé Contrasts: Popeye-Nurse | |
| Control of Work | Gregory, Popeye, Carl Sagan, Team Player, Mouse, Fido, Scrooge, Nurse | .0066 |
| | Scheffé Contrasts: Popeye-Nurse Gregory-Nurse | |
| Cooperation | Fido, Mouse, Carl Sagan, Nurse, Scrooge, Gregory, Popeye, Team Player | .0576 |
| Workload | Team Player, Popeye, Nurse, Scrooge, Carl Sagan, Mouse, Fido, Gregory | .0016 |
| | Scheffé Contrasts: Gregory-Nurse | |
| Adequacy of Tools and Equipment | Fido, Scrooge, Gregory, Team Player, Popeye, Mouse, Carl Sagan, Nurse | .0564 |
| Job Content Clarity | Carl Sagan, Scrooge, Gregory, Popeye, Mouse, Fido, Team Player, Nurse | .0181 |
| | Scheffé Contrasts: Carl Sagan-Nurse | |

1. F Tests across the leader clusters were not statistically significant at the .05 level for the following five worker scales: Organizational Identification, Organizational Commitment, Self-Esteem, Job Significance, and Feedback. They are not, therefore, displayed in this Exhibit.

2. Scheffé contrasts were tested at the .10 level.

**Exhibit 14.20**
**Differences in Leadership Traits by Organizational Type**

### LEADER TRAIT: Practicality-Unconventionality

| Organizational Type | N | Mean[*] | S.D. |
|---|---|---|---|
| ERATO | 8 | 2.04 | 10.2 |
| Small Universities | 10 | 1.72 | 12.5 |
| Government Laboratories | 49 | .50 | 10.3 |
| National Telegraph and Telephone | 8 | .43 | 9.1 |
| Corporations | 64 | .23 | 9.3 |
| Universities | 9 | -4.94 | 8.5 |
| Total | 148 | .21 | 9.8 |

F Ratio= .6034          F Probability= .6974

### LEADER TRAIT: Intimacy-Relationship

| Organizational Type | N | Mean | S.D. |
|---|---|---|---|
| National Telegraph and Telephone | 8 | 4.05 | 6.6 |
| Government Laboratories | 49 | 2.46 | 10.0 |
| Corporations | 64 | 0.37 | 9.4 |
| ERATO | 8 | -1.52 | 8.3 |
| Small Universities | 10 | -3.27 | 8.7 |
| Universities | 9 | -8.15 | 4.5 |

F Ratio= 2.71          F Probability= .0228

### LEADER TRAIT: Gentility-Firm-mindedness

| Organizational Type | N | Mean | S.D. |
|---|---|---|---|
| Universities | 9 | 3.89 | 9.1 |
| National Telegraph and Telephone | 8 | 2.59 | 8.3 |
| Government Laboratories | 49 | 2.19 | 9.1 |
| Small Universities | 10 | .26 | 9.6 |
| Corporations | 64 | -1.54 | 9.7 |
| ERATO | 8 | -3.24 | 10.0 |
| Total | 148 | | |

F Ratio= 1.46          F Probability= .2064

[*] The exhibit reveals the rank orders of the average magnitudes of each of the leader traits in each of the organizational types. Scores were normalized with a mean of zero and standard deviation of 1. For ease of interpretation, however, both means and standard deviations were multiplied by 10.

**Exhibit 14.20** (continued)

### LEADER TRAIT:  Rationality-Affect

| Organizational Type | N | Mean | S.D. |
|---|---|---|---|
| Small Universities | 10 | 6.54 | 5.1 |
| Corporations | 9 | 1.03 | 9.8 |
| ERATO | 8 | .32 | 7.5 |
| Universities | 9 | -1.25 | 10.7 |
| Government Laboratories | 49 | -1.35 | 9.9 |
| National Telegraph and Telephone | 8 | -2.50 | 7.5 |
| Total | 148 | .25 | 9.6 |

F Ratio= 1.42          F Probability= .2214

### LEADER TRAIT:  Introversion-Extroversion

| Organizational Type | N | Mean | S.D. |
|---|---|---|---|
| Government Laboratories | 49 | 2.42 | 8.8 |
| ERATO | 8 | .62 | 12.4 |
| Small Universities | 10 | .09 | 8.8 |
| Corporations | 64 | -.48 | 9.4 |
| National Telegraph and Telephone | 8 | -1.13 | 11.5 |
| Universities | 9 | -2.78 | 10.2 |
| Total | 148 | .41 | 9.4 |

F Ratio= .81          F Probability= .5487

### LEADER TRAIT: Extemporaneity-Premeditation

| Organizational Type | N | Mean | S.D. |
|---|---|---|---|
| ERATO | 8 | 5.62 | 10.8 |
| National Telegraph and Telephone | 8 | 4.54 | 10.1 |
| Corporations | 64 | .47 | 10.2 |
| Universities | 9 | -.04 | 7.2 |
| Government Laboratories | 49 | .90 | 8.2 |
| Small Universities | 10 | -1.10 | 10.4 |
| Total | 148 | .38 | 9.5 |

F Ratio= 1.03          F Probability= .3399

### LEADER TRAIT:  Ideation-Literal

| Organizational Type | N | Mean | S.D. |
|---|---|---|---|
| ERATO | 8 | 3.23 | 10.4 |
| Small Universities | 10 | 1.28 | 12.2 |
| Government Laboratories | 49 | .55 | 9.8 |
| Corporations | 64 | 2.64 | 9.8 |
| Universities | 9 | -.55 | 11.3 |
| National Telegraph and Telephone | 8 | -2.84 | 8.1 |
| Total | 148 | .14 | 9.9 |

F Ratio= .37          F Probability= .8698

**Exhibit 14.20 (continued)**

### LEADER TRAIT:  Consideration-Reasonableness

| Organizational Type | N | Mean | S.D. |
|---|---|---|---|
| National Telegraph and Telephone | 8 | 5.12 | 5.1 |
| Government Laboratories | 49 | 1.42 | 10.0 |
| Universities | 9 | 1.10 | 10.8 |
| Corporations | 64 | -.16 | 9.6 |
| Small Universities | 10 | 4.06 | 8.9 |
| ERATO | 8 | 8.16 | 5.0 |
| Total | 148 | 0.0 | 9.8 |

F Ratio= 2.20          F Probability= .0572

The data require an unusual mode of interpretation partly because of the relatively small sample sizes. On only one scale (Intimacy-Relationship) do the differences among the kinds of organizations reach statistical significance in a one-way analysis of variance, and even for this scale, post-hoc Scheffe tests show no two groups are significantly different at the probability level of .05. However, when the same one-way analysis of variance is performed on the three primary groups—government institutes, universities, and corporations, the F Ratio for this variable is 5.08, with the F Probability reaching $< .008$, and a post-hoc Scheffe contrast showing a difference between government institutes and universities at the .05 level. Considering these data, university R & D leaders would appear to be more social in their interactions with their workers than are leaders in the government sector. This more relaxed relationship is not unexpected in the more collegial setting of a university, especially where section size is smaller.

A superficial conjecture might lead to the expectation of differences in the eight scales across these organizational types if sample sizes were larger. One might well ask, for example, whether the organization of the work in the three main sectors—corporations, universities, and government institutes—might lead to an expectation that there would be different leadership dispositions in each. That is, it would not be unreasonable to expect that the more practical orientations and shorter time frames in corporations would require a different kind of leader than would be needed in universities, where the orientation may be more basic and the time frame longer.

These same data are presented in aggregate tabular form in Exhibit 14.21. Exhibit 14.22 gives the rank orders of the means by kind of organization.

Two reasons are suggested as explanations of why these differences are not manifested in the data. The first has to do with the homogeneous nature of the Japanese culture; the second with the modes of administrative succession in the organizational ladder.

As reported in Chapters 3, 4, and 5, the common heritage and high uniformity of family socialization and educational indoctrination make differences in so-

**Exhibit 14.21**

**Aggregate Mean Scores of Organizational Types on MBTI Adjusted Scales[1]**

| | N | Practicality-Unconventionality | Intimacy-Sociability | Gentility-Firm-mindedness | Rationality-Affect | Introversion-Extroversion | Extemporaneity-Premeditation | Ideation-Literal | Consideration-Reasonableness |
|---|---|---|---|---|---|---|---|---|---|
| ERATO | 8 | 20.4 | -15.1 | -32.4 | 3.2 | 6.2 | 56.2 | 32.3 | -81.6 |
| CORP. | 64 | 2.3 | 3.7 | -15.4 | 10.3 | -4.8 | 4.7 | -2.6 | -1.6 |
| GOV'T | 49 | 5.0 | 24.6 | 21.9 | -13.5 | 24.2 | -9.3 | 15.5 | 14.2 |
| UNIV. | 9 | -49.4 | -81.5 | 38.9 | -12.4 | -23.8 | -0.3 | -5.5 | 11.0 |
| SM. UNI. | 10 | 17.2 | -32.7 | 2.6 | 65.4 | 0.9 | -11.0 | 12.8 | -40.06 |
| NTT | 8 | 4.3 | 40.5 | 25.9 | -25.0 | -11.3 | 45.4 | -28.4 | 51.2 |
| Total | 148 | 2.1 | 4.0 | 2.8 | 2.5 | 4.1 | 3.8 | 1.4 | 0.3 |
| S.D. | | 98.0 | 94.0 | 98.0 | 96.0 | 94.0 | 95.0 | 99.0 | 98.0 |
| F Ratio | | .60 | 2.71 | 1.46 | 1.42 | .80 | 1.03 | .37 | 2.20 |
| F Probability | | .70 | .03 | .21 | .22 | .55 | .40 | .87 | .06 |

1. Means and standard deviations have been multiplied by ten to make the table more readable.

**Exhibit 14.22**
**Rank Orders of Organizational Types on MBTI Adjusted Scales[1]**

| | Practicality-Unconventionality | Intimacy-Sociability | Gentility-Firm-mindedness | Rationality-Affect | Introversion-Extroversion | Extemporaneity-Premeditation | Ideation-Literal | Consideration-Reasonableness |
|---|---|---|---|---|---|---|---|---|
| ERATO | 6 | 4 | 6 | 3 | 2 | 1 | 1 | 1 |
| CORP. | 2 | 3 | 5 | 2 | 4 | 3 | 4 | 3 |
| GOV'T | 4 | 2 | 3 | 5 | 1 | 5 | 3 | 5 |
| UNIV. | 1 | 6 | 1 | 4 | 6 | 4 | 5 | 4 |
| SM. UNI. | 5 | 5 | 4 | 1 | 3 | 6 | 2 | 2 |
| NTT | 3 | 1 | 2 | 6 | 5 | 2 | 6 | 6 |

1. Since as noted above, the differences between the means for the six types of organizations are generally not significant, rank orders must be viewed with some considerable caution.

ciety less pronounced, or at least to Western eyes, less visible. The preparation for work life that takes place in the early years and the reinforcement of the traditions of Japan (despite Western influences) make for a consistency of organizational forms and behaviors *across* organizational types. Indeed, such consistency appears to be maladaptive to the needs of the society. Although environmental scanning has reached a fine art in Japan, the responsiveness of the organizational design to the results of that process may be somewhat inhibited by cultural tradition and social influences. Hence, the finding of no differences in leader types across corporations, universities, and government institutes reflects not only the reality, but a problem to be addressed.

Further, as noted in Chapter 4, the system of higher education dominates the talent allocation process, assigning its college graduates to entry-level positions in the various organizational sectors across the country. There is a moderate prestige ranking among organizations both within and across these sectors, with the university sector having a slight edge over the others, mostly because of its emphasis on basic research. (''Theory'' has higher prestige in the United States as well.) Within the corporate sector, the larger, more well-known and stable firms attract the best and brightest students. In the university sector, the imperial universities gather the best university graduates, while in the government sector, the most desirable positions are in prestigious departments in national planning.

Native, inborn traits of leadership, however, are held by the Japanese to be evenly distributed across the population in Japan. The Japanese believe that all people start with equal talents at birth and have equivalent opportunities to achieve (thus accounting in part for the extreme maternal concern and ego investment in education for their offspring). Thus, success for the Japanese is considered to be almost completely a matter of diligence at school and work (see Chapter 4). By the end of college, then, there has been some considerable differentiation of achievement on the basis of the hard work at schooling (though, to be sure, most of that work took place prior to entrance at college). College graduates are then chosen for work on three grounds: (1) the prestige of their college; (2) the number and influence within the organization of previous graduates from the college; and (3) the fit in personality between the candidate and the ''personality'' of the particular organization, that is, projections of his ability to adapt to the style of organizational behavior, in both its formal work requirements and technology and its informal norms of behavior. However, since organizational designs and organizational culture *in general* are relatively constant across organizational types, the movement from college to work setting is not likely to extract from the universities workers with traits that are qualitatively more suited for one or another organizational type.

The second reason for the absence of a finding of differences lies in the processes of administrative succession in Japanese organizations, in this case, the R & D laboratory section.[5] As noted earlier, leaders ''emerge'' in Japan. There is generally no abrupt, one-time decision that elevates any one person to an opening in an organization. Rather, the organization as a whole, at all levels, gradually becomes aware of the leadership potential of each of its employees. Leadership at the lower levels prior to official appointment is also carried out in the many formal and informal interactions that characterize Japanese enterprise (including union activity). There are countless occasions during the typical business day when groups of workers aggregate for a social or recreational respite. These may revolve around a favorite television soap opera (a good many offices today have television sets in them), or an afternoon tea, or predinner snack, or a group exercise or athletic activity. Workers come to know and respect those among their peers who have leadership skills. Although the actual selection of a person for formal appointment is preceded by the Japanese equivalent of trial balloons, there is almost always agreement on the person or persons who are eligible. This practice is common *across* organizational types. The skills of leadership (especially in R & D) are not so much technical knowledge or expertise in the field—corporate, university, or government institute (though certainly some reasonably high level of intelligence is necessary), but a combination of traits and associated behaviors that have been shown to be successful in the organization; behaviors that reinforce the traditions and rituals held in high esteem by the employees and those that may be seen as temporally responsive to the times.

Almost regardless of type of organization, typical modes of decision making require that many people be gathered together on frequent occasions so that different kinds of expertise can be brought to bear on the problem at hand. The leader, therefore, is less an initiator or director of activities and more a coordinator; less a ''stroker'' (since this need is filled by the group in Japanese society) and more an integrator. Japanese culture, then, is a constant. Organizational contingencies extract from the employee masses, in Jeffersonian fashion, an elite group whose traits match the needs of the particular organization rather than the type of organization.

This discussion is intended to show that the commonality of leader traits across the organizational types is attributable to the commonality of the frameworks, regardless of the objectives of the organization. In sum, both the Japanese organizational culture and the similarity of research as an activity across the organizational types explains the lack of findings of significant differences in the various settings.

Having said this, it should be pointed out that there is no implication whatsoever that there is no variance within organizations or, indeed, across organizations within sectors. Certainly, there is ''good'' leadership and ''bad'' leadership among corporations, or among universities, or among government laboratories, as reported earlier. The rank orders, though statistically only marginally different, reveal some possible differences. Using only the top and bottom ranks as indicative of a predominant disposition in a particular kind of organization, it would appear that larger university leaders are highest on practicality and gentility and more extroverted. Smaller university laboratory leaders, in contrast, are ranked highest on rationality and premeditation, a more conservative posture reflecting, perhaps, a more careful approach toward projects whose payoffs may be more distant in time. NTT leaders score at the top or bottom of the six groups on four of the eight traits. They tend toward ideational, intuitive thinking, high affect and close interpersonal relationships on the job. The public service orientation of NTT requires a larger view of the external environment than may be provided by leaders with these orientations. Government R & D leaders are distinctive only in their more ideational thinking, judging from the rank orders above. The laboratory leaders in the corporate sector are not distinguished in the rank orderings by any particular set of characteristics (though that, itself, may be indicative of a distinctive complex of personality traits).

## LEADER-WORKER ATTITUDE RELATIONSHIPS

Even though there were practically no differences in the adjusted MBTI traits across the more commonly found organizational types, it is still of interest to determine whether some of the leader traits may have had independent or multivariate impacts on the attitudes of the workers for the sample as a whole. A simple correlation matrix of leader traits by JDS scale scores revealed twenty correlations that were statistically significant. However, the average magnitude of the statistically significant correlations was so low as to be unremarkable. The largest correlation was .15, revealing a slight relationship between the trait of "ideational-literal" and worker scores on "role clarity." These are displayed in Exhibit 14.23.

Disaggregating the sample into the three major groups—corporations, universities, and government institutes—resulted in little improvement in the correlations for corporations and government institutes. Although the statistically significant figures were often different from those for the sample as a whole, again the magnitude of the significant correlations were low—in the range of .09 to −18 for corporations and .12 to −19 for government institutes—thus explaining relatively little of the variance. On the other hand, separating out the university responses was much more productive. Exhibit 14.24 gives the statistically significant correlations.

According to university research and development workers, under leaders who are more practically oriented, identification with and pride in their organization and personal satisfaction is lower. However, commitment to the organization is reduced when leaders are extemporaneous in their orientations. The effects of different kinds of leaders on the diversity of the task for this group are difficult to interpret. On the one hand, diversity is enhanced when leaders are more unconventional and ideational and more open and interactive with a wide group of workers. On the other hand, diversity is also increased when leaders are less demonstrative and more firm-minded and reasonable rather than considerate. Apparently, leaders need to be highly interactive and open to new ideas, yet able to make firm decisions without regard to individual worker feelings. This

**Exhibit 14.23**

**Matrix of Correlations of Revised MBTI Scale Scores and Revised Hackman-Oldham Scale Scores**

|    | PU | IR | GF | RA | IE | EP | IL | CR | OI | SA | ID | WD | CW | SE | FB | CO | WL | TO | JC | JS |
|----|----|----|----|----|----|----|----|----|----|----|----|----|----|----|----|----|----|----|----|----|
| PU |    |    |    |    |    |    |    |    |    |    |    |    |    |    |    |    |    |    |    |    |
| IR | 26 | X  |    |    |    |    |    |    |    |    |    |    |    |    |    |    |    |    |    |    |
| GF | 02 | -15 | X |    |    |    |    |    |    |    |    |    |    |    |    |    |    |    |    |    |
| RA | -20 | 10 | -31 | X |    |    |    |    |    |    |    |    |    |    |    |    |    |    |    |    |
| IE | 23 | 39 | -03 | 10 | X |    |    |    |    |    |    |    |    |    |    |    |    |    |    |    |
| EP | -05 | 14 | -12 | 07 | -02 | X |    |    |    |    |    |    |    |    |    |    |    |    |    |    |
| IL | -19 | 07 | -20 | 33 | 08 | 19 | X |    |    |    |    |    |    |    |    |    |    |    |    |    |
| CR | 17 | -09 | 32 | -34 | 03 | 09 | -26 | X |    |    |    |    |    |    |    |    |    |    |    |    |
| OI | -04 | 08 | -05 | 06 | 00 | 05 | 00 | -05 | X |    |    |    |    |    |    |    |    |    |    |    |
| SA | -06 | -02 | 02 | 10 | 00 | 09 | 14 | -01 | 59 | X |    |    |    |    |    |    |    |    |    |    |
| ID | 04 | -04 | -02 | -03 | -03 | -01 | -02 | 00 | -23 | -12 | X |    |    |    |    |    |    |    |    |    |
| WD | -08 | -08 | -02 | 11 | 06 | 10 | -09 | 02 | 34 | 57 | 01 | X |    |    |    |    |    |    |    |    |
| CW | -11 | -06 | -01 | 10 | -01 | 07 | 07 | -03 | 06 | 32 | 04 | 41 | X |    |    |    |    |    |    |    |
| SE | 02 | 01 | -01 | 04 | -07 | 00 | 03 | -07 | 25 | 43 | 12 | 32 | 08 | X |    |    |    |    |    |    |
| FB | -03 | 00 | -05 | 02 | -01 | 02 | 00 | 01 | 33 | 26 | -09 | 21 | 06 | 11 | X |    |    |    |    |    |
| CO | 04 | 06 | -05 | 02 | 00 | 10 | 02 | -04 | 49 | 42 | -13 | 24 | 10 | 17 | 41 | X |    |    |    |    |
| WL | 02 | -01 | -03 | 01 | 06 | -10 | 05 | -09 | -03 | -03 | 09 | 03 | -20 | 06 | 09 | -08 | X |    |    |    |
| TO | -00 | 04 | 03 | 02 | -02 | 12 | 05 | 00 | 33 | 29 | -10 | 22 | 14 | 14 | 18 | 34 | -12 | X |    |    |
| JC | -04 | -05 | 03 | 11 | -02 | 07 | 15 | -09 | 10 | 41 | 03 | 41 | 46 | 24 | 11 | 15 | -02 | 17 | X |    |
| JS | -01 | -06 | 04 | 03 | -03 | 04 | -02 | -08 | 34 | 32 | -01 | 30 | -02 | 22 | 31 | 32 | 27 | 11 | 13 | X |

**Exhibit 14.24**

**Statistically Significant Correlations between Adjusted MBTI Scale Scores and Hackman-Oldham Adjusted Scale Scores (University Laboratories Only)**

|  | (r) | (p) |
|---|---|---|
| **Practicality-Unconventionality** |  |  |
| Organizational Identification and Pride | -.38 | .004 |
| Personal Satisfaction | -.37 | .004 |
| Work Diversity | -.28 | .029 |
| Control Over Task | -.32 | .014 |
| **Intimacy-Relationships** |  |  |
| Organizational Identification and Pride | -.32 | .014 |
| Personal Satisfaction | -.39 | .003 |
| Work Diversity | -.29 | .022 |
| Control Over Task | -.43 | .001 |
| **Gentility-Firm-mindedness** |  |  |
| Work Diversity | -.33 | .011 |
| **Rationality-Affect** |  |  |
| Self-Esteem | -.28 | .027 |
| Job Content Clarity | .24 | .048 |
| **Introversion-Extroversion** |  |  |
| Work Diversity | .34 | .009 |
| **Extemporaneity-Premeditation** |  |  |
| Organizational Commitment | -.30 | .020 |
| Workload | .48 | .000 |
| **Ideational-Literal** |  |  |
| Interdependence | .24 | .050 |
| Work Diversity | .26 | .037 |
| Job Content Clarity | .26 | .040 |
| **Consideration-Reasonableness** |  |  |
| Work Diversity | -.30 | .018 |

finding would seem to confirm those of Pelz and Andrews (1976) who found that complete freedom of choice for workers resulted in lower productivity than did some modicum of external control.

A second statistical manipulation of these same data proved to be somewhat more revealing. In an effort to determine whether the distribution of responses on the adjusted Hackman-Oldham worker scales may have had insufficient variance to reveal the differential impact of the leader traits, the workers were divided on the basis of their scores on each of the twelve worker scales into two groups. One group comprised workers who scored 1½ standard deviations or more above the mean scale score; the other was made up of those who scored 1½ standard deviations or more below the mean. One-way analyses of variance were then run to examine the differences between the high and low outlying groups on each of the leader scales. A typical question proposed, for example, was "is there a difference in the strength of their leader's 'intimacy-relationships' trait between the high and low scoring worker groups on the worker 'personal satisfaction' scale?" More plainly, do workers in groups expressing more personal satisfaction have leaders who are higher in intimacy or in relationships orientation? A number of statistically significant relationships (most at the .05 level or well below) emerged from this analysis. In Exhibit 14.25 the independent and dependent variables and their F ratios are listed. Some caution in interpreting these data must be exercised, since only about 10 percent of the data (the outlying groups at each extreme of the distribution) are being examined. Presenting these data in a slightly different form results in the somewhat more easily interpretable set of data in Exhibit 14.26.

Looked at in this way, a pattern of relationships is revealed. The first four of the variables to be discussed fall into the job characteristics category in the original Hackman-Oldham classification. "Job content clarity," for example, for Japanese R & D workers is related to the leader characteristics of ideational-literal and rationality-affect. Somewhat surprisingly, therefore, workers report more job content clarity when leaders are less literal in their perceptions, more ideational. It should be noted, however, that jobs in Japanese organizations tend not to be closely defined. Many workers may be involved in any project, with those having interest, background, and expertise contributing to the solutions of problems regardless of formal job title. A leader, consequently, who is highly literal in his approach to work may not be as flexible as required in the definitions of jobs. Furthermore, the variable itself—job content clarity—comprises items that suggest feedback available from the work itself, rather than from other workers. In sum, workers are permitted much freedom on the job in Japan, and the clarity of the work stems more from their ability to become involved in jobs that have some clear meaning than from any bureaucratically defined job description.

Work diversity for workers is related to the leader traits of Ideational-Literal, Extemporaneity-Premeditation, and Rationality-Affect. This syndrome is quite similar to the one above. The work diversity scale is defined by conditions such as job variety, opportunity for creativity, use of high skills, high challenge, and work simplification (negative). All of these are occasioned by leaders whose traits speak to strong theoretical, if nonconventional thinking, not tied to rigid planning.

Task control for R & D workers is related to leaders who are introverted. The worker variable in this case is comprised of feelings of autonomy as well as identification with a complete job. Introverted leaders tend to be quiet and reserved, closed to others, keeping their feelings to themselves. It is difficult to make sense of this relationship, and we reserve further comment on this and the last pair—worker perceptions of tool and equipment adequacy to leader extemporaneity-premeditation.

In the Hackman and Oldham rationale, these job conditions should, under

**Exhibit 14.25**
**Adjusted MBTI Leader Traits and Associated Adjusted Hackman-Oldham Variables**

### Leader Scale: Extemporaneity-Premeditation

1. Worker Scale: Personal Satisfaction

|  | N | Mean | F Ratio | F Probability |
|---|---|---|---|---|
| Worker High Group* | 35 | 5.86 | 8.0326 | .0057 |
| Worker Low Group** | 55 | 5.22 | | |

2. Worker Scale: Work Diversity

|  | N | Mean | F Ratio | F Probability |
|---|---|---|---|---|
| Worker High Group | 14 | 6.07 | 11.2575 | .0013 |
| Worker Low Group | 51 | 5.08 | | |

3. Worker Scale: Adequacy of Tools and Equipment

|  | N | Mean | F Ratio | F Probability |
|---|---|---|---|---|
| Worker High Group | 28 | 5.71 | 9.8495 | .0025 |
| Worker Low Group | 45 | 5.00 | | |

### Leader Scale: Ideational-Literal

1. Worker Scale: Personal Satisfaction

|  | N | Mean | F Ratio | F Probability |
|---|---|---|---|---|
| Worker High Group | 35 | 4.43 | 4.8988 | .0295 |
| Worker Low Group | 55 | 4.00 | | |

2. Worker Scale: Job Clarity

|  | N | Mean | F Ratio | F Probability |
|---|---|---|---|---|
| Worker High Group | 25 | 4.60 | 12.1195 | .0009 |
| Worker Low Group | 43 | 3.77 | | |

3. Worker Scale: Work Diversity

|  | N | Mean | F Ratio | F Probability |
|---|---|---|---|---|
| Worker High Group | 14 | 4.36 | 3.6993 | .0590 |
| Worker Low Group | 51 | 3.80 | | |

*1½ standard deviations above the mean
**1½ standard deviations below the mean

**Exhibit 14.25 (continued)**

### Leader Scale: Introversion-Extroversion

1. Worker Scale: Organizational I.D. and Commitment

|                    | N  | Mean | F Ratio | F Probability |
|--------------------|----|------|---------|---------------|
| Worker High Group  | 32 | 6.16 | 3.1954  | .0782         |
| Worker Low Group   | 39 | 6.67 |         |               |

2. Worker Scale: Task Control

|                    | N  | Mean | F Ratio | F Probability |
|--------------------|----|------|---------|---------------|
| Worker High Group  | 35 | 6.60 | 3.9712  | .0493         |
| Worker Low Group   | 57 | 6.05 |         |               |

### Leader Scale: Rationality-Affect

1. Worker Scale: Work Diversity

|                    | N  | Mean | F Ratio | F Probability |
|--------------------|----|------|---------|---------------|
| Worker High Group  | 14 | 7.36 | 5.9173  | .0178         |
| Worker Low Group   | 51 | 6.47 |         |               |

2. Worker Scale: Job Content Clarity

|                    | N  | Mean | F Ratio | F Probability |
|--------------------|----|------|---------|---------------|
| Worker High Group  | 25 | 7.28 | 3.3423  | .0720         |
| Worker Low Group   | 43 | 6.67 |         |               |

### Leader Scale: Consideration-Reasonableness

1. Worker Scale: Job Significance (JB — neg loadings in FA)

|                    | N  | Mean | F Ratio | F Probability |
|--------------------|----|------|---------|---------------|
| Worker High Group  | 38 | 4.24 | 3.5186  | .0640         |
| Worker Low Group   | 53 | 4.62 |         |               |

ideal conditions, lead to positive psychological states. In this research, however, not only are the conditions directly related to these states, but so also are the characteristics of leaders. "Job significance" for Japanese R & D workers is related to the leader characteristic of "Consideration versus Reasonableness." That is, workers in R & D laboratories tend to feel their jobs are more significant when their leaders express some higher degree of interpersonal caring rather than a more impersonal or rational interaction style. More will be said later about the responsibilities of section leaders for the affective condition of workers. Briefly, it should be noted here that the "stroking function" in Japanese organizations is often split among the immediate supervisor, the group, and the

**Exhibit 14.26**
**Summary of Correlations of Adjusted MBTI Leader Traits and High (or Low)**
**Scoring Groups with Adjusted Hackman-Oldham Scales[1]**

| Associated Adjusted MBTI Leader Traits | Adjusted Hackman-Oldham Worker Attitudes Scales | |
|---|---|---|
| | Job Characteristics | P |
| Intimacy/Sociability | Organizational I.D. | < .05 |
| Rationality/Affect | Personal Satisfaction | < .01 |
| Extemporaneity/Premeditation | Personal Satisfaction | < .05 |
| Ideational/Literal | Personal Satisfaction | < .00 |
| Practicality/Unconventionality (-) | Work Diversity | < .05 |
| Intimacy/Sociability (-) | Work Diversity | < .05 |
| Rationality/Affect | Work Diversity | < .00 |
| Extemporaneity/Premeditation | Control | < .05 |
| Introversion/Extroversion (-) | Self-Esteem | < .05 |
| Consideration/Reasonableness (-) | Self-Esteem | < .05 |
| Extemporaneity/Premeditation | Cooperativeness | < .01 |
| Extemporaneity/Premeditation (-) | Workload | < .01 |
| Consideration/Reasonableness (-) | Workload | < .01 |
| Gentility/Firm-mindedness (-) | Tool Adequacy | < .01 |
| Extemporaneity/Premeditation | Tool Adequacy | < .01 |
| Rationality/Affect | Job Clarity | < .01 |
| Extemporaneity/Premeditation | Job Clarity | < .05 |
| Ideational/Literal | Job Clarity | < .00 |
| Consideration/Reasonableness (-) | Job Clarity | < .05 |
| Consideration/Reasonableness (-) | Job Meaningfulness | < .05 |

1. Negative correlations are marked with a minus sign. None of the twenty statistically significant correlations reached a magnitude of greater than .15. Levels of statistically significant differences from zero are noted.

next-higher-up bureaucrat, with the last having responsibilities for the long-term personal welfare of each individual worker.

The end result of carefully constructed job design should be motivated, satisfied, and productive workers. Here, in this research, leader characteristics are added as additional variables, independently affecting these end-result variables. The findings here indicated that the personal satisfaction of workers may be affected by two leader characteristics. The more extemporaneous versus premeditated the leader is, the more satisfied workers are. That is, the more the leader is able to "flow" with the work, rather than premeditate and plan it carefully, the more the workers are pleased. In a similar way, R & D leaders who are intuitive or ideational rather than literal in their personalities tend to have more satisfied workers. In Japanese R & D laboratories, then, workers appreciate more the leaders who are able to exhibit a more flexible and intuitive approach to work and whose demeanor is more open and expressive in contrast to those who are more concerned with careful planning and who share their feelings only with a few intimates.

## DIFFERENCES ACROSS INDUSTRY TYPES

As noted in the chapter on methods, the sample was selected from four industries: electronics, iron and steel, transportation, and chemicals. Research and development processes in these industries are different in many ways, reflecting the differences in markets, technologies, and freight of tradition. Of interest in the data analysis was whether leadership traits and conflict management practices would differ across industries and whether worker responses to leadership and other conditions would vary.

In the findings, there were no statistically significant differences in leader traits as measured by the adjusted MBTI. There were, however, interesting variations in the demographic characteristics of the leaders. For example, as revealed in Exhibit 14.27, R & D leaders in the chemical industry are significantly younger than in other fields, while in iron and steel, the leaders are older. (Interestingly, R & D workers as well as leaders are significantly younger in the chemical industry.)

While there was no statistically significant difference (F probability = .08) in the number of years the current director of the R & D laboratory section had been the incumbent, the data seemed to suggest that in iron and steel, directors had served for the shortest time (about 2½ years), while for electronics, the period was over 4½ years). Similarly, though the statistics cannot support a firm conclusion, it appears as though R & D units in the transportation field begin the fewest projects each year (11), with iron and steel starting the most (19). However, there also was no statistically significant difference in the number of projects under way at any one time (grand mean: 29).

Perceptions of the leaders of the availability of funds for research varied across the institution types also. Leaders in transportation firms, for example, viewed past funding quite pessimistically compared to others, but for the future, it is the iron and steel firm leaders who see prospects as quite dim (Exhibit 14.28).

Research and development in the United States is conducted in the context of a nexus of professional contacts articulated through professional associations, corporate contracts, and government funding agencies. Most research leaders and workers outside of the university are closely connected with people and discoveries at the universities. In contrast, in Japan, the extensiveness of contacts with university researchers by leaders in the corporate sector differ by industry. Exhibit 14.29 reveals that R & D leaders in the chemical industry are more than twice as likely to be involved with university researchers than are those in electronics.

**Exhibit 14.27**
**Differences in Mean Age of Leaders across Industry Types**

| Industry | Number | Mean Age | S.D. |
|---|---|---|---|
| Electronics | 19 | 47 | 5 |
| Iron and Steel | 20 | 50 | 5 |
| Transportation | 12 | 47 | 4 |
| Chemicals | 7 | 43 | 3 |

(Total N represents the number of leaders in the corporate sector only).

F Probability: .0133
Post Hoc Scheffé ($<.05$):  Iron and Steel-Chemicals

Crucial to the ability of an industry to maintain its competitiveness is the balance in projects devoted to basic, applied, or developmental research. No significant differences were found across the industries examined in this research. Exhibit 14.30 reveals the data. Note that the numbers are quite small, so statistical significance may be an unnecessarily restrictive constraint in interpreting the data. However, no firm conclusions can, of course, be drawn from these findings.

Attention might be directed, however, to the "apparent" large emphasis in the transportation industry on applied research compared with the others. The relatively low emphasis in the electronic industry on basic research is similarly notable.

## NOTES

1. As noted in Chapter 13, overall research directors were asked to distribute questionnaires to two different section leaders—one rated as high here addresses differences in the responses from each group.

2. Note the following discussion ignores the magnitudes of the responses. High-quality leaders *may* tend more than low-quality to do something without saying that both agree very little with the statement.

3. It should be noted that these responses are biased by ambitions and expectancies. Thus "pessimism" for a high-quality R & D section may reflect a judgment that prior adequate funding levels may be reduced in the future, while a low-quality R & D section, with a history of relatively low funding, may see a continuation of that low level with less pessimism. This is an artifact of all questionnaire design.

4. Because cell sizes were small, statistically significant findings were difficult to obtain. Hence, conclusions about these data must be guarded. *If*, however, in a larger sample the same percentage distribution occurred, the findings would be of some considerable interest. This speculation is especially worth remarking when the absolute quantitative figures are large.

5. Small Ns require that this finding be quite tentative.

**Exhibit 14.28**
**Retrospective and Prospective Views of the Availability of R & D Funding**

|  | Availability of Funds in the Past | | | Availability of Funds in the Future | |
|---|---|---|---|---|---|
|  | Number | Mean[1] | S.D. | Mean | S.D. |
| Electronics | 19 | 2.3 | 1.9 | 2.3 | 1.0 |
| Iron and Steel | 20 | 2.2 | .8 | 2.9 | 1.1 |
| Transportation | 12 | 2.8 | .9 | 2.0 | .6 |
| Chemicals | 7 | 1.6 | .6 | 2.0 | .6 |

F Probability:

| Funds Past: | .0187 | (No significant Scheffé contrasts) |
|---|---|---|
| Funds Future: | .0266 | (No significant Scheffé contrasts) |

1. Higher mean indicates a perception of *declining* availability of funds.

**Exhibit 14.29**
**Percent of Time Meeting with University Personnel**

| Industry | Number | Mean % | S.D. |
|---|---|---|---|
| Electronics | 18 | 5 | 5 |
| Iron and Steel | 18 | 7 | 4 |
| Transportation | 12 | 8 | 6 |
| Chemicals | 7 | 12 | 3 |

F Probability: .03
Scheffé Contrast ($< .05$): Electronics-Chemicals

**Exhibit 14.30**
**Emphasis on Basic, Applied, or Developmental Research**

| Industry | Number | Mean Basic | Mean Applied | Mean Developmental |
|---|---|---|---|---|
| | | (%) | (%) | (%) |
| Electronics | 18 | 7 | 39 | 56 |
| Iron and Steel | 18 | 15 | 42 | 55 |
| Transportation | 12 | 11 | 59 | 41 |
| Chemicals | 7 | 9 | 44 | 48 |

(Percentages do not add to 100% because of rounding).

F Probabilities:

| | |
|---|---|
| Basic: | $< .31$ |
| Applied: | $< .11$ |
| Develop.: | $< .29$ |

# Conflict Management

A significant question in the design for this research was how conflict was managed in different kinds of R & D organizations—government institutes, university laboratories, and corporate sections. Since the organizational cultures in these three types of organizations might be expected to be quite different, so also might the modes by which workers choose to resolve experienced conflicts, or, what has been labeled in Chapter 11 ''disputes'' in the light of conflict ''denial.'' Whether these conflict management modes are ''healthy'' in terms of their effects on worker motivation and productivity is certainly of interest. Both the differences across kinds of organizations and the effects of different modes of conflict resolution are discussed below.

## WORKER CONFLICT MANAGEMENT PREFERENCES
## ACROSS KINDS OF ORGANIZATIONS

The choices given by R & D workers in response to the questions in the Thomas-Kilmann Conflict Management instrument differed across four of the major kinds of organizations in the sample. These differences are revealed in Exhibit 15.1.

As will be noted, eleven of the thirty Thomas-Kilmann scale items discriminated significantly ($p = <.05$) across the four organizational kinds. Faced with the question of Competing versus Accommodating (question number 3), corporate workers appear more inclined to ''Compete'' than do government R & D workers (74% versus 61%). Relatedly, as evident in the answers to question numbers 6 and 9, corporate workers are most Competitive and least likely to Avoid conflict. Given an opportunity to compromise by proposing a middle ground rather than Competing by pressing to get points made (as in question

**Exhibit 15.1**

**Differences in Conflict Management Styles across Types of Organizations[1]**
**(Percent Worker Responses)**

| Question Number | Government (N=234) | University (N=88) | Corporation (N=372) | ERATO (N=45) |
|---|---|---|---|---|
| 1. | | | | |
| Avoid | 12 | 11 | 13 | 13 |
| Accommodate | 88 | 89 | 87 | 87 |
| Chi-Square | 0.18 | | | |
| Significance | 0.98 | | | |
| 2. | | | | |
| Compromise | 59 | 61 | 50 | 51 |
| Collaborate | 41 | 39 | 50 | 49 |
| Chi-Square | 6.83 | | | |
| Significance | 0.08 | | | |
| 3. | | | | |
| Compete | 61 | 69 | 74 | 69 |
| Accommodate | 39 | 31 | 26 | 31 |
| Chi-Square | 11.74 | | | |
| Significance | 0.01* | | | |
| 4. | | | | |
| Compromise | 33 | 33 | 24 | 24 |
| Accommodate | 37 | 67 | 76 | 76 |
| Chi-Square | 7.30 | | | |
| Significance | 0.06 | | | |
| 5. | | | | |
| Collaborate | 9 | 8 | 16 | 18 |
| Avoid | 91 | 92 | 84 | 82 |
| Chi-Square | 7.80 | | | |
| Significance | 0.05 | | | |

* 3
Compete          "I am usually firm in pursuing my goals."
Accommodate      "I might try to soothe the other's feelings and preserve the friendship."

1. The complete questionaire item is provided only for questions where the differences across organizational types was statistically significant.

number 13), government and university R & D workers tend to be less likely to Compete than corporations or ERATO. Indeed, ERATO's distinctive attitude (almost half, 47%, would Compete) on this item is worth noting. Where self-assertiveness is not conceptually an option in the Kilmann-Thomas instrumentation (as in items 15 and 16), corporate R & D workers, on the one hand, are most likely to accommodate by soothing feelings rather than avoiding tensions,

**Exhibit 15.1 (continued)**

| Question Number | Government (N=234) | University (N=88) | Corporation (N=372) | ERATO (N=45) |
|---|---|---|---|---|
| **6.** | | | | |
| Avoid | 67 | 67 | 53 | 58 |
| Compete | 33 | 33 | 47 | 42 |
| Chi-Square | 13.04 | | | |
| Significance | 0.01* | | | |
| **7.** | | | | |
| Avoid | 53 | 50 | 53 | 71 |
| Compromise | 47 | 50 | 47 | 29 |
| Chi-Square | 6.01 | | | |
| Significance | 0.11 | | | |
| **8.** | | | | |
| Compete | 66 | 76 | 65 | 69 |
| Collaborate | 34 | 24 | 35 | 31 |
| Chi-Square | 4.04 | | | |
| Significance | 0.26 | | | |
| **9.** | | | | |
| Avoid | 81 | 84 | 71 | 84 |
| Compete | 19 | 16 | 29 | 16 |
| Chi-Square | 13.53 | | | |
| Significance | 0.00*** | | | |
| **10.** | | | | |
| Compete | 67 | 80 | 75 | 76 |
| Compromise | 33 | 21 | 25 | 24 |
| Chi-Square | 7.56 | | | |
| Significance | 0.06 | | | |

* 6

| Avoid | "I try to avoid creating unpleasantness for myself." |
|---|---|
| Compete | "I try to win my position." |

** 9

| Avoid | "I feel that differences are not always worth worrying about." |
|---|---|
| Compete | "I make some effort to get my way." |

while, on the other hand, they are most likely to avoid conflict by convincing others of the merits of their positions rather than accommodating by trying not to hurt the other's feelings. University R & D workers tend to do the opposite. Subtlely buried in these questions, however, is "aggressiveness" as a disposition. Thus, in 15, corporate workers will be more likely to actively preserve a relationship, rather than withdraw, while in 16, their very avoidance is aggressive, "convince" being an active verb. University workers appear, in other words, to be more willing to play passive roles in conflict management. This

**Exhibit 15.1 (continued)**

| Question Number | Government (N=234) | University (N=88) | Corporation (N=372) | ERATO (N=45) |
|---|---|---|---|---|
| **11.** | | | | |
| Collaborate | 33 | 35 | 43 | 40 |
| Accommodate | 67 | 65 | 57 | 60 |
| Chi-Square | 6.52 | | | |
| Significance | 0.09 | | | |
| **12.** | 34 | 32 | 33 | 16 |
| Avoid | 66 | 68 | 67 | 84 |
| Compromise | | | | |
| Chi-Square | 5.86 | | | |
| Significance | 0.12 | | | |
| **13.** | | | | |
| Compromise | 84 | 82 | 74 | 53 |
| Compete | 16 | 18 | 26 | 47 |
| Chi-Square | 23.68 | | | |
| Significance | 0.0000* | | | |
| **14.** | | | | |
| Collaborate | 83 | 94 | 83 | 84 |
| Compete | 17 | 06 | 17 | 16 |
| Chi-Square | 7.72 | | | |
| Significance | 0.02 | | | |
| **15.** | | | | |
| Accommodate | 48 | 35 | 54 | 47 |
| Avoid | 52 | 65 | 46 | 53 |
| Chi-Square | 10.20 | | | |
| Significance | 0.02** | | | |

* 13
| | |
|---|---|
| Compromise | "I propose a middle ground." |
| Compete | "I press to get my points made." |

** 15
| | |
|---|---|
| Accommodate | "I might try to soothe the other's feelings and preserve our relationship." |
| Avoid | "I try to do what is necessary to avoid tensions." |

pattern is repeated in questions 19, 20, and 30, where the slightly more assertive, aggressive, and competitive orientation in the corporate sector is manifested. While for the entire sample, conflict avoidance is preferred, for corporate R & D workers there is a slightly higher preference for Competing versus Accommodating, Accommodating versus Avoiding, and Collaborating versus Compromising or Accommodating. The shorter time perspective of projects in the corporate sector and the overall ambiance of corporate competitiveness gives this empirical finding some intuitive validity.

**Exhibit 15.1 (continued)**

| Question Number | Government (N=234) | University (N=88) | Corporation (N=372) | ERATO (N=45) |
|---|---|---|---|---|
| **16.** | | | | |
| Accommodate | 70 | 78 | 60 | 67 |
| Avoid | 30 | 22 | 40 | 33 |
| Chi-Square | 14.59 | | | |
| Significance | 0.00* | | | |
| **17.** | | | | |
| Compete | 60 | 65 | 71 | 64 |
| Avoid | 40 | 35 | 29 | 36 |
| Chi-Square | 7.81 | | | |
| Significance | 0.05 | | | |
| **18.** | | | | |
| Accommodate | 13 | 10 | 10 | 7 |
| Compromise | 87 | 90 | 90 | 93 |
| Chi-Square | 1.69 | | | |
| Significance | 0.64 | | | |
| **19.** | | | | |
| Collaborate | 25 | 32 | 36 | 27 |
| Avoid | 75 | 68 | 64 | 73 |
| Chi-Square | 9.57 | | | |
| Significance | 0.02** | | | |
| **20.** | | | | |
| Collaborate | 32 | 24 | 40 | 30 |
| Compromise | 68 | 76 | 60 | 70 |
| Chi-Square | 11.18 | | | |
| Significance | 0.01*** | | | |

* 16

| Accommodate | "I try not to hurt the other's feelings." |
|---|---|
| Avoid | "I try to convince the other person of the merits of my position." |

** 19

| Collaborate | "I attempt to get all concerns and issues immediately out in the open." |
|---|---|
| Avoid | "I try to postpone the issue until I have had some time to think it over." |

*** 20

| Collaborate | "I attempt to immediately work through our differences." |
|---|---|
| Compromise | "I try to find a fair combination of gains and losses for both of us." |

## THE RELATIONSHIP OF WORKER CONFLICT MANAGEMENT PREFERENCES TO WORKER CONDITIONS AND ATTITUDES

How R & D leaders address and manage conflict could have a profound effect on how their subordinates feel and behave at work. Since the Japanese R & D

**Exhibit 15.1 (continued)**

| Question Number | Government (N=234) | University (N=88) | Corporation (N=372) | ERATO (N=45) |
|---|---|---|---|---|
| **21.** | | | | |
| Accommodate | 73 | 64 | 71 | 64 |
| Collaborate | 27 | 36 | 29 | 36 |
| Chi-Square | 3.69 | | | |
| Significance | 0.30 | | | |
| **22.** | | | | |
| Compromise | 76 | 75 | 74 | 73 |
| Compete | 24 | 25 | 26 | 27 |
| Chi-Square | 0.25 | | | |
| Significance | 0.97 | | | |
| **23.** | | | | |
| Collaborate | 88 | 92 | 88 | 89 |
| Avoid | 12 | 8 | 12 | 11 |
| Chi-Square | 1.35 | | | |
| Significance | 0.72 | | | |
| **24.** | | | | |
| Accommodate | 85 | 90 | 85 | 86 |
| Compromise | 15 | 10 | 15 | 14 |
| Chi-Square | 1.31 | | | |
| Significance | 0.73 | | | |
| **25.** | | | | |
| Compete | 20 | 18 | 30 | 36 |
| Accommodate | 80 | 82 | 70 | 64 |
| Chi-Square | 13.68 | | | |
| Significance | 0.00* | | | |
| **26.** | | | | |
| Compromise | 37 | 39 | 40 | 36 |
| Collaborate | 63 | 61 | 60 | 64 |
| Chi-Square | 0.55 | | | |
| Significance | 0.91 | | | |

* 25
Compete        "I try to show him the logic and benefits of my position."
Accommodate    "In approaching negotiations, I try to be considerate of the other person's wishes."

unit leader is typically reluctant to intervene directly, "disputes" must be managed by the workers themselves. Japanese workers themselves, as noted in earlier chapters, are hesitant to assert themselves during disputes. The result often means that poor ideas go unchallenged, and good ideas go unimproved or are rejected. Yet this "normal" pattern does not always take place in R & D units.

**Exhibit 15.1 (continued)**

| Question<br>Number | Government<br>(N=234) | University<br>(N=88) | Corporation<br>(N=372) | ERATO<br>(N=45) |
|---|---|---|---|---|
| 27. | | | | |
| Avoid | 68 | 73 | 63 | 64 |
| Accommodate | 32 | 27 | 37 | 36 |
| Chi-Square | 3.50 | | | |
| Significance | 0.32 | | | |
| 28. | | | | |
| Compete | 86 | 94 | 90 | 96 |
| Collaborate | 14 | 6 | 10 | 4 |
| Chi-Square | 6.51 | | | |
| Significance | 0.09 | | | |
| 29. | | | | |
| Compromise | 20 | 22 | 19 | 16 |
| Avoid | 80 | 78 | 81 | 84 |
| Chi-Square | 0.61 | | | |
| Significance | 0.89 | | | |
| 30. | | | | |
| Accommodate | 43 | 46 | 30 | 32 |
| Collaborate | 57 | 54 | 70 | 68 |
| Chi-Square | 15.58 | | | |
| Significance | 0.00* | | | |

* 30
Accommodate     "I try not to hurt the other's feelings."
Collaborate      "I always share the problem with the other person so that we can work it out."

Just as there are norms about conflict management that dictate leader behavior, so also are there expectations among workers about how to resolve conflicts. In this section, the results of the analysis of the data on the relationship between conflict management preferences of R & D workers and their attitudes toward their work environments are presented. The correlations between the responses to the Thomas-Kilmann conflict questions and the Hackman-Oldham worker attitude questions are explored.

When a correlation matrix of the questions in each data set was produced, the results were initially disappointing. Although there were a moderate number of correlations that were statistically different from zero, the magnitude of the correlations was quite low—of the order of .10 to .14. As a consequence, separate matrices were called for each of the subsamples—government, university, and corporate sectors. The result was again not revealing of any relationships of consequence between worker conflict management choices and worker motivation and related attitudes for the government and corporate sectors. As Exhibit 15.2 reveals, only one pair of items for government institutes was statistically significant, as were five pairs for the corporate sector.

The few pairs with significant correlations are difficult to make meaningful. However, in the government institutes, it would appear that when workers choose to avoid controversy, rather than to compromise, worker interdependence is higher. Of course, the causal arrow may be in the other direction. It may not be the attitudes toward conflict management that dictate the organizational design but the requisites of work that constrain the modes of adjudicating conflict. That is, if workers are required to spend significant amounts of time in interaction, an avoidance of conflict may arise out of the recognition of the sheer inefficiency of frequent and protracted conflict. Conceivably, on the other hand, norms of conflict avoidance in the workplace, in the interests of continued comity in interdependent relations when carried to the extreme, could result in lowered creativity. In the Japanese R & D setting, then, the placidity of interpersonal relations may not be functional for the desired aims of the unit.

In the corporate sector, taking the more important findings from Exhibit 15.2, worker-perceived job clarity seems to be more closely associated ($r = -22$) with compromise rather than assertiveness (see Item 10). That is, in the presence of the usual loose definition of roles in Japanese corporations, corporate R & D workers with low role clarity tend to be more inclined to be tentative and compromising rather than firm when there are disputes. On the other hand, when roles are clearer, workers can be and are more assertive. In other words, the tight circumscription of roles may create a defensiveness about role boundaries and a firm protectionist attitude with respect to tasks that are allegedly "owned" by the worker. What is of interest in general with respect to R & D management is the relationship between collective norms and needed work behaviors. While especially in applied research and development, the give-and-take of collaboration requires a submersion of personal ego over individual contribution, the generation of norms that foster excessive submissiveness or excessive compromise may result in the loss of original ideas that deserve to be fought for.

Relatedly, again from Exhibit 15.2, accommodating to the other person's point of view is associated with lower perceptions of work overload (Item 27; $r = -20$). That is, Japanese corporate workers who tend to prefer to avoid controversies, rather than try to accommodate others, tend to perceive themselves as having too much work. Withdrawal from controversy for R & D workers in Japanese corporate R & D, then, is found more among workers who see themselves with too much to do. Such withdrawal may or may not be functional, depending on the issue. That is, in the face of perceived overload, some workers may abandon their creative ideas rather than try to work out some accommodation with others with whom they may differ.

For the university R & D workers, there were more numerous significant findings. For eleven of the Hackman-Oldham scale items, there were significant correlations with the Thomas-Kilmann Conflict Questionnaire items. In addition to the item-to-scale correlations, for the university sector, the conflict manage-

**Exhibit 15.2**

**Correlations of Conflict Management Choices with Worker Attitudes: Government Institutes and Corporate Sectors[1]**

### GOVERNMENT INSTITUTES (N=202)

A. Thomas-Kilmann Conflict Questionnaire:
   **Item 12**
   1.   I sometimes avoid taking positions which would create controversy.
   2.   I will let him have some of his positions if he lets me have some of mine.

B.   Revised Hackman-Oldham Worker Attitude Questionnaire Scale: **Interdependence**

Correlation coefficient: -.22
Significance: p = <.001

### CORPORATIONS (N=301)

A. Thomas-Kilmann Conflict Questionnaire:
   **Item 01**
   1.   There are times when I let others take responsibility for solving the problem.
   2.   Rather than negotiate on things which we disagree, I try to stress those things upon which we both agree.

B. Revised Hackman-Oldham Worker Attitude Questionnaire Scale: **Adequacy of Tools and Equipment**

Correlation coefficient: .25
Significance: p = <.000

A. Thomas-Kilmann Conflict Questionnaire:
   **Item 10**
   1.   I am firm in pursuing my goals
   2.   I try to find a compromise solution.

B. Revised Hackman-Oldham Worker Attitude Questionnaire Scale: **Job Clarity**

Correlation coefficient: -.22
Significance: p = <.000

A. Thomas-Kilmann Conflict Questionnaire:
   **Item 13**
   1.   I propose a middle ground.
   2.   I press to get my points made.

1. Only correlations greater than .20 are listed.

**Exhibit 15.2 (continued)**

    B. Revised Hackman-Oldham Worker Attitude Questionnaire Scale:
        **Adequacy of Tools and Equipment**

                    Correlation coefficient:  .24
                    Significance: $p = <.000$

  A. Thomas-Kilmann Conflict Questionnaire:
      **Item 25**
      1.      I try to show him the logic and benefits of my position.
      2.      In approaching negotiations, I try to be considerate of the other person's wishes.

  B. Revised Hackman-Oldham Worker Attitude Questionnaire Scale:
      **Job Clarity**

                    Correlation coefficient: -.22
                    Significance: $p = <.000$

  A. Thomas-Kilmann Conflict Questionnaire:
      **Item 27**
      1.      I sometimes avoid taking positions that would create controversy.
      2.      If it makes the other person happy, I might let him maintain his views.

  B. Revised Hackman-Oldham Worker Attitude Questionnaire Scale:
      **Work Overload**

                    Correlation coefficient: -.20
                    Significance: $p = <.000$

ment items were also used in regression equations to predict the dependent worker attitudes (see Exhibit 15.3). It should be noted at the outset that the correlations for all eleven dependent variables range from .25 to $-.56$. Only statistically significant correlations are presented.

With respect to the dependent variable, "Organizational Identification," the magnitudes of the correlations were in the .30 range. The proportion of variance explained by the worker conflict management style preferences in the regression equation was 46 percent. Some further teasing out of the meaning of the items included in the regression is needed. It would appear that no one style predominates, but of particular note is the absence of an item manifesting a competitive orientation.

Only 24 percent of the variance in "Personal Satisfaction" is explained by the set of conflict management variables. Avoiding and Accommodating seem to be most highly related, but, anomalously, Competing (the negative correlation for item 09) appears also to be related.

Organizational Commitment can be partially explained by the combined variables in the Conflict Management set (R Square = .37). Again, however, no interpretation of the particular set in the equation is immediately apparent. All five conflict management styles play some part in the prediction.

A smaller number of items explains "Interdependence" (R Square = 55%).

**Exhibit 15.3**
**Relationships of Conflict Management Choices with Worker Attitudes**

University Sector  (N=48)

I. Revised Hackman-Oldham Worker Attitude Questionnaire Scale:
   **Organizational Identification**

| Thomas-Kilmann Conflict Questionnaire Items: | Correlation Coefficient | Significance |
|:---:|:---:|:---:|
| 07 | .30 | <.02 |
| 13 | .28 | <.28 |
| 15 | .36 | <.01 |
| 20 | .29 | <.29 |
| 23 | .30 | <.02 |
| 30 | .35 | <.01 |

Multiple Regression[1]:
.45TK15 + .29TK14 + 19.3 = Org. ID
Multiple R = .46
F = 5.9
Significance F = <.01

II. Revised Hackman-Oldham Worker Attitude Questionnaire Scale:
   **Personal Satisfaction**

| Thomas-Kilmann Conflict Questionnaire Items: | Correlation Coefficient | Significance |
|:---:|:---:|:---:|
| 01 | .39 | <.00 |
| 09 | -.38 | <.00 |
| 13 | .30 | <.02 |
| 15 | .40 | <.00 |
| 20 | .33 | <.01 |
| 23 | .26 | <.04 |
| 30 | .26 | <.04 |

Multiple Regression:
.31TK15 + .30TK01 + 6.7 = Personal Satisfaction
Multiple R = .49
R square = .24
F = 7.2
Significance F = <.00

1. Items entered into regression equation only if contribution to explained variance is greater than .05 level of significance.

The three items connote Compromise, Collaboration, and Accommodation, with Competing and Avoiding not entering the equation. Thus, using the Thomas-Kilmann model, interdependence is connected in the minds of this university sample with attending to the wishes of the other in a relationship with more attention to other than to self—a finding not inconsistent with the usual expectations of "collegiality" (a condition more desired than practiced in both U.S. and Japanese universities).

**Exhibit 15.3 (continued)**

III. Revised Hackman-Oldham Worker Attitude Questionnaire Scale:
   **Organizational Commitment**

| Thomas-Kilmann Conflict Questionnaire Items: | Correlation Coefficient | Significance |
|:---:|:---:|:---:|
| 02 | .39 | <.00 |
| 06 | -.37 | <.01 |
| 07 | -.32 | <.01 |
| 10 | .28 | <.03 |
| 13 | -.31 | <.02 |
| 19 | .27 | <.03 |
| 21 | .29 | <.02 |
| 23 | -.29 | <.02 |
| 24 | -.29 | <.02 |

Multiple Regression:
   $.38TK02 - .34TK06 + 31TK10 + 16.3 = $ Org. Commitment
   Multiple R = .61
   R square = .37
   F = 8.7
   Significance F = <.0001

IV. Revised Hackman-Oldham Worker Attitude Questionnaire Scale:
   **Interdependence**

| Thomas-Kilmann Conflict Questionnaire Items: | Correlation Coefficient | Significance |
|:---:|:---:|:---:|
| 13 | .28 | <.03 |
| 23 | .34 | <.01 |
| 24 | .27 | <.03 |

Multiple Regression:
   $.34TK23 + .57TK24 + 36TK19 - 4.0 = $ Interdependence
   Multiple R = .55
   R square = .31
   F = 6.5
   Significance F = <.0010

Forty-one percent of the variance in ''Work Diversity'' can be explained with the items in the H-O conflict management scale. In this case again, a mixed bag of items appears in the regression equation. However, the negative correlations tend to be more associated with competitive behavior. From this, it might be inferred that university R & D work that provides opportunities for diverse behaviors is associated with worker attitudes that favor more competitive conflict management modes. In other words, in work settings where workers have a variety of tasks rather than a narrowly circumscribed set, there is more of a likelihood of role conflict with others. Under these conditions, workers (at least these Japanese university R & D workers) are inclined to work out differences in more self-serving ways. The orientation toward basic rather than applied

**Exhibit 15.3 (continued)**

V. Revised Hackman-Oldham Worker Attitude Questionnaire Scale:
   **Work Diversity**

| Thomas-Kilmann Conflict Questionnaire Items: | Correlation Coefficient | Significance |
|---|---|---|
| 01 | .38 | < .00 |
| 02 | -.28 | < .03 |
| 04 | -.40 | < .00 |
| 07 | -.27 | < .03 |
| 09 | -.46 | < .00 |
| 14 | -.25 | < .05 |
| 20 | .34 | < .01 |
| 22 | -.25 | < .05 |

Multiple Regression:
   $-.48TK09 - .59TK14 - .42TK29 + 54.8 = $ Work Diversity
   Multiple R = .64
   R square = .41
   F = 10.2
   Significance F = < .0000

VI. Revised Hackman-Oldham Worker Attitude Questionnaire Scale:
   **Control**

| Thomas-Kilmann Conflict Questionnaire Items: | Correlation Coefficient | Significance |
|---|---|---|
| 01 | .44 | < .00 |
| 09 | -.56 | < .00 |
| 20 | .45 | < .00 |
| 25 | .28 | < .28 |
| 30 | .25 | < .04 |

Multiple Regression:
   $-.56TK09 + 38.7 = $ Control
   Multiple R = .56
   R square = .32
   F = 21.2
   Significance F = < .0000

research may enhance this. However, as noted in earlier chapters, organizational roles in Japanese organizations are generally loosely defined. Further, strong norms enforce collaborative interactions. Under these circumstances, it is likely that among those with more diversity in their work the preference for competitive problem solving and conflict management must be suppressed. Once again, ideas that have innovative potential may be inhibited by historical patterns of collectivistic behavior, *despite* the presence of at least some individualistic proclivities.

Control over work, the next variable, appears to be dominated by the strong

**Exhibit 15.3 (continued)**

VII. Revised Hackman-Oldham Worker Attitude Questionnaire Scale:
   **Self-Esteem**

| Thomas-Kilmann Conflict Questionnaire Items: | Correlation Coefficient | Significance |
|---|---|---|
| 02 | .49 | < .00 |
| 08 | -.51 | < .00 |
| 16 | .54 | < .00 |
| 19 | .36 | < .01 |
| 21 | .31 | < .02 |
| 22 | .27 | < .03 |
| 25 | -.47 | < .00 |

Multiple Regression:
   .43TK16 - 41TK08 + .24TK04 + 20.3 = Self-Esteem
   Multiple R = .70
   R square = .49
   F = 14.9
   Significance F = < .0000

VIII. Revised Hackman-Oldham Worker Attitude Questionnaire Scale:
   **Workload**

| Thomas-Kilmann Conflict Questionnaire Items: | Correlation Coefficient | Significance |
|---|---|---|
| 01 | .32 | < .01 |
| 19 | -.36 | < .01 |
| 20 | .24 | < .05 |
| 24 | .40 | < .00 |
| 26 | -.35 | < .01 |
| 27 | .48 | < .00 |
| 29 | -.27 | < .03 |
| 30 | .25 | < .04 |

Multiple Regression:
   .48TK27 - .38TK09 - .28TK17 + 16.1 = Workload
   Multiple R = .60
   R square = .37
   F = 8.5
   Significance F = < .0002

negative correlation of −56 for Item 09, supported by a correlation of .25 for Item 25, both connoting a preference for competitive conflict management. On the other hand, the other items entering into the regression equation suggest different persuasions. Hence, no conclusions about the relationships between conflict management style preferences and control over work can be drawn without more investigation into the nuances of these items.

Three items contribute most strongly toward the prediction of worker Self-

**Exhibit 15.3 (continued)**

IX. Revised Hackman-Oldham Worker Attitude Questionnaire Scale:
   **Cooperation**

| Thomas-Kilmann Conflict Questionnaire: | Correlation Coefficient | Significance |
|---|---|---|
| 02 | -.26 | < .04 |
| 21 | -.29 | < .02 |

Multiple Regression:
   .34TK07 + 13.8 = Cooperation
   Multiple R = .34
   R square = .11
   F = 5.8
   Significance F = < .02

X. Revised Hackman-Oldham Worker Attitude Questionnaire Scale:
   **Adequacy of Tools and Equipment**

| Thomas-Kilmann Conflict Questionnaire Items: | Correlation Coefficient | Significance |
|---|---|---|
| 13 | .31 | < .02 |
| 21 | -.25 | < .05 |

Multiple Regression:
   .30TK13 + 6.2 = Adequacy of Tools and Equipment
   Multiple R = .31
   R square = .10
   F = 4.9
   Significance F = < .03

XI. Revised Hackman-Oldham Worker Attitude Questionnaire Scale:
   **Job Clarity**

| Thomas-Kilmann Conflict Questionnaire Items: | Correlation Coefficient | Significance |
|---|---|---|
| 14 | -.32 | < .02 |
| 27 | -.31 | < .02 |

Multiple Regression:
   -.31TK 14 + 25.8 = Job Clarity
   Multiple R = .31
   R square = .10
   F = 5.1
   Significance F = < .03

Esteem: Item 16 (Accommodate versus Compete), r = .54; Item 08 (Compete versus Collaborate), r = −51; and Item 02 (Compromise versus Collaborate), r = .49. Forty-nine percent of the variance in the dependent variable was explained with all of the items in the regression equation. Once again, Japanese self-esteem in the university setting is seen to be related more to giving in than to individual success.

Workload (more properly, perceived work overload) is also related to several of the conflict management items. Here, the explained variance is only 37 percent, with Avoiding (r = .48) constituting the more significant relationship. It might be suggested that one way for Japanese R & D workers to deal with the threat of work overload is to give in to their colleagues. Such a coping mechanism is not, of course, unique to the Japanese setting, nor to R & D, but as noted above, the enormous effort in Japanese organizations that goes into collaboration may force some workers to withdraw from potentially fruitful relationships where their own ideas might win out in a competition driven by their own assertiveness.

The remaining dependent variables can be explained by some of the conflict management variables, but the order of magnitudes of the correlations and the explained variance from the regressions is relatively low.

In sum, the attitudes toward conflict management in Japanese R & D follow directly from the values described in earlier chapters that are the products of culture, family, education, and organizational expectations. The denial of conflict engenders an avoidance of conflict management behaviors that appear to be self-serving, even when individual workers may prefer a more competitive approach. The impact of conflict management styles on (or at least their relationship to) worker attitudes reflects the cultural importance of *amae* and *on*—dependence and duty. The result of these influences on both conflict management style and worker behavior may be a sacrifice of the individuality necessary for sustained commitment to innovative ideas. The question for Japanese policy makers is how to develop that commitment without sacrificing the positive benefits that have so long enabled Japanese organizations to reach success. In the next chapter, workers report on what they see as desirable managerial behaviors that may move the system toward the accommodation of past and future values.

# Worker Preferences for Leader Types

At the end of the questionnaires administered to leaders and workers was a section which asked for their opinions in general about preferred traits and behaviors of leaders in research and development laboratories in Japan. Below, a summary of the comments offered by the workers (not the leaders) is presented. The raw data in the form of general comments were translated, the content analyzed, then organized into categories. The comments are diverse, and they may not be representative of the attitudes of all workers in the sample. They are revealing, however, of some underlying concerns that might well be investigated in future studies.

Four separate but overlapping areas of desired leadership characteristics or behavior were expressed by R & D workers. They cover the following areas:

1. Desirable personal characteristics of leaders
2. Desirable behaviors of leaders
3. Desirable characteristics of the R & D group
4. Desirable characteristics of the larger organization

Each of the categories of expressed desired behaviors is listed in Exhibit 16.1.

As can be seen, the desirable personal characteristics fall into three classes: (1) values, beliefs, and dispositions; (2) knowledge, and (3) skills and abilities. In the first class, the general impression is that workers want leaders who are strong, trustworthy, and self-confident, yet aware of and respectful of subordinates as individuals. With respect to desired knowledge, workers believe their leaders should have a breadth of understanding and knowledge, yet simultaneously should be at least as proficient as their subordinates in their areas of

**Exhibit 16.1**
**Desired Leader Characteristics and Behavior and Group and Organizational Characteristics Espoused by R & D Workers**

I.      PERSONAL CHARACTERISTICS OF LEADERS CONSIDERED IMPORTANT

A. Values
     Belief in fairness and equality
     Respect for individuality
     Adaptability — "make people relax or be hard on them"
     Combination of warm heart and intelligence
     Well-balanced personality
     Youth (outmoded technology is no good)
     Strong individual character
     Trustworthiness
     Belief in own deserved respect from subordinates
     Willingness to compromise after discussion with subordinates

B. Knowledge
     Knowledge of broad areas of science
     Knowledge of project (greater than workers) with respect to objectives, background, significance, schedule, effects
     Capacity to understand work content (note: workers complain that managers do not understand their work)
     Technical and theoretical proficiencies in subordinate staff specialties

C. Skills and Abilities
     Ability to understand personalities and abilities
     Ability to understand purposes of research and communicate them
     Capacity to understand original ideas
     Capacity to estimate/project results of R & D
     Ability to see the long-term perspective
     Ability to dream
     Prophetic vision
     Ability to present proposals clearly — quality alone without clarity is not sufficient
     Good communication skills (harmony)

II.      BEHAVIORS OF LEADERS CONSIDERED IMPORTANT

A. Proactive Leader Behavior

     1. Vis-à-Vis Individuals in Group:
        a. Initiating Behaviors (Cognitive)
           Anticipate problems and need for changes (especially in applied and developmental research)
           Explain errors
           Exchange opinions

**Exhibit 16.1 (continued)**

> Give attention to individuals one-on-one, not
> > in group
> Provide technical training
> Balance theory and practice
> Balance ideal and practical reality

  b. Consideration Behaviors
  Praise worker achievement

2. Vis-à-Vis the **Group as a Whole:**

  a. Initiating Behaviors (Cognitive)
  Stimulate staff with ideas
  Encourage free thought and challenge
  Conduct staff "show and tell"
  > (e.g., where staff give presentations about the background,
  > motivation and procedures that resulted in their success.
  > Group members to stimulate one another).
  Present research objectives
  Present ideas concretely

  b. Consideration Behaviors — Morale and Action-Inducing
  Encourage honesty (from the heart) even during working hours
  Encourage motivation
  Generate enthusiasm
  Listen to staff opinion
  Help workers realize their hopes
  Get workers to think together and take action together

3. Aimed at Human Resource Development
  Bring out 100% of researcher potential
  Personal growth
  Through education and training, discover differences in abilities
  Use in-house education as a means to assess talent at an early stage
  Identify worker dreams, harmonize them and develop potential

B. Reactive "Behaviors" (not proactive)
  Do not meddle
  Minimum management
  Let people try
  Permit worker mistakes or success
  Leave methods to staff

**Exhibit 16.1 (continued)**

III.    CHARACTERISTICS OF THE **GROUP** CONSIDERED
        IMPORTANT

A. Social Concerns
   Knowledge of contribution to society
   Workers who want to benefit society

B. Abilities
   Quality of individual researchers
   Full utilization of existing skills
   Workers who grasp essence of work

C. Group Involvement
   Recognition of group objectives

D. Commitment
   Motivation
   Enthusiasm

E. Climate
   Supportive climate for research and creativity
   Physical and mental environment
   Easy communication
   Growth in research skills and knowledge

IV.    CHARACTERISTICS OF **ORGANIZATION** TO WHICH GROUP
       BELONGS — CONSIDERED IMPORTANT

A. **Externally Related**
       Adequate market research
       Selection of research that can be accepted by society
       Identification of larger organizational strategy
       Continuing calculation of impact on society
       Public relations for research results

B. **Internally Related**
       Careful ongoing project evaluation
       Short project length
       Budget flexibility
       Efficiency — output/input
       Communication with and education of superiors
       Identify superior's organizational strategy

specialization. Whether such breadth is possible may be questionable, given the diversity of science and the rapidly emerging technologies. It may be that Japanese workers so need to respect their leaders that they have unrealistic expectations as to their possible competencies.

Concerning the third set of characteristics, R & D workers want leaders with three basic sets of skills and abilities: intelligence, long-range vision and imagination, and communication skills. As noted in earlier chapters, intelligence as a trait is usually cited as a necessary but not sufficient characteristic of leadership. The idea that leaders (at least in R & D) must be able to project themselves into an unknown future and to shape ideas concerning it does not come out as strongly in the theoretical literature on leadership, though the more pragmatic messages certainly imply that such capacity is necessary. In the dissection of the traits that emerged from the revised MBTI (see pages 186–196), there are several that suggest the possibility that such a disposition may be present among these R & D leaders.

Communication is similarly cited as desirable. Notably absent as an expressed desirable "trait" is any kind of disposition for succorance. While Japanese workers may desire and expect "stroking" behaviors from leaders that mirror parent-child socialization patterns (see below), they do not see this as a personality characteristic. This curious anomaly may be due to a cultural need to see leaders as reflecting the strength of the subordinates. To suggest that a leader must be considerate is to suggest in addition that subordinates "need" consideration. Not only would such a need probably be construed as weakness (perhaps in all cultures, not just the Japanese), but in Japan it would imply that certain individuals may call attention to themselves. Such is undesirable, as noted in earlier chapters.

The "behaviors" that R & D subordinates desire of their leaders fall into several categories: proactive and reactive, and within the first category, with respect to individuals contrasted to groups. When leaders interact with individuals, they should be "educators," according to these respondents. That is, they should explain both the reality of day-to-day technical needs as well as lay out the domains of the theories that may be relevant. Praise is cited in these open-ended comments as desirable, though as noted above, publicly singling out individual achievement is not usually recommended. This comment doubtless refers to individual commendation delivered soto voce.

Workers believe in dealing with the unit as a whole, in contrast with individuals within it, and leaders should be capable of both stimulating new ideas and generating high morale. Leaders should be able to present research ideas and objectives clearly and concretely. At the same time, they are responsible for building morale and motivation. Again, these twin themes of leadership—initiating structure and consideration—are not unique to Japan or to R & D.

A third category of proactive behavior desired of leaders is directed toward human resource development. Reflecting the strong expectation in Japan of corporate responsibility for caring for individual workers, this group of respondents personifies that responsibility by expecting R & D leaders to be attentive to each person's individual strengths, both real and potential, and to his ambitions.

Among the comments in this last section of the questionnaire was a category that appeared to indicate worker concern with characteristics of the group, rather than with the leader's responsibility toward it. The implication, of course, is that the leader is, indeed, to be held accountable for these characteristics. Chief among the desirable group traits is a culture that supports commitment to the group, motivation toward group-determined objectives, and support for creativity in research. Also desired are high-quality workers who can utilize their skills. Finally, good groups, according to these respondents, recognize their responsibility for the social welfare of the Japanese society in general. This latter reinforces both the Hackman and Oldham conceptualizations of "work significance" in their motivation model and the observations made in Chapter 15 concerning the Japanese worker's need to feel responsible for the well-being of the group and larger society.

Finally, these comments point to desirable characteristics of the organization in which the R & D unit is set. This set of recommendations addresses both external and internal conditions of the organization. R & D researchers express concerns that the organization be sensitive to the needs of society, anticipating those that can and should be met by the organization. At the same time, workers want to be sure that the contributions of the organization to that society are assessed and that the organization gets credit for them. Internally, researchers want their projects to be subject to continuous evaluation so that projects can be terminated or times to completion extended, and budgets can be adjusted for maximum efficiency. Communication between the larger organization and the research and development operation is also needed.

# VI

# Conclusions and Recommendations

# 17

# Conclusions and Recommendations

There is little doubt that Japanese research and development in the last two decades has been enormously successful, especially in applied domains. Technological progress stemming from research and development has been estimated to contribute over 50 percent to the increase in Japan's Gross National Product (Science and Technology Agency 1987, 15; cf. Martin & Irvine 1989). While a variety of factors comprise the ingredients of effective research and development, it is incontrovertible that leadership plays a significant part. In this book, some important personality characteristics of leaders in Japanese R & D laboratory sections identified through an extensive research effort have been discussed and analyzed. While the research shows that there do not appear to be significant differences in personality traits among leaders across government, university, and corporation laboratories, there are some indications that the new, more open-ended, government-sponsored laboratories (ERATO) may have distinctive leader types.

If there are few differences *across* organizational types, there are many differences in leadership styles in Japanese R & D in general. Eight distinctive types or clusters of personality traits were isolated from questionnaire data received from R & D leaders. The clusters represent leaders who are predominantly gregarious, or dogged, or "mousy," or succorant, or imaginative, or extroverted, and so on. The research demonstrates, in other words, that Japanese R & D leaders are not homogeneous in the personalities. Moreover, for some of these clusters, there were important impacts on (or at least relationships with) subordinate worker attitudes, values, commitments, and satisfactions.

No one leader cluster was found to have a monopoly of desirable or influential characteristics with respect to these worker variables. This absence of domination of any one type is explained by variations in situational demands in R & D settings and by the distinctively Japanese pattern of allocating many parts of the traditional leadership roles to the workers themselves. Because of space limitations, the special roles played by the workers could not be discussed at length in the book. So also, the lack of confirmation of the existence of the four leader styles (NF, SF, NT, ST) requisite to the complement of organizational prerequisites (AGIL) attests to the complexity of leadership requirements in organizations, and as well, perhaps, to the cross-cultural differences in both organizational leaders and organizations. For this sample in Japan, there is no simple matching of leader to internal or external contingency that will result in greater efficiency or effectiveness. Multiple-trait leaders in Japanese R & D attempt to deal with all four organizational prerequisites and allocate tasks in those that do not match their personalities to other persons or to the group.

In addition to worker self-management, Japanese organizations are much more heavily normed than those in the United States. In Stephen Kerr's terms (Kerr 1978) there are more and stronger "substitutes for leadership"—organizational characteristics other than interpersonal interactions that constrain workers to behave in ways deemed organizationally desirable. It can be said unequivocally that in Japan these "substitutes" also take on a much richer variety than is presently known. It remains to explore the interaction of these substitutes with the leader types identified so far through this research.

## SOCIALIZATION AND LEADERSHIP

A persistent theme in this book has been the profound influence that culture, family, and education have on both leaders and workers. The leadership roles played out by managers of R & D units clearly mirror prior relationships they have had with their extended families, with each of their parents, with siblings, and with teachers. As Fukutake (1981) notes, "Parents . . . have been unable to break away from pampering the child in early childhood, as they themselves were pampered. They cannot shift to democratic or autonomous discipline that will make the child capable of independent self-control as he grows older" (p. 45). The expectations such preadult interactions engender, especially in a homogeneous society, are molded into societal and organizational norms that severely constrain any who would deviate. Yet there are some leaders (and presumably, some workers) who do depart and with good effect in their organizations. (We can not speculate about the effects on their individual psyches.) For example, of the eight unique clusters of leader types identified in Chapter 12, it would appear that "Fido," "Scrooge," and "Popeye" in the Japanese setting most significantly affect R & D output via their influence on the motivation of workers (though for quite different reasons in each case). In addition to technological, organizational, and work design requirements, the social dynamics of the particular work group "educe" the leader type which is appropriate to the organization in Japan, and in turn the roles played by the second in command, the *nyobu yaku*. As Craig (1970a) notes, the personality and environment are in intimate relationship. There is, he reports, an "obvious cor-relation between the shame orientation, the weakness of self, and the depth and sensitivity of individual involvement in the group." Further,

The Japanese leader is a member of the group rather than one who stands above the group. He is held responsible for the actions of the group, both by higher authority and by the group itself. And he must be responsive to the demands of the group. If he can do this, it matters little whether he is brilliant or even especially capable, for among his followers there will be brilliant men who can do the work. In the typical Japanese group the followers will be given considerable freedom as long as they do their work.

## GROUP VALUES, NORMS, AND LEADERSHIP

To some degree the course of change from the organic solidarity (Durkheim 1933) that now characterizes Japanese work units toward the more mechanical solidarity that is more typical in the West requires a release of the bonds of community that so tightly constrain relationships and behavior. In Peter Blau's terms, institutions will move from "integrative" to "distributive" exchange relationships (Blau 1964) or, as Etzioni (1961) puts it, from "normative" to "utilitarian" conditions. These latter are more calculative—more cognitive and measured in terms of the balance between personal and group advancement. For the Japanese this would mean a raising to consciousness of the gaps between their real interests and those of the organization, between their *honne* and their *tatemae*. As noted in Chapter 8, for the most part, Japanese workers are not aware of that gap. To admit it would be to cause considerable personal anguish in the individual—the anguish of individuality and the apartness that individu-ality brings. As Hamilton and Sanders (1992, 56) note, truth or sincerity in social relationships in Japan means "doing or saying what one should in the face of pressures that could include one's own desires." With the coherent and omni-present life development socialization processes experienced by young Japanese, it is psychologically easier in adulthood to remain unaware of disjuncture be-tween personal and social expectations.

Surely, no one would wish on the Japanese a total shift to Western-style organizations, with their plethora of distrust and self-serving behavior. In Amer-ica, workers are aware of the gaps between what they want and what is in the organization's interest. They choose often to deal with it, however, not by denial but by subterfuge, if not sabotage, all with personal psychic and organizationally negative consequences.

Nevertheless, one of the costs of greater creativity and innovation in Japan may lie in the loosening of the sense of "responsibility" that the Japanese feel for others in their organization and for the organization itself. This is not to suggest that workers need act less "responsibly." Rather, it is to suggest that the very conception of responsibility needs to be broadened to include individual as well as corporate growth. In the long run, if each individual conscientiously balances his obligations to self and others, both individual and society will prosper. Bending too far to the idiographic side is dangerous. The greatest threat to meritocratic social systems is that the centrifugal force toward maximization of individual gain usually (if temporarily and cyclically) moves the norms and behaviors of citizens well beyond the requirements for collaborative, integrative interaction. The result is the excess of capitalism that exploits the less powerful or the dissolution to anarchy that opens the society's resource doors to whoever is able to walk through.

## INDIVIDUALITY AND R & D SUCCESS

What late-twentieth-century Western scholars mean by "individualism" is significantly different from what scholars in earlier generations meant by it. As Malraux (1926) noted, the heyday of individualism in the West took place in the passion and openness of the late nineteenth century, while in his day (and today) we suffer from a "failure of individualism." The issue of the meaning of individualism is complicated not only by time but by cross-cultural incomparabilities. Since individualism appears to be linked to creativity and innovation in R & D, it is important to consider the inhibitions to individualism and the changes both necessary and possible to introduce it into R & D units.

Japanese suggestion systems, which are fairly widespread throughout the country, are one form of the institutionalization of individualism, though the suggestions tend to be arguments for small incremental change, and the motivation to make suggestions is still to conform to expectations of the group in socially acceptable ways. Dramatically deviant ideas receive relatively little attention because the risk of peer opprobrium is too great. Change as a way of thinking and doing must become an important value, and the promise of enhanced social status its progenitor.

Although recent trends may portend significant changes in Japan youth, the creative young Japanese person generally is still *not* frustrated by the lack of reward for individual effort, since as noted above, he has been socialized not to expect the reward until later in life. Furthermore, the reward comes at least in some significant measure from his feeling of contribution to group harmony and achievement. This is reinforced by his sense of hard work and commitment to group aims, an effort that by itself is partially self-rewarding, even in the absence of visible evidence of its positive effect on the group (though to be sure, his own extraordinary effort itself must be perceived by the worker as visible to others). To be singled out for special reward while young would be to subject the rewarded person to charges of violation of local egalitarian norms and the cultural value of respect for the elderly.

Thus, the institutionalization of a reward system in R & D that recognizes individual achievement alone will be difficult to implement (cf. King 1990). More promising is a system that rewards not only the achievement and not only the effort that produced it, but the creative deviation from standard thinking or doing. These differences must be considered by leaders and workers *not* as expressions of immature individualism but as mature contributions to the group. *Wa* thus takes a longer-term perspective. The goal becomes not immediate, ongoing harmony and the avoidance or denial of conflict, but group welfare over the longer term. Difference is tolerated and encouraged as part of *wa*, and is not perceived and punished as a violation of it.

## CONFLICT MANAGEMENT IN R & D

While the finer tuning of the Japanese culture as a whole would make one think that conflicts would be more frequently perceived and manifested, the Japanese have had a long history of successful internal conflict management that has generated a remarkably stable system with a high degree of comity. The resolution mechanisms that Deutsch (1987) identifies, those that are both functional and dysfunctional, are all present in Japanese society, so that ostensible stability and calm come at some collective psychic cost. As Lebra (1989, 56 ff.) notes with respect to the dichotomy of harmony and conflict in Japan, the two are not mutually exclusive. Lebra goes on:

In fact, the logic of bipolarization may well be reversed: the more harmony-oriented, the more conflict-sensitive.

The norm of harmony may be precisely what makes people more aware of conflicts with others, conflicts between their self-interest and obligations, and so forth.

The success of the mechanisms described in Chapter 11 has enabled conflict denial, as defined here, to be a viable cognitive option for most Japanese, including those in R & D centers. The functions of conflict denial for the Japanese R & D manager permit the Japanese an optimism about problem solving that makes it possible for them to be highly successful researchers in the applied and developmental domains. It permits them further to engage in lengthy discussions that aim at total consensus because they have a record of success at that process.

## ORGANIZATIONAL DESIGN AND R & D LEADERSHIP

The Japanese research and development organization represents perhaps the ultimate in sociotechnical design. It merges the technology of research and development with the Japanese social system, its values, norms, affective interpersonal relationships, and so on. Integrative rather than distributive solutions to conflict are more possible in the Japanese R & D setting because "real" conflict is denied.

To some extent the shift to individuality and rewards for deviance is likely to follow in the near future from increasing sophistication of information technology (Nakatani 1988, 78). Smaller organizations, which have been accorded lower status in Japanese society, can now be more successful by product development and marketing that addresses a narrow range of consumer needs assessed through new, inexpensive knowledge search and acquisition tools. One result will be smaller, flatter organizations with rewards based not on seniority but on individual merit. The role of leadership in the generation of manifested individuality is significant. Good leaders are both role models and culture (norm) definers/promulgators. The emergence of a new breed of leaders in Japan may start with the small firms, that is, not the larger, prestigious ones into which the best college graduates aspire to enter.

## THE R & D LEADER

From the long history of research studies, leadership appears to include a combination of genetic and acquired or learned traits plus proactive behaviors—roughly initiating structure and consideration—set in the context of a variety of constraining or supporting conditions (e.g., resource availability, norms, communication). There is also evidence that organizational characteristics call for leaders with capacities to meet the special needs of problem, place, and time. There is considerable research support for the proposition that leadership can have a profound effect on performance in academic settings (Knorr et al. 1979). From the findings from this research, it is clear that a variety of types of leaders are present in Japanese R & D and that these types have varying effects on quite different aspects of both the organizational conditions for research productivity and the worker mental conditions that can maximize innovation and creativity in those organizational settings.

Japanese education is geared to the development of two somewhat contradictory, Jungian types among leaders: Sensation-Intuition and Sensation-Thinking. The Confucian-related pattern of discrete, logical, deliberate, sequential steps, with measured responses and careful scrutiny of results to correct deviance, contributes to a dampening of the more free-spirited, combinatorial, cognitive processes that Postmodernists and artificial intelligence researchers tell us also characterize human thought. The union of sensation and intuition is brought on by the Japanese person's learned need to be sensitive to others and to the culture as a whole. Both of these acquired habits of mind engender a tolerance for delayed personal gratification. For research and development breakthroughs, it may be that these habits of the heart and mind are ill-suited. Although critical of the Western model of creativity, Tatsuno (1990) describes it as follows:

In the West, creativity is viewed as an epiphany, and only one phase in the creative process—the generation of new ideas that trigger dramatic breakthroughs—is emphasized. In contrast to the incrementalism of Japan's adaptive creativity, Western creativity is rapid-fire, awe-inspiring, and often engenders the zeal of religious faith. Westerners delight in spectacular displays of genius by individuals. Despite the months or years of tedious groundwork, we believe that breakthroughs are the ultimate proof of creativity. Anything short of spectacular quantum leaps is considered "ho-hum" science. (p. 49)

While there are some hints at recognition of the need for the development of more paradigmatic thinking and breakthroughs (*hassoo*) that recognize those paradigms, the interest is minimal and itself is derivative of Western methods (e.g., brainstorming). There is also a growing core of younger, dissatisfied scientists (*shinjinrui*—a new breed) pressing (as much as possible in Japan) for change. But without significant social and cultural transformation, these young people may continue to be frustrated. While outlining ways to overcome the many obstacles to increasing creativity in the laboratory, Tatsuno (1990) hints at some merging of "scientific rationality with Buddhist philosophy to arrive at creative new solutions that are "heir to Japan's historical search for *wakon yosai*—a satisfying union of Western science and Eastern philosophy" (p. 42). What this misses, of course, is a uniquely Japanese approach to generating breakthroughs. That itself would require a breakthrough, so the Japanese are hoisted on their own petard unless serious efforts are made in other sectors of the society to change modes of thinking and interacting.

Note that the question of greater individuality has been considered here in terms of its potential benefit in permitting creative ideas (however deviant they may seem), to be presented openly for consideration. Recall, however, that where R & D focuses on basic research, such strength of individual conviction is beneficial in the competition for new ideas. It needs to be said, of course, that idea generation is only one part of innovation. As Kanter (1983; 1988) observes, it is a process that takes place over a period of time and is carried out by different individuals. In Chapter 10, the issues of technology transfer were discussed. It was clear from that discussion that the management of innovation from idea creation to marketing is a skill well mastered by the Japanese. The focus in this book, however, is on leadership's facilitation of the formation of more productive creative processes among R & D researchers themselves—on what Barry Staw (1990) and others have called "intrapreneurs," "idea generators," and "idea champions."

## JAPANESE LEADERSHIP IN ACTION—FACE RELATIONS

The most significant difference between Japanese and American leaders lies in the legitimacy of assertiveness. In America, aggressive, proactive, interventionist leadership is viewed as admirable and is accepted by workers as a valid exercise of formal authority. In Japan, on the other hand, such behavior would be seen as a violation of cultural norms. As Stewart (1985) notes:

The Japanese consider it brash for an individual to make definite decisions regarding her or himself or others. It is offensive for an individual to urge the acceptance of her or his opinion as a course of action. He or she must use circumlocution and maintain a rather strict reserve.

The individual Japanese is subjugated to the group and, when faced with a decision leading to action, he or she shrinks and may go to what seem fantastic lengths to avoid making the decision. Even if he should commit himself verbally to a course of action, he will frequently end by doing nothing. He lacks a sense of personal responsibility; he feels only a sense of group responsibility. If at all possible he will try to throw the onus of decision responsibility on a group or at least on some other person.

The subtlety of manifested leadership in Japan, regardless of the dominant trait cluster of the leader, requires special modes of analysis. Irving Goffman's depiction of a "face engagement" (Goffman 1963; cf. Ekman 1982) suggests that leadership expressed in face-to-face interactions "comprise all those instances of two or more participants in a situation joining each other openly in maintaining a single focus of cognitive and visual attention—what is sensed as a single *mutual activity*, entailing preferential communication rights" (p. 89, emphasis in original).

Face relations in R & D units, especially those with applied, collaborative modes of interaction, play an important part in the exercise of leadership. Masatsugu (1982) reminds us that in Japanese, the word for face is *kao*, but it connotes not only the physiognomy of the part above the neck but the "totality of the individual." Interestingly, the different parts of the leadership role, for example, internal and cross boundary concerns, have their counterparts in the characterization of the face. Thus, the person who exercises internal leadership in conflict management and the promotion of a harmonious organizational culture is said to occupy one face role called *kao-yaku*. On the other hand, the person who represents the organization (in this case, the R & D unit) to its outside constituencies is called a *kao-pasu* or "face pass." By virtue of the recognition he has in the outside world, he gains favors in that world. So also can others who "borrow" his face (*kao-o kariru*), that is, who use their acquaintance with the *kao-pasu* to introduce or advance themselves. When reputation, so dear to the Japanese, is threatened, the expression *kao-ni-kakawaru* (it will damage my reputation) is sometimes employed to indicate the concern.

In the end, then, leadership in Japan is by nuance—nuance perceived and nuance transmitted. It is an esthetic condition, a Zen relationship acted out virtually without conscious differentiation of leaders and followers (cf. Bateson 1979; Kobayashi 1990). Can such leader behaviors be taught and learned? Probably not through any formal system, but behaviors are conditioned by culture. So also are esthetic standards. What is functional and beautiful is temporally and culturally bound. It is likely that as Japan becomes even more integrated with the West and its culture changes, so also will face relations. "Nuance" may be replaced by more direct expressions of feeling and attitude.

## POLICY IMPLICATIONS OF RESEARCH FINDINGS

From the time of Compte and Durkheim in the era of modern sociology, there have been attempts to find ways of restoring the balance between the disordering elements of society and the needs of humankind for social comity. There have also been contrary attempts to find ways of upsetting the balance in the interests of social progress. Early sociologists saw the answer to the balance problem in the bonding of human beings through affection and solidarity as the "system" answers the need for both external productivity and internal cohesion. National and organizational policy makers must recognize the stage of cultural evolution in which the country as a whole finds itself before policy can be made and effectuated. With due awareness of this need, there are a number of ways in which the findings from this research can be used in policy development, at both a national and local level.

There is some question whether the same means of removing blocks to creativity and innovation as are used in the West will be successful in Japan. As King and Anderson (1990) note, too little attention has been paid to the problems of conformity or norm-formation that enhance or inhibit creativity, even in Western settings. Since these problems are even more pronounced in Japan, it is clear that some considerable research is needed on this subject.

This research has both practical and theoretical implications. In the first instance, socialization and educational goals must be reconceived. Both the parental role and the educational system must be involved. As noted above, Fukutake (1981) points to the extraordinary challenge that this represents. He suggests further that Japan is in a state of social flux. Modern parents are unsure about their roles. This confusion may represent an opportunity rather than a liability. Education, for example, may have to develop new ways of socializing young people to engage in "lateral thinking" (De Bono 1971). Furthermore, as Merry White (1987) notes, effort alone (*gambatte*) may no longer be the sufficient condition for respect and status in the emerging Japanese society. Standing out rather than standing in may need to be made socially desirable in early school years in order for creative departures to be assayed later in life. Second, the findings offer some sense of the kinds of leaders that would be optimum in a variety of typical situations. If different leaders are significantly different in their effectiveness and efficiency, then it is important to be able to select those who properly meet organizational needs for each. The research reported here identifies the characteristics of leaders found to be successful. This information can be used by those who choose leaders (either by selection or election). As Kilmann (1977) and Mitroff (1983) note, at least four quite different kinds of leadership are needed to maximize internal and external efficiency and effectiveness. There remains, of course, the problem of identifying leaders with the special clusters of traits that can be canonically connected with characteristics of groups of subordinates.

On the theoretical side, there is an evident need for developing new insights about the relationships between internal/external orientations, especially in the light of the distribution of leadership responsibilities to self-managed teams (cf. Goodman, Devadas, & Hughson 1988). Further, presently, very little is known about the substitutes for leadership as various types of leaders may complement them under a complex set of contingencies. It is especially propitious to explore these matters in Japan where culture plays such a significant part in the dynamics of "group" leadership, by which is meant not leadership of the group but leadership by the group. Much remains to be sorted out in the integration of personality, small group dynamics, and organizational effectiveness.

A second use of the findings is by leaders now in office, as they seek to become more effective or efficient. While some social science research suggests that leadership style is relatively inflexible because of personality invariance, other research says that leaders can and should adapt their behavior to the needs of the time. In knowing what kinds of leadership style and conflict management work best, current leaders may be able to adjust their behavior accordingly.

A third by-product of this research lies in the possibility of task design. Long-standing published research indicates that the proper design of work is important in sustaining subordinate motivation. The findings from this study should enable leaders better to match the design of work settings to both the needs of the workers and the requirements for effectiveness.

Another implication of the research findings may lie in the advancement of educational policy. It is conceivable that students can be made aware of the nature of alternative leadership dispositions and can be taught different conflict management modes that have been shown to be effective.

A final implication of the research has to do with the formation of national labor and educational policy. Cooperation by the corporate sector with MITI-funded basic research priorities is declining as corporations themselves take on high-risk projects that they see as critical to their long-term futures. Government laboratories and universities have not been able to take up the slack, despite such projects as ERATO. The prosperity of any country is at least partially conditioned on the wisdom and skill with which national leaders are able to identify and control the flow of talented young people into positions of responsibility (as, for example, into leadership positions in research and development). The findings from this research should provide useful data for the purpose of determining allocations of funds for education and training, and as well, perhaps, to facilitate the cross-institutional employment mobility of skilled leaders.

In the end, it is the motivational theory of Hackman and Oldham—the job characteristics approach—to which we must turn to understand best how multiple leaders are effective in Japanese R & D. Recall that three critical psychological states are necessary for workers to be motivated and to produce high-quality work: experienced meaningfulness, experienced responsibility, and knowledge of results. Hackman and Oldham suggest that task design can provide these conditions. Thus, task variety, task identity, task significance, autonomy, and feedback are critical to the achievement of the important psychological states.

But in Japan (and most assuredly in other countries as well) the normative and goal contexts in which task design features are laid out are equally important. Without identity within the institution and its goals, without a matching organizational culture, and without supportive peer norms, workers will not produce at high-quality levels. The Hackman and Oldham scheme is Western and individualistic in ideology and psychological assumptions. In Japan, where individual identity is so closely tied to (if not isomorphic with) the group and organizational ideologies, goals, and conceptualizations of success, leaders have somewhat different roles. There, the assumption is that the cultural and normative setting will always be supportive of management goals; hence, leaders spend less time having to proselytize and socialize. These activities are performed by members of the organization.

The devolution to the group of many responsibilities of leadership includes accountability. Thus, it is to the group that management turns for social control and adherence to organizational standards. Unfortunately, a potential concomitant side effect of group control is social loafing and deindividuation. For Japan to motivate R & D workers, leaders must find ways not to permit workers to submerge themselves in the group and accept unquestioningly group directives for performance.


## GOVERNMENT SUPPORT FOR RESEARCH AND DEVELOPMENT

There is a clear awareness of the need for a radical transformation in the conduct of research in Japan. The Science Council has recently pointed to the importance of developing a research agenda that recognizes the social and cultural requirements not of this generation, but of the next. They also lament the brain drain which draws talented people away from the universities and into private business. The Miyazawa administration, in its revised *Outline of Policies Governing Science and Technology* (Spring 1992), recommended an immediate doubling of expenditures for research and development. In an editorial in the *Asahi Shimbun*, the recommendation is made to "diversify academic institutions through sweeping reforms, such as dismantling the outmoded Meiji era system that continues to put the former imperial universities at the pinnacle of the nation's institutions of higher learning, and by elimination of the distinction between national and private universities." (*Asahi Shimbun* 1992). It is not clear, however, whether Japanese industry values the input of the Japanese government. As Frost (1987) notes, corporate R & D conducted under government funding is peripheral at best to the central concerns of the organization. Major corporations in Japan outspend their U.S. counterparts in investment in R & D and are weaning themselves away from reliance on the government.

## LABOR-MANAGEMENT RELATIONS

Little has been said thus far on the nature of industrial and labor relations in Japan, though the subject is a large and important one. Much of the modern manifestations of paternalism and personality development were central to the management-labor conflict that arose in the early part of the twentieth century. Some would assert that current Japanese organization and leadership is not primarily a function of ancient tradition but a product of a new industrial ideology consciously promulgated by a semibureaucratic agency, the *Kyoochookai*, or Cooperation and Harmony Society. To counter the influence of both the scientific management principles of Frederick Taylor and the increased individualism of capitalism in general, the Kyoochookai members promoted a reconstructed, Confucianism-based ideology of harmony and organic solidarity. (For further information, see Kinzley 1991.) As this book clearly illustrates, however, it would appear to be the more deep-seated and long-standing ancient traditions and mores that define the leader and his relationships to workers in modern Japan.

## CONCLUSION

In the end, the Japanese, thankfully, remain enigmatic and ever-fascinating. To engage in research on their culture and on one of their important developing institutions—the research and development enterprise—constitutes an activity of great wonderment and surprise and engenders a profound examination of one's self and one's own society. But the theory of Japanese management still constitutes a ''jungle'' (Keys & Miller 1984). The jungle is complicated by a prematurely, or perhaps sagely forward-looking, postmodernist Japan in which ambiguity and nonlinearity are accepted as a matter of course. The power of intuitive/feeling type leaders (NFs) to deal with such a culture heuristically (cf. Nutt 1989) suggests that their personalities may be better suited to leadership needs in the twenty-first century.

As noted at the outset of this book, it is hoped that the images and messages about Japan have some reasonable verisimilitude and offer some passage through the jungle. But it is not absolutely necessary that they be accurate for the insights about Japan to be useful. Japan and the United States have much in common and much that is different. It is important and necessary to see the potential for the importation of ideas from other cultures, to test their validity in research, and to utilize them in practice if possible. But it is also wise to exult in the continuation of the diversity of humankind. Japan and its people are unique. One hopes that they and we will always be so.

# References

Abegglen, James C., 1958. *The Japanese Factory: Aspects of Its Social Organization.* Glencoe, IL: The Free Press.

Abegglen, James C. & George Stalk, Jr., 1985. *Kaisha, The Japanese Corporation.* New York: Basic Books.

Abernathy, W. & J. Utterback, 1978. "Patterns of Industrial Innovation," *Technology Review, 80* (June), 2–9.

Adler, Nancy J., 1991. *International Dimensions of Organizational Behavior.* Second Edition. Boston: PWS-Kent Publishing Company.

Adler, Nancy & Dafna N. Izraeli (eds.), 1988. *Women in Management Worldwide.* Armonk, NY: M. E. Sharpe.

Alder, Nancy & Robert Doktor, 1986. "From the Atlantic to the Pacific Century: Cross-Cultural Management Reviewed," *Journal of Management, 12*, 2 (Summer), 295–318.

Ajzen, Icek & M. Fishbein, 1973. "Attitudinal and Normative Variables as Predictors of Specific Behaviors," *Journal of Personality and Social Psychology, 27*, 41–57.

Ajzen, Icek & M. Fishbein, 1980. *Understanding Attitudes and Predicting Social Behavior.* Englewood Cliffs, NJ: Prentice-Hall.

Akio, Yamanouchi, 1986. "Kigyo Henkaku no Gijitsu Management," in *Management of Organizational Change in R & D.* Tokyo: Nihon Keizai Shimbunsha.

Aldag, Ramon J., Steve H. Barr, & Arthur P. Brief, 1981. "Measurement of Perceived Job Characteristics," *Psychological Bulletin, 90*, 3 (November), 415–431.

Aldrich, Howard E., 1979. *Organizations and Environments.* Englewood Cliffs, NJ: Prentice-Hall.

Alexander, Jeffrey C. & Paul Colomy, 1985. " 'Institutionalization' and 'Collective Behavior': Points of Contact Between Eisenstadt's Functionalism and Symbolic Interactionism," in Erik Cohen, Moshe Lissak, & Uri Almagor (eds.), *Compar-*

*ative Social Dynamics, Essays in Honor of S. N. Eisenstadt.* Boulder, CO: West-
view Press, pp. 337–345

Algera, Jen A., 1981. " 'Objective' and Perceived Task Characteristics as a Determinant
of Reactions by Task Performers," *Journal of Occupational Psychology, 56*, 95–
105.

Algera, Jen A., 1990. "The Job Characteristics Model of Work Motivation Revisited,"
in Ewe Kleinbeck, Hans-Henning Quast, Henk Thierry, & Hartmut Hacker (eds.),
*Work Motivation.* Hillsdale, NJ: Lawrence Erlbaum Associates, Publishers.

Allison, David (ed.), 1969. *The R & D Game: Technical Men, Technical Managers, and
Research Productivity.* Cambridge, MA: M.I.T. Press.

Allport, Gordon, 1979. *The Nature of Prejudice.* Reading, MA: Addison-Wesley.

Amabile, T. M., 1982. "Children's Artistic Creativity: Detrimental Effects of Competition in a Field Setting," *Personality and Social Psychology Bulletin, 8*, 573-578.

Amabile, T. M. 1983. *The Social Psychology of Creativity.* New York: Springer Verlag.

Amano, Iduo, 1979. "Continuity and Change in the Structure of Japanese Higher Edu-
cation," in William K. Cummings, Iduo Amano, & Kazuyuki Kitamura (eds.),
*Changes in the Japanese University, A Comparative Perspective.* New York:
Praeger.

American Association for the Advancement of Science, 1987. *AAAS Report XII, Research
and Development FY 1988.* Washington, DC: American Association for the Advancement of Science.

Anderson, Alun M., 1984. *Science and Technology in Japan.* Harlow, Essex, England:
Longman Group Ltd.

Andrews, Frank M., 1979a. "Motivating Diversity and the Performance of Research
Units," in F. M. Andrews (ed.), *Scientific Productivity, The Effectiveness of Re-
search Groups in Six Countries.* Cambridge, England: Cambridge University
Press.

Andrews, Frank M. (ed.), 1979b. *Scientific Productivity, The Effectiveness of Research
Groups in Six Countries.* Cambridge, England: Cambridge University Press.

Ansari, Mahfooz A., 1990. *Managing People at Work, Leadership Styles and Influence
Strategies.* Newbury Park, CA: Sage Publications.

Aoki, Masahiko, 1986. "Implications of the Information and Incentive Structures of the
Japanese Firm to the Nature and Direction of Its R & D Activities." Paper delivered at the NIRA Conference on Networking of Innovative Organizations, December 18–19, Tokyo, Japan.

Argyris, Chris, 1957. *Personality and Organization.* New York: Garland.

Argyris, Chris & Donald A. Schön, 1978. *Organizational Learning: A Theory of Action
Perspective.* Reading, MA: Addison-Wesley.

Arimoto, Akira, 1978. "The Academic Structure in Japan: Institutional Hierarchy and
Academic Mobility." Yale Higher Education Group Working Paper YHERG–27,
New Haven (August).

Aron, A., E. N. Aron, M. Tudor, & C. Nelson, 1991. "Close Relationships as Including
Other in the Self," *Journal of Personality and Social Psychology, 60*, 241–253.

*Asahi Shimbun*, 1992. Cited in *Japan Access, 3*, 31 (August 17), 10.

Azar, E. E. & J. W. Burton (eds.), 1986. *International Conflict Resolution: Theory and
Practice.* Brighton, England: Wheatsheaf; Boulder, CO: Lynne Rienner.

Azumi, Koya, Frank Hull, & Kiyonori Sakakibara, 1986. "The Most and the Least

Innovative R & D Operations in Japan: Preliminary Findings," *Hitotsubashi Journal of Commerce and Management, 21*, 1 (December), 45–60.

Bachnik, Jane M., 1983. "Recruitment Strategies for Household Succession: Rethinking Japanese Household Organization," *Man, 18*, 1 (March), 160–182.

Bachnik, Jane M. & Charles J. Quinn (eds.), 1994. *Situated Meaning: Inside and Outside in Japanese Self, Society and Language*. Princeton, NJ: Princeton University Press.

Badaway, M. K., 1982. *Developing Managerial Skills: Succeeding as a Technical Manager*. New York: Van Nostrand.

Bailyn, Lotte, 1985. "Autonomy in the Industrial R & D Lab," *Human Resource Management, 24*, 2, (Summer), 129–146.

Bairy, Maurice, 1969. "Motivational Forces in Japanese Life," in Robert J. Ballon (ed.), *The Japanese Employee*. Tokyo: Sophia University.

Baker, Norman R., E. P. Winkofsky, Lynn Langmeyer, & Dennis J. Weseney, 1980. "Idea Generation: A Procrustean Bed of Variables, Hypotheses, and Implications," *TIMS Studies in the Management Sciences, 15*, 33–51.

Bales, Robert F., 1950. *Interaction Process Analysis*. Reading, MA: Addison-Wesley.

Bales, Robert F., 1953. "The Equilibrium Problem in Small Groups," in Talcott Parsons, Robert F. Bales, and Edward A. Shils, *Working Papers in the Theory of Action*. Glencoe, IL: The Free Press.

Bales, Robert F., 1965. "Adaptive and Integrative Changes as Sources of Strain in Social Systems," in A. Paul Hare, E. F. Borgatta, and Robert F. Bales (eds.), *Small Groups: Studies in Social Interaction*. Revised Edition. New York: Knopf.

Baliga, B. Rajaram & James G. Hunt, 1988. "Life Cycle Approach to Leadership," in James G. Hunt, B. Rajaram Baliga, H. Peter Dachler, & Chester A. Schriesheim (eds.), *Emerging Leadership Vistas*. Lexington, MA: Lexington Books.

Ballon, Robert J., 1969. "Participative Employment," in Robert J. Ballon (ed.), *The Japanese Employee*. Tokyo: Sophia University.

Bandura, A., 1982. "Self-Efficacy Mechanisms in Human Agency," *American Psychologist, 37*, 122–147.

Barker, James R., 1993. "Tightening the Iron Cage: Concertive Control in Self-Managing Teams," *Administrative Science Quarterly, 38*, 3 (September), 408–437.

Barnard, Chester, I., 1938. *The Functions of the Executive*. Cambridge, MA: Harvard University Press.

Barnard, Chester I., 1986. "Collectivism and Individualism in Industrial Management," in William B. Wolf & Haruki Iino (eds.), *Philosophy for Managers: Selected Papers of Chester I. Barnard*. Tokyo: Bunshido Publishing Company, pp. 9–27.

Barney, Jay B. & Barry Baysinger, 1988. "The Organization of Schumpeterian Innovations." Strategy Group Working Paper Series, No. 88–001, Department of Management, College of Business Administration, Texas A & M University.

Barnlund, Dean C., 1959. "A Comparative Study of Individual, Majority, and Group Judgment," *Journal of Abnormal and Social Psychology, 58*, 55–60.

Barnlund, Dean C., 1975. *Public and Private Self in Japan and the United States, Communicative Styles of Two Cultures*. Tokyo: The Simul Press, Inc.

Barnlund, Dean C., 1989. "Public and Private Self in Communicating with Japan," *Business Horizons, 32*, 2 (March-April), 32–40.

Barrett, Gerald V. & Bernard M. Bass, 1976. "Cross Cultural Issues in Industrial and Organizational Psychology," in Marvin E. Dunnette (ed.), *Handbook of Industrial and Organizational Psychology.* Chicago: Rand McNally College Publishing Company.

Barrow, Jeffrey, 1977. "The Variables of Leadership," *Academy of Management Review,* 2, 2 (April), 231–251.

Bartholomew, James R., 1982. "Science, Bureaucracy, and Freedom in Meiji and Taishoo Japan," in Tetsuo Najita & J. Victor Koschmann (eds.), *Conflict in Modern Japanese History.* Princeton, NJ: Princeton University Press.

Bass, Bernard M., 1985. *Leadership and Performance Beyond Expectations.* New York: The Free Press.

Bass, Bernard M., 1990. *Bass and Stogdill's Handbook of Leadership.* Third Edition. New York: The Free Press.

Bass, Bernard M., 1991. "Debate" on "Ways Men and Women Lead," *Harvard Business Review, 69,* 1 (January-February), 151–152.

Bass, Bernard M., Philip C. Burger, Robert Doktor, & Gerald V. Barrett, 1979. *Assessment of Managers, An International Comparison.* New York: The Free Press.

Bateson, Gregory, 1979. *Mind and Nature.* New York: Dutton.

Battelle Institute, 1973. *Science, Technology and Innovation.* Washington, DC: National Science Foundation.

Baum, Howell S., 1985. "The Psychodynamics of Subordinacy: Implications for Administration." Paper presented at the Annual Meeting of the American Political Science Association, New Orleans, August 29–September 1.

Beck, John C. & Martha N. Beck, 1994. *The Change of a Lifetime, Employment Patterns Among Japan's Managerial Elite.* Honolulu: University of Hawaii Press.

Befu, Harumi, 1971. *Japan: An Anthropological Introduction.* New York: Harper & Row.

Befu, Harumi, 1980. "A Critique of the Group Model of Japanese Society," *Social Analysis, 5/6* (December), 29–43.

Befu, Harumi, 1986. "The Social and Cultural Background of Child Development in Japan and the United States," in Harold Stevenson, Hiroshi Azuma, & Kenji Hakuta (eds.), *Child Development and Education in Japan.* New York: W. H. Freeman and Company, pp. 13–27.

Befu, Harumi, 1990. "Four Models of Japanese Society and Their Relevance to Conflict," in S. N. Eisenstadt & Eyal Ben-Ari (eds.), *Japanese Models of Conflict Resolution.* London: Kegan Paul International, pp. 213–238.

Bellah, Robert N., 1985. *Habits of the Heart.* New York: Harper & Row, Publishers.

Bellah, Robert N., Richard Madsen, William M. Sullivan, Ann Swidler, & Steven M. Tipton (eds.), 1987. *Individualism & Commitment in American Life, Readings on the Themes of Habits of the Heart.* New York: Harper & Row, Publishers.

Bem, Daryl J. & Andrea Allen, 1974. "On Predicting Some of the People Some of the Time: The Search for Cross-Situational Consistencies in Behavior," *Psychological Review, 81,* 6, 506–520.

Benfari, Robert, 1991. *Understanding Your Management Style: Beyond the Myers-Briggs Type Indicators.* Lexington, MA: Lexington Books.

Benne, Kenneth D. & Paul Sheats, 1948. "Functional Roles of Group Members," *Journal of Social Issues, 4,* 2.

Bennett, Dudley, 1976. *TA and the Manager.* New York: AMACOM.

Bennett, John W. & Iwao Ishino, 1963. *Paternalism in the Japanese Economy, Anthropological Studies of Oyabun-Kobun Patterns.* Minneapolis: University of Minnesota Press.

Bennis, Warren G., 1984. "Transformative Power and Leadership," in T. J. Sergiovanni & J. E. Corbally (eds.), *Leadership and Organizational Culture*. Urbana: University of Illinois Press, pp. 64–71.

Bennis, Warren G. & Burt Nanus, 1985. *Leaders: The Strategies for Taking Charge*. New York: McGraw Hill Book Company.

Bennis, Warren G. & Herbert A. Shepard, 1976. "A Theory of Group Development," in Graham S. Gibbard, John J. Hartman, & Richard D. Mann (eds.), *Analysis of Groups*. San Francisco: Jossey-Bass Publishers.

Bergen, A. & R. Miyajima, 1986. "Productivity and the R & D Production Interface in Japan," *R&D Management, 16*, 1, 15–24.

Berger, Peter L., 1963. *Invitation to Sociology*. New York: Doubleday & Company.

Bergen, S. A., 1990. *R & D Management, Managing Projects and New Products*. New Revised Edition. Oxford, England: Basil Blackwell Ltd.

Berne, Eric, 1961. *Transactional Analysis in Psychotherapy*. New York: Grove Press.

Berne, Eric, 1964. *Games People Play, The Psychology of Human Relationships*. New York: Grove Press.

Bernstein, Paula, 1985. *Family Ties, Corporate Bonds*. New York: Doubleday & Company.

Bess, James L., 1977. "The Motivation to Teach," *Journal of Higher Education, 48*, 1 (May/June), 243–258.

Bess, James L., 1983. "Faculty Perspectives on Administrator Effectiveness (II): The Influence of Personality Type." Paper presented at the annual meeting of the American Educational Research Association, Montreal.

Bess, James L., 1988. *Collegiality and Bureaucracy in the Modern University*. New York: Teachers College Press.

Bess, James L. (ed.), 1982. *Motivating Professors to Teach Effectively*. New Directions for Teaching and Learning, #14. San Francisco: Jossey-Bass.

Bess, James L. (ed.), 1984. *College and University Organization: Insights from the Behavioral Sciences*. New York: New York University Press.

Beyer, Janice M., 1981. "Ideologies, Values and Decision Making," in Paul C. Nystrom & William H. Starbuck (eds.), *Handbook of Organizational Design*, Vol. 2. Oxford, England: Oxford University Press, pp. 166–202.

Bhagat, R. S., 1982. "The Role of Subjective Culture in Organizations: A Review and Directions for Future Research," *JAP Monograph, 67*, 653–685.

Bird, Allan, 1992. "Power and the Japanese CEO," *Asia Pacific Journal of Management, 7*, 2, 1–20.

Bisno, Herb, 1988. *Managing Conflict*. Beverly Hills, CA: Sage Publications.

Blake, Robert R. & Jane S. Mouton, 1964. *The Managerial Grid*. Houston: Gulf Publishing.

Blalock, Hubert M., Jr., 1987. "A Power Analysis of Conflict Processes," in Edward J. Lawler & Barry Markowsky (eds.), *Advances in Group Processes, 4* (Summer). New York: JAI Press, pp. 1–40.

Blau, Peter M., 1956. *Bureaucracy in Modern Society*. New York: Random House.

Blau, Peter M., 1964. *Exchange and Power in Social Life*. New York: John Wiley & Sons.

Blumer, Herbert, 1969. *Symbolic Interactionism*. Englewood Cliffs, NJ: Prentice-Hall.

Bond, Michael H. & Daisuke Shiraishi, 1974. "The Effect of Body Lean and Status of an Interviewer on the Non-Verbal Behavior of Japanese Interviewees," *International Journal of Psychology, 9*, 2, 117–128.

Bond, Michael H., Hiroaki Nakazato, & Daisuke Shiraishi, 1975. "Universality and Distinctiveness in Dimensions of Japanese Person Perception," *Journal of Cross-Cultural Psychology, 6*, 3 (September), 346–375.

Borisoff, Deborah & David A. Victor, 1989. *Conflict Management: A Communications Skills Approach.* Englewood Cliffs, NJ: Prentice-Hall.

Borland, Alan, 1988. *In Search of Self in India and Japan.* Princeton, NJ: Princeton University Press.

Borton, Hugh (ed.), 1951. *Japan.* Ithaca, NY: Cornell University Press.

Botkin, James, Dan Dimancescu, & Ray Stata, 1984. *The Innovators, Rediscovering America's Creative Energy.* New York: Harper & Row, Publishers.

Bowker, R. R., 1986. *Industrial Research Laboratories of the United States, Including Consulting Research Laboratories.* Washington, DC: National Research Council of the National Academy of Sciences.

Bowonder, B. & T. Miyake, 1992. "A Model of Corporate Innovation Management: Some Recent High Tech Innovations in Japan," *R & D Management, 22*, 4 (October), 319–335.

Bowring, Richard & Peter Kornicki (eds.), 1993. *The Cambridge Encyclopedia of Japan.* New York: Cambridge University Press, p. 238.

Bozeman, Barry, Michael Crow, & Albert Link, 1984. *Strategic Management of Industrial R & D.* Lexington, MA: Lexington Books.

Branscomb, Lewis & Fumio Kodama, 1993. *Japanese Innovation Strategy: Technical Support for Business Visions.* Cambridge, MA: Center for Science and International Affairs.

Breaugh, J. A., 1985. "The Measurement of Work Autonomy," *Human Relations, 38*, 551–570.

Breaugh, J. A., 1989. "The Work Autonomy Scales: Additional Validity Evidence," *Human Relations, 42*, 1033–1056.

Bridges, William, 1992. *The Character of Organizations: Using Jungian Type in Organizational Development.* Palo Alto, CA: Consulting Psychologists Press.

Brief, Arthur P. & R. J. Aldag, 1981. "The 'Self' in Work Organizations: A Conceptual Review," *Academy of Management Review, 6*, 75–88.

Brislin, Richard W., Walter J. Lonner, & Robert M. Thorndike, 1973. *Cross-Cultural Research Methods.* New York: John Wiley & Sons.

Brown, Karen A., T. D. Klastorin, & Janet L. Valluzzi, 1990. "Project Performance and the Liability of Group Harmony," *IEEE Transactions on Engineering Management, 37*, 2 (May), 117–125.

Brown, L. David, 1983. *Managing Conflict at Organizational Interfaces.* Reading, MA: Addison-Wesley Publishing Company.

Buber, Martin, 1970. *I and Thou.* New York: Scribner.

Buckley, P. J. & H. Mirza, 1985. "The Wit and Wisdom of Japanese Management: An Iconoclastic Analysis," *Management International Review, 25*, 3, 16–32.

Burgoon, Judee K., 1985. "Nonverbal Signals," in Mark L. Knapp & Gerald R. Miller (eds.), *Handbook of Interpersonal Communication.* Beverly Hills, CA: Sage Publications, pp. 344–390.

Burns, T. & G. M. Stalker, 1961. *The Management of Innovation.* London: Tavistock Publications.

Bush, Vannevar, 1946. *Endless Horizons*. Washington, DC: Public Affairs Press.

Calder, Bobby J., 1977. "An Attribution Theory of Leadership," in Barry M. Staw & Gerald R. Salancik (eds.), *New Directions in Organizational Behavior*. Chicago: St. Clair Press.

Cameron, Kim S. & David A. Whetten, 1984. "Models of the Organizational Life Cycle: Applications to Higher Education," in J. L. Bess (ed.), *College and University Organization: Insights from the Behavioral Sciences*. New York: New York University Press.

Cantor, Leonard, 1985. "Vocational Education and Training: The Japanese Approach," *Comparative Education, 21*, 1, 67–76.

Caraley, Demetrios, 1982. *Doing More With Less: Cutback Management in New York City*. New York: Graduate Program in Public Policy Administration, Columbia University.

Chang, C. S., 1982. "Individualism in the Japanese Management System," in Sang M. Lee & Gary Schwendiman (eds.), *Japanese Management: Cultural and Environmental Considerations*. New York: Praeger.

Chanin, M., 1984. "A Study of the Relationship Between Jungian Personality Dimensions and Conflict Handling Behavior," *Human Relations, 37*, 863–879.

Charon, Joel M., 1985. *Symbolic Interactionism, An Introduction, an Interpretation, an Integration*. Second Edition. Englewood Cliffs, NJ: Prentice-Hall.

Chemers, Martin M., 1984. "The Social, Organizational, and Cultural Context of Effective Leadership," in Barbara Kellerman (ed.), *Leadership, Multidisciplinary Perspectives*. Englewood Cliffs, NJ: Prentice-Hall.

Child, John, 1981. "Culture, Contingency and Capitalism in the Cross-National Study of Organizations," *Research in Organizational Behavior, 3*, 303–356.

Christopher, Robert C., 1983. *The Japanese Mind: The Goliath Explained*. New York: Simon & Schuster.

Clark, Burton R., 1979. "The Japanese System of Higher Education in Comparative Perspective," in William K. Cummings, Iduo Amano, & Kazuyuki Kitamura (eds.), *Changes in the Japanese University, A Comparative Perspective*. New York: Praeger, pp. 217–240.

Clark, Rodney, 1979. *The Japanese Company*. New Haven, CT: Yale University Press.

Coan, Richard W., 1978. "Review of the Myers-Briggs Type Indicator," in Oscar F. Buros (ed.), *The Eighth Mental Measurement Yearbook*. Vol. 1. Highland Park, NJ: The Gryphon Press, pp. 973–975.

Cohen, Allan R. & David L. Bradford, 1989. "Influence Without Authority: The Use of Alliances, Reciprocity, and Exchange to Accomplish Work," *Organizational Dynamics* (Winter).

Cohen, Bernard P., Ronald J. Kruse, & Michael Anbar, 1982. "The Social Structure of Scientific Research Teams," *Pacific Sociological Review, 25*, 2 (April), 205–232.

Cohen, David, Marilye Cohen, & Herbert Cross, 1981. "A Construct Validity Study of the Myers-Briggs Type Indicator," *Educational and Psychological Measurement, 42*, 3 (Autumn), 883–891.

Coles, James S. (ed.), 1984. *Technological Innovation in the '80s*. Englewood Cliffs, NJ: Prentice-Hall/Spectrum.

Comrey, Andrew L., 1983. "An Evaluation of the Myers-Briggs Type Indicator," *Academic Psychology Bulletin, 5*, 1 (March), 115–129.

Conger, Jay A., Rabinda N. Kanungo & Associates (eds.), 1988. *Charismatic Leadership.* San Francisco: Jossey-Bass.

Cooley, Charles, 1909. *Social Organization.* New York: Scribners.

Cooley, Charles, 1983. *Human Nature and the Social Order.* New Brunswick, NJ: Transaction Books.

Cornwell, John M. & William P. Dunlap, 1994. "On the Questionable Soundness of Ipsative Data: A Response to Savilee and Willson," *Journal of Occupational and Organizational Psychology, 67,* Part 2 (June), 89–100.

Coser, Lewis A., 1956. *The Functions of Social Conflict.* Glencoe, IL: The Free Press.

Coser, Lewis A., 1968. "Conflict: III. Social Aspects," in David L. Sills (ed.), *International Encyclopedia of the Social Sciences, 3.* New York: Crowell Collier and Macmillan, pp. 232–236.

Cotton, John L., 1993. "Self-Directed Work Teams," in *Employee Involvement: Methods for Improving Performance and Work Attitudes.* Newbury Park, CA: Sage, ch. 10.

Cotton, John L., D. A. Vollrath, K. L. Froggatt, M. L. Lengnick-Hall, & K. R. Jennings, 1988. "Employee Participation: Diverse Forms and Different Outcomes," *Academy of Management Review, 13,* 8–22.

Cousins, S., 1989. "Culture and Self-perception in Japan and the United States," *Journal of Personality and Social Psychology, 56,* 124–131.

Craig, Albert M., 1970a. "Introduction: Perspectives on Personality in Japanese History," in Albert M. Craig & Donald H. Shively (eds.), *Personality in Japanese History.* Berkeley: University of California Press, pp. 1–28.

Craig, Albert M., 1970b. "Kido Kooin and Ookubo Toshimichi: A Psychohistorical Analysis," in Albert M. Craig & Donald H. Shively (eds.), *Personality in Japanese History.* Berkeley: University of California Press, pp. 264–308.

Cresswell, John W., 1985. "Faculty Research Performance: Lessons from the Sciences and Social Sciences," Report #4, ASHE-ERIC Higher Education Reports, 1985. Washington, DC: Association for the Study of Higher Education.

Cummings, Larry L. & Barry M. Staw (eds.), 1990. *Leadership, Participation and Group Behavior.* Greenwich, CT: JAI Press.

Cummings, Thomas G., 1981. "Designing Effective Work Groups," in Paul C. Nystrom & William H. Starbuck (eds.), *Handbook of Organizational Design,* Vol. 2. New York: Oxford University Press, pp. 250–271.

Cummings, Thomas G. & Sursh Srivastva, 1976. *Management of Work: A Socio-Technical Systems Approach.* Kent, OH: Comparative Administration Research Institute, Kent State University Press.

Cummings, William K., 1980. *Education and Equality in Japan.* Princeton, NJ: Princeton University Press.

Cummings, William K., Amano Iduo, & Kazuyuki Kitamura (eds.), 1979. *Changes in the Japanese University, A Comparative Perspective.* New York: Praeger.

Cutler, Robert S., 1987. "Impressions, Observations and Comments on Science and Technology in Japan." Paper, Department of General Systems Studies, College of Arts and Sciences, The University of Tokyo, Komaba, Meguro-ku, Tokyo, Japan.

Dachler, H. Peter, 1984. "Chapter 5 Commentary: On Refocusing Leadership from a Social Systems Perspective of Management," in James G. Hunt, Dian-Marie Hosking, Chester A. Schriesheim, & Rosemary Stewart (eds.), *Leaders and Man-*

*agers, International Perspectives on Managerial Behavior and Leadership.* New York: Pergamon Press, pp. 115–134.

Dahrendorf, R., 1969. *Class and Class Conflict in Industrial Society.* Stanford, CA: Stanford University Press.

Dansereau, Fred, Jr., George Graen, & William J. Haga, 1983. "A Vertical Dyad Linkage Approach to Leadership Within Formal Organizations: A Longitudinal Investigation of the Role Making Process," in Robert W. Allen & Lyman W. Porter (eds.), *Organizational Influence Processes.* Glenview, IL: Scott, Foresman & Co.

Davis, Nanette J., 1980. *Sociological Constructions of Deviants, Perspectives and Issues in the Field.* Second Edition. Dubuque, Iowa: Wm. C. Brown Company Publishers.

Davison, M. L., 1983. *Multidimensional Scaling.* New York: John Wiley & Sons.

Deal, Terrence E. & Allan A. Kennedy, 1982. *Corporate Cultures: The Rites and Rituals of Corporate Life.* Reading, MA: Addison-Wesley.

DeBono, Edward, 1971. *Lateral Thinking for Management: A Handbook of Creativity.* New York: American Management Association.

Deci, Edward L., 1971. "The Effects of Externally Mediated Rewards and Controls on Intrinsic Motivation," *Journal of Personality and Social Psychology, 18,* 105–115.

Deci, Edward L., 1975. *Intrinsic Motivation.* New York: Plenum.

Deci, Edward L. & Richard M. Ryan, 1982. "Intrinsic Motivation to Teach: Possibilities and Obstacles in Our Colleges and Universities," in J. L. Bess (ed.), *New Directions for Teaching and Learning: Motivating Professors to Teach Effectively,* no. 10 (June).

Deci, Edward L. & Richard M. Ryan, 1985. *Intrinsic Motivation and Self-Determination in Human Behavior.* New York: Plenum Press.

De Mente, Boye De, 1981. *The Japanese Way of Doing Business.* Englewood Cliffs, NJ: Prentice-Hall.

Dermer, Jerry (ed.), 1986. *Competitiveness Through Technology.* Lexington, MA: D.C. Heath.

Derra, Skip, 1989. "Honoring the Stars of Research," *Research & Development, 31,* 8 (August), 49–52.

de Tocqueville, Alexis, 1966. *Democracy in America,* trans. George Lawrence and ed. J. P. Mayer & Max Lerner. New York: Harper & Row, Publishers.

Deutsch, Morton, 1973. *The Resolution of Conflict: Constructive and Destructive Processes.* New Haven, CT: Yale University Press.

Deutsch, Morton, 1980. "Fifty Years of Conflict," in L. Festinger (ed.), *Retrospectives on Social Psychology.* New York: Oxford University Press, pp. 46–77.

Deutsch, Morton, 1987. "A Theoretical Perspective on Conflict and Conflict Resolution," in Dennis J. D. Sandole & Ingrid Sandole-Staroste (eds.), *Conflict Management and Problem Solving: Interpersonal to International Applications.* New York: New York University Press, pp. 38–49.

Deutscher, Irwin, 1968. "Asking Questions Cross-Culturally: Some Problems of Linguistic Comparability," in Howard S. Becker, Blanch Geer, David Riesman, & Robert Weiss (eds.), *Institutions and the Person.* Chicago: Aldine Publishing Company.

De Vos, George A., 1976. "The Interrelationship of Social and Psychological Structures in Transcultural Psychiatry," in W. P. Lebra (ed.), *Culture-Bound Syndromes,*

*Ethnopsychiatry, and Alternative Therapies.* Honolulu: University of Hawaii Press.

De Vos, George A., 1985. "Dimensions of the Self in Japanese Culture," in Anthony J. Marsella, George De Vos, & Francis L. K. Hsu (eds.), *Culture and Self, Asian and Western Perspectives.* New York: Tavistock Publications, pp. 141–184.

De Vos, George A., 1986. "Child Development in Japan and the United States: Prospectives (sic) of Cross-Cultural Comparisons, Development in Japan and the United States," in Harold Stevenson, Hiroshi Azuma, & Kenji Hakuta (eds.), *Child Development and Education in Japan.* New York: W. H. Freeman and Company, pp. 291–298.

Dewey, John, 1929. *The Quest for Certainty: A Study of the Relationship of Knowledge and Action.* New York: Minton, Balch.

Dewey, John, 1962. *Individualism—Old and New.* New York: Capricorn Books.

Diehl, Anders, 1984. "On Japanese Creativity," in E. Eto & K. Katsui (eds.), *R & D Management Systems in Japanese Industry.* Amsterdam, Holland: Elsevier Science Publishers B.V.

Dienesch, Richard M. & Robert C. Liden, 1986. "Leader-Member Exchange Model of Leadership: A Critique and Further Development," *Academy of Management Review, 11,* 3, 618–634.

Dill, David D., 1985. "Theory Versus Practice in the Staffing of R & D Laboratories," *R & D Management, 15,* 3 (July), 227–241.

Dimmock, Hedley G., 1987. *Groups: Leadership and Group Development.* San Diego: University Associates.

Doi, Takeo, 1973. *The Anatomy of Dependence.* Tokyo: Kodansha.

Doi, Takeo, 1986. *The Anatomy of Self.* Tokyo: Kodansha.

Doktor, Robert H., 1990. "Asian and American CEO's: A Comparative Study," *Organizational Dynamics, 18,* 3 (Winter), 46–56.

Donohue, William A., 1985. "Ethnicity and Mediation," in William B. Gudykunst, Lea P. Stewart, & Stella Ting-Toomey (eds.), *Communication, Culture and Organizational Processes.* Beverly Hills, CA: Sage.

Dore, Ronald P., 1973. *British Factory, Japanese Factory; The Origins of Diversity in Industrial Relations.* Berkeley: University of California Press.

Dore, Ronald P., 1982. "Foreword," in Tadashi Fukutake, *The Japanese Social Structure: Its Evolution in the Modern Century,* trans. Ronald P. Dore. Tokyo: University of Tokyo Press.

Dore, Ronald P. (ed.), 1967. *Aspects of Social Change in Modern Japan.* Princeton, NJ: Princeton University Press.

Dorfman, Peter W. & Jon P. Howell, 1988. "Dimensions of National Culture and Effective Leadership Patterns," *Advances in International Comparative Management, 3,* 127–150.

Dossett, Dennis L. & Jeho Lee, 1991. "Cultural Versus Organizational Differences in the Perception of Work Autonomy." Paper presented at the annual meeting of the Academy of Management, Miami Beach.

Drew, David E., 1985. *Strengthening Academic Science.* New York: Praeger.

Driver, Michael, 1984. "Decision Style and Organizational Behavior: Implications for Academia," in J. L. Bess (ed.), *College and University Organization: Insights from the Behavioral Sciences.* New York: New York University Press.

Duke, Benjamin, 1986. *The Japanese School: Lessons for Industrial America.* New York: Praeger.

Dunham, Randall B., Ramon J. Aldag, & Arthur P. Brief, 1977. "Dimensionality of Task Design as Measured by the Job Diagnostic Survey," *Proceedings*, annual meeting of the Academy of Management, Kansas City, pp. 89–93.

Dunnette, Marvin E. (ed.), 1976. *Handbook of Organizational and Industrial Psychology.* Chicago: Rand McNally College Publishing Company.

Durkheim, Emile, 1933. *The Division of Labor in Society*, trans. George Simpson. New York: The Free Press.

Earley, P. Christopher, 1989. "Social Loafing and Collectivism: A Comparison of the United States and the People's Republic of China," *Administrative Science Quarterly, 34,* 4 (December), 565–581.

Earley, P. Christopher, 1993. "East Meets West Meets Mideast: Further Explorations of Collectivistic and Individualistic Work Groups," *Academy of Management Journal, 36,* 2, 319-348.

Ekman, Paul, 1973. "Cross-Cultural Studies of Facial Expression," in Paul Ekman (ed.), *Darwin and Facial Expression: A Century of Research in Review.* New York: Academic Press, pp. 169–222.

Ekman, Paul (ed.), 1982. *Emotion in the Human Face.* New York: Cambridge University Press.

Ekman, Paul & W. V. Friesen, 1969. "The Repertoire of Nonverbal Behavior: Categories, Origins, Usage, and Coding," *Semiotica, 1,* 49–98.

Ekman, Paul & W. V. Friesen, 1971. "Constants Across Cultures in the Face and Emotion," *Journal of Personality and Social Psychology, 17,* 124–129.

Ellul, Jacques, 1964. *The Technological Society*, trans. John Wilkinson. New York: Alfred A. Knopf.

Emery, F. E. & E. L. Trist, 1960. "Socio-technical Systems," in *Management Sciences Models and Techniques*, Vol. 2. London: Pergamon Press.

England, George W. & Anant R. Negandhi, 1979. "National Contexts and Technology as Determinants of Employee's Perceptions," in George W. England, Anant R. Negandhi, & Bernhard Wilpert (eds.), *Organizational Functioning in a Cross-Cultural Perspective.* Kent, OH: Kent State University Press, pp. 175-190.

England, George W. & Raymond Lee, 1974. "The Relationship Between Managerial Values and Managerial Success in the United States, Japan, India, and Australia," *Journal of Applied Psychology, 59,* 4 (August), 411–419.

Epstein, Seymour, 1979. "The Stability of Behavior: I. On Predicting Most of the People Much of the Time," *Journal of Personality and Social Psychology, 37,* 7 (July), 1097–1126.

Epton, S. R., R. L. Payne, & A. W. Pearson (eds.), 1983. *Managing Interdisciplinary Research.* Chichester, England: John Wiley & Sons.

Erez, Miriam & P. Christopher Earley, 1993. *Culture, Self-Identity, and Work.* New York: Oxford University Press.

Eto, Hajime & Konomu Matsui (eds.), 1986. *R & D Management Systems in European Research Centres, A Directory of Organizations in Science, Technology, Agriculture, and Medicine.* Harlow, Essex, England: Burnt Mill.

Etzioni, Amitai, 1961. *A Comparative Analysis of Complex Organizations.* New York: The Free Press.

Fairhurst, Gail, 1993. "The Language of Self-Managing Teams." Paper presented at the annual meeting of the Academy of Management, Atlanta, GA.

Farmer, Richard N., 1984. "Understanding the Ways of Understanding: Cross-Cultural Management Methodology Reviewed," in Richard N. Farmer (ed.), *Advances in International Comparative Management*, Vol. 1.

Farrell, Ronald A. & Victoria L. Swigert (eds.), 1975. *Social Deviance*. Philadelphia: Lippincott.

Fiedler, Fred W. & Joseph E. Garcia, 1987. *New Approaches to Effective Leadership*. New York: John Wiley & Sons.

Fiedler, Fred W., Martin M. Chemers, & Linda Mahar, 1976. *Improving Leadership Effectiveness*. New York: John Wiley & Sons.

Fishbein, Martin & Icek Ajzen, 1975. *Belief, Attitude, Intention, and Behavior: An Introduction to Theory and Research*. Reading, MA: Addison-Wesley Publishing Company.

Fiske, Edward B., 1987a. "Study, Drawing Lessons for U.S., Cites Rigor of Japanese Schooling," *New York Times*, January 4, pp. A1, 10.

Fiske, Edward B., 1987b. "Comparing the U.S. and Japan," *New York Times*, January 6, pp. C1, 8.

Fitzpatrick, Mary Ann & Diane M. Badzinski, 1985. "All in the Family: Interpersonal Communication in Kin Relationships," in Mark L. Knapp & Gerald R. Miller, *Handbook of Interpersonal Communication*. Beverly Hills: Sage Publications, pp. 687–736.

Flynn, David M., 1982. "Japanese Values and Management Processes," in Sang M. Lee & Gary Schwendiman (eds.), *Japanese Management: Cultural and Environmental Considerations*. New York: Praeger, pp. 72–81.

Follett, Mary Parker, 1942. *Dynamic Administration: The Collected Papers of Mary Parker Follett*, ed. Henry C. Metcalf & L. Urwick. New York: Harper & Brothers.

Foster, W. F., 1989. "Toward a Critical Practice of Leadership," in J. Smyth (ed.), *Critical Perspectives on Educational Leadership*. London, England: Falmer, pp. 39–62.

Frame, J. Davidson, 1987. *Managing Projects in Organizations*. San Francisco: Jossey-Bass.

Freidson, Eliot, 1975. *Doctoring Together, A Study of Professional Social Control*. New York: Elsevier.

Freud, Sigmund, 1989. *Group Psychology and the Analysis of the Ego*, translated and edited by James Strachey. New York: W. W. Norton.

Fried, Yitzhak & Gerald R. Ferris, 1987. "The Validity of the Job Characteristics Model: A Review and Meta-Analysis," *Personnel Psychology, 40*, 287–322.

Friedrich, Carl J., 1959. *Community*. New York: Liberal Arts Press.

Friedrich, Carl J., 1972. *Tradition and Authority*. New York: Praeger.

Frost, Ellen L., 1987. *For Richer, For Poorer*. New York: Council on Foreign Relations.

Fukutake, Tadashi, 1981. *Japanese Society Today*. Second Edition. Tokyo: University of Tokyo Press.

Fulton, Oliver & Martin Trow, 1975. "Research Activity in American Higher Education," in Martin Trow (ed.), *Teachers and Students, Aspects of American Higher Education*. New York: McGraw-Hill Book Company.

Fusfield, Herbert I., 1986. *The Technical Enterprise*. Cambridge: Ballinger Publishing Company.

Fusfield, Herbert I. & Carmela S. Haklisch, "Cooperative R & D for Competitors," *Harvard Business Review, 63*, 6 (November-December), 60.

Fusfield, Herbert I., Richard N. Langlois, & Richard R. Nelson, 1991. *The Changing Tide, Federal Support of Civilian Sector R & D*. New York: New York University, Center for Science and Technology Policy.

Gabrenya, William K. R., Jr., Bibb Latane, & Yue-Eng Wang, 1983. "Social Loafing in Cross Cultural Perspective," *Journal of Cross-Cultural Psychology, 14*, 368–384.

Gamson, William, 1968. *Power and Discontent*. Homewood, IL: The Dorsey Press.

Gans, Herbert J., 1988. *Middle American Individualism: The Future of Liberal Democracy*. New York: The Free Press.

Gaston, Jerry, 1973. *Originality and Competition in Science*. Chicago: The University of Chicago Press.

Gaston, Jerry, 1978. *The Reward System in British and American Science*. New York: John Wiley & Sons.

George, Jennifer M., 1991. "Extrinsic and Intrinsic Origins of Perceived Social Loafing in Organizations." Paper presented at the Annual Meeting of the Academy of Management, Miami Beach, August.

Gerstenfeld, Arthur, 1970. *Effective Management of Research and Development*. Reading, MA: Addison-Wesley.

Gerstner, Charlotte R. & David V. Day, 1994. "Cross-Cultural Comparison of Leadership Prototypes," *Leadership Quarterly, 5*, 2, 121–134.

Getzels, Jacob W. & Egon G. Guba, 1957. "Social Behavior and the Administrative Process," *The School Review, 65* (Winter), 423–41.

Ghiselli, Edward E., 1966. *The Validity of Occupational Aptitude Tests*. New York: John Wiley & Sons.

Gibbard, Graham S., 1976. "Individuation, Fusion, and Role Specialization," in Graham S. Gibbard, John J. Hartman, & Richard D. Mann (eds.), *Analysis of Groups*. San Francisco: Jossey-Bass.

Gibbs, Jack P., 1981. *Norms, Deviance, and Social Control, Conceptual Matters*. New York: Elsevier.

Glick, William H., G. Douglas Jenkins, Jr., & Nina Gupta, 1986. "Method Versus Substance: How Strong Are Underlying Relationships Between Job Characteristics and Attitudinal Outcomes?" *Academy of Management Journal, 29*, 3 (September), 441–464.

Goffman, Irving, 1959. *The Presentation of Self in Everyday Life*. Revised and Enlarged Edition. Garden City, NY: Doubleday.

Goffman, Irving, 1963. *Behavior in Public Places*. Glencoe, IL: The Free Press.

Goleman, Daniel, 1990. "The Group and the Self: New Focus on a Cultural Rift," *New York Times*, December 25, pp. 37, 41.

Goodman, Paul S., Elizabeth Ravlin, & Marshall Schminke, 1990. "Understanding Groups in Organizations," in Larry L. Cummings & Barry M. Staw (eds.), *Leadership, Participation and Group Behavior*. Greenwich, CT: JAI Press, pp. 333–385.

Goodman, Paul S., Rukmini Devadas, & Terri L. Griffith Hughson, 1988. "Groups and Productivity: Analyzing the Effectiveness of Self-Managing Teams," in John P. Campbell, Richard J. Campbell & Associates, *Productivity in Organizations*. San Francisco: Jossey-Bass.

Gough, Harrison, G. & Donald G. Woodworth, 1960. "Stylistic Variations Among Professional Research Scientists," *Journal of Psychology, 49*, 87–98.

Gouldner, Alvin, 1954. *Patterns of Industrial Bureaucracy.* Glencoe, IL: The Free Press.

Graen, George & James F. Cashman, 1975. "A Role-Making Model of Leadership in Formal Organizations: A Developmental Approach," in James G. Hunt & Lars L. Larson (eds.), *Leadership Frontiers.* Kent, OH: Comparative Administration Research Institute, Kent State University.

Graen, George & T. A. Scandura, 1987. "Toward a Psychology of Dyadic Organizing," in Larry L. Cummings & Barry M. Staw (eds.), *Research in Organizational Behavior*, Vol. 9. Greenwich, CT: JAI Press, pp. 175–208.

Graen, George, T. A. Scandura, & M. R. Graen, 1986. "A Field Experimental Test of the Moderating Effects of Growth-Need Strength on Productivity," *Journal of Applied Psychology, 71*, 484–491.

Graham, Margaret B. W., 1985. "Industrial Research in the Age of Big Science," in Richard S. Rosenbloom (ed.), *Research on Technological Innovation, Management and Policy*, Vol. 2. Greenwich, CT: JAI Press.

Graubard, Stephen R., 1990. "Showa: The Japan of Hirohito," *Daedalus, 119* (Summer), 3.

Graumann, Carl F., 1986. "Changing Conceptions of Leadership: An Introduction," in Carl F. Graumann & Serge Moscovici (eds.), *Changing Conceptions of Leadership*. New York: Springer-Verlag.

Greenhaigh, Leonard, 1986. "SMR Forum: Managing Conflict," *Sloan Management Review, 27*, 4 (Summer), 45–51.

Greenwald, A. G., 1982. "Ego Task Analysis: An Integration of Research on Ego Involvement and Self-Awareness," in Albert H. Hastorf & Alice M. Isen (eds.), *Cognitive Social Psychology*. New York: Elsevier/North-Holland.

Guillet de Monthoux, Pierre, 1989. "Modernism and the Dominating Firm—on the Managerial Mentality of the Swedish Model." Paper prepared for the Young-Rubicam Seminar, "Convergences et Divergences Culturelles en Europe," Paris, 1989. Stockholm: Department of Business Administration, University of Stockholm.

Hackman, J. Richard, 1976. "Group Influences on Individuals," in Marvin E. Dunnette (ed.), *Handbook of Industrial and Organizational Psychology.* Chicago: Rand McNally College Publishing Company, pp. 1455–1525.

Hackman, J. Richard & Charles G. Morris, 1975. "Group Tasks, Group Interaction Process, and Group Performance Effectiveness: A Review and Proposed Integration," in Leonard Berkowitz (ed.), *Advances in Experimental Social Psychology*, Vol. 8. New York: Academic Press, pp. 45–99.

Hackman, J. Richard & Greg R. Oldham, 1974. "The Job Diagnostic Survey: An Instrument for the Diagnosis of Jobs and the Evaluation of Job Redesign Projects." Technical Report #4, Department of Administrative Sciences, Yale University, May.

Hackman, J. Richard & Greg R. Oldham, 1976. "Motivation Through the Design of Work: Test of a Theory," *Organizational Behavior and Human Performance, 16*, 250–279.

Hackman, J. Richard & Greg R. Oldham, 1980. *Work Redesign.* Reading, MA: Addison-Wesley.

Hackman, J. Richard & Richard E. Walton, 1986. "Leading Groups in Organizations," in Paul S. Goodman and Associates, *Designing Effective Work Groups*. San Francisco: Jossey-Bass Publishers, pp. 72–119.

Hagen, Everett E., 1962. *On the Theory of Social Change*. Homewood, IL: The Dorsey Press.

Hagstrom, Warren O., 1965. *The Scientific Community*. New York: Basic Books.

Haire, Mason, Edwin E. Ghiselli, & Lyman W. Porter, 1963. "Cultural Patterns in the Role of the Manager," *Industrial Relations, 2,* 2 (February).

Hamabata, Matthews Masayuki, 1990. *Crested Kimono. Power and Love in the Japanese Business Family*. Ithaca, NY: Cornell University Press.

Hamilton, V. Lee & Joseph Sanders, 1992. *Everyday Justice, Responsibility and the Individual in Japan and the United States*. New Haven, CT: Yale University Press.

Hara, Reinosuke, 1992. "Management of R & D in Japan," Bulletin #87, Institute of Comparative Culture Business Series, Sophia University, Tokyo.

Hare, A. Paul, 1960. "Elements of Social Interaction," in A. Paul Hare, *Handbook of Small Group Research*. New York: The Free Press, pp. 7–22.

Harman, Harry H., 1976. *Modern Factor Analysis*. Third Edition. Chicago: University of Chicago Press.

Harman, Lesley D., 1985. "Acceptable Deviance in Social Control: The Case of Fashion and Slang," *Deviant Behavior, 6,* 1–15.

Harris, D. B., 1982. "How National Cultures Shape Management Styles," *Management Review* (July), 58–61.

Harris, M., 1981. *Cultural Materialism: The Struggle for a Science of Culture*. New York: Random House.

Harvard College, 1980. "Note on Japanese Management and Employment Systems," Boston: Harvard Business School.

Hasegawa, Keitaro, 1986. *Japanese-Style Management*. Tokyo: Kodansha International, Ltd.

Hattori, I., 1978. "A Proposition on Efficient Decision-Making in the Japanese Corporation," *Columbia Journal of World Business* (Summer), 7–15.

Hawkins, Richard & Gary Tiedeman, 1975. *The Creation of Deviance*. Columbus: Charles E. Merrill Publishing Company.

Hayashi, Shuji, 1988. *Culture and Management in Japan*. Tokyo: University of Tokyo Press.

Hayashi, Takeshi, 1990. *The Japanese Experience in Technology: From Transfer to Self-Reliance*. Tokyo: United Nations University Press.

Hayes, Robert H. & Steven C. Wheelwright, 1979. "Link Manufacturing Process and Product Life Cycles," *Harvard Business Review* (January-February).

Hechter, Michael, 1987. *Principles of Group Solidarity*. Berkeley: University of California Press.

Heelas, Paul & Andrew Lock (eds.), 1981. *Indigenous Psychologies: The Anthropology of the Self*. London: Academic Press.

Heine, Patricke Johns, 1963. "The Problem of Personality in Sociological Theory," in Joseph M. Wepman & Ralph W. Heine (eds.), *Concepts of Personality*. Chicago: Aldine Publishing Company, pp. 385–407.

Hellriegel, Don, John W. Slocum, & Richard W. Woodman, 1989. *Organizational Behavior*. Fifth Edition. St. Paul: West Publishing Company.

Hennessey, B., 1982. "Effects of Reward and Task Label on Children's Creativity in Three Domains." Unpublished manuscript, Brandeis University.

Henwood, Felicity, 1984. *Science, Technology, and Innovation: A Research Bibliography*. New York: St. Martin's Press.

Hersey, Paul & Kenneth H. Blanchard, 1969. "Life Cycle Theory of Leadership," *Training and Development Journal, 23*, 26-34.

Hersey, Paul & Kenneth H. Blanchard, 1988. *Management of Organizational Behavior: Utilizing Human Resources*. Fifth Edition. Englewood Cliffs, NJ: Prentice-Hall.

Herzberg, Frederick, 1966. *Work and the Nature of Man*. Cleveland: World Publishing Company.

Hideki, Yukawa, 1987. "Modern Trend of Western Civilization and Cultural Peculiarities in Japan," in Charles A. Moore (ed.), *The Japanese Mind, Essentials of Japanese Philosophy and Culture*. Honolulu: University of Hawaii Press, pp. 52–65.

Hill, Melvyn A., 1984. "The Law of the Father, Leadership and Symbolic Authority in Psychoanalysis," in Barbara Kellerman (ed.), *Leadership, Multidisciplinary Perspectives*. Englewood Cliffs, NJ: Prentice-Hall, pp. 23–38.

Himes, Joseph S., 1980. *Conflict and Conflict Management*. Athens: The University of Georgia Press.

Hirsch, Sandra & Jean Kummerow, 1989. *Lifetypes*. New York: Warner Books.

Hirschman, A. O., 1970. *Exit, Voice, and Loyalty: Responses to Decline in Firms, Organizations, and States*. Cambridge, MA: Harvard University Press.

Hochschild, Arlie R., 1983. *The Managed Heart*. Berkeley: University of California Press.

Hoffman, L. R., 1959. "Homogeneity of Member Personality and Its Effect on Group Problem-Solving," *Journal of Abnormal and Social Psychology, 58*, 27–32.

Hoffman, L. R. & N.R.F. Maier, 1961. "Quality and Acceptance of Problem Solutions by Members of Homogeneous and Heterogeneous Groups," *Journal of Abnormal and Social Psychology, 62*, 401–407.

Hofstede, Geert, 1976. "Nationality and Espoused Values of Managers," *Journal of Applied Psychology, 61*, 2 (April), 148–155.

Hofstede, Geert, 1980a. *Culture's Consequences: International Differences in Work-Related Values*. Beverly Hills, CA: Sage Publications.

Hofstede, Geert, 1980b. "Motivation, Leadership and Organization: Do American Theories Apply Abroad?" *Organizational Dynamics* (Summer), 42–63.

Hofstede, Geert, 1983. "The Cultural Relativity of Organizational Practice and Theories," *Journal of International Business Studies, 14*, 2, 75–89.

Hofstede, Geert, 1984. "The Cultural Relativity of the Quality of Life Concept," *Academy of Management Review, 9*, 3, 389–398.

Hollander, E. P., 1958. "Conformity, Status, and Idiosyncrasy Credit," *Psychological Review, 65*, 117–127.

Hollander, E. P., 1979. "Leadership and Social Exchange Processes," in K. Gergen, M. S. Greenberg, & R. H. Willis (eds.), *Social Exchange: Advances in Theory and Research*. New York: Winston-Wiley, pp. 103–118.

Hollander, E. P. & J. W. Julian, 1970. "Studies in Leader Legitmacy, Influence and Innovation," in L. Berkowitz (ed.), *Advances in Experimental Social Psychology, 5*. New York: Academic Press, pp. 34–69.

Holloway, Susan D., 1988. "Concepts of Ability and Effort in Japan and the United States," *Review of Educational Research, 58*, 3 (Fall), 327–345.

Homans, George C., 1950. *The Human Group*. New York: Harcourt Brace & Company.

Horio, Teruhisa, 1988. *Educational Thought and Ideology in Modern Japan: State Authority and Intellectual Freedom,* trans. Steven Platzer. Tokyo: University of Tokyo Press.

House, Robert J., 1971. ''A Path Goal Theory of Leader Effectiveness,'' *Administrative Science Quarterly, 16*, 321–338.

House, Robert J. & Jitendra V. Singh, 1987. ''Organizational Behavior: Some New Directions for I/O Psychology,'' *Annual Review of Psychology, 38*, 669–718.

House, Robert J. & L. A. Wigdor, 1967. ''Herzberg's Dual-Factor Theory of Job Satisfaction and Motivation: A Review of the Evidence and a Criticism,'' *Personnel Psychology, 20*, 369–390.

House, Robert J. & Mary L. Baetz, 1990. ''Leadership: Some Empirical Generalizations and New Research Directions,'' in Larry L. Cummings & Barry M. Staw (eds.), *Leadership, Participation and Group Behavior.* Greenwich, CT: JAI Press, pp. 1–83.

House, Robert J., Allen C. Filley, & Steven Kerr, 1971. ''Relation of Leader Consideration and Initiating Structure to R & D Subordinates' Satisfaction,'' *Administrative Science Quarterly, 16*, 1 (March), 19–30.

House, Robert J., William D. Spangler, & James Woycke, 1991. ''Personality and Charisma in the U.S. Presidency: A Psychological Theory of Leader Effectiveness,'' *Administrative Science Quarterly, 36*, 364–396.

Howat, Gary & Manuel London, 1980. ''Attributions of Conflict Management Strategies in Supervisor-Subordinate Dyads,'' *Journal of Applied Psychology, 65*, 2 (April), 172–175.

Hoy, Frank & Don Hellriegel, 1982. ''The Kilmann & Herden Model of Organizational Effectiveness Criteria for Small Business Managers,'' *Academy of Management Journal, 25*, 2, 308–322.

Hoy, Wayne H. & Cecil G. Miskel, 1991. *Educational Administration, Theory, Research, and Practice*. Fourth Edition. New York: McGraw-Hill.

Hsu, Francis L. K. 1965. ''The Effect of Dominant Kinship Relationships on Kin and Non-Kin Behavior: A Hypothesis,'' *American Anthropologist, 67*, 3, 638–661.

Hsu, Francis L. K., 1975. *Iemoto: The Heart of Japan*. New York: John Wiley & Sons.

Hsu, Francis L. K., 1985. ''The Self in Cross-Cultural Perspective,'' in Anthony J. Marsella, George De Vos & Francis L. K. Hsu (eds.), *Culture and Self, Asian and Western Perspectives*. New York: Tavistock Publications, pp. 24–55.

Hui, C. Harry & Harry C. Triandis, 1986. ''Individualism-Collectivism: A Study of Cross-Cultural Researchers,'' *Journal of Cross-Cultural Psychology, 17*, 2 (June), 225–248.

Hui, C. Harry & Harry C. Triandis, 1991. ''Cultural Differences in Reward Allocation: Is Collectivism the Explanation?'' *British Journal of Social Psychology, 30*, 2 (June), 145–157.

Hunt, James G., 1984. ''Organizational Leadership, The Contingency Paradigm and its Challenges,'' in Barbara Kellerman (ed.), *Leadership, Multidisciplinary Perspectives*. Englewood Cliffs, NJ: Prentice-Hall, pp. 113–138.

Hunt, James G., 1991. *Leadership, A New Synthesis*. Newbury Park, CA: Sage Publications.

Hunt, James G., B. Rajaram Baliga, H. Peter Dahler, & Chester A. Schriesheim (eds.), 1988. *Emerging Leadership Vistas*. Lexington, MA: Lexington Books.

Hunt, James G., Dian-Marle Hosking, Chester A. Schriesheim, & Rosemary Stewart (eds.), 1984. *Leaders and Managers, International Perspectives on Managerial Behavior and Leadership.* New York: Pergamon Press.

Hunt, Sonja M., 1984. "The Role of Leadership in the Construction of Reality," in Barbara Kellerman (ed.), *Leadership, Multidisciplinary Perspectives.* Englewood Cliffs, NJ: Prentice-Hall, pp. 157–178.

Huszczo, G. E., 1990. "Training for Team Building," *Training and Development Journal* (February), 37–43.

Idaszak, Jacqueline R. & Fritz Drasgow, 1987. "A Revision of the Job Design Survey: Elimination of a Measurement Artifact," *Journal of Applied Psychology, 72,* 10, 69–74.

Idaszak, Jacqueline R., William P. Bottom, & Fritz Drasgow, n.d. "A Test of the Measurement Equivalence of the Revised Job Diagnostic Survey: Past Problems and Current Solutions." Unpublished paper, Department of Psychology, University of Illinois, Urbana-Champaign.

Ilgen, Daniel R. & John R. Hollenbeck, 1991. "The Structure of Work: Job Design and Roles," in Marvin D. Dunnette & Leaetta M. Hough (eds.), *Handbook of Industrial and Organizational Psychology.* Second Edition. Vol. 2. Palo Alto, CA: Consulting Psychologists Press, pp. 165–207.

Industrial Research Institute, 1986. *Trip Report, I.R.I. Study Mission to Japan.* New York: Industrial Research Institute.

Irvine, John, 1984. *Foresight in Science, Picking the Winners.* London: Frances Pinter.

Irvine, John, 1988. *Evaluating Applied Research: Lessons from Japan.* London: Pinter Publishers.

Isaksen, S. G. (ed.), 1988. *Frontiers of Creativity Research: Beyond the Basics.* Buffalo, NY: Bearly.

Ishide, Takeshi, 1984. "Conflict and Its Accommodation: *Omote-Ura* and *Uchi-Soto* Relations," in Ellis S. Krauss, Thomas Rohlen, & Patricia Steinhoff, *Conflict in Japan.* Honolulu: University of Hawaii Press.

Jackson, D. J. & D. F. Alwin, 1980. "The Factor Analysis of Ipsative Measures," *Sociological Methods and Research, 9,* 218–238.

Jacobs, David, 1974. "Dependency and Vulnerability: An Exchange Approach to the Control of Organizations," *Administrative Science Quarterly,* 45–59.

Jain, R. K. & H. C. Triandis, 1990. *Management of Research and Development Organizations, Managing the Unmanageable.* New York: John Wiley & Sons.

James, William, 1975. *Pragmatism.* Cambridge, MA: Harvard University Press.

Janis, Irving L., 1972. *Victims of Groupthink.* Boston: Houghton Mifflin.

Japan Times, 1985. *Top 2,000 Japanese Companies, 1985.* Tokyo: The Japan Times, Ltd.

Japanese Association of Corporate Executives (Kaizai Doyukai), 1988. "1987 White Paper on Business Corporations, A Strategic Personnel System Based on Individuality," cited in *Japan Times,* February 2.

Japanese Working Group on the Innovation Cycle, 1986. "The Innovation Spiral: A New Look at Recent Technological Advances," paper presented to the 2nd U.S.–Japan Conference on High Technology and the International Environment, November 9–11, Kyoto, Japan.

Jelinek, Mariann & Claudia Bird Schoonhoven, 1990. *The Innovation Marathon: Lessons from High Technology Firms.* Oxford, England: B. Blackwell.

Johnson, Frank A., 1993. *Dependency and Japanese Socialization: Psychoanalytic and*

*Anthropological Investigations into "Amae."* New York: New York University Press.

Johnson, Frank A., Anthony J. Marsella, & Colleen L. Johnson, 1974. "Social and Psychological Aspects of Verbal Behavior in Japanese-Americans," *American Journal of Psychiatry, 131*, 5 (May), 580–583.

Johnson, Howard W., Chairman, Panel on Advanced Technology Competition and the Industrialized Allies, 1983. *International Competition in Advanced Technology, Decisions for America.* Washington, DC: National Academy Press.

Johnston, Wesley J. & Thomas V. Bonoma, 1979. "Leaders and Followers," in Gerald Zaltman (ed.), *Management Principles for Non-Profit Agencies and Organizations.* New York: AMACOM, pp. 38–70.

Jones, Gareth R., 1984. "Task Visibility, Free Riding, and Shirking: Explaining the Effect of Structure and Technology on Employee Behavior," *Academy of Management Review, 9*, 4, 684–695.

Jones, Lyle V., Gardner Lindzey & Porter E. Coggeshall, 1982. *An Assessment of Research Doctorate Programs in the United States.* Washington, DC: National Academy Press, 1982.

Jung, C. G., 1923. *Psychological Types or the Psychology of Individuation*, trans. H. Godwin Baynes. London: Routledge & Kegan Paul, Ltd.

Kagano, Tadao, Ikujiro Nonaka, Kiyonori Sakakibara, & Akihiro Okumura, 1983–84. "Strategic Adaptation to Environment: Japanese and U.S. Firms Compared," *Japanese Economic Studies, 12*, 2 (Winter), 33–80.

Kahn, Herman & Thomas Pepper, 1980. *The Japanese Challenge.* New York: William Morrow and Company.

Kanabayashi, Masayoshi, 1988. "Bucking Tradition, In Japan, Employees Are Switching Firms for Better Work, Pay," *Wall Street Journal, CCXII*, 71 (October 11), pp. 1, 19.

Kanfer, Ruth, 1990. "Motivation Theory and Industrial and Organizational Psychology," in Marvin E. Dunnette & Leaetta M. Hough (eds.), *Handbook of Industrial and Organizational Psychology.* Second Edition. Vol. 1. Palo Alto, CA: Consulting Psychologists Press, pp. 75–170.

Kanter, Rosabeth Moss, 1983. *The Change Masters.* New York: Simon & Schuster.

Kanter, Rosabeth Moss, 1988. "When a Thousand Flowers Bloom: Structural, Collective, and Social Conditions for Innovation in Organization," in Barry M. Staw & Larry L. Cummings (eds.), *Research in Organizational Behavior, 10.* Greenwich, CT: JAI Press, pp. 169–211.

Katovich, Michael A., 1987. "Identity, Time, and Situated Activity: An Interactionist Analysis of Dyadic Transactions," *Symbolic Interaction, 10*, 2, 187–208.

Katsuto, Uchihashi, 1987. "Toward Methodology Innovation in Industry," *Japan Quarterly, XXXIV*, 1 (January-March), 2–7.

Katz, Daniel & Robert L. Kahn, 1978. *The Social Psychology of Organizations.* Second Edition. New York: John Wiley & Sons.

Katz, Ralph (ed.), 1988. *Managing Professionals in Innovative Organizations.* Cambridge, MA: Ballinger Publishing Company.

Katzell, Raymond A. & Donna E. Thompson, 1990. "An Integrative Model of Work Attitudes, Motivation, and Performance," *Human Performance, 3*, 2, 63–85.

Kawai, Kazuo, 1967. *Japan's American Interlude.* Chicago: University of Chicago Press.

Keller, Robert, 1992. "Transformational Leadership and the Performance of Research and Development Project Groups," *Journal of Management, 18*, 3, 489–501.

Kellerman, Barbara (ed.), 1984. *Leadership: Multidisciplinary Perspectives.* Englewood Cliffs, NJ: Prentice-Hall.

Kelly, H. H. & W. Thibaut, 1969. "Group Problem Solving," in G. Lindsey & E. Aronson (eds.), *The Handbook of Social Psychology.* Second Edition. Vol. 4. Reading, MA: Addison-Wesley.

Kenrick, Douglas T. & David C. Funder, 1988. "Profiting from Controversy, Lessons from the Person-Situation Debate," *American Psychologist, 43*, 1 (January), 23–34.

Kenrick, Douglas T. & D. O. Stringfield, 1980. "Personality Traits and the Eye of the Beholder: Crossing Some Traditional Philosophic Boundaries in the Search for Consistency in All of the People," *Psychological Review, 87*, 88–104.

Kerr, Steven & J. M. Jermier, 1978. "Substitutes for Leadership: Their Meaning and Measurement," *Organizational Behavior and Human Performance, 22*, 375–403.

Kets de Vries, Manfred F. R., 1984. *The Neurotic Organization.* San Francisco: Jossey-Bass.

Keys, J. Bernard & Thomas R. Miller, 1984. "The Japanese Management Theory Jungle," *Academy of Management Review, 9*, 2, 342–353.

Kida, Hiroshi, 1986. "Japan's Science Policy." Unpublished paper, Tokyo, National Institute for Educational Research, September 2.

Kidder, Tracy, 1981. *The Soul of a New Machine.* Boston: Little, Brown.

Kikuchi, Seishi, 1951. "Scientific Research," in Hugh Borton (ed.), *Japan.* Ithaca, NY: Cornell University Press.

Kilmann, Ralph H., 1977. *Social Systems Design, Normative Theory and the MAPS Design Technology.* New York: North-Holland.

Kilmann, Ralph H. & Kenneth W. Thomas, 1975. "Interpersonal Conflict-Handling Behavior as a Reflection of Jungian Personality Dimensions," *Psychological Reports, 37*, 3 (December), Part I, 971–980.

Kilmann, Ralph H. & Kenneth W. Thomas, 1977. "Developing a Forced-Choice Measure of Conflict-Handling Behavior: The 'Mode' Instrument," *Educational and Psychological Measurement, 37*, 309–325.

Kilmann, Ralph H. & R. P. Herden, 1976. "Toward a Systematic Methodology for Evaluating the Impact of Interventions on Organizational Effectiveness," *Academy of Management Review, 1*, 3, 87–98.

Kimura, B., 1973. *Hito to Hito no Aida* (In-Between Persons). Tokyo: Baifukan.

King, Nigel, 1990. "Innovation at Work: The Research Literature," in Michael A. West and James L. Farr, *Innovation and Creativity at Work, Psychological and Organizational Strategies.* New York: John Wiley & Sons.

King, Nigel & Neil Anderson, 1990. "Innovation in Working Groups," in Michael A. West and James L. Farr (eds.), *Innovation and Creativity at Work, Psychological and Organizational Strategies.* New York: John Wiley & Sons, pp. 81–100.

Kinzley, W. Dean, 1991. *Industrial Harmony in Modern Japan, The Invention of a Tradition.* London: Routledge.

Kipnis, D., S. M. Schmidt, & I. Wilkinson, 1980. "Interorganizational Influence Tactics: Explorations in Getting One's Way," *Journal of Applied Psychology, 65*, 440–452.

Kitaoji, Hisonabu, 1971. "Structure of the Japanese Family," *American Anthropologist, 73*, 5 (October), 1036–1057.

Kitsuse, John I. & Anne Murase, 1987. "Reform of Education System, Who Wants It?" *The Japan Times* (February 15), pp. 6–7.

Klett, C. J. & D. W. Yaukey, 1959. "A Cross-Cultural Comparison of Social Desirability," *Journal of Social Psychology, 49,* 19–26.

Kline, Stephen J., 1985. "Innovation Is Not a Linear Process," *Research Management* (July/August).

Knoke, David, 1990. *Organizing for Collective Action, The Political Economies of Associations.* New York: Aldine de Gruyter.

Knoke, David & Christine Wright-Isak, 1982. "Individual Motives and Organizational Incentive Systems," *Research in the Sociology of Organizations, 1,* 209–254.

Knorr, K. D., R. Mittermeir, G. Aichholzer, & G. Waller, 1979. "Leadership and Group Performance: A Positive Relationship in Academic Research Units," in F. M. Andrews (ed.), *Scientific Productivity.* Cambridge: Cambridge University Press, pp. 95–117.

Knowles, Henry P. & Borje O. Saxberg, 1971. *Personality and Leadership Behavior.* Reading, MA: Addison-Wesley.

Kobayashi, Victor N., 1990. "Ecological Perspectives on *Kyooyoo* and Esthetic Quality: Japan and America," *Senri Ethnological Studies, 28,* 83–89.

Kojima, Hideo, 1984. "A Significant Stride Toward the Comparative Study of Control," *American Psychologist, 9* (September), 972–973.

Kolb, Deborah M. & Linda L. Putnam, 1992. "The Multiple Faces of Conflict in Organizations," *Journal of Organizational Behavior, 13,* 3 (May), 311–324.

Kondo, Dorinne K., 1990. *Crafting Selves. Power, Gender, and Discourses of Identity in a Japanese Workplace.* Chicago: University of Chicago Press.

Kono, Toyohiro, 1984. *Strategy and Structure of Japanese Enterprises.* Armonk, NY: M. E. Sharpe.

Korman, A. K., 1966. " 'Consideration,' 'Initiation of Structure,' and Organizational Criteria," *Personnel Psychology, 18,* 349–360.

Kornhauser, W., 1962. *Scientists in Industry: Conflict and Accommodation.* Berkeley: University of California Press.

Kotter, John P., 1990. *A Force for Change, How Leadership Differs from Management.* New York: The Free Press.

Krantz, James, 1989. "The Managerial Couple: Superior-Subordinate Relationships as a Unit of Analysis," *Human Resource Management, 28,* 2 (Summer), 161–175.

Krauss, Ellis S., Thomas Rohlen, & Patricia Steinhoff, 1984. *Conflict in Japan.* Honolulu: University of Hawaii Press.

Kraut, Allen I., 1975. "Some Recent Advances in Cross-National Management Research," *Academy of Management Journal, 18,* 3 (September), 538–549.

Kruglanski, A. W., 1975. "The Endogenous-Exogenous Partition in Attribution Theory," *Psychological Review, 82,* 387-406.

Kubiak, W. David, 1988a. "E Pluribus Yamoto: The Culture of Corporate Beings," *Kyoto Journal, 6* (Spring), 13.

Kubiak, W. David, 1988b. "The Japanese Art of Mindbinding," *Kyoto Journal,* 7 (Summer), 42–47.

Kudoh, Tsutomu & David Matsumoto, 1985. "Cross-Cultural Examination of the Semantic Dimensions of Body Postures," *Journal of Personality and Social Psychology, 48,* 6, 1440–1446.

Kumagai, Fumie, 1981. "Filial Violence: A Peculiar Parent-Child Relationship in the

Japanese Family Today," *Journal of Comparative Family Studies, 12*, 3 (Summer), 337–349.

Lambright, W. Henry & Albert H. Teich, 1981. "The Organizational Context of Scientific Research," in Paul C. Nystrom & William H. Starbuck (eds.), *Handbook of Organizational Design*. Vol. 2. Oxford, England: Oxford University Press.

Latane, Bibb, 1986. "Responsibility and Effort in Organizations," in Paul S. Goodman (ed.), *Designing Effective Work Groups*. San Francisco: Jossey-Bass.

Latane, Bibb, K. D. Williams, & Stephen Harkins, 1979. "Many Hands Make Light Work: The Causes and Consequences of Social Loafing," *Journal of Personality and Social Psychology, 37*, 822–832.

Lawler, Edward E. III, 1973. *Motivation in Work Organizations*. Monterey, CA: Brooks/Cole Publishing Company.

Lawler, Edward E. III, 1986. *High Involvement Management*. San Francisco: Jossey-Bass.

Lawless, David J., 1983. "Organizational Structure and Basic Units in Higher Education Institutions," *International Journal of Institutional Management in Higher Education, 7*, 2 (July), 137–147.

Lawrence, Paul R. & Jay W. Lorsch, 1967. "Differentiation and Integration in Complex Organizations," *Administrative Science Quarterly, 12* (June), 1–47.

Lebra, Takie Sugiyama, 1976. *Japanese Patterns of Behavior*. Honolulu: University of Hawaii Press.

Lebra, Takie Sugiyama, 1984. *Japanese Women: Constraint and Fulfillment*. Honolulu: University of Hawaii Press.

Lebra, Takie Sugiyama, 1989. "Nonconfrontational Strategies for Management of Interpersonal Conflicts," in Ellis Krauss, Thomas P. Rohlen, & Patricia Steinhoff (eds.), *Conflict in Japan*. Honolulu: University of Hawaii Press, pp. 41–60.

Lebra, Takie Sugiyama & William P. Lebra (eds.), 1986. *Japanese Culture and Behavior: Selected Readings*. Revised Edition. Honolulu: University of Hawaii Press.

Lee, Sand M. & Gary Schwendiman (eds.), 1982. *Japanese Management: Cultural and Environmental Considerations*. New York: Praeger.

Lee, T. H., J. C. Fisher, & T. S. Yau, 1986. "Is Your R and D on Track?" *Harvard Business Review 84*, 1, 34ff.

Lepper, M. R., D. Greene, & R. E. Nisbett, 1973. "Undermining Children's Intrinsic Interests with Extrinsic Rewards: A Test of the 'Overjustification' Hypothesis," *Journal of Personality and Social Psychology, 28*, 129–137.

Lewin, Kurt, Ronald Lippitt, & Robert K. White, 1939. "Patterns of Aggressive Behavior in Experimentally Produced Social Climates," *Journal of Social Psychology, 10*, 271-301.

Lewis, Catherine, 1986. "Children's Social Development in Japan: Research Directions," in Harold Stevenson, Hiroshi Azuma, & Kenji Hakuta (eds.), *Child Development and Education in Japan*. New York: W. H. Freeman & Company, pp. 186–200.

Lewis, Darrell R. & W. W. Becker, Jr. (eds.), 1979. *Academic Rewards in Higher Education*. Cambridge, MA: Ballinger Publishing Co.

Likert, Rensis, 1961. *New Patterns of Management*. New York: McGraw-Hill Book Company.

Likert, Rensis, 1967. *The Human Organizations*. New York: McGraw-Hill Book Company.

Lincoln, James R. & Arne L. Kalleberg, 1985. "Work Organization and Commitment," *American Sociological Review*, 50, 6 (December), 738–760.

Linowes, Richard G., 1993. "The Japanese Manager's Traumatic Entry into the United States: Understanding the American-Japanese Cultural Divide," *Academy of Management Executive*, 7, 4, 21–40.

Little, Blair, 1984. "Significant Issues for the Future of Product Innovation," *Journal of Innovative Product Management*, 1, 1 (January), 56–66.

Locke, Edwin A. & Gary P. Latham, 1990. *A Theory of Goal Setting and Task Performance*. Englewood Cliffs, NJ: Prentice-Hall.

Lohr, Steve, 1984. "The Japanese Challenge, Can They Achieve Technological Supremacy?" *The New York Times Magazine*, July 8, p. 18.

London, Manuel & Gary Howat, 1978. "The Relationship Between Employee Commitment and Conflict Resolution Behavior," *Journal of Vocational Behavior*, 13, 1 (August), 1–14.

Luthans, Fred, Harriette S. McCaul, & Nancy G. Dodd, 1985. "Organizational Commitment: A Comparison of American, Japanese, and Korean Employees," *Academy of Management Journal*, 28, 1, 213–219.

McCall, Morgan W., Jr. & Michael M. Lombardo (eds.), 1978. *Leadership, Where Else Can We Go?* Durham: Duke University Press.

McCaulley, Mary H., 1981. *Jung's Theory of Psychological Types and the Myers-Briggs Type Indicator*. Gainesville, FL: Center for the Application of Psychological Type.

MacDuffie, John Paul, 1988. "The Japanese Auto Transplants: Challenges to Conventional Wisdom," *ILR Report*, 26, 1 (Fall), 12–18.

McCrae, Robert R. & Paul T. Costa, Jr., 1984. "Personality is Transcontextual: A Reply to Veroff," *Personality and Social Psychology Bulletin*, 10, 2 (June), 175–179.

McGown, Valerie, 1980. "Paternalism: A Definition," *Social Analysis*, 5/6 (December), 102–124.

McGregor, Douglas, 1960. *The Human Side of Enterprise*. New York: McGraw-Hill Book Company.

McKie, J. W., 1974. *Social Responsibility in the Business Predicament*. Washington, DC: Brookings.

McLuhan, Marshall, 1964. *Understanding Media: The Extensions of Man*. New York: McGraw-Hill.

McMillan, Charles J., 1985. *The Japanese Industrial System*. Second Edition. New York: Walter de Gruyter.

McWilliams, Wilson C., 1973. *The Idea of Fraternity in America*. Berkeley: University of California Press.

Mainichi Weekly, 1986. "Japanese Sports Training Questioned," *Mainichi Weekly* (October 4), no. 749.

Malraux, Andre, 1926. *La Tentation de L'Occident*. Paris: B. Grasset.

Mann, Leon, 1980. "Cross-Cultural Studies of Small Groups," in Harry C. Triandis & Richard W. Brislin, *Social Psychology, Handbook of Cross-Cultural Psychology*. Vol. 5. Boston: Allyn and Bacon, pp. 155–209.

Mann, Richard D., 1959. "A Review of the Relationships Between Personality and Performance in Small Groups," *Psychological Bulletin*, 56, 241–270.

Manz, Charles C. & Henry P. Sims, Jr., 1987. "Leading Workers to Lead Themselves:

The External Leadership of Self-Managing Work Teams,'' *Administrative Science Quarterly, 32* (March), 106–128.

March, James G. & Herbert Simon, 1958. *Organizations*. New York: John Wiley & Sons.

March, James G. & Zur Shapira, 1987. ''Managerial Perspectives on Risk and Risk Taking,'' *Management Science, 33*, 11 (November), 1404–1418.

Marcson, Simon, 1960. *The Scientist in American Industry*. New York: Harper & Brothers.

Marquis, Donald G., 1969. ''The Anatomy of Successful Innovations,'' *Innovation, 7* (November), 28–37.

Marsland, Stephen E., 1980. ''Note on Japanese Management and Employment Systems,'' Harvard Business School Case Note 481–009, Harvard College, Cambridge, MA.

Martin, Ben R. & John Irvine, 1989. *Research Foresight, Priority-Setting in Science*. London: Pinter Publishers.

Maruo, Naomi, 1982. ''The Japanese Model of Labour-Management Relations and Worker's Participation,'' in Veljko Rus, Akihiro Ishikawa, & Thomas Woodhouse (eds.), *Employment and Participation, Industrial Democracy in Crisis*. Tokyo: Chuo University Press, pp. 135–163.

Maruyama, Magorah, Ross E. Mouer, & Yoshio Sugimoto, 1983. ''Theories of Japanese Culture,'' *Current Anthropology, 24*, 5 (December), 658–659.

Masatsugu, Mitsuyuki, 1982. *The Modern Samurai Society*. New York: AMACOM.

Matsumoto, David, 1989. ''Cultural Influences on the Perception of Emotion,'' *Journal of Cross-Cultural Psychology, 20*, 1 (March), 92–105.

Matsushita, Konosuke, 1975. *Thoughts on Man*. Tokyo: PHP Institute International. (Originally published in Japanese as *Ningen o Kangaeru*)

Maynard, Senko Kumiya, 1989. *Japanese Conversation: Self-contextualization Through Structure and Interactional Management*. Vol. 35 in the Series, Advances in Discourse Processes, Roy O. Freedle (ed.). Norwood, NJ: Ablex Publishing Corporation.

Mazur, Allan, 1985. ''A Biosocial Model of Status in Face-to-Face Primate Groups,'' *Social Forces, 64*, 377–402.

Mead, George Herbert, 1934. *Mind, Self and Society*, ed. C. W. Morris. Chicago: University of Chicago Press.

Meindl, James R., 1993. ''Reinventing Leadership: A Radical, Social Psychological Approach,'' in J. Keith Murnighan (ed.), *Social Psychology in Organizations, Advances in Theory and Research*. Englewood Cliffs, NJ: Prentice-Hall, pp. 80–117.

Merton, Robert K., 1957. *Social Theory and Social Structure*. Revised Edition. Glencoe, IL: The Free Press.

Miller, Danny, 1986. ''Chief Executive Personality (MBTI) and Corporate Strategy in Small Firms,'' *Management Science, 32*, 1389–1409.

Miller, Donald B., 1986. *Managing Professionals in Research and Development*. San Francisco: Jossey-Bass.

Miller, Lynn E., & Joseph E. Grush, 1988. ''Improving Predictions in Expectancy Theory Research: Effects of Personality, Expectancies, and Norms,'' *Academy of Management Journal, 31*, 1, 107–122.

Mintzberg, Henry, 1973. *The Nature of Managerial Work*. New York: Harper & Row, Publishers.

Mintzberg, Henry, 1983a. *Power In and Around Organizations*. Englewood Cliffs, NJ: Prentice-Hall.

Mintzberg, Henry, 1983b. *Structure in Fives. Designing Effective Organizations*. Englewood Cliffs, NJ: Prentice-Hall.

Mischel, W., 1983. ''Alternatives in the Pursuit of the Predictability and Consistency of Persons: Stable Data That Yield Unstable Interpretations,'' *Journal of Personality*, *51*, 578–604.

Misumi, Jyuji, 1985. *The Behavioral Science of Leadership*. Ann Arbor: The University of Michigan Press.

Misumi, Jyugi & Mark F. Peterson, 1985. ''The Performance-Maintenance (PM) Theory of Leadership: Review of a Japanese Research Program,'' *Administrative Science Quarterly*, *30*, 2 (June), 198–223.

Mitroff, Ian I., 1983. *Stakeholders of the Organizational Mind*. San Francisco: Jossey-Bass.

Mitroff, Ian I. & Ralph H. Kilmann, 1975. ''Stories Managers Tell: A New Tool for Organizational Problem Solving,'' *Management Review*, *64*, 7, 18–28.

Moeran, Brian, 1984a. ''Individual, Group and *Seishin*: Japan's Internal Cultural Debate,'' *Man (N.S.)*, *19*, 2 (June), 252–266.

Moeran, Brian, 1984b. *Lost Innocence, Folk Craft Potters of Onta, Japan*. Berkeley: University of California Press.

Mohr, L. B., 1969. ''Determinants of Innovation in Organizations,'' *American Political Science Review*, *63*, 163–173.

MOMBUSHO, 1965. *Higher Education in Postwar Japan, The Ministry of Education's 1964 White Paper*, trans. and ed. John E. Blewett. Sophia, Japan: Sophia University Press.

MOMBUSHO, 1983. *An Outline of the University-Based Research System in Japan*. Tokyo: Ministry of Education, Science and Culture.

MOMBUSHO, 1984. *Higher Education in Japan with Particular Reference to the Role and Functions of Universities*. Tokyo: MOMBUSHO.

Monson, T. C., J. W. Hesley, & L. Chernick, 1982. ''Specifying When Personality Traits Can and Cannot Predict Behavior: An Alternative to Abandoning the Attempt to Predict Single Act Criteria,'' *Journal of Personality and Social Psychology*, *43*, 385–399.

Morioka, Kiyomi, 1986. ''Privatization of Family Life in Japan,'' in Harold Stevenson, Hiroshi Azuma, & Kenji Hakuta (eds.), *Child Development and Education in Japan*. New York: W. H. Freeman and Company, pp. 63–73.

Morishima, Motohiro, 1987. Personal Communication, November 10.

Morishima, Motohiro & Takao Minami, 1983. ''Task Interdependence and Internal Motivation: Application of Job Characteristic Model to 'Collectivist' Cultures,'' *Tetsugaku (Philosophy)*, *77*, 133–147.

Moritani, Masanori, 1981. ''What Sustains Japanese Technology?'' Tokyo: Nomura Research Institute.

Moritani, Masanori, 1982. *Japanese Technology*. Tokyo: The Simul Press.

Moses, Rafael, 1989. ''Denial in Political Process,'' in E. L. Edelstein, Donald L. Nathanson, & Andrew M. Stone (eds.), *Denial, A Clarification of Concepts and Research*. New York: Plenum Press, pp. 287–297.

Mouer, Ross & Yoshio Sugimoto, 1986. *Images of Japanese Society, A Study in the Structure of Social Reality*. London: KPI Limited.

MOW International Research Team, 1987. *The Meaning of Working*. New York: Academic Press.

Mower, Judith C. & David Wilemon, 1989. "Rewarding Technical Teamwork," *Research Technology Management*, *32*, 5 (September-October), 24–29.

Mroczkowski, Tomasz & Masao Hanaoka, 1989. "Continuity and Change in Japanese Management," *California Management Review*, *31*, 2 (Winter), pp. 39–53.

Mura, David, 1988. "A Japanese-American in Tokyo," *Partisan Review*, *55*, 1, 113–122.

Murayama, Motofusa, 1982a. "The Japanese Business Value System," in Sang M. Lee & Gary Schwendiman (eds.), *Japanese Management: Cultural and Environmental Considerations*. New York: Praeger, pp. 89–116.

Murayama, Motofusa, 1982b. "*Kazokushigi* and *Shudanshugi* Management Approaches: Source of Concept Variance in Japanese Business Settings," in Sang M. Lee & Gary Schwendiman (eds.), *Japanese Management: Cultural and Environmental Considerations*. New York: Praeger, pp. 171–198.

Murnighan, J. Keith & Donald E. Conlon, 1991. "The Dynamics of Intense Work Groups: A Study of British String Quartets," *Administrative Science Quarterly*, *36*, 2 (June), 2, 165–186.

Myers, Isabel, 1962. *The Myers-Briggs Type Indicator*. n.p.: Isabel Briggs-Myers.

Nadler, Lawrence B., Marjorie Keeshan Nadler, & Benjamin J. Broome, 1985. "Culture and the Management of Conflict Situations," in William B. Gudykunst, Lea P. Stewart, & Stella Ting-Toomey (eds.), *Communication, Culture, and Organizational Processes*. Beverly Hills, CA: Sage Publications, pp. 87–113.

Nagi, Saad Z. & Ronald G. Corwin, 1972. *The Social Contexts of Research*. New York: Wiley-Interscience.

Najita, Tetsuo & J. Victor Koschmann (eds.), 1982. *Conflict in Modern Japanese History, The Neglected Tradition*. Princeton, NJ: Princeton University Press.

Nakamura, Hajime, 1967. "Basic Features of the Legal, Political and Economic Thought of Japan," in Charles A. Moore (ed.), *The Japanese Mind*. Honolulu: University of Hawaii Press.

Nakamura, Hajime, 1987. "Legal, Political, and Economic Thought" in Charles A. Moore (ed.), *The Japanese Mind, Essentials of Japanese Philosophy and Culture*. Honolulu: University of Hawaii Press, pp. 143–163.

Nakane, Chie, N., 1986. "Criteria of Group Formation," in Takie Sugiyama Lebra & William P. Lebra (eds.), *Japanese Culture and Behavior, Selected Readings*. Revised Edition. Honolulu: University of Hawaii Press, pp. 171–187.

Nakane, Chie, 1988a. "Hierarchy in Japanese Society," in Daniel I. Okimoto & Thomas P. Rohlen (eds.), *Inside the Japanese System*. Stanford: Stanford University Press, pp. 8–14. (from her *Japanese Society*)

Nakane, Chie, 1988b. Cited in W. David Kubiak, "E Pluribus Yamoto: The Culture of Corporate Beings," *Kyoto Journal*, 6 (Spring), p. 13.

Nakatani, Iwao, 1988. *The Japanese Firm in Transition*. Tokyo: Asian Productivity Organization.

Nanus, Burt, 1992. *Visionary Leadership*. San Francisco: Jossey-Bass.

National Academy Press, 1983. *International Competition in Advanced Technology: Decisions for America*. Washington, DC: National Academy Press.

National Governors' Association and The Conference Board, 1987. *The Role of Science and Technology in Economic Competitiveness.* Final Report prepared for the National Science Foundation. N.p.

National Science Foundation, 1983. *The Process of Technological Innovation: Reviewing the Literature.* Washington, DC: National Science Foundation.

Nichols, Rodney, W., 1992. *Science and Technology in United States International Affairs.* New York: Carnegie Commission on Science, Technology and Government.

Noguchi, Yoshi, 1992. "Dropping Out of Tokyo's Rat Race," *New York Times Forum* (March 1), p. 17.

Nonaka, Ikujiro & Johny K. Johansson, 1985. "Organizational Learning in Japanese Companies," in Robert Lamb & Paul Shrivastava (eds.), *Advances in Strategic Management, 3,* pp. 277–296.

Nutt, Paul C., 1989. *Making Tough Decisions.* San Francisco: Jossey-Bass.

Nystrom, Harry, 1979. *Creativity and Innovation.* New York: John Wiley & Sons.

Odaka, Kunio, 1982. "The Japanese Style of Workers' Self-Management: From the Voluntary to the Autonomous Group," in Veljko Rus, Akihiro Ishikawa, & Thomas Woodhouse (eds.), *Employment and Participation, Industrial Democracy in Crisis.* Tokyo: Chuo University Press, pp. 225–235.

Ohmae, Kenichi, 1985. *Triad Power: The Coming Shape of Global Competition.* New York: The Free Press.

Ohsawa, Takeshi, 1975. "The Use of the MBTI in Japan." Paper presented at the First National Conference on the Uses of the Myers-Briggs Type Indicator. Gainesville: University of Florida.

Ohsawa, Takeshi, 1981. "A Profile of Top Executives of Japanese Companies." Paper presented at the Fourth Biennial Conference on the Myers-Briggs Type Indicator, Stanford, California, Stanford University.

Oldham, Greg R. & J. Richard Hackman, 1981. "Relationships Between Organizational Structure and Employee Reactions: Comparing Alternative Frameworks," *Administrative Science Quarterly, 26,* 1 (March), 66–83.

Oldham, Greg R., J. Richard Hackman, & Lee P. Stepina, 1978. "Norms for the Job Diagnostic Survey." Technical Report No. 16, School of Organization and Management, Yale University, July.

Oster, Harriet, 1989. "Processing Facial Affect," in A. W. Young & H. D. Ellis (eds.), *Handbook of Research on Face Processing.* New York: Elsevier Science Publishers B.V. (North-Holland), pp. 107–161.

OSTP, 1985. *Biennial Science and Technology Report to the Congress: 1983–84.* Washington, DC: USGPO.

OSTP, 1991. *Biennial Science and Technology Report to the Congress, 1990–91.* Washington, DC: USGPO.

Ouchi, William C., 1978. "The Transmission of Control Through the Organizational Hierarchy," *Academy of Management Journal, 21,* 2, 173–192.

Ouchi, William C., 1980. "Markets, Bureaucracies and Clans," *Administrative Science Quarterly, 25,* 129–141.

Ouchi, William C., 1981. *Theory Z: How American Business Can Meet the Japanese Challenge,* Reading, MA: Addison-Wesley.

Ouchi, William C., 1984. *The M-Form Society.* Reading, MA: Addison-Wesley.

Parsons, Talcott, 1949. *Essays in Sociological Theory: Pure and Applied.* Glencoe, IL: The Free Press.

Parsons, Talcott, 1951. *The Social System.* Glencoe, IL: The Free Press.

Parsons, Talcott & Edward A. Shils, 1951. "Personality as a System of Action," in Talcott Parsons & Edward A. Shils (eds.), *Toward a General Theory of Action.* New York: Harper & Row, Publishers.

Parsons, Talcott, Robert F. Bales, & Edward A. Shils, 1953. "Phase Movement in Relation to Motivation, Symbol Formation, and Role Structure," in Talcott Parsons, Robert F. Bales, & Edward A. Shils, *Working Papers in the Theory of Action.* New York: The Free Press.

Pascale, Richard T. & Anthony G. Athos, 1981. *The Art of Japanese Management.* New York: Simon and Schuster.

Passin, Herbert, 1965. *Society and Education in Japan.* Tokyo: Kodansha International, Ltd.

Payne, Roy, 1990. "The Effectiveness of Research Teams: A Review," in M. A. West & J. L. Far (eds.), *Innovation and Creativity at Work.* Chichester, England: John Wiley & Sons.

Peak, Lois, 1991. *Learning to Go to School in Japan: The Transition from Home to Preschool.* Berkeley: University of California Press.

Pei, M., 1965. *The Story of Language.* Philadelphia: J. B. Lippincott.

Pelz, Donald, 1952. "Influence: A Key to Effective Leadership in the First Line Supervisor," *Personnel, 29,* 209–217.

Pelz, Donald C., 1967. "Creative Tensions in the R & D Climate," *Science, 157,* 160–165.

Pelz, Donald C., 1978. "Environments for Creative Performance Within Universities," in Samuel Messick and Associates, *Individuality in Learning.* San Francisco: Jossey-Bass.

Pelz, Donald C. & Frank M. Andrews, 1976. *Scientists in Organizations.* Revised Edition. Ann Arbor: Institute for Social Research, University of Michigan.

Pelz, Donald C., Herbert Meyer, & Saul W. Gellerman, 1975. *Organizing the Organization for Better R & D.* New York: AMACOM.

Perrow, Charles, 1970. *Organizational Analysis: A Sociological View.* Belmont, CA: Wadsworth Publishing Company.

Perrow, Charles, 1986. *Complex Organizations: A Critical Essay.* Third Edition. New York: Random House.

Peterson, Mark F., Mary Yoko Brannen, & Peter B. Smith, 1992. "Japanese and United States Leadership: Issues in Current Research," *Advances in International Comparative Management, 9,* 57–82.

Pfeffer, Jeffrey, 1977. "Power and Resource Allocation in Organizations," in Barry M. Staw & Gerald R. Salancik (eds.), *New Directions in Organizational Behavior.* Chicago: St. Clair Press, pp. 233–265.

Pfeffer, Jeffrey & Gerald R. Salancik, 1978. *The External Control of Organizations: A Resource Dependent Perspective.* New York: Harper & Row.

Pierce, Jon L., Donald G. McTavish, & Kjell R. Knudsen, 1986. "The Measurement of Job Characteristics: A Content and Contextual Analytic Look at Scale Validity," *Journal of Occupational Behaviour, 7,* 299–313.

Pierre, Andrew J. & Frank Press, 1987. *A High Technology Gap, Europe, America and Japan.* New York: Council on Foreign Relations.

Pinder, Craig C., 1984. *Work Motivation.* Glenview, IL: Scott, Foresman.

Pittenger, David J., 1993. "The Utility of the Myers-Briggs Type Indicator," *Review of Educational Research, 63,* 4 (Winter), 467–488.

Podsakoff, P. M., 1982. "Determinants of a Supervisor's Use of Rewards and Punishments: A Literature Review and Suggestions for Further Research," *Organizational Behavior and Human Performance, 29,* 58–83.

Pollack, Andrew, 1993a. "Japanese Starting to Link Pay to Performance, Not Tenure," *New York Times International* (October 2).

Pollack, Andrew, 1993b. "Japanese, in a Painful Recession, Trim Industrial Research Outlays," *New York Times* (November 29), pp. D1, 3.

Pondy, Louis, R., 1967. "Organizational Conflict: Concepts and Models," *Administrative Science Quarterly, 12,* 2 (September), 296–320.

Porter, Lyman W., Robert W. Allen, & Harold L. Angle, 1991. "The Politics of Upward Influence in Organizations," in Barry M. Staw & Larry L. Cummings (eds.), *Personality and Organizational Influence.* Greenwich, CT: JAI Press, pp. 139–180.

Price, Derek John de Solla, 1963. *Little Science, Big Science.* New York: Columbia University Press.

Price-Williams, D. R., 1985. "Cultural Psychology," in Gardner Lindzey & Elliot Aronson (eds.), *Handbook of Social Psychology.* Vol. II. New York: Random House, pp. 993–1042.

Pucik, Vladimir & Nina Hatvany, 1983. "Management Practices in Japan and Their Impact on Business Strategy," in Robert Lamb (ed.), *Advances in Strategic Management, 1,* 103–131.

Rahim, M. Afzalur, 1986. *Managing Conflict in Organizations.* New York: Praeger.

Rahim, M. Afzalur, 1983a. *Rahim Organizational Conflict Inventory—I.* Palo Alto: Consulting Psychologists Press.

Rahim, M. Afzalur, 1983b. *Rahim Organizational Conflict Inventory—II, Forms, A, B, & C.* Palo Alto, CA: Consulting Psychologists Press.

Rauch, Jonathan, 1992. *The Outnation, A Search for the Soul of Japan.* Boston: Harvard Business School Press.

Redl, Fritz, 1942. "Group Emotion and Leadership," *Psychiatry, 5,* 573–596.

Reischauer, Edwin O., 1977. *The Japanese.* Cambridge, MA: Belknap Press.

Reischauer, Edwin O., 1988. *The Japanese Today: Change and Continuity.* Cambridge, MA: Belknap Press.

Renwick, Patricia A., 1975. "Perception and Management of Superior-Subordinate Conflict," *Organizational Behavior and Human Performance, 13* (June), 444–456.

Rickards, Tudor, 1991. "Innovation and Creativity: Woods, Trees and Pathways," *R&D Management, 21,* 2, 97–108.

Ridgeway, Cecilia L., 1987. "Nonverbal Behavior, Dominance, and the Basis of Status in Task Groups, *American Sociological Review, 52,* 5 (October), 683–694.

Riesman, David, 1954. *Individualism Reconsidered.* Glencoe, IL: The Free Press.

Riesman, David with Nathan Glazer & Reuel Denney, 1961. *The Lonely Crowd.* New Haven, CT: Yale University Press.

Riggs, Henry E., 1984. "Innovations: A United States-Japan Perspective." Unpublished paper presented to the United States-Japan Project on High Technology.

Robbins, Stephen, 1974. *Managing Organizational Conflict.* Englewood Cliffs, NJ: Prentice-Hall.

Roberts, Karlene H., 1970. "On Looking at an Elephant: An Evaluation of Cross-Cultural Research Related to Organizations," *Psychological Bulletin*, *74*, 327–350.

Roberts, Karlene H. & Nakiye A. Boyacigiller, 1984. "Cross-National Organizational Research: The Grasp of Blind Men," *Research in Organizational Behavior*, *6*, 423–475.

Roberts, Karlene H. & William Glick, 1981. "The Job Characteristics Approach to Task Design: A Critical Review," *Journal of Applied Psychology*, *66*, 2 (April), 193–217.

Rogers, Everett M., 1983. *Diffusion of Innovations*. Third Edition. New York: The Free Press.

Rohlen, Thomas P., 1974. *For Harmony and Strength: Japanese White Collar Organization in Anthropological Perspective*. Berkeley: University of California Press.

Rohlen, Thomas P., 1975. "The Company Work Group," in Ezra F. Vogel (ed.), *Modern Japanese Organization and Decision-Making*. Berkeley: University of California Press, pp. 185–209.

Rohlen, Thomas P., 1983. *Japan's High Schools*. Berkeley: University of California Press.

Roman, Mel & Patricia E. Raley, 1980. *The Indelible Family*. New York: Rawson, Wade Publishers.

Ronen, Simcha, 1977. "Similarities Among Countries Based on Employee Work Values and Attitudes," *Columbia World Journal of Business* (Summer), 89–96.

Rosenberg, S., D. E. Erlick, & L. Berkowitz, 1955. "Some Effects of Varying Combinations of Group Members on Group Performance Measures and Leadership Behaviors," *Journal of Abnormal and Social Psychology*, *51*, 195–203.

Rosener, Judy B., 1990. "Ways Women Lead," *Harvard Business Review*, *68*, 6 (November-December), 119–125.

Rost, Joseph C., 1991. *Leadership for the Twenty-First Century*. New York: Praeger.

Rothbaum, Fred, John R. Weisz, & Samuel S. Snyder, 1982. "Changing the Self: A 2-Process Model of Perceived Control," *Journal of Personality and Social Psychology*, *42*, 1 (January), 5–37.

Rothschild-Whitt, Joyce, 1979. "The Collectivist Organization: An Alternative to Rational-Bureaucratic Models," *American Sociological Review*, *44*, 4 (August), 509–527.

Rowe, David C., 1987. "Resolving the Person-Situation Debate, Invitation to an Interdisciplinary Dialogue," *American Psychologist*, *42*, 3 (March), 218–227.

Ryooichi, Iwauchi, 1985. "Educational Background as a Credential," *The East*, *21*, 3 (June), 6–8.

Saito, Kazuaki, 1985. "Heroes and Hero-Worship, Ivan Morris' Views on the Japanese Fascination with Failure," in Nippon Steel Corporation, *Inside the Japanese, Essays from Japan*. Tokyo: Public Relations Corporate Secretariat, Nippon Steel Corporation, n.p.

Sakakibara, Kiyonori, 1988. "Increasing Basic Research in Japan: Corporate Activity Alone Is Not Enough." Working Paper No. 8802, Hitotsubashi University.

Sakuta, Keiichi, 1978. "The Controversy Over Community and Autonomy," in J. Victor Koschmann, *Authority and the Individual in Japan*. Tokyo: University of Tokyo Press.

Salaman, Graeme, 1980. "Organizations as Constructors of Social Reality (II)," in G.

Salaman & K. Thompson (eds.), *Control and Ideology in Organizations.* Cambridge, MA: The MIT Press.

Salancik, Gerald R. & Jeffrey Pfeffer, 1978. ''A Social Information Processing Approach to Job Attitudes and Job Design,'' *Administrative Science Quarterly, 23,* 2 (June), 224–253.

Sampson, Edward E., 1988. ''The Debate on Individualism, Indigenous Psychologies of the Individual and Their Role in Personal and Societal Functioning,'' *American Psychologist, 43,* 1 (January), 15–22.

Sarason, I., 1975. ''Personality Research: Components of Variance Attributable to the Person and Situation,'' *Journal of Personality and Social Psychology, 32,* 199–204.

Sasaki, Naoto, 1981. *Management and Industrial Structure in Japan.* Oxford, England: Pergamon Press.

Sashkin, Marshall, 1987. ''Explaining Excellence in Leadership in Light of Parsonian Theory.'' Paper presented at the annual meeting of the American Educational Research Association, Washington, DC, April 24.

Sashkin, Marshall & R. M. Fulmer, 1988. ''Toward an Organizational Leadership Theory,'' in James G. Hunt, B. R. Baliga, H. P. Dachler, & E. A. Schriesheim (eds.), *New Vistas in Leadership.* Boston: Lexington, pp. 51–65.

Sato, Kimimasa, 1991. ''It's Time for University Executives to Wake up from Deep Sleep,'' Tokyo: *Asahi Evening News,* June 2.

Sato, Nancy E., 1990. ''Japanese Education Where It Counts: In the Classroom.'' Paper presented at the annual meeting of the American Educational Research Association, Boston.

Sato, Ryuzo, 1985. ''The Technology Game and Dynamic Comparative Advantage: An Application to U.S.–Japan Competition.'' Working Paper No. 2, New York University, Center for Japan–U.S. Business and Economic Studies.

Saville, P. & E. Willson, 1991. ''The Reliability and Validity of Normative and Ipsative Approaches in the Measurement of Personality,'' *Journal of Occupational Psychology, 64,* 219–238.

Schein, Edgar H., 1985. *Organizational Culture and Leadership.* San Francisco: Jossey-Bass.

Schmitt, Roland W., 1985. ''Successful Corporate R & D,'' *Harvard Business Review, 63,* 3 (May/June), 124–128.

Schneider, Benjamin, 1990. ''Interactional Psychology and Organizational Behavior,'' in Barry M. Staw and Larry L. Cummings (eds.), *Personality and Organizational Influence.* Greenwich, CT: JAI Press, pp. 51–81.

Schoonhoven, Claudia B. & Maryann Jelinek, 1990. ''Dynamic Tension in Innovative High Technology Firms: Managing Rapid Technological Change through Organizational Structure,'' in M. A. Von Glinow & S. A. Mohrman, *Managing Complexity in High Technology Industries: Systems and People.* Oxford, England: Oxford University Press, pp. 90–118.

Schriesheim, Chester A., Terri A. Scandura, & Linda L. Neider, 1991. ''Leader-Member Exchange as a Predictor and Moderator of Delegation.'' Paper presented at the annual meeting of the Academy of Management, Miami Beach.

Schumpeter, J. A., 1939. *Business Cycles.* New York: McGraw-Hill Book Company.

Schwartz, B., 1983. ''George Washington and the Whig Conception of Heroic Leadership,'' *American Sociological Review, 48,* 1, 18–33.

Science and Technology Agency, 1987. "Toward the Internationalization of Japan's Science and Technology (Summary)," STA White Paper on Science and Technology, 1987. Tokyo: Science and Technology Agency.

Seligman, Martin E. P., 1991. *Learned Optimism*. New York: Alfred A. Knopf.

Selznick, Philip, 1949. *TVA and the Grass Roots*. Berkeley: University of California Press.

Selznick, Philip, 1957. *Leadership in Administration*. New York: Harper & Row.

Sethi, S. Prakask, 1975. *Japanese Business and Social Conflict: A Comparative Analysis of Response Patterns with American Business*. Cambridge, MA: Ballinger.

Sethi, S. Prakask, Nobuaki Namiki, & Carl L. Swanson, 1984. *The False Promise of the Japanese Miracle*. Boston: Pitman Publishing Company.

Shane, Scott, 1993. "Cultural Influences on National Rates of Innovation," *Journal of Business Venturing*, 8, 1 (January), 59–73.

Shartle, C. L., 1956. *Executive Performance and Leadership*. Englewood Cliffs, NJ: Prentice-Hall.

Shenhav, Yehouoda, 1991. "Expected Managerial Careers Within Growing and Declining R & D Establishments," *Work and Occupations*, 18, 1 (February), 46–71.

Shepard, H. A., 1956a. "Creativity in R/D Teams," *Research and Engineering* (October), 10–13.

Shepard, H. A., 1956b. "Supervisors and Subordinates in Research," *Journal of Business*, 29, 4, 261–267.

Shibata, Yusaku, 1984. "Toward a Policy Guidance System for Complex Innovation," in Hajime Eto & Konomu Matsui, *R & D Management Systems in Japanese Industry*. Amsterdam, The Netherlands: Elsevier Science Publishers B.V. (North-Holland).

Shields, James J., Jr. (ed.), 1989. *Japanese Schooling, Patterns of Socialization, Equality and Political Control*. University Park: The Pennsylvania State University Press.

Shigaki, Irene, 1983. "Child Care Practices in Japan and the United States: How Do They Reflect Cultural Values in Young Children?" *Young Children*, 38, 13–24.

Shimada, Haruo, 1985. "The Perceptions and the Reality of Japanese Industrial Relations," in Lester C. Thurrow (ed.), *The Management Challenge*. Cambridge, MA: The MIT Press.

Shimahara, Nobuo K., 1979. *Adaptation and Education in Japan*. New York: Praeger.

Shishin, Alex, 1988. "Japanese Education and the Authoritarian Group Dynamic," *Kyoto Journal*, 7 (Summer), 48–49.

Shrivastava, Paul & Ian Mitroff, 1983. "Frames of References Managers Use: A Study in the Applied Sociology of Knowledge," in Robert Lamb (ed.), *Advances in Strategic Management*, 1, 161–182.

Shrivastava, Paul & W. E. Souder, 1985. "Phase Transfer Models for Technological Innovation," in Robert Lamb & Paul Shrivastava (eds.), *Advances in Strategic Management*, 3, 135–147.

Silverman, Bernard S., 1982. "The Bureaucratic State in Japan: The Problem of Authority and Legitimacy," in Tetsuo Najita & J. Victor Koschmann (eds.), *Conflict in Modern Japanese History, The Neglected Tradition*. Princeton, NJ: Princeton University Press.

Simmel, Georg, 1955. *Conflict and the Web of Group-Affiliations*, trans. Kurt H. Wolff & Reinhard Bendix. Glencoe, IL: The Free Press.

Simons, Carol, 1987. "They Get By With a Lot of Help from Their *Kyoiku* Mamas," *Smithsonian, 17*, 12 (March), 44–53.

Sims, H. P., A. D. Szilagyi, & A. T. Keller, 1976. "The Measurement of Job Characteristics," *Academy of Management Journal, 19*, 196–213.

Singer, Kurt, 1973. *Mirror, Sword, and Jewel: A Study of Japanese Characteristics.* New York: George Braziller.

Singleton, John, 1989. "*Gambaru*: A Japanese Cultural Theory of Learning," in James J. Shields, Jr. (ed.), *Japanese Schooling, Patterns of Socialization, Equality and Political Control.* University Park: The Pennysylvania State University Press, pp. 8–15.

Slater, Philip E., 1966. *Microcosm, Structural, Psychological and Religious Evolution in Groups.* New York: John Wiley & Sons.

Slaughter, Sara & James Utterback, 1990. "U.S. Research and Development: An International Comparative Analysis," *Business in the Contemporary World, 2* (Winter), 27–35.

Smith, Clagett G. & Oguz N. Ari, 1968. "Organizational Control Structure and Member Consensus," in Arnold S. Tannenbaum, *Control in Organizations.* New York: McGraw-Hill Book Company.

Smith, Ken G., Ken A. Smith, Judy D. Olian, Henry P. Sims, Jr., Douglas P. O'Bannon, & Judith A. Scully, 1994. "Top Management Team Demography and Process: The Role of Social Integration and Communication," in *Administrative Science Quarterly, 39*, 3 (September), 412–438.

Smith, Kenwyn K. & David N. Berg, 1987. *Paradoxes of Group Life, Understanding Conflict, Paralysis, and Movement in Group Dynamics.* San Francisco: Jossey-Bass.

Smith, Robert J., 1983. *Japanese Society, Tradition, Self and the Social Order.* Cambridge, England: Cambridge University Press.

Staw, Barry M., 1976. *Intrinsic and Extrinsic Motivation.* Morristown, NJ: General Learning Press.

Staw, Barry M., 1983. *Psychological Foundation of Organizational Behavior.* Second Edition. Glenview, IL: Scott, Foresman.

Staw, Barry M., 1984. "Motivation Research vs. the Art of Faculty Management," in J. L. Bess (ed.), *College and University Organization: Insights from the Behavioral Sciences.* New York: New York University Press.

Staw, Barry M., 1990. "An Evolutionary Approach to Creativity and Innovation," in Michael A. West & James L. Farr, *Innovation and Creativity at Work, Psychological and Organizational Strategies.* New York: John Wiley & Sons, pp. 287–308.

Staw, Barry M., Lance E. Sandelands, & Jane E. Dutton, 1981. "Threat-Rigidity Effects in Organizational Behavior: A Multilevel Analysis," *Administrative Science Quarterly, 26*, 501–524.

Steers, Richard M. & Lyman W. Porter, 1975. *Motivation and Work Behavior.* New York: McGraw-Hill Book Company.

Stein, M. I., 1975. *Stimulating Creativity.* Vol. 2. *Group Procedures.* New York: Academic Press.

Stevenson, Harold & James W. Stigler, 1992. *The Learning Gap.* New York: Summit Books.

Stewart, Edward C., 1985. "Culture and Decision-Making," in William B. Gudykunst,

Lea P. Stewart & Stella Ting-Toomey (eds.), *Communication, Culture and Organizational Processes.* Beverly Hills, CA: Sage Publications, 177–211.

Stinchcombe, Arthur L., 1990. "Turning Inventions into Innovations, Schumpeter's Organizational Sociology Modernized," in Arthur L. Stinchcombe, *Information and Organizations.* Berkeley: University of California Press, pp. 152–193.

Sullivan, Jeremiah J., 1983. "A Critique of Theory Z," *Academy of Management Review,* 8, 1 (January), 132–142.

Sullivan, Jeremiah, Teruhiko Suzuki, & Yasumasa Kondo, 1985. "Managerial Theories of the Performance Control Process in Japanese and American Work Groups." Paper presented at the annual meeting of the Academy of Management, San Diego.

Sundstrom, E., K. P. DeMeuse, & D. Futrell, 1990. "Work Teams, Applications and Effectiveness," *American Psychologist,* 45, 120–133.

Suzuki, Takao, 1978. *Japanese and the Japanese: Words in Culture.* Tokyo: Kodansha International.

Tachibanaki, Toshiaki, 1984. "Labor Mobility and Job Tenure," in Masahiko Aoki (ed.), *The Economic Analysis of the Japanese Firm.* Amsterdam: North-Holland.

Takagi, Haruo, 1985. *The Flaw in Japanese Management.* Ann Arbor: UMI Research Press.

Tatsuno, Sheridan M., 1990. *Created in Japan, From Imitators to World-Class Innovators.* New York: Harper & Row, Publishers.

Teitaroo, Suzuki Daisetz, 1987. "Reason and Intuition in Buddhist Philosophy," in Charles A. Moore (ed.), *The Japanese Mind, Essentials of Japanese Philosophy and Culture.* Honolulu: University of Hawaii Press, pp. 66–109.

Thamhain, Hans J. & David L. Wilemon, 1977. "Leadership, Conflict, and Program Management Effectiveness," *Sloan Management Review,* 19, 1 (Fall), 69–89.

Thamhain, Hans J. & David L. Wilemon, 1983. "Building High Performing Engineering Project Teams," *IEEE Transactions on Engineering Management,* EM–34, 3, 130–137.

Thamhain, Hans J. & Gary R. Gemmill, 1974. "Influence Styles of Project Managers: Some Project Performance Correlates," *Academy of Management Journal,* 17, 2 (June), 216–233.

Thibaut, John W. & Harold H. Kelley, 1959. *The Social Psychology of Groups.* New York: John Wiley & Sons.

Thomas, Alan Berkeley, 1988. "Does Leadership Make a Difference to Organizational Performance?" *Administrative Science Quarterly,* 33, 3 (September), 388–400.

Thomas, Kenneth, 1976. "Conflict and Conflict Management," in Marvin E. Dunnette (ed.), *Handbook of Industrial and Organizational Psychology.* New York: Rand McNally and Company, pp. 889–935.

Thomas, Kenneth W. & Ralph H. Kilmann, 1974. *Thomas-Kilmann Conflict MODE Instrument.* Tuxedo, NY: XICOM.

Thomas, Kenneth W. & Ralph H. Kilmann, 1978. "Comparison of Four Instruments Measuring Conflict Behavior,"*Psychological Reports,* 42, 1139–1145.

Thompson, James P., 1960. "Organizational Management of Conflict," *Administrative Science Quarterly,* 4 (March), 389–409.

Thompson, James P., 1967. *Organizations in Action.* New York: McGraw-Hill Book Company.

Thompson, James P. & Arthur Tuden, 1959. *Comparative Studies in Administration*. Pittsburgh: University of Pittsburgh Press.

Tjosvold, Dean, 1989. "Interdependence and Power Between Managers and Employees: A Study of the Leader Relationship," *Journal of Management, 15*, 1, 49–62.

Tjosvold, Dean & D. W. Johnson, 1978. "Effects of Controversy on Cognitive Perspective Taking," *Journal of Educational Psychology, 69*, 679–685.

Tobin, Joseph J., David Y. H. Wu, & Dana H. Davidson, 1989. *Preschool in Three Cultures, Japan, China and the United States*. New Haven, CT: Yale University Press.

Toennies, F., 1957. *Community and Society (Gemeinschaft und Gesellschaft)*, trans. C. P. Loomis. East Lansing: Michigan State University Press.

Tominaga, Keii (ed.), 1984. *Daigaku Hyoka no Kenkyu* (A Study on the Evaluation of Japanese Universities). Tokyo: University of Tokyo Press.

Tooyoo, Keizai, 1985. "Company Ratings and Financial Data by Company," *Tookei Geppoo* (Statistical Monthly), *44*, 8.

Triandis, Harry C., 1972. *The Analysis of Subjective Culture*. New York: John Wiley & Sons.

Triandis, Harry C., 1990. "Cross-cultural Studies of Individualism and Collectivism," in J. Berman (ed), *Nebraska Symposium on Motivation*. Lincoln: University of Nebraska Press.

Triandis, Harry C., Christopher McCusker, & C. Harry Hui, 1990. "Multimethod Probes of Individualism and Collectivism," *Journal of Personality and Social Psychology, 59*, 5 (November), 1006–1020.

Triandis, H. E., E. R. Hall, & R. B. Ewen, 1965. "Member Heterogeneity and Dyadic Creativity," *Human Relations, 18*, 33–55.

Trice, Harrison M. & Janice M. Beyer, 1991. "Cultural Leadership in Organizations," *Organizational Science, 2*, 2 (May), 149–169.

Trist, E. L., 1963. *Organizational Choice: Capabilities of Groups at the Coal Face Under Changing Technologies: The Loss, Re-Discovery and Transformation of a Work Tradition*. London: Tavistock Publications.

Trist, E. L. & K. W. Bamforth, 1951. "Some Social and Psychological Consequences of the Long Wall Method of Coal Getting," *Human Relations, 4*, 3–38.

Tsuji, Kiyoaki, 1968. "Decision-Making in the Japanese Government: A Study of Ringisei," in Robert E. Ward (ed.), *Political Development in Modern Japan*. Princeton, NJ: Princeton University Press, pp. 457–475.

Tung, Rosalie L., 1984. *Key to Japan's Economic Strength: Human Power*. Lexington, MA: Lexington Books.

Turney, Jon (ed.), 1984. *Sci-Tech Report*. New York: Pantheon.

Turquet, Pierre M., 1976. "Leadership: The Individual and the Group," in Graham S. Gibbard, John J. Hartman, & Richard D. Mann (eds.), *Analysis of Groups*. San Francisco: Jossey-Bass, pp. 349–371.

Tushman, Michael L. & William L. Moore, 1988. *Readings in the Management of Innovation*. Second Edition. Cambridge, MA: Ballinger.

Tyler, Tom R., 1993. "The Social Psychology of Authority," in J. Keith Murnighan (ed.), *Social Psychology in Organizations, Advances in Theory and Research*. Englewood Cliffs, NJ: Prentice-Hall.

Tyler, Tom R. & E. Allen Lind, 1992. "A Relational Model of Authority in Groups," in M. Zanna (ed.), *Advances in Experimental Social Psychology*, 25. New York: Academic Press, pp. 151–191.

Ullman-Margalit, Edna, 1977. *The Emergence of Norms*. Oxford, England: Clarendon Press.

Uno, Yoshiyasu & Robert Rosenthal, 1972. "Tacit Communication Between Japanese Experimenters and Subjects," *Psycholgia*, 15 (December), 213–222.

U.S. News & World Report, 1987. "The Brain Battle," *U.S. News and World Report*, 102, 2 (January 19), 58–65.

Ushiogi, Morikazu, 1993. "Graduate Education and Research Organization in Japan," in Burton R. Clark (ed.), *The Research Foundations of Graduate Education: Germany, Britain, France, United States, Japan*. Berkeley: University of California Press.

Valentine, James, 1990. "On the Borderlines: The Significance of Marginality in Japanese Society," in Eyal Ben-Ari, Brian Moeran, & James Valentine (eds.), *Unwrapping Japan*. Honolulu: University of Hawaii Press, pp. 36–57.

Van de Ven, Andrew H., 1986. "Central Problems in the Management of Innovation," *Management Science*, 32, 5, 590–607.

Van de Ven, Andrew H. & Diane L. Ferry, 1980. *Measuring and Assessing Organizations*. New York: John Wiley & Sons.

VanGundy, Arthur B., 1984. *Managing Group Creativity, A Modular Approach to Problem Solving*. New York: AMACOM.

van Wolferen, Karel, 1989. *The Enigma of Japanese Power, People and Politics in a Stateless Nation*. New York: Knopf.

Veroff, J., 1983. "Contextual Determinants of Personality," *Personality and Social Psychology Bulletin*, 9, 331–343.

Villere, Maurice F., 1981. *Transactional Analysis at Work*. Englewood Cliffs, NJ: Prentice-Hall.

Vogel, Ezra F., 1979. *Japan As No. 1*. Cambridge, MA: Harvard University Press.

Vogel, Ezra F. (ed.), 1975. *Modern Japanese Organization and Decision-Making*. Berkeley: University of California Press.

von Cranach, Mario, 1986. "Leadership as a Function of Group Action," in Carl F. Graumann & Serge Moscovici (eds.), *Changing Conceptions of Leadership*. New York: Springer-Verlag.

Vroom, Victor H., 1984. "Leaders and Leadership in Academe," in J. L. Bess (ed.), *College and University Organization: Insights from the Behavioral Sciences*. New York: New York University Press.

Vroom, Victor H. & Philip W. Yetton, 1973. *Leadership and Decision-Making*. Pittsburgh: University of Pittsburgh Press.

Wagner, J. A. & Michael K. Moch, 1985. "Individualism-Collectivism—Concept and Measure," *Group and Organization Studies*, 11, 3, 280–304.

Wakabayabayashi, Mitsuru, 1987. "Internalization of Japanese Corporations: Personnel and Human Resource Management Practices of Japanese Firms in Foreign Countries," *Bulletin of the Faculty of Education*, Nagoya University, 34, 173–187.

Wakabayabayashi, Mitsuru, George Graen, Michael Graen, & Martin Graen, 1988. "Japanese Management Progress: Mobility Into Middle Class Management," *Journal of Applied Psychology*, 73, 2 (May), 217–227.

Wallace, Jennifer J., 1989. " 'But You Don't Live Here, Man': Negotiating Social Reality at the Rosebush Hotel," *Symbolic Interaction*, 13, 2, 241–255.

Wallach, M. A., N. Kogan, & D. J. Bem, 1962. "Group Influence or Individual Risk Taking," *Journal of Abnormal and Social Psychology, 65,* 75–86.

Walton, Richard E., 1969. *Interpersonal Peacemaking: Confrontations and Third-Party Consultation.* Reading, MA: Addison-Wesley.

Walton, Richard E. & P. R. McKersie, 1965. *A Behavioral Theory of Labor Negotiations: An Analysis of a Social Interaction System.* New York: McGraw-Hill Book Company.

Walton, Richard E. & J. Richard Hackman, 1986. "Groups Under Contrasting Management Strategies," in Paul S. Goodman and Associates, *Designing Effective Work Groups.* San Francisco: Jossey-Bass, pp. 168–201.

Watanabe, Chihiro, Irawan Santoso, & Tjahya Widayanti, 1991. *The Inducing Power of Japanese Technological Innovation.* London: Pinter Publishers.

Watanabe, Masao, 1990. *The Japanese and Western Science,* trans. Otto T. Benfey. Philadelphia: University of Pennsylvania Press.

Waterman, A. S., 1981. "Individualism and Interdependence," *American Psychologist, 36,* 762–773.

Watt, John, 1989. *Individualism and Educational Theory.* Dordrecht, The Netherlands: Kluwer Academic Publishers.

Weber, Max, 1947. *The Theory of Social and Economic Organization,* trans. A. M. Henderson & Talcott Parsons. New York: The Free Press.

Weber, Max, 1952. *On Charisma and Institution Building: Selected Papers,* ed. S. N. Eisenstadt. Chicago: University of Chicago Press.

Weick, Karl E., 1977. "Enactment Processes in Organizations," in Barry M. Staw & Gerald R. Salancik (eds.), *New Directions in Organizational Behavior.* Chicago: St. Clair Press, pp. 267–300.

Weick, Karl E., 1984. "Contradictions in a Community of Scholars: The Cohesion-Accuracy Tradeoff," in James L. Bess (ed.), *College and University Organization.* New York: New York University Press.

Weiss, Howard M. & Seymour Adler, 1990. "Personality and Organizational Behavior," in Barry M. Staw & Larry L. Cummings (eds.), *Personality and Organizational Influence.* Greenwich, CT: JAI Press, pp. 1–50.

Weisz, John R., Fred M. Rothbaum, & Thomas C. Blackburn, 1984. "Standing Out and Standing In, The Psychology of Control in America and Japan," *American Psychologist, 39,* 9 (September) 955–969.

West, Michael A., 1990. "The Social Psychology of Innovation in Groups," in Michael A. West & James L. Farr (eds.), *Innovation and Creativity at Work, Psychological and Organizational Strategies.* New York: John Wiley & Sons, pp. 309–333.

West, Michael A. & James L. Farr (eds.), 1990. *Innovation and Creativity at Work: Psychological and Organizational Strategies.* New York: John Wiley & Sons.

Westney, D. Eleanor, 1994. "The Evolution of Japan's Industrial Research and Development," in Masahiko Aoki & Ronald Dore, *The Japanese Firm, The Sources of Competitive Strength.* New York: Oxford University Press, pp. 154–177.

Westney, D. Eleanor & Kiyonori Sakakibara, 1986. "The Role of Japan-Based R & D in Global Technology Strategy," in Mel Horwitch (ed.), *Technology in the Modern Corporation.* New York: Pergamon Press, pp. 217–232.

Wheeler, Donald F., 1976. "The Structure of Academic Governance in Japan." Yale Higher Education Program, Working Paper YHEP-9, New Haven, CT.

White, Merry, 1987. *The Japanese Educational Challenge, A Commitment to Children.* New York: The Free Press.

White, Merry & R. LeVine, 1986. "What is an Ii Ko?" in R. Stevenson, H. Azuma, & K. Hakuta (eds.), *Child Development and Education in Japan.* New York: W. H. Freeman.

Whitely, W. & George W. England, 1977. "Managerial Values as a Reflection of Culture and the Process of Industrialization," *Academy of Management Journal, 20,* 439–453.

Wilkins, Leslie T., 1965. "The Deviance-Amplifying System," in Leslie T. Wilkins, *Social Deviance.* London: Tavistock Publications Limited, pp. 87–94.

Willis, David B. & Patricia Horvath, 1988. "The Teaching Profession: A View from Japan," *Educational Leadership* (November), 64–68.

Womack, Deanna F., 1988. "Assessing the Thomas-Kilmann Conflict Mode Survey," *Management Communications Quarterly, 1,* 3 (February), 321–349.

Woodman, Richard W., John E. Sawyer, & Rickey W. Griffin, 1993. "Toward a Theory of Organizational Creativity," *Academy of Management Review, 18,* 2, 293–321.

Woodward, Joan, 1965. *Industrial Organization.* London: Oxford University Press.

Yamada, Tadayoshi, 1985. "Productivity Improvement at Nippon Steel," in Eric G. Flamholtz & T. K. Das (eds.), *Human Resource Management and Productivity, The State of the Art and Future Prospects.* II. International Perspectives. Los Angeles: Institute of Industrial Relations, University of California, pp. 5–19.

Yamagishi, Toshio, 1988. "Exit from the Group as an Individualistic Solution to the Free Rider Problem in the United States and Japan," *Journal of Experimental Social Psychology, 24,* 6 (November), 530–542.

Yamanouchi, Akio, 1986. "Kigyo Henkaku no Gijitsu Management," in *Management of Organizational Change in R & D.* Tokyo: Nihon Keizai Shimbunsha.

Yammarino, Francis J. & Thomas J. Naughton, 1992. "Individualized and Group-Based Views of Participation in Decision-Making," *Group and Organizational Management, 17,* 4 (December), 398–413.

Yoo, Takeuchi, 1984. "Peer Pressure in Japanese Organizations," *Japan Echo, 11,* 3, 53–59.

Yoshino, M. Y., 1968. *Japan's Managerial System.* Cambridge, MA: MIT Press.

Yukl, Gary, 1989. "Managerial Leadership: A Review of Theory and Research, Special Issue: Yearly Review of Management," *Journal of Management, 15,* 2 (June), 251–289.

Zammuto, Raymond, Manuel London, & Kendrith M. Rowland, 1979. "Effects of Sex on Commitment and Conflict Resolution," *Journal of Applied Psychology, 64,* 2 (April) 227–231.

Zeugner, John F., 1984. "The Puzzle of Higher Education in Japan," *Change Magazine, 16,* 1 (January/February), 24–31.

Zuckerman, Harriet, 1977. *Scientific Elites: Nobel Laureates in the United States.* New York: The Free Press.

Zuckerman, M. J., F. Porac, D. Lathin, R. Smith, & E. L. Deci, 1978. "On the Importance of Self-Determination for Intrinsically Motivated Behavior," *Personality and Social Psychology Bulletin, 4,* 443–446.

# Index

**About the Author**

JAMES L. BESS is Professor of Higher Education at New York University. Formerly director of NYU's Program in Higher Education, and former director of Institutional Research at the State University of New York–Stony Brook, he is the author or editor of numerous books, articles, and monographs.

ISBN 0-89930-915-1

EAN

9 780899 309156

90000>

HARDCOVER BAR CODE